HEGEMONIES OF LANGUAGE AND
THEIR DISCONTENTS

CARLOS G. VÉLEZ-IBÁÑEZ

HEGEMONIES OF LANGUAGE AND THEIR DISCONTENTS

⁊⁊

The Southwest North American Region Since 1540

THE UNIVERSITY OF
ARIZONA PRESS

TUCSON

The University of Arizona Press
www.uapress.arizona.edu

ISBN-13: 978-0-8165-3711-2 (cloth)
ISBN-13: 978-0-8165-3920-8 (paper)

Cover design by Leigh McDonald

Publication of this book is made possible in part by the proceeds of a permanent endowment created with the assistance of a Challenge Grant from the National Endowment for the Humanities, a federal agency.

Library of Congress Cataloging-in-Publication Data
Names: Vélez-Ibáñez, Carlos G., 1936– author.
Title: Hegemonies of language and their discontents : the Southwest North American region since 1540 / Carlos G. Vélez-Ibáñez.
Description: Tucson : The University of Arizona Press, 2017. | Includes bibliographical references and index.
Identifiers: LCCN 2017010447 | ISBN 9780816537112 (cloth : alk. paper)
Subjects: LCSH: Language policy—Mexico—History. | Language policy—United States—History. | Spanish language—Political aspects—Mexican-American Border Region. | English language—Political aspects—Mexican-American Border Region. | Indians of North America—Cultural assimilation—Mexico, North. | Indians of North America—Cultural assimilation—Southwest, New. | Hegemony.
Classification: LCC P119.32.M6 V45 2017 | DDC 306.440979—dc23 LC record available at https://lccn.loc .gov/2017010447

This work is dedicated to three great intellects, all of whom unfortunately are no longer present. Yet their fine works provide us with continuing inspiration and narratives that upend peoples without histories. To Michael Kearney, mi amigo querido and stimulator of grand ideas and transnational thought; to Arturo Rosales, mi primo and an extraordinary Chicano historian; and to Eric R. Wolf, mentor from afar and an amazing original thinker and anthropologist, my deepest respect to you all.

To Alma Rubinoskas
With respect,
Carl Wm. K. —
9-9-20

CONTENTS

7. Bilinguality, Dual Languages, Translanguality, and Heritage Maintenance: Contending Approaches and an Ethnographic Assembly of Funds of Knowledge and a Dual Language Translanguage Model

Conclusion

ILLUSTRATIONS

ACKNOWLEDGMENTS

THIS WORK COULD NOT HAVE BEEN RESEARCHED AND WRITTEN without the strong support from Arizona State University and especially Patrick Kenney, the dean of the College of Liberal Arts and Sciences, and President Michael Crow, whose penchant for innovation provides us all with the space and place to tinker with the basis of thinking. My research sabbatical provided me the opportunity to spend half a year ensconced in the Zimmerman Library at the University of New Mexico and specifically in its Center for Southwest Research and Special Collections; its fine staff, including Samuel Sisneros, Nancy Brown-Martínez, and Christopher Geherin, escorted me through the mysteries of the fine Spanish and Mexican collections. To Samuel, who is able to decipher the most difficult of Spanish colonial paleography with its penchant for abbreviations, inverted letters, and idiosyncratic interpretations of spellings and syntax, I offer profound thanks; I still send him occasional phrases and words that stump even the most initiated. He was crucial in identifying pertinent documents that were most helpful, especially those on the Genizaros and the trilingual Ute-Spanish-English dictionary. To both him and Nancy, my deep appreciation for leading me to wonderful sources otherwise hidden from my neophyte view. I thank Chris for his patience and direction to sources with which I was unfamiliar. I hope I reciprocated to some degree. As important, thanks to the Southwest Hispanic Research Institute, under whose auspices I served as a visiting scholar, and especially to Maurice Kivlighan, who made my stay an easy and supported one. For her support, thanks also to Professor Barbara Reyes, the SHRI interim director. To my colleagues at UNM, on whom I first tried my rather strange ideas about the region and its peoples: Felipe González, José Rivera, and Michael Trujillo, *mil gracias por todo.* The work of editing and commentary by Luis Plascencia, to whom I am extremely grateful, produced a much clearer and hopefully connected work, as did commentary by my graduate students who suffered through an earlier draft. I very much appreciated the reviewers of the manuscript and their recommendations, and I followed most.

I could not have really begun to learn about the Matachine Complex without the unfailing good humor, wry insights, and extraordinary memory of all things Mexicano from New Mexico and its deeply embedded religiosity of Charles Aguilar—an extraordinary *rezador* and master of the funds of knowledge of the Bernalillo and most other Indigenous and Mexicano ritual complexes of New Mexico and Chihuahua. His rabbinical presence provided much of the cultural and historical glue necessary for the entire complex and community to function, and I passed some of my more esoteric interpretations by him. And certainly not last are the matachines of Bernalillo, who allowed me in their midst and responded to my at times naïve and probably boring inquiries.

Last but not least, I dedicate this work to all my family and especially to Nayely Luz Vélez-Cruz, my last kid and a very special young woman and extraordinary scholar-to-be; to my wife, María Luz Cruz Torres, an amazing anthropologist in her own right; to my daughters, Carmelita, Lucy, and Mariel, my overachieving spawns; and to Miguel and Carlos, who have gone through much and emerged sound and accomplished—my respect, love, and affection to all. To Damian, who has happily found his way, my respect and affection. To all four of my grandchildren, read and learn and embrace the courage of your ancestors, *Mexicano, español, e indígena.*

HEGEMONIES OF LANGUAGE AND
THEIR DISCONTENTS

"Las Tres Culturas," El Santuario de Chimayó, Chimayó, New Mexico, August 15, 2015, photograph by the author.

INTRODUCTION

༈

*In the beginning was the Word, and the Word was with God, and the Word was
God, and it was in English y en español.*
DOUAY-RHEIMS BIBLE WITH POETIC LICENSE

T HE "TRES CULTURAS" SCULPTURE adorning the opposite page is a recent
representation struck for the Sanctuary of Chimayó in New Mexico a few years
ago and provides a glimpse of the manner in which hegemony is innocently represented as if it were a neutral, congealed rendering of three "cultures"—by the open-
armed and rather stunted standing Indigenous person accepting the "word" from the
reader, the kneeling Hispano/Mexicano figure submitting with his hand on his face
in either rapture or shame, and, last, the reader of the word by a Western Anglo cow-
boy figure who, in the sculpture, is the only one with a seating arrangement and thus
of important status. Each has been sculpted so that the Anglo figure is tallest, the
stunted Indigenous figure is taller than the Hispano while standing but shorter than
the Anglo, and the kneeling Hispano/Mexicano is below them both. This sculptural
innocence cast in Mexico for the pastor of the sanctuary provides a seeming perfectly
harmonious acceptance of and gratitude for the English word being imparted. Yet
each cultural representation in their situated and unequal arrangement and the action
of transmitting the English word together form a symbolic representation of hundreds
of years of distributed language hegemony, but not their discontents. Yet only a few
years before the political bifurcation of the border region, another sculpture might
have arranged the Hispano/Mexicano as the reader of the word *en español* to the
shortened Indigenous figure, but certainly not their discontents. The known Middle
American practice by imperial regimes of burning the codices of other conquered
regimes and creating the new word of mythic legitimacy would seem to be an equivalent practice.[1] But what is most telling is the complete absence of the presence of any
African-origin representation; this denotes its absence not just from the historical
record of the region but also from the consciousness of the sculptor.[2]

In part, this mythic stone representation contributes to the masking of the "hidden histories" of populations, as Wolf (1983, 2010) has so eloquently phrased the process of denying, siloing, and creating caricatures of conquered populations and the ensuing processes of hegemonizing, homogenizing, and labeling such populations, which he states "are thought by many to have no history" (1983). From my point of view, removing and excising the languages of such populations contribute immensely to this erasing process. The remedy seems to lie not just in recovering those histories but also in telling the tale of how such ahistoricism takes place through the hegemonizing process—and more important, how those same populations create their own histories by expressing their discontents. As Schneider and Rapp (1995) have so eloquently stated, the way in which to accomplish this "is defining written and oral historical 'records' as among the sources to be mined by anthropologists. It means systematic use of archaeology, linguistics, ethnographic observations, and interviewing to discern a richer past. And it means listening for the histories that others produce for themselves" (7). But from my point of view it also means bringing to bear the most relevant theories, methodologies, and instruments of application to usefully advantage the population of that rearticulated history, and occasionally dipping into ethnobiography for gauging the proximity of our findings to that which we think is closer to what we think we have experienced. Lastly, in translating Spanish colonial materials and others to English, this text in fact does continue to privilege English over Spanish, and by doing so, as one of the blind reviewers of this book stated, "falls into the same trap of erasure and hegemonic practices." I agree that this does contribute to the privileging of English, but there are conditions that are not possible to remedy. That is, there are a number of works cited that were already translated to English by their sources from the colonial and Mexican periods, and so therefore, for consistency, this would require retranslating them to Spanish, the permissions for which would require extensive and time-consuming communications. Second, this would also require in some cases visiting the original Spanish colonial texts, many of which are in Spanish archives, another set of explorations that are not possible. Finally, this note itself unmasks the privileging inherent in my translating the Spanish texts. It is hoped that this removes a layer of that privilege and its inherent hegemonic structure. But we must be reminded that the Spanish texts themselves are part of that colonial and Mexican hegemony, translated or not.

Nevertheless, I seek to understand the long process of establishing language hegemonies by penetrating imperial and national states in the Southwest North American Region (SWNAR) and unlayering the hidden histories behind that from the Spanish colonial period to the present transnational and transborder periods of the United States and Mexico. I use the term *Southwest North American Region*, as will be developed, in favor of others such as the *Borderlands*, *Greater Mexico*, the *Great North*, or the *Spanish Frontier*, among others, to denote the huge transborder swath of ecology made up of subecologies, over which political and economic methods of human control and extraction, including a bifurcating border, have been impressed. Briefly, it is proposed that Southwest North America excludes Mesoamerica, which is roughly central Mexico and parts of Central America south from southern Sinaloa west to León, Guanajuato, and including Tampico, Tamaulipas.

Therefore, the SWNAR in the present would include four U.S. states and six northern Mexican states, and most importantly shares a common ecology of deserts, valleys, rivers, mountain ranges, marine zones, and flora and fauna. These are part of an interdependent (albeit asymmetrical) political economy, including Indigenous populations, the offspring of European populations (variously known as Españoles Mexicanos during the colonial area and Mexicanos during the national era), and the early presence of African-origin populations. Three hundred years later, new English-speaking populations spread themselves west in the aftermath of the American-Mexican War to the present, depending on which side of the region is referenced. Because of the imposition of the political line, the region after its establishment will be regarded as the "northern and southern regions" of the larger entity. I will develop this construct further in the following chapters.

The development of the manner in which languages and their attending ideological constructs were imposed upon resident populations from 1540 to the present basically pertains to this regional arena and is at the crux of this work, recognizing the earlier 1521 conquest of Tenochtitlan. Through the lenses of the Spanish colonial penetration by explorers and colonists, the national impositions of conquest by the United States, and continued imposition by the Mexican state in the SWNAR region, we will attempt to analyze the suppositions, ideologies, premises, and mechanisms by which Spanish and English became situated among Native peoples and later Mexican national populations during the nineteenth century and continuing with their descendants and migrating populations crossing the bifurcated but brittle border.

But it is apparent, from the title of this work, *Language Hegemonies and Their Discontents: The Southwest North American Region Since 1540*, that these impositions are not linear, nor are they necessarily easily or readily accepted by those subject to these processes. Instead this process is hydra-headed, complex, reactive, and accommodated at times but forcefully rejected at others. In many ways such impositions create dynamics totally in opposition to their intended function and lead to such actions as physical and linguistic revolts, hybridic versions, multilayered capacities of use and misuse, revitalizations, and intended tongue-in-cheek, recalcitrant, and often manipulative strategies of undermining the very process of linguistic erasure and imposition. At other times the hegemonies imposed on populations are strategically embraced by the subjects of the imposition, who then act to undermine them through legal and quasi-legal measures. As will be discussed below, these impositions and their reactions are "distributed" and are neither binary nor one-sided, except temporarily as the well-known accommodations and negotiations made early in the conquest by Mesoamerican elites such as the Tlaxcalans. They themselves penetrated the SWNAR with the first Spanish colonization by Juan de Oñate y Salazar in 1598, and probably earlier with Francisco Vásquez de Coronado's exploration in 1540.[3] I will provide case studies that hopefully represent the enormous range of possibilities from the Spanish colonial period to the present. What becomes very apparent is that such populations did not simply limp away, and at times I will provide autoethnographic and "witness" narratives of others to support the various contentions that emerge.

For the Spanish colonial period (1540–1821), we will explore the distribution of language hegemony through attention to the central mechanisms of imposition: the missions, the military, and the civil authority and their multiple methods, including literacy, performance, music, and legal constraints on communication. Once the short Mexican period terminated with the imposition of the region by the American-Mexican War (1846–1848) and the Gadsden Purchase in 1853, the northern and southern regions developed parallel but different processes linguistically and in terms of policies and approaches. English became the dominant language imposed on both Native peoples and Mexicans who remained after both the Treaty of Guadalupe Hidalgo and the Treaty of the Mesilla, and transborder Mexican populations were subjected to this dominance as well. Native peoples in the northern region were treated in the same manner as were Mexicans but with special tools such as boarding schools and English-only residences through forced acculturation. In the southern region, language impositions of Spanish over Indigenous languages continued between the mid-nineteenth century and the Mexican Revolution but in part this was integral to the emergence of "mestizos"—that is, those populations genetically and culturally the descendants mostly of Spanish, Indigenous, and/or African admixture, which by 1810 constituted 40 percent of the Mexican population (McCaa 2000, 265). Such mestizaje in the northern region was very similar but again bifurcated by the imposition of the border so that English imposition, although very much a politically imposed strategy, was strengthened by the large-scale migration of Americans to the northern region, especially after 1880 with development of the railroad and the wholesale migration of non-Mexican and non-Indigenous women from the midwestern, southern, and eastern United States. We will take up this demographically oriented discussion in later chapters, but all processes, both hegemonic and their discontents, are distributional, nonbinary, and not neither/nor or either/or.

We will approach this in chapter 1 by first considering the various ways to think about the discontents of language hegemony and ideologies as foundations for what follows. We will take a "distributional" approach that attempts to avoid the pitfalls of characterizing these phenomena either as homogeneous or as one of the dark saturation of imposition without the ray of the light of multifaceted discontents. But these are often naturalized by what Mary Pratt (1992) has termed the "seeing man" syndrome, which is the wholesale naturalization and moral centering of imposition by a colonial process and into the present. It is a way of representing the impositions and hegemony of colonizers "to secure their innocence" and thus obviate and mask their overbearing presence.

This discussion will provide a brush stroke of ideas and approaches from linguistic, cultural, and evolutionary anthropology, as well as from more philosophically inclined thinkers such as William Roseberry, James C. Scott, Eric R. Wolf, Raymond Williams, and Antonio Gramsci. Integrated within this discussion is a call to think about what we think and to simply gauge what enormously important impact one set of people has in trying to engage another set to change its way of communication by changing its language—the interesting, almost absent means of sharing not just simple information about the day's events but as, or more importantly *of*, our senses of ourselves and those events. In other words, these are the language images that communicate our relation to what we are saying and what we are saying in relation to ourselves, whether it be passionate, or befuddled, or suspicious, or objective, or neutral, or insightful, or merely uninformed and dumb. Language transmits those thoughts to different degrees coupled with movement and frowns or smiles, or shaking of the shoulders, or finger pointing. All contribute to the message about ourselves in some form or another. These approaches are ensconced within a broader material, physical, and regional context that shape and influence their possible usefulness for our purposes.

We will then unravel the political ecology of the SWNAR as a laboratory in which these foundations may fruitfully adhere as a means of explaining how and why this regional approach makes sense and, more importantly, how human populations of the region interacted, bumped, and changed each other, and we will take a small genetic transmission journey to support these underlying demographic and economic patterns of exchange and hegemony. We will develop the underlying broad "megascripts" that became the normalized premises and orientations guiding language hegemony with the Spanish colonial version steeped in medieval religiosity and biological pretense, the Mexican version steeped in incipient Europeanization and later nascent nationalism and mestizaje, and the American version steeped in manifest destinies of cultural and racial superiority embedded in economic ideologies of expansion, wealth, capitalism, and highly defended immigrant mentalities.

In chapter 2 we interrogate the hydra-headed approaches of Spanish colonial language impositions on Native peoples with a discussion of the mechanisms and premises used by the "seeing men": missionary agents, civil authorities, and the military and their attending discontents. It is here that the distributional model of hegemony and their discontents are amplified and discussed with operational processes suggested. From the Pueblo Revolt to the bilingual Pimas of Sonora answering in Pima to Spanish confessional interrogations, such discontents vary but reflect in kind the many examples of the common daily expressions of dissatisfaction as well as the use of Spanish legal methods to balance juridical issues. Some joined wholeheartedly to obtain or retain privilege within the Spanish colonial context as the literature will reveal. Nevertheless, *en toto* these are distributed by context, historical relations, negotiations, and partial to seemingly complete acceptance.

Chapter 3 emphasizes the use of performances as basic mechanisms of colonial language hegemony and, as importantly, the manner in which Indigenous populations resisted, accommodated, and used these impositions, and further how, in the present, some of these performances are crucial to language and cultural stability among New Mexicans. This chapter focuses on detailed discussions of the Matachine Complex among both the Rarámuri (Tarahumara) of Chihuahua and the Hispano/Mexicanos in New Mexico; both provide insights into the processes by which these performances became "owned" by both and eventually became ritual statements of cultural integrity as matachines turned themselves into "seeing men," upending the meaning and functions of the mediums of transmission. This illustrates again how such hegemonic practices are "distributed" and the range of their discontents. This chapter will integrate ethnographic fieldwork gathered in New Mexico during the period of August 1, 2014, to January 10, 2015, to augment the literature discussed.

Chapter 4 takes up the important bifurcating processes emerging from the American-Mexican War and the Gadsden Purchase and their resulting political, economic, and educational processes in the northern region, as well as their parallel but entirely different developments in the southern region, all up through the middle of the twentieth century. This chapter emphasizes the differential approaches of hegemonic practices imposed over both Indigenous and Mexican-origin populations in the north and those over Indigenous populations in the south, as well as the manner in which the political ecology of the region served as crucial causative factors and their attending discontents. We will glimpse the often psychically harmful programs instituted, from the "1C" programs that segregated Mexican-origin children, to the practice of corporal punishment for forbidden Spanish being spoken in English-only boarding schools and similar practices in boarding schools for Indigenous children.

Chapter 5 provides a glimpse of the education narratives based on the eugenics movement of the early twentieth century and their curricular and language consequences. These represent the institutional narratives of the "seeing man" in educational terms, which are offset by the inherited ideological narratives of optional scripts. We will explore the emergence of optional narratives transmitted through the Mexican

Revolution, such as the Indianist philosophy, historical confrontation, and the philosophically transcendent idea of the mestizo in the form of cultural nationalism as introduced by Octavio Romano-V. These, as will be discussed, are strong narratives to the megascripts of the "American Dream," but I will introduce two other equally strong constructs that seem to be absolutely in opposition. First is the Mexican feminist revolutionary narrative that was carried, practiced, and integrated by women into the ideological premises of already existing Mexican populations in the very early twentieth century and that strongly influenced Chicana feminism fifty-five years later. The second was carried by about one hundred thousand men and women bringing their conservative Catholic beliefs while fleeing from the Cristero Rebellion of the 1920s; these beliefs proved to be important sources for Mexican Catholic parochial education in Arizona, Texas, and California and for the formation of Mexican-origin middle classes. Many of these ideological narratives were expressed by Mexican-origin newspapers, and these were inherited and created by new generations of Chicanas and Chicanos.

Chapter 6 traces the genesis of the English-only phenomenon and its political demography in the northern region and explores bilingualism and Spanish as secondary in a "white" context as explained by Jane Hill (n.d.) and others. This phenomenon is a well-articulated "seeing man" discourse accentuated with elaborate rationales blended with the missionary zeal of its inducers, and it appeals to the linguistic salvation of children. This chapter also takes up the dynamic and continuous asymmetry of the spread of English south in the region and the manner in which English has become a second but not secondary language. The chapter discusses how the region enjoys three processes simultaneously—the growth of bilingualism and the new demography, the English-only penchant, and the penetrations of English south—each with their own contradictions to the other.

Chapter 7 focuses on an analysis of the most recent advances in dual language programs, their underlying neurological and linguistic rationales and program achievements, and their possible advantages by the use of "funds of knowledge" methodology as developed by a variety of researchers—all based on regional and cultural capital approaches to the changing transnational and transborder economic and ecological processes in the twenty-first century. These are in fact "seeing" language from other-than-colonial projects and rationales and blend what we know are closer to approximations between learning to learn without compromise and accentuation of what others see as beneficial to the steady and possible positive expansion of the various selves of ourselves. I proffer a concluding chapter that attempts to tie all the many hydra-headed elements that comprise this discussion and provides a glimpse of what may be possible for the future of the region and its many peoples.

1

HEGEMONIES OF LANGUAGE

꣸

Theoretical Outlines of Language Impositions and Their
Distributions—A Political Ecology of Southwest North America

I knew something wasn't quite right when the bubble-nosed principal yanked me
out of the line of first grade children waiting to walk into their classroom in Tuc-
son. He pulled me to his office, where he rationalized his punishment by prefacing
the "swats" I was to receive with a statement that it was a school rule not to speak
Spanish or any "other tongue." I had no idea what this meant at the time, even
after the three hits with the smooth-ended paddle he used to impress me with what
I didn't understand. I have been trying, I think, to understand this for the next
many years that I have lived.

ME, REFLECTION AND RECOLLECTION ON HOW TO
BEGIN THIS BOOK, AUGUST 30, 2015

ATTEMPTING TO INFUSE CONTROL OVER OTHERS by violence or persuasion, and everything in between, by a population with a very different language
and view of the world is a daunting task. Such processes we may regard as attempts to
impose "language hegemony"—that is, the sometimes attempted replacement of one
language over the other and/or sometimes the restriction of a subordinated language
to domains defined by the other. I will elaborate this further. Certainly the Catholic
imperial Spanish Crown was no stranger to this process when it undertook the colonization of what we now term North America, Central America, and South America.
In Spain, almost parallel to its being jelled as a unified kingdom, non-Muslims had
been engaged for seven hundred years in the opposite task of ridding themselves of
the occupation of the Islamic Empire and its grand influences. On the eastern side of
the North American continent, the English version of this task of colonization was
one less of linguistic replacement than simple mercantile expansion and territorial
occupation without the stress or limitations of missionization and conversion, focusing instead on the expulsion of Indigenous peoples. This strategy was also mostly
followed by their American descendants except for later in the late nineteenth century,
and it was similarly followed in the American-Mexican War with Mexicans. That said,

however, like the Spaniards, most American policies to the present followed "one language only" approaches for those who remained and for those who migrated and resettled back into lands segmented by the newly constructed border.

The "cultural bumping" of human populations, as I have said elsewhere (Vélez-Ibáñez 1996), is very much a project of different cultural populations seeking to expand and mostly overwhelm populations already present. The colonial project from the sixteenth century to almost the present is one in which empires led by armies of soldiers, merchants, farmers, wealth seekers, missionaries, and governments spread over vast reaches of the then-known world—from Europe and the teeny island of England to every continent across the Pacific, Atlantic, and Indian Oceans, the Mediterranean, and the Caribbean and countless seas such as the Sea of Cortez and too many others to enumerate. Colonialism produced "master narratives" that became the "master's narratives" and justified expansion by creating funds of knowledge (to be discussed in chapter 7) that rationalized it like a historical rendering, and numerous literary narratives upheld and legitimized that rationalization for overwhelming one or more populations over others. These became the "megascripts" that were normalized and became part of the conscious and unconscious grand premises that guided the basis of overwhelming others.

By "megascripts" I mean ideologically driven, always incomplete, naturalized rationalizations of power, dominance, and exploitation buttressed by local and regional scripts. These may be constituted and expressed as "normalized" rationalizations, values, beliefs, rituals, symbols, and accepted "civil" discourses of many sorts.[1] Thus, the overwhelming medieval megascript of the Spanish colonial period was an underlying and unswerving commitment to a rigid Counter-Reformation Catholicism ensconced within a militarized experience formed by seven hundred years of combat and violence with the Islamic Empire in southern Spain—all coupled with a benevolent bent based on the salvation of the souls of populations who had not invited their "conversions," with some exceptions, as will be discussed. These are in fact the "seeing man" scripts promulgated and communicated by different forms. Within the written, oral, performed, and pronounced discourses arising from such a narrative, the cultural glue of a privileged caste, an emotional and affective commitment to the presence of the devil and witchcraft, the salvation of unconverted souls, the search for wealth and control of resources of humans, their physical and psychic spaces, and a right of fire and sword all written for an unyielding and contradictory medieval Catholic script. It has rationalized many times, with contradictory medieval logic, multitudes of both paternalistic and protective strategies toward Native peoples, as well as the willingness to visit atrocious violence on any resisting populations. Pushed along by profit-motivated individuals who funded many of the exploratory as well as colonizing efforts, and by an increasingly bankrupt Crown, the Spanish framework took hold. But it was both fragile and prone to negotiations and modifications by Indigenous peoples, as exemplified by the Tlaxcalans early in the conquest, who negotiated their autonomy without encomienda for their having helped the Crown defeat the Aztecs (Sabes 2010, 22).

Later, the Mexican Republic's impositions (1821), to different degrees to the present, were organizationally very much reminiscent of the Spanish script but coupled with a republican political agenda based on private ownership, individual rights, and a laissez-faire economy but often interrupted by revolts and political intrigue. Likewise, the English-speaking populations of the British Crown, moving across the Atlantic and penetrating the East Coast with its new colonies, entertained very different megascripts to rationalize its presence, including ideologies of commerce pushed by charter companies under Crown license, Puritanism, elimination of witchcraft and devil worship, and, most importantly, a quest for territory to establish individual farms for unwanted populations such as prisoners where the indentured servants and later African slaves could be utilized in what became plantation economies. Later American versions propelled these megascripts with an aggressive and violent expansion under the guise of Manifest Destiny and coupled to ideologies of individual freedom, republicanism, and contradictions like the Three-Fifths Compromise—which guided the allocation of legislative representation and taxes—the expulsion of Indigenous peoples, the invasion of Mexico, and their corporal demise when either expedient or important. All were buttressed to an increasingly massive immigration movement of English speakers and Europeans in the nineteenth century, from 8,400 annually in 1820 to almost 800,000 in 1880.[2]

Language was used in all of their communicative formats and mediums, including schooling, books, letters, announcements, instructions, pronouncements, declarations, constitutions, amendments, ritualizations, performances, epic poems, memorials, biographies, musical compositions, and histories, to convey these scripts. Such mediums sometimes communicated violently and without recourse, sometimes with appeal to life after death, sometimes with offers that could not be resisted, and many times with narratives that were ingenious, subtle, structurally hidden, and much beyond the purview of those being affected.

Simultaneously, those subjected to such processes did not sit idly by but many times joined those master narratives—and the language that represented them—and, with that, gaining the overwhelming power to overpower others. Sometimes they submitted but did not surrender. Sometimes they integrated and negotiated these megascripts of newly imposed rules, regulations, laws, economies, physical controls, and territorial redefinitions with new names and explicit boundaries, and, in interesting and mostly contradictory ways, they sometimes adopted, adjusted, and adapted these narratives until they seemed to be their own, and they strongly identified with that which originally sought to overwhelm them and displace local narratives of beliefs and values. Many times they fought for the very agents that would lead them to linguistic and cultural submission, or so it seemed.

However, there is an underlying human dynamic that was present throughout all these processes and that is that "living action . . . can never be the logical consequence of any grand design" (Turner 1974, 13). Whatever the megascript, these are filled in the first place with contradictions and conflicts of rationalizations, applications, and negotiations over space and time. These underlie most repetitive attempts of the megascripts being established through schooling, examples, dictums, pronouncements, regulations, laws, organizational and administrative structures, doctrines, celestial beliefs, practices, and, most importantly, rituals and performance—all are fragile and incomplete and dialectical. Built into their formats are all the ingredients for their failure and partial success. These dynamics are such that when impressed on others, those so affected during the process of their application are not without discontent as well. Rather, in reflecting on van Gennep's ideas on rites of passage, Turner states a wonderful insight into these processes: "[I]n all ritualized movements there was at least a moment when those being moved in accordance with a cultural script were liberated from normative demands, when they were, indeed, betwixt and between successive lodgments in jural political systems. In this gap between ordered worlds almost anything may happen" (13). The attempted imposition of already incomplete megascripts and their underlying contradictory demands for adherence and performance either by acquiescence, acceptance, or force, as well as their "cultural bumping" against other similarly creating "native" ones, would seem to be the perfect laboratory for almost anything happening.[3] And it did—and for the culturally bumped, and for those bumping, the emergence of liminal spaces, places, and senses of selves and their attending communicative modes unfolded and continues to do so among myriad populations worldwide to the present moment, and certainly for this region. What is fascinating is that such processes are also indicated genetically and are, in their distribution of DNA, "between and betwixt"—even though all the populations that moved across the Atlantic were themselves part of earlier such processes, but claims to "purity of blood" trumped their genetic history, of which, of course, they were unaware. I take these processes up more fully in chapters 2 and 3.

I am mostly concerned with the way in which such processes emerged for the almost five hundred years between the Spanish colonial period to the English-speaking present in the space I label the Southwest North American Region (SWNAR). I will expand this notion later, but it basically comprises what we regard as the southwestern United States and northern Mexican states—but these political boundaries are not the most definitive aspects of the concept. Instead, I take a multilayered political ecology approach that seems to support this idea and will be discussed fully.

But for this explanatory journey, we need to be guided by some major concepts about the way in which we think we think and the way in which we approach the question of the hegemony of language and its discontents.

THINKING ABOUT WHAT WE THINK WE THINK

I take this step to think about what we think to simply gauge the enormously important impact one set of people has in trying to engage another set to change its way of communication by changing its language—the interesting, almost absent means of sharing not just simple information about the day's events but also—and perhaps more importantly—about our senses of those events and of ourselves. As I have stated in the introduction, those are language images that communicate our relation to what we are saying and what we are saying in relation to ourselves, whether it be passionate, or befuddled, or suspicious, or objective, or neutral, or insightful, or merely uninformed and dumb. Language transmits this to different degrees, coupled with movement and frowns or smiles, or the shaking of the shoulders or the pointing of a finger, or as might be the case for some, the expression may be stone cold, even though a twitch may give it all away. All contribute to the message about ourselves in some form or another.

We can partially appreciate how important this is can be if we borrow insights from evolutionary anthropologists like Terrance W. Deacon (2012). Through a number of studies, he lays the foundation for what it means to be an individual organism and with organizational complexities and, by inference, what this means for language development. For him, individuation is responsible not only for its organizational designs but also for its own maintenance and perpetuation, which he refers to as "teleodyamics—that both delineates and creates the individuality that is the organism itself. Organism functions are indirectly self-referential and self-projecting" (Deacon 2012, 465), so we create ourselves biologically and cognitively in relation to others. This self-creative process of self-sustainability and portability more importantly provides the basis of considering how agency is an expanding "built-in" requirement for the selves of ourselves to evolve, develop, and expand our capacities for the further individuation of the agent itself. This process is, however, an ahistoric one and not muddled by historical realities such as colonization, invasions, or attempted linguistic replacement. But that is a further narrative, so for the moment we will keep this theoretically "clean."

This direction proposed by Deacon is in part a response to earlier biocognitive orientations proposed by the biologists Maturana and Varela beginning in 1972 and continuing through the present. Their notion of *autopoiesis* (meaning self-creation) provided a substantial advance in complex systems thinking—this concept is one in which each living being is creating itself as it emerges or, as Deacon describes it, "the core self-referential dynamics of both life and mind that constitutes an observational perspective" (2012, 6).[4] According to Mingers (1990, 319), this perspective in regard to language is one in which the "development of language is a subject-dependent domain rather than a domain of reality." From this complex adaptive systems approach, in which both biological and cognitive systems are interactive systems for the individual to emerge and interact with other autopoiesis systems such as cultural and social domains, linguistic behavior is connotative and not prescriptive (329). According to Mingers, the process of using language—or "languaging"—occurs only when the linguistic behaviors become coordinated, emerging only when the nervous system has so developed itself "that it can interact with its own symbolic descriptions" (1991, 329). This can only occur if there is a "consensual coordination of action," so language is always an activity, especially intersecting the "self" and the myriad domains of action. Agency, it would seem to follow, is one in coordinated conjunction between selves, associated others, and their structures of commonalities identified in the flow of the actions.

Yet Deacon, in a very simple but elegant suggestion, states that the "theory . . . avoids the challenges posed by phenomena whose existence is determined with respect to something displaced, absent, or not yet actualized, because these are defined in internalized self-referential form" (2012, 6). In essence, Deacon does not deny the promise of the autopoeises construct and does not eliminate the active languaging processes of human self-referencing and entering structures of commonality in other domains, which kick off responses as well as "shudderings" internally and in relation to others. These are necessary but not sufficient to explain the recurring existences and emergence of "absential" phenomena where there is no there, there. Thus from both Deacon's and my point of view, agency transcends the necessary "presence" or stimulation of other actions that are always incomplete anyway. For Deacon and myself, "*Such concepts as information, function, purpose, meaning, intention, significance, consciousness, and value are intrinsically defined by their fundamental incompleteness*" (Deacon 2012, 23; italics original). As such, "intentionality" is the motor for agency, and when that very deeply embedded absential potential is denied or obstructed, what makes us "us" is put into question, even though it is not "there" and absent. The sources for such potential emerges within social relations.

That agency is greatly tested and emerges in social relations in which we have to give and take in order to get what we would like or what we would give because the basis of our capacity to continue to garner or give—the basis of human groups—is social reciprocity.[5] Without self-referencing and other referencing to decide intentions and to signal those intentions through language, our capacity for our various selves to grow and expand may be placed in jeopardy or stasis, or may make us pretty crazy. These potentials to signal reciprocity then emerge in not just the relationship and in action but in the various "ourselves" and the "others" on whom we depend for social identity and simple sociability—the core of being able to get and give things while simultaneously "not there."

One way in which such capacities, either by volition or as unintended consequences, are endangered is by making those relationships so damaging and oppressive that the organism simply becomes confused about its selves, denies that such endangerment is occurring (which is not sustainable), or somehow blends the oppressive messages and actions to become part of internal and intentional selves. Such relationships may not, in the long term, be healthy for the organism as a whole. It may very well be that such a process empties our capacity for the functioning absenteeism of the "not there." It may also call into question our capacity to continue an emerging autopoeises that is not tangled and mangled like the tangles of synaptic plasticity impacted by dementia and Alzheimer's disease.

And, of course, among the other multitudes of possible responses to such circumstances is that the organism joins with others of like selves and, through symbolic communication, acts out against such oppression through physical violence, ritual adaptation, syncretic mixing, and/or resigned acceptance but hardly ever surrenders. And much later, in the concluding chapters, I will develop how "languaging" ideas may be useful in forming "translanguaging" processes and programs in response to negative language policies and practices.[6] Given these general ideas then, what does occur when the major means of communication for reciprocity, for group life, and certainly about the senses of selves and their absent spaces becomes the object of replacement, denigration, substitution, or erasure of the modus operandi of one group over another? Simultaneously, what are the responses of those so affected, and how are both impositions and responses distributed over time and place?

This is the central focus for this work, which involves the attempts by European colonial powers to hegemonize the very means of communication and development of selves in the newly "discovered" continent—that is, a continent unknown to them but obviously well discovered by the thousands of years of presence by populations misnamed "Indians." However, this is not just their story but also that of other populations who themselves were part of the original oppressors who themselves had to undergo similar processes and continue to do so, sometimes voluntarily and sometimes not. These are Mexicans, whom I refer to as "Mexican-origin," regardless of which side of the newly bifurcated line dividing the Southwest North American Region they reside. The narrative of language hegemony in this context, however, cannot quite yet be told, since we need to have a general agreement on terms as to what this means, their parameters, and how this couples to the very brief exploration of the various selves involved.

THE DISTRIBUTIONS OF LANGUAGE
HEGEMONY AND THEIR DISCONTENTS[7]

In his 1983 speech to the faculty senate of the City University of New York, Eric R. Wolf stated that "it is only when we integrate our different kinds of knowledge that the people without history emerge as actors in their own right. When we parcel them out among the several disciplines, we render them invisible—their story, which is also our story, vanishes from sight" (Wolf 1983, 1). For Wolf, parceling out people who have not been afforded the respect of broad and deep historical treatments is an artifact of disciplinary silos that exclude the rich textures of experience in favor of a Europeanized penchant for reducing populations conquered and studied to types or superficial sketches to be replaced by homogeneously defined states, empires, and nations. Such peoples "are thought by many to have no history" (ibid.). From the point of view of this book, such a process is also deeply tied to removing the manner in which such hidden populations communicated with each other and with others not unlike themselves. This is an attempt to render such populations mute without the ability to "talk back," therefore guaranteeing their absence from a more nuanced and enriched narrative all buttressed by "seeing men" moralizations. As we will see in later chapters, the historicized Mexican origin narratives in the region are quite at variance with the siloed descriptions and examinations of Mexican children in the same chapter, who were not only ahistoricized by educational studies of their inferiority but homogenized to sketches of themselves. Homogenization, ahistoricization, and hegemonization run together in attempting to remove entire populations from existentially and historically derived selves. Trying to substitute the languages of "others" is simultaneously an attempt to dehistoricize them. We will take up the task of balancing things a bit in the ensuing chapters.

This process, then, of attempted replacement and simultaneous substitution of language of one population over the other we may regard as "language hegemony" or, if we take a more active approach, "languaging hegemony"—all the diverse processes seeking to end, bend, and twist a conquered population's means of communication. Or, if we were to follow Wolf's wonderful phrase that also titled his fine book, *Europe and the People Without History* (2010), we will be examining this process through language and cultural lenses—that is, the hegemonies of language suppression and replacement of a people's language are not clean processes but very messy and filled with contradictions and oppositions. Eventually these lead to attempts by those so affected to create their own narratives as part of their discontents, as is this work. In part, the counterpoint of these hegemonic processes are the discontents that are distributed throughout the unwritten local record of populations but told in daily narratives.

But since the notion of "hegemonies" is fairly unfamiliar to most audiences, we will look at some traditional notions that capture both processes and attention to keeping unsiloed. William Roseberry states its parameters: "I propose that we use the concept [hegemony] *not* to understand consent but to understand struggle; the ways in which the words, images, symbols, forms, organizations, institutions, and movements used by subordinate populations to talk about, understand, confront, accommodate themselves to, or resist their domination are shaped by the process of domination itself" (1994, 360–61; italics original).

But as Roseberry would agree, this struggle—which undergirds the works by Gramsci (1971, 1973), is elaborated by Williams (1977), and is deliberated by Derrida (1974)—is part of the daily interaction within and between different cultural populations from childhood through adulthood, between the narratives told in households and the narratives told in schools and institutions, within and between contending rituals, between children and children and between adults and adults, and, importantly, between children and adults, and between major means of communication and populations being convinced to be coerced or convinced to consent to the efficacy of the message givers from ancient empires through modern nation-states. Or, to state it in a more complex adaptive sense, the struggle is one of creating structures of commonality, in which the organism being impressed will somehow agree to eventually respond to the imposing organism's pitch so that the two can emerge in some kind of mutual and potential development. However, such a process is not only of long duration but beset with incompleteness, contradictions, and oppositions, that, even while seemingly adoptive and adaptive, are "shudderings" rather than integrations for further emergence, given the impact of hegemonic processes.

One important early intellectual guide to this notion of "hegemony" is the work of James C. Scott. His early work was very much oriented toward the resistance of rural peasants and sought to note how "the distinctive patterns of belief and behavior which are valued by the peasantry of an agrarian society" constitute "a pattern of structural, stylistic, and normative opposition to the politico-religious tradition of ruling elites" (Scott 1977a). Therefore, much of this original work was focused on patron-client, face-to-face relationships and not systemic responses to oppression. His focus was on the anthropological idea of the "little tradition" of folk beliefs and practices as main carriers of resistance. He rearticulated this position in later works in which he focused on "structures of personal domination, such as serfdom and slavery" (Scott 1990, 62). Here he departed from Foucault, who was focused on the "'impersonal,' 'scientific,' disciplinary forms of the modern state" (Scott 1990, 62) and who focused on power relations not as "a binary structure with 'dominators' on the one side and 'dominated' on the other" (Foucault 1980, 142). Foucault stated that this "was not a relation between a political structure, a government, a dominant social class, the master facing the slave, and so on" (ibid.). Rather, the practice and exercise of using power has as its mirrored processes resistance as a normative consequence so that "a whole field of responses, reactions, results, and possible inventions may open up [in contexts of power expression]" (Foucault 1982, 220). From the point of view of my work, "discontent" is both a feature of power relations and the use of myriad forms of adaptation, invention, and multiple strategies and tactics to take advantage of opportunities, structures, networks, and relationships, as well as the means and media of communication in order to do so. The expression of power is both systemic and personal; it is both impersonal and personal; it is both dyadic and carried over multitudes of networks of relations and nodes of transmission. It is "local" and "intermediary," and it is "national" and "transnational," and it relocates itself through multitudes of institutional mediums and local networks of communications. These are "articulated" up and down and across through multiple paid and unpaid agents from teachers to politicians and from friends to enemies. Discontent is also as varied as it is the expression of power. Discontent may range from symbolism to an AK-47, but it, too, is articulated in various forms, formats, and mediums, and sometimes it results in the elimination of the entire powerful apparatus, like that which occurred during the Pueblo Revolt (1680) or the Mexican Revolution (1910). But there is a hidden dimension that the powerful enjoy in the initial stages of their hegemonizing and homogenizing and ahistoricizing processes that those in contention do not have.

Numerous commentators beside those mentioned above have taken on the task of probing these processes, including those who think about "posthegemony" notions that, although intellectually interesting, are not too well supported by ethnographic reality as far as I can see.[8] But I am going to pick and choose those most helpful, and among these is the insightful work by Mary Louise Pratt, *Imperial Eyes: Travel Writing and Transculturation* (1992). Among other valuable concepts, she uses the term *anticonquest* in a refreshing but not obvious manner and states that this is the idea of "the strategies of representation whereby European bourgeois subjects seek to secure their innocence in the same moment they assert European hegemony" (7). From initial contact by the Spanish imperial "seeing man," who is the "European male subject of European landscape discourse—he whose imperial eyes passively look out and possess" (7), upon entering this "new world," the "pan or palo" (bread or stick) approach is rendered. As will be noted in the discussion relating to Juan de Oñate y Salazar's performative entrance in crossing the Río Grande from El Paso del Norte, standard celestial references and disclaimers of biblical proportions leading to perpetual sustenance by a Catholic God and his son and mother and accompanying angels, saints, and cherubims were coupled with claims of legal control over life, limb, and space, which, unfulfilled or disobeyed, could only lead to serious corporal punishments and resistance met by fire and sword. Throughout most communications, there will always be present this "anti-conquest" patina, either expressed or implied. From such contradictions emerge the structure of hegemonic development and their discontents. Most imperial or national hegemonic processes seem to have as their underlying frame of reference a presented rationale. This was couched in the language of innocence, salvation, spiritual connection, a betterment formula of some sort, and, of course, purity of intention balanced by instruments guaranteeing obeisance, obedience, and replacement by purchase, violence, "brainwashing," and an exchange for life and limb against its opposite. These colonial "seeing man" narratives were part of the many declarations made by the Spanish colonial regime such as the Rights of Vassalage and the Acts of Possession and Obedience. As will be discussed, these were formulaic declarations of hegemony of body, territory, and mind of Indigenous peoples couched in legalese and sacred references, with an underlying threat of arms and fire. Such processes, however, transcend epoch or period. The seeing man position extends certainly into the modern period of rationalized hegemonization expressed by such rationales as "manifest destiny," masking the slavery orientations of almost every American president throughout the eighteenth and nineteenth centuries, except for both of the Adamses and Lincoln. The seeing man blinds himself by his rationalizations and his ideological meganarratives in order to be supported in committing the worst of atrocities and to support rationalizations for the religious conversion of "others" to be saved. The seeing man extends into the twentieth century and into the present as liberal concerns about the efficacy of language for "second language" speakers by privileging it as the first; the ensuing labels of seeming scientific categories such as "ESL" and a plethora of others visited upon children become markers of concern and educational programming, masking its underlying "whiteness" and noblesse oblige. Each of the following chapters provide different versions and formats of the seeing man phenomenon that undergird the capacity of both naturalizing and making possible the distribution of hegemonic practices and their language impositions and distributions. But as will be shown, such hegemonic processes are deliberately and sometimes unconsciously undermined by those who can "see" through the seeing man phenomenon.

But there are dimensions of the notion of hegemony that I would like to take up, especially in relation to what I would suggest are the "distributions of hegemony," the impact of their impositions, and the "distributions of discontent" that are as variable as the populations and contexts in which these emerge. By "distributions of hegemony," I mean the multiple and unequal dissemination and use of coercive actions of violence, mechanisms, mediums, events, methods, and ideologies by which impositions are delivered by imperial or national authorities in order to control and/or exploit the populations undergoing such processes.[9] These are mitigated as Foucault would suggest: "a whole field of responses, reactions, results, and possible inventions may open up" (Foucault 1982, 220). Thus the "distributions of discontent" refers to the multiple, varied, and complex expressions of struggles that mirror the processes of hegemonic distributions and are as diverse. They range from passive nonresponses to seeming domination, to physical and symbolic violence and rebellion. A well-known example in the region is the use of "Spanglish"—what may be termed as a kind of "fractual recursivity"—which Zentella defines as (in the case of Spanglish) "the alternation of several dialects of Spanish and English [that] so challenges the notion of bounded languages and identities that any effort to halt the crossing of linguistic boundaries [will prove] as foolhardy as the proverbial finger in the dike" (Zentella 2003, 61). From one perspective, it is basically the adaptation of using English verbs and nouns in the syntax of Spanish, although I would suggest it is a matter of context and intent, such as a gardener using *rakiar* for 'raking,' or of intentional joking by using twists on words such as *Trumpudo* for 'Trump' or *El jello port car* for 'The yellow car port'.[10] And the crossing occurs daily under the noses of the correctional authorities and is judged as inferior and impure—neither the King's English nor the Castellano of the Royal Academy of Spain. It is in fact a kind of thumbing of the fickle finger at the most unconscious level, and to do it well takes great skill in both languages. Nevertheless, it is coercively treated in most institutional settings but not without a price. "Spanglish-ing" of course is part of the larger phenomenon of the not too often admired "code-switching" and a bane to both English and Spanish language teachers in the region.[11]

The coercive aspects are one part of the Gramscian formula, with the other being what I would term *legitimacy* or a complex unity of coercion and consent in situations of domination.[12] These distributions of hegemony and distributions of discontent are allied and mirrored process that may occur simultaneously to the attempted domination or even after established acquiescence of those being dominated. However, coercive actions such as violence, physical segregation, enslavement, and other equally untempered approaches will more than likely be short-term solutions to the establishment of some sort of hegemony. Unless such coercions turn into internalized legitimate rationalizations over time and are seemingly adopted by those dominated, then it is highly likely that constant rebellion in multiple forms will become normative, such as in many of the conflicts between the Spanish empire and multitudes of Indigenous peoples.[13] On the other hand, when coercion was coupled with processes leading to eventual acceptance, then coercion and control eventually become internalized as legitimacy and "freedom" and are naturalized as if they had always existed. In such settings, the coercion/legitimacy arc is a "distributed" one in which hegemony and discontentment are its underlying initiating mirrored platforms.

Hegemonic impositions then are deeply and profoundly historical, ecological, economic, cultural, social, and psychological but also distributional in force, density, intensity, and internalization. Yet fragile or overwhelming hegemonic processes seep into the very consciousness to different degrees of that which makes us "us" and them "them" and the "there's" of absent spaces and places, more so as fractured versions of the original impositions. And, of course, actual physical places and spaces become imbued with what they are called, termed, or categorized, so "El Río Grande" in Spanish masks the Pueblo names for "big river," such as those in Tewa or Jemez, but is also imbued with sacra.[14] The English version of "Rio Grande" shortened the Spanish name and made it mostly a connotation instead of a denotation.

But such processes are compounded theoretically and operationally. As Deacon (2012, 7) suggests, "Like meanings and purposes, consciousness may not be something *there* in any typical sense of being materially or energetically embodied, and yet may still be materially causally relevant." The means of transferring the "not there" is another "not there" phenomenon—language, whether written, spoken, heard, or imagined, is materially and causally relevant, as Deacon would say. From my point of view, language, like consciousness, has an "unnoticed option" in that it, too, is defined by its absential character, yet it deeply impacts the material, social, emotive, and cultural worlds of our species, of which I have always tried to make sense in a material way. But the ringer is that language, like consciousness, is not also not there, and what is not there as well is "me," to paraphrase Deacon. This wonderful space and not space is among the great contradictions as possibilities for invention, innovation, and experimentation but also perhaps a source of denial when their opposites occur, such as imposition, oppression, and exploitation, justified by stints of elaborated ritualization and ideological convictions. From my point of view, the "me" is probably in others and "they" in what I consider the "me" with all of their attending spaces/not spaces, so that for millennia this funny species has set up all sorts of parameters for those "me's" and the "not there" meanings and the sounds and patterns that we call language and for our capacity for absent representations. Therefore, language impositions and their myriad attending behaviors have profound possible shatterings and generative possibilities to the not present "there," and in a way, that is what my not there "me" is interested in.

This work is one of continuing development in which I am trying to understand how language imposition takes shape of the "me's" and the others when peoples meet, collide, fight, resist, accommodate, and cooperate. The "me" of me is, very much like everyone else, a complex of deeply pushed "not there's" emergent from an experimental imagining that I have termed the Southwest North American Region (SWNAR). I will get there in a bit, but this is also part of a many-layered experience of having been born by accident in Saint Joseph's Hospital in Nogales, Arizona, and it would seem to be a kind of "not there" memory that pushed me forward to this moment of incipient explanations. Let me expand.

TRANSBORDER CLASS EXISTENCES:
A BIT OF AUTOETHNOBIOGRAPHY

For autobiographic context, I was raised in Tucson, Arizona; I was carried there, in fact, after being born in a bit of a rush in Nogales, Arizona—a border town parallel to its Mexican counterpart of Nogales, Sonora. Neither of these towns existed prior to the carving of this part of the border region in 1853, and in reality they were not invented until late in the nineteenth century.[15] While living in Tucson, my parents and sister, and I in the womb, were visiting relatives in Magdalena, Sonora—a town founded by the famous missionary Eusebio Kino, and a 120-mile trek south that my parents and, later, I made at least once every month or so; in turn my cousins and uncles from both sides of the family visited us, and some also went to school in Tucson.

However, on this trek on October 27, 1936, we were returning to Tucson and a few miles south of the border line—as my mother stated, "Siempre eras muy inquieto" (You were always very restless)—my mother went into labor and evidently barely made it to Saint Joseph's Hospital in Nogales, Arizona. There, after I was born, she said that I was placed in a crib next to the window that faced the cyclone fence separating Sonora and Arizona and that my feet were pointed south and my head was facing north. After some rest and recuperation, we all returned to Tucson where, for the next many years, I lived a basically transborder existence of very dense cross-border relations and visits and rituals and boyhood escapades, and, more than anything else, I learned and experimented. I was exposed in this many-layered region to cultural and social contradictions and commonalities, to bi- and trilingualism, and to many-layered cultural dimensions of expectations, values, and coding for and about behaviors.

In Tucson during the summer heat, we played baseball on a rocky, barren lot behind my house that was bounded by a local cement pond about two feet deep that belonged to the local water company. We lived a sound working-class life of limited income, homemade toys, and a five-block walk to the local elementary school where we were spanked for every word of Spanish heard by the principal—but that is a later story. What made this all a bit dizzy is that when we visited Magdalena, we changed class; my uncle was a doctor in a huge house with laundry rooms in the back in which washerwomen scrubbed my five cousins' clothes and ours as well. In the kitchen, the cook and maid sat while all the rest of us ate our breakfast, lunches, and dinners in the dining area. When, as a five-year-old, I curiously asked the question of why they were not sitting with the rest of the family in the dining room, the response was a muted one communicated only by disapproving looks. Past Magdalena, as a fifteen-year-old, I visited Mexico City, where my other cousins and aunts lived in interesting splendor; this was accentuated by a visit to a huge marketplace where I looked at some leather objects. A Mexican teenager struck up a kid's conversation with me when my Mexico

City aunt guided me away, stating that "no es de tu clase" (he is not of your class). But on my return to Tucson, I still continued to play *pelota* in back of my house, and my father continued bringing home his $75 a week paycheck, and my mother made ends and bills meet with eggs from our chickens and my eating Rainbow bread— white and filled with air and great by itself dipped in Del Monte Catsup—while my older sister Lucy read *Don Quixote* in Spanish while listening to Glenn Miller, Pérez Prado, and Luis Arcaraz.

The many "me's" for those of us raised in the region were created and distributed by the constant noise and clamor of many times opposing and sometimes parallel cultural notions of living and dying, and the language used to convey all this was sometimes Spanish and sometimes English, and for some it was the O'odham spoken by the Tohono O'odham and Pima Ayto. This was multidirectional but always done with a certain pride of being able to negotiate and manipulate the sounds and the meanings and the "there's" and "not there's."

For the "me's," and for many who were part of this region, and certainly for the anthropologists like me who look at ten-thousand-year periods as fairly recent, the newly attempted imposed versions of language and culture and consciousnesses were but a few hours old or, in more generational modes, two grandmothers ago from the present. Consequently, this part of the "me's," absent or not, was the most recent layer added to many layers of many years enjoyed by populations of the region in contact, conflict, intermixing, and bumping into each other and imposing their will and language and cultural mechanisms on the other. In this manner, the continuous process of "teleodynamics," in which living organisms as described by Deacon simultaneously individuate and make imperative contextual shifts, developments, and simultaneous growth on which that individuation is dependent, including "even human consciousness" (2012, 265), is a many-layered and often contradictory one. This is too often imposed or demanded so that communication learned early and often is braked and negatively soaked with admonitions and often pain. For me, this has taken place, as it has for millions, in what I refer to as the Southwest North American Region.

THE SOUTHWEST NORTH AMERICAN REGION (SWNAR)[16]

We take this side road to understand the hegemonies of language and their discontents in that this discussion primarily takes place in what I have termed the Southwest North American Region. The reasons are many for this small trek, not the least of which are that much of the impositions of language and their reactions took place among populations that had for thousands of years sought to create ways of extracting natural resources from the region and that had a huge repertoire of languages. However, that region changed drastically with the European inundations in the sixteenth to eighteenth centuries and the nineteenth-century American expansion. The linguistic map was to be changed forever.

The region that I term the SWNAR has characteristics that can be broadly described by, first, a complicated but persistent ecology formed by the various subecologies that transcend the present southern border and limit as well as make possible the human inventions long imposed in the region; second, the three-hundred-year-old struggle and accommodation of Spanish/Mexican and Indigenous relationships that were endemic and embedded in the structure of the imperial Spanish mandate to explore, conquer, missionize, and colonize; third, the crucial and important imposition of the region into northern and southern regions as a consequence of the American-Mexican War and the Tratado de la Mesilla or the Gadsden Purchase; fourth, the ongoing struggle and accommodation in the southern part between ascendant national Mexican mestizos and Indigenous populations; and fifth, the ongoing struggle and accommodation in the northern part of the tripartite struggle between hegemonic American populations and Mexican-origin and Native peoples. Lastly, this imposition is crosscut by the economic integration of an asymmetrical political economy and its large-scale population movements between regions.[17]

The ecological basis of the region transects the boundary lines and extends both north and south. It includes shared coastal regions east and west; the grand Sonoran Desert, which encompasses almost 311,000 square kilometers; and the Madrean Archipelago formed by the convergence of the Rocky Mountains to the north and composed of fifty-five Sky Island ranges and complexes (separate ranges joined by topography and oak woodland), with thirty-five of them in Sonora. It also encompasses the Sierra Occidental to the south, with the Chihuahuan Desert, with an area of 362,000 square kilometers to the east (Geo Mexico 2014) and the Sonoran Desert to the west (Ruhlam et al. 2014), the southern Texas plains and interior plains and hills subregion, and maritime ecologies on the Atlantic and Pacific Oceans.

The detailed specifics of the region are treated elsewhere, but suffice it to say that for our purposes the region ecologically and geographically excludes Mesoamerica but not its influences, which is roughly central Mexico and parts of Central America, southern Sinaloa west to León, and Guanajuato, and it includes Tampico, Tamaulipas. Therefore, the SWNAR in the present would include roughly four U.S. states and six northern Mexican states but more importantly shares a common ecology of diverse deserts, valleys, rivers, mountain ranges, and flora and fauna— as figure 1 illustrates—and is altogether larger in circumference than Spain, Great Britain, France, Italy, and Germany.

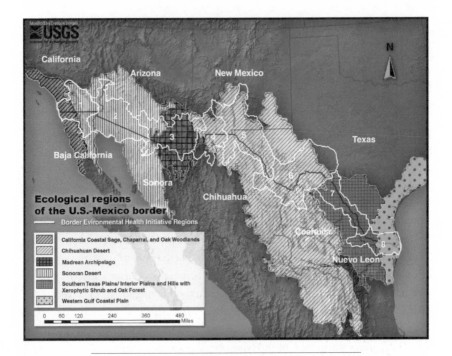

FIGURE 1. Ecological regions. Redrawn by Enrique Borges.

It is presently characterized with an interdependent political economy, albeit asymmetrical cultural populations, including Indigenous populations and the offspring of European populations variously known as Españoles Mexicanos during the colonial era and Mexicanos during the national era, with the addition of English-speaking populations as the aftermath of the American-Mexican War to the present, depending which side of the region is referenced. Because of the imposition of the political line, the region after its establishment will be regarded as the "northern" and "southern" regions of the larger entity.

But the imposition of the region via the American-Mexican War dictated the imposition of the American narrative and became the overarching megascript of the northern region that is followed to this day and commonly obfuscates a much more complex series of processes. Yet the American presence, as well as its industrial form of economic organization accompanied by its overwhelming mythic narrative, is an important additive to the populations already in contention. Based on an eastern prism of explanation and expectations, including demands of linguistic singularity, cultural assimilation, and, without doubt in many parts of the northern side of the region, political control and social hierarchy based on class, race, and ethnicity, new contiguities were created and enforced in multifaceted ways.

The southern region also establishes its own mythic hierarchy reminiscent of the Spanish caste. Although no longer was its central prism based on the peninsular Spaniard or criollos. Instead, the hierarchy became a nationalized cultural version of the mestizo in which after the Mexican revolution becomes its dynamic defining mechanism and after which national policies favored these populations over Indigenous ones and conflicts over land, language, culture, water, and natural resources ensued throughout Sonora, Chihuahua, Nuevo León, Tamaulipas, and Baja California, and I would certainly include the northern half of Sinaloa.

But even bifurcated by imposed borders and the establishment of what I would suggest is at best and always has been a brittle border, the region has always been crosscut by economy, migrations, interests, institutions, and the creations of crosscutting kinship, multilayered cultural phenomena, and material expressions, within which are contained the actual manifestations of contending and integrating dynamics. In reality, in the present this space and place is a transborder region of trade, exchange, and trilinguality to different degrees and hierarchy. Thus languages spoken, used, and imposed very much are arranged and distributed not by national boundaries per se but also by the necessities of use due to these realities of a complex political ecology that emerged and continues to this moment.

TRANSBORDER LINGUISTIC AND CULTURAL PHENOMENA: TWO CASE STUDIES OF SONORA

To illustrate the brittleness of the border and the dynamics of economy on language hegemony, two case studies are introduced: first, a brief case study of Adalberto Vélez García, who as a youngster was sent by his father to Tucson to live with his maternal grandaunts and uncles to learn English in 1907 and illustrates the transborder processes of culture and language change; second, the linguistic and cultural phenomena described by Tinker Salas (1997) of the "Sonorenses Americanizados." The two coincide generationally, geographically, and culturally and illustrate the processes of the manner in which a bifurcated region emerged but simultaneously developed economic, cultural, linguistic practices, and relations that crosscut and integrate the political divisions defined by treaties. But these also provide insights into the manner in which often subtle but important cultural and linguistic practices reveal the hegemonic influences of the dominant political entity.

ADALBERTO VÉLEZ GARCÍA: 1900–1987

At age seven, Adalberto Vélez García was sent to Tucson to live with his maternal aunts and uncles to learn English from his home in Magdalena, Sonora, sixty miles south of the U.S.-Mexico border. This was only fifty-four years after his great-uncle saw the last Mexican flag lowered in Tucson. Ostensibly this decision of sending Adalberto to his relatives was made in order to enable his father to later open a carriage and wagon factory in Tucson. This long-range strategy of sending sons early in their lives to learn English and trades and American notions of production was not an uncommon one, as will be seen.

In the late 1890s and through the early 1900s, only a few short years before the Mexican Revolution, Manuel Vélez Terán, his father, owned a carriage manufacturing "factory" in Magdalena, in which he employed fifty men making surreys, stagecoaches, and more importantly heavy mining wagons for the mines in Arizona and Sonora. This was a morphed blacksmith and wheelwright shop using more assembly processes than the singly made wagon or surrey, an innovation that came straight from Manuel's visits to his relatives in Tucson and watching American production processes there.[18] Manuel had an arrangement to sell his wagons to Federico Ronstadt, his compadre (co-godparent) in Tucson and owner of F. Rondstadt Hardware and Machinery Company. Federico José María Ronstadt was born of a German father in Las Delicias, Sonora, and a Mexican mother, Margarita Redondo, who was a cousin to Francisca García Gil, both having been born in Tubutama, Sonora, and related by marriage and consanguinity. Francisca was Adalberto's mother and Manuel Vélez Terán's wife.

Federico earlier in 1882 had also been sent to Tucson to learn blacksmithing and wheelwright trades.[19] A few years later Manuel sold his wagons to Rondstadt, but Manuel Vélez Terán's manufacturer's nameplate was replaced on the wagon hub with Ronstadt's, and thus the wagon became an American product not unlike the maquiladoras of the present. But what figure 2 also reveals is that while the wagon hub shown here was made of Mexican mesquite and imported Norwegian iron for its surrounding braces in Magdalena, the name plate lists not Manuel Vélez Terán in the Mexican manner of naming but rather "Manuel A. Vélez" with the initial "A" standing for his middle name of "Adalberto." This was the American manner of naming even in Magdalena, Sonora, Mexico, 120 miles south of Tucson and was a mark of what will be discussed as "Sonorenses Americanizados" in the ensuing case study. However, what is important to note that this was an early indication of the "Americanization" of this subregion and very likely occurred in others.

In the following years, Adalberto not only learned the language. Like all transborder peoples of the period, he traveled back and forth between Tucson and Magdalena. He attended elementary and secondary schools in Tucson, married Luz Ibáñez

FIGURE 2. Hub of a wagon made in 1904 in Magdalena, Sonora. Photo by the author.

Maxemin in Magdalena and as a backup in Tucson as well, and he lived out his long life as an automobile mechanic. This latter occupation he had partially learned from his older brothers, who, after the invention of the automobile, closed the wagon factory and opened a garage in Magdalena while Adalberto in Tucson went to school, worked as a telegram delivery boy, and worked at La Bonanza Department Store as a clerk (figure 3).

On visits of as long as a year, he practiced the mechanics of automobile repair in Magdalena while for equally long periods he became completely bilingual in English and Spanish and worked in Tucson. He could never facilitate his father's wish to open a wagon factory in Tucson, especially since the automobile and eventually the truck replaced the need for surreys, stagecoaches, or wagons throughout the region.

FIGURE 3. Adalberto G. Vélez, second from right: La Bonanza Clothing Store, 1916, Tucson, Arizona, with the owner, Carlos Jácome (center), and with unknown Sonorense and Anglo employees. Photo by the author.

However, as for many Mexicans, the linguistic imposition marked his identity in the northern region so that Adalberto Vélez García became better known to his fellow workers as "Ed" because they couldn't pronounce his name, and so his named changed from his home context to the public one. His surname of course is Vélez but because of the influence of the American patronymic custom of dropping the maternal surname, he shortened García to "G," thus privileging his paternal surname of "Vélez." Moreover, he used his maternal name as an abbreviation instead of as a surname and placed it in the middle between his name and his father's surname, thus creating a hybridic version of both a Mexican and American version of naming. He followed the same pattern followed by his own father who had been "Americanized" 120 miles south from Tucson in the Mexican state of Sonora.

He was never unemployed, even during the Great Depression, and in the midst of transborder economic woes, two world wars, and frequent visits and stays across the imposed bifurcated line, he and his wife of more than fifty years raised their two children in Tucson, Arizona, both of whom were fluent bilinguals in reading, speaking, and writing learned early from a Tucsonan father and Mexican mother.

THE SONORENSES AMERICANOS

But Adalberto's cultural and economic landscape was much larger than Tucson, for his cultural emergence may be understood most clearly within what Miguel Tinker Salas has described "Sonorenses Americanos" and the manner in which American economic penetration filled the linguistic and cultural landscape of Sonoran Mexicans to the point that parts of the population were referred to as "Sonorenses Americanos." That is, Mexicans from Sonora or from Tucson who became American citizens expressed and negotiated a complex of practices derived from both American English and Mexican Spanish on a daily basis. What must be understood is that in many places of the newly minted now American towns and cities like Tucson, the cultural and linguistic life was Sonoran Mexican and not American. The ink on the Treaty of the Mesilla, which incorporated southern Arizona and New Mexico into the United States, was barely dry only forty-six years before Adalberto was born and it was one of the older uncles and aunts with whom he stayed that saw the last Mexican flag come down in Tucson in 1858. For Sonorenses born in Tucson or born in Magdalena, Tucson was a Mexican town during this period of the early 1900s but impacted by the new immigrants from the east and the thriving trade between Sonora and now Arizona.

For Sonorenses born in either, most continued to function in two environments, influencing events in southern Arizona as well as in Sonora (Tinker Salas 1997, 104). Thus when Sonorenses went back home to Sonora to visit relatives or the opposite of relatives from Sonora visiting relatives who only a few years before had been Mexican citizens and now nominally American ones and incorporating English into their discourse, neither thought little of it since in fact this was not but a recently purchased portion of Sonora bought at the point of gun.[20] The process of becoming an American citizen and learning English "did not imply a dramatic change in their lifestyle or culture. Sonorans constituted the majority of the population throughout the region, and their culture pervaded the social organization of life in most areas (1997, 105).

But this influence of American culture can be further noted, extending into Sonora, and can be seen in the following photograph of Adalberto Velez's kin in Magdalena, Sonora, in approximately 1890. It shows his mother's cousin (older woman seated) surrounded by Adalberto's cousins and one sister (tallest standing). What is most

FIGURE 4. "Royal Baking Soda" flower planter. Photo courtesy of Dr. F. Arturo Rosales, who is a relative of his as well.

telling of the continuing influence is of course the wooden box being used as a flower planter but attached to the post with the lettering of "Royal Baking Soda" many times used for flower tortillas in figure 4.

Thus until Sonorans were inundated with American immigrants from the East and Midwest in Tucson (and schooling did not have yet the devastating effect on language loss and retention until the 1940s), Sonorenses Americanizados continued to be Sonorenses and spoke Spanish with ease, read poetry and *Don Quixote*, attended plays in Spanish at the Teatro Carmen, and wrote letters in Spanish to relatives just 120 miles south of their homes in Tucson—even though, little by little (and sometimes in punctuated ways such as the use of corporal punishment), language loss and the imposition of English was ensured.[21]

These processes, however, were characteristic and the cases in point could be multiplied all along the 2,000-mile bifurcating line from the nineteenth century forward in the northern region and southern parts of the SWNAR. These layered innovations of language and culture are not only adjustments but also responses to and conflict with homogenous "seeing men" propositions that transcend political borders, institutional safeguards, and quotidian demands for acquiescence, since the dynamics of the region demand very adaptive means of adjusting "selves" to the "others'" senses of ourselves while standing off the impacts of these imposing processes themselves.

The transnationalization of the region from both north and south directions became an integral part of the SWNAR and language very much becomes a transborder phenomenon of great complexity and of linguistic hierarchies filled with contradictions and oppositions. But these are part and parcel of the continuing economic integration of the region divided not only by an increasingly militarized fence but more importantly by a lack of true understanding and simple knowledge like that treated here. But we have much more to excavate of the processes leading to this present that will in fact provide direction and understanding to the manner in which hegemonies of language and their accompanying discontents become distributed from the Spanish colonial period to the present.

2

PRE-HISPANIC PRACTICES, HYDRA-HEADED SPANISH COLONIAL APPROACHES, AND THEIR DISCONTENTS

※

The Cross, the Pen, the Sword, and Indigenous Daggers

I N THE PREVIOUS CHAPTER I laid out the essentials of what I have termed the Southwest North American Region (SWNAR). The elements that comprise the region contribute to the substance of relations between populations and made possible the manner in which language hegemony was attempted and distributed. The process involved at least two major populations during the colonial and national periods, and in the present. My initial focus is the Spanish colonial impacts and their distribution, and by "distribution" I mean that language hegemonies, their accompanying megascripts, and their methods employed were hardly ever homogeneous, complete, accepted, learned, and used by the heterogeneity of populations upon which they were imposed. To gain a sense of this linguistic heterogeneity before the arrival of Europeans, it is imperative to gain a sense of the language maps and their heterogeneity so that we do not lose sight of the reality of the difficulty facing the Spanish colonial powers, but as well the reality of the broad language repertoires facing their attempts. We will explore briefly the pre-European language practices in the region in order to gain a fundamental understanding of the multiplicity of impacts of European impositions and the manner in which those so impacted articulated their responses and negotiations and attention from the colonial period to Mexican Independence (1521–1821). We need to know what was there in order to know what the colonial inundation tried to drown, so that there is no room for considering the region as an empty space or place.

PRE-HISPANIC LANGUAGE
COMMUNICATION OF THE REGION

The SWNAR's language repertoire has been recently gauged by David L. Shaul (Shaul 2014, 14–15) and that which he refers to as "western North America" is made up of six language families and language stocks including Uto-Aztecan, Athabaskan, Hokan, Penutian, Algic, and Tanoan. *Families* and *stocks of languages* are linguistic terms that include many different languages that in fact share such linguistic elements that are peculiar to a broader category like those listed for the region. However, in the example of Uto-Aztecan that ranges from California to Central America, it is composed of at least eight subfamilies, and some of these are composed of subfamilies themselves. Using the Takic subfamily as an example, it has two subfamilies. One of them, Cupan, has three languages without considering attending dialects. The other, Serran, is made up of two others not including dialects (2014, 26). Hopi, for example, which is spoken in twelve pueblo villages in northeastern Arizona and which is itself a subfamily of Uto-Aztecan, has three dialects distributed among three mesas: first, second, and third, but the variances between them are small (118). But none of these languages can ever be considered as isolated. Rather, due to changes in ecology, raiding, exchange, and commerce from multiple directions and borrowing from others as well as elimination due to climatic or ecological necessities, the pre-Hispanic transborder region demanded linguistic and other means of communication between these various populations who spoke one of many dialects and languages of the region. Later, by the turn of the eighteenth century when Spanish inroads had already been made into Texas and New Mexico, according to Hämäläinen (2008), "Comanches were able to conduct most of their business at New Mexico's border fairs in their own language, and many of the comancheros and ciboleros who visited Comancheria to trade and hunt were fluent in the Comanche language" (171).

The point of this exercise is that the region is made up of many languages, many mutually unintelligible, but given the enormous trade and exchange systems, as well as south-to-north and north-to-south migrations of peoples of the region, communication must have been regularized by one or more communication modes. This is an ancient complex of necessary communications and spread, especially by Uto-Aztecan languages through the southern parts of the SWNAR from and by Mesoamerican sources.

Early twenty-first-century scholarship includes the work by Hill (2001), LeBlanc (2003, 2008), and Mabry and Doolittle (2008),[1] with the latter not precluding a north–south process; nevertheless, all do support the hypothesis that farmer foragers around 4000 B.C. spread from Mesoamerica to the SWNAR, although contested by some archeologists.[2] In addition, LeBlanc (2008, 130–31) provides a linguistic, archae-ological, and genetic discussion supporting "a fairly good case for an Uto-Aztecan-speaking farmer spread [from Mesoamerica] resulting in the wide distribution of a lan-guage family...about 4000 years ago."[3] But the most impressive proposition to return to Hill's work (2001), as presented by Mabry, Carpenter, and Sánchez (2008) com-bines linguistic analysis and radio carbon dates on cultigens summarized as follows:

> Maize was introduced to the U.S. Southwest [for me SWNAR] by a single northward
> migration of Proto-Uto-Aztecan (PUA) agriculturalists who originated in Central Mex-
> ico, 2. the PUA Community included the domesticators of maize, 3. the initial expan-
> sion of Proto-Uto-Aztecans into the Southwest occurred between 4,000 and 3,000
> years ago, 4. the PUA expansion into the Southwest occurred in a leap frog pattern
> from oasis to oasis, 5. The PUA community practiced irrigation, 6. The PUA commu-
> nity began to break up between the arrival of maize and beans, and 7. the historically
> non-agricultural Aztecan peoples in the extreme north abandoned agriculture during
> prehistoric times. (158)[4]

This view of early contacts but not necessarily the origins of maize is supported by the works of Haury (1986) and Di Peso (1974), as well as Riley's (2005) recent dis-cussion of the Paquimé Complex situated in the northern part of Chihuahua. Riley states that at its apex between A.D. 1060 and 1340, the complex consisted of around eighty-eight acres in the region of Casas Grandes in Chihuahua and that "Paquimé represented the most overt Mesoamerianization in all of Aztlán. Here were not only indications of Mesoamerican religious beliefs but also of Mesoamerican social and political systems, attenuated to be sure, but in place and operating." From ball courts to mounds faced with masonry, a possible astronomical observatory, stratified living quarters of many kinds, elaborate galleries, and with a complex water and sewage sys-tem, Paquimé housed a population of several thousand (2005, 117). What language was spoken is unsure but Riley (177) indicates that it might be a Taracahitan language closely related to Opata of Sonora but certainly derived as one of the Uto-Aztecan branches.

Ancient contact from Mesoamerican sources to and from the region were part and parcel, for example, of the turquoise trade during Postclassic periods from the Northern region of SWNAR to Tula, which passed through the now Mexican states of Zacatecas and Durango (Weigand: 1997, 28; 2008, 348–50). From Weigand we know that the great mining centers—La Quemada, Chalchihuites of Zacatecas, and mining appear-ing in Durango, Chihuahua, Sonora, and what is now Arizona and New Mexico—all associated with the trade of turquoise. Its widespread use increased communi-cation among monumentalist centers among the desert and Mountain Mogollon, the Hohokam, and Anasazi. Equally long-distance trade of the Scarlet Macaw from perhaps as far south as the lowland country of Veracruz may have been possible (Riley 2005, 137–38) or raised or bred at Paquimé but as well brought from southern SWNAR, such as in southern Tamaulipas to the complex site of Pueblo Bonito (the largest Chaco site of the tenth century), to which traders traversed hundreds of miles and required linguistic or sign communication (Vélez-Ibáñez 1996, 31). Without delving into the enormous archaeological literature indicating the transfer of motifs, ideas, and practices between and among Native peoples west-to-east and back and south-to-north and back, we may conclude that many populations of the SWNAR region did in fact interact directly in some cases or indirectly in others with complex systems further into what is known as Mesoamerica and that there is sufficient evidence to conclude that for at least 1,696 years the pre-Hispanic (SWNAR region) was part of a series of exchange systems made up of centers of production, trade, and redistribution (Vélez-Ibáñez, 34–35). In fact, Mabry and Doolittle (2008, 64) state that the "social processes involved on the early agricultural frontier in the U.S.-Mexico Borderlands and the rest of *southwestern North America* [my italics] should be *reconceptualized* [my italics] as including both diffusions and migrations and both hunter-gatherers with their own knowledge of native plant husbandry and farmers introducing domesticated cultigens into new environmental setting." My contention and framework extends from these periods to the present as they did for Stoddard (2005, 10–17).

With different nuances, Hill's and her supporters' very original hypotheses may be questioned, as well as the nuances of discussions concerning specific dating, materials examined, and meanings and derivations by scholars; however, none are sufficient to negate nor reduce these propositions' contributions to our understanding of ancient contacts between populations prior to the arrival of Europeans and support especially focused theoretical orientations of political ecology connecting the region's material and physical geography, its modes of productive characteristics, and their linguistic associations. For these scholars the settings for their discussion, and certainly for this broader work, all seek a much more inclusive ecology and conceptualization for considering the spread of languages, their specific associations with the geography, and the results of such innovations as the introduction of maize agriculture in ancient times and multiple modes of production in the present.

LANGUAGE NECESSITIES IN TRADE AND WAR

Such a complex of trade and exchange demanded and required linguistic and cultural accommodation and communication, even though warring and raiding was also part of the communication linkages between pre-European peoples. Trade required common understandings of value, of desired goods, of price setting, and, as importantly, some sort of reciprocal exchange systems created between frequent traders. In such contexts, multilingualism was more the norm than the exception. On the other hand, wars and conflicts and raiding were also part of the huge expanse of the different microecological niches making up the region. Access to natural resources, control of territories, need for genetic partners, and the cultural demands of warrior-based societies initiated conflicts between sedentary and later highly mobile horse-dependent peoples of the region. But both trade and warring demanded communication for the former to take place and for the latter to end without annihilation. In fact, taking captives, especially of women, demanded their use as biological partners, increasing biodiversity, and importantly the opportunity to exchange languages. Offspring may have become bilingual as did their parents. As will be discussed below, multiple means of such communication were available so that it is highly likely that one or more means of language use was prevalent including: a lingua franca, or more, bilingualism, sign language, and long distant telegraph: smoke signals from specialized signal towers.

Trade and war, then, and the latter especially in the form of raiding, were the basic dynamics of the pre-Hispanic era as Athabaskan and Uto-Aztecan and other speakers met in many regions of SWNAR, such as in the Chama Valley of eastern New Mexico around the ancient Pueblo of Abiqui. Ebright and Hendricks (2006, 16) point out that "Abiqui was the center of *la tierra de Guerra* ["land of war": my translation and italics], at the same time as it was the focus of trading networks among Pueblos, Apaches, and Navahos . . . and represented a middle ground before Spanish contact . . ."[5] As Ramón A. Gutiérrez (1991) describes Pueblo approaches to warfare, this was considered the primary function of men. As part of the ritual process, young men had to establish their warrior competency. To accomplish this, a young man created a senior-junior relationship with a "warrior-father" to instruct him not only in the skills necessary to achieve mastery in the craft but also all of the rituals, performances, songs, and narratives associated with becoming a warrior.[6] In fact, most tribal peoples of the region, from band-organized "acephalous" tribal units to complex Pueblo-stratified systems of moieties, clans, lineages, and sundry other societies, usually had a "Peace Chief" or head and a "War Chief" or head, each with very different functions but both selected based on individual achievement and reputation.[7] Women served crucial functions, from serving as Shamans to defending hearths during attacks by other peoples. They served as bridges during actual conflicts in sealing off trade exchanges from the violence of men killing men. Warring for all, whether against others like them or unlike them, was part of the survival landscape for most people of the region.

But war was not a necessary condition. Neighboring tribes had speakers who were bilinguals, such as reported by Father Eusebio Kino in Sonora, who in his long and intense missionary travels reported that the Opas (Opata) and Cocomaricopoas spoke very different languages from that of the Pimas (living around present-day Phoenix) and stated, "though it is very clear, as there were some who knew both languages very well" (Bolton 1919, 128). From Kino we have an indication that Native leaders were also likely to be bilingual when he describes how Yumans asked that he visit them and that Kino spoke "leisurely with this governor, who knew very well both the Pima and Yuma languages . . ." (Bolton 1919, 250).

Carroll L. Riley (1971, 286) states that when Spanish explorers in the middle of the sixteenth century traveled up through Sinaloa—the area directly south of Sonora—they were in contact with ". . . people who spoke varying dialects, some of which were related to Aztec . . . and with considerable use of Nahuatl as far north as the Piaxtla River," which is north of present-day Mazatlán. Given that these explorers traveled with bilingual Nahuatl-Spanish speakers from central Mexico, communication was made much easier, especially so in learning routes north, water availability, and food resources, whether from hunting or traded or extracted from Indigenous villages. In fact, as early as 1540, Francisco Vásquez de Coronado's penetration included 2,000 "*indios amigos*" (Indian friends), 800 of whom were Nahuatl-speaking warriors and porters from Central Mexico. Another 500 were recruited from Jalisco, Nayarit, and Sinaloa, and the rest from other places for a total of 2,000 Indigenous peoples without whom the entire expedition could not have been carried out (Flint 2009, 66,73).

However, there seems to be also the circumstance in which one language was well known over a wide area as a kind of lingua franca, like Pima, which is Indigenous to Sonora (including much of now Arizona) through Sinaloa. Riley (1971) observes the following in describing Cabeza de Vaca's description of the language used by his companions upon meeting Spanish slave raiders after almost eight years of walking throughout the SWNAR between 1528 and 1536:

> They were speaking a language called *Primahaitu* which, according of Cabeza de Vaca, had been in use by Indians for the last four hundred leagues. The statement is somewhat ambiguous, but it meant that over a long stretch of back trail, the Spaniards had been able to communicate in a trade jargon or a lingua franca. The four hundred leagues (ca. 1200 miles) probably should not be taken too literally. The language itself was most likely Pima. This does hint at widespread linguistic contact in that part of the world. (288)

Moreover, the other form of communication was sign language. It was extensively used by Plains Tribal groups, who covered a geographic area from Canada through southern Texas and northern Mexico (Davis and Supalla (1995, 80).[8] More specifically, Foster (1995, 208–9) traced Fray Gaspar José de Solís's diaries of his inspection of the Franciscan missions in Texas in February 1768 and returning to Zacatecas seven months later from where he had begun.[9] Among his many observations of numerous Native peoples of Texas, Solis wrote that many different groups who together congregated near one of the major rivers (the Brazos) could not communicate with each other verbally but instead used sign language, which allowed them to communicate with each other for entire days. Foster states that according to Solis, one of the first responsibilities of new priests was to learn Native signs (Foster 1995, 208–9).

In fact, Plains Indians like the Comanche who entered Texas and New Mexico interacted both violently and in trade with Pueblo Indians of New Mexico with linguistic, ritual, and sign forms of expression exchanged as well. The coexistence of Spaniard and Comanche slave raids combined so that each sold slaves in the annual trade fairs held in such places as Taos, New Mexico. Such interactions encouraged not only the capture of slaves and the trading of goods, but also the capture of each other's modes of language as well as communicating by the use of sign language. This interaction is recalled even to this day. Spanish/Mexican[10] and Indigenous Pueblos reenact the taking of their respective populations by Comanches through ritualized dances.[11] As Richard I. Ford summarizes multilingual practices in the colonial and Mexican periods for New Mexico: "The most common languages used by Indians who did not know each other's language was Spanish and Navajo . . . Spanish, known to some degree by people in the Rio Grande Pueblos and even by the Jicarilla Mescalero, and some Comanche, was the lingua franca of New Mexico" (720).

However, long-distance communication by smoke signals was also employed, especially within areas controlled by the same group or statelets. According to Riley (1971, 161), this form of telegraph was very functional with the emergence of complex "statelets" in Sonora controlling segments of the Sonora, Moctezuma, Yaqui, and Bavispe River systems and valleys. Warlike and aggressive, these stratified and agricultural semiurban towns consisted of several hundred houses to small homesteads with extensive planted fields and trade and exchange between statelets. There were two confederations, one under the control of Senora (Sonora) in three of the valleys mentioned above and a second controlled by Oera and linguistically split between Opata and Pima (both Uto-Aztecan languages). The telegraphic system was built around the need for defense as well as for trade and functioned to assemble the federated leagues composing the political structure of these statelets described by Baltasar Obregón in his History/Memoir of 1584. He describes the setting and system of communication in this manner as quoted by Riley (1971, 163):

> This league and alliance was summoned by means of messengers and many high columns of smoke. News of the battle fought by the Senora [Sonora] group against the Northern Confederacy was spread for 300 leagues [2.63 miles and 4.23 km per league], and it reached Cinaro within two days . . . through the wiles of the devil or through smoke

signals. This seems more likely because the natives spend hours communicating with each other, town to town, province to province. Thus by those signals and messages the news, as I understand, reached the province of Cinaro, three hundred leagues distant from Sahuaripa, in two days. (Riley 1971, 163)

Two hundred years later, on September 22, 1776, while American revolutionaries were engaged in conflict with their colonial masters, Friars Francisco Atanasio Domínguez and Silvestre Vélez de Escalante of the misnamed "Escalante-Domínguez" Expedition[12] were trekking about in mountainous Utah and reported

From the highest part of the last ridge-cut we saw a large number of big smoke signals being sent up, not too far away in the sierra itself and in front of us. Silvestre the guide said they belonged to some of this people possibly out hunting. We returned the message with others to avoid being mistaken, should they have seen us, for hostile people and so have them run away or welcome us with arrows. Again, they began sending up bigger smoke clouds at the pass through which we had to go toward the lake, and this made up believe that they had already seen us, for this is the handiest and the regular signal used for anything worth knowing about all the peoples in this part of America. (Chávez 1995, 13)

Oral messages were also a means of communication. However, when quantities regarding days, amounts, or agreements were to be made, a system of knotted maguey fibers was employed. This form of counting was prevalent throughout the region since the Pueblo Revolt of 1680, many leagues away from Sonora. Its main leader and organizer, Popé from San Juan Pueblo, used this means when dispatching runners so that "the cord was passed through all the pueblos of the kingdom so that the ones which agreed to it might untie one knot in sign of obedience, and by the other knots they would know the days which were lacking; and this was to be done on pain of death to those who refused to agree to it."[13]

Yet most communications were not necessarily associated with the control of other Indigenous peoples but rather engaged in a combination of trade, exchange, and war, as has been noted. Such a dynamic consisted, for the most part, in periods of peace punctuated by fierce combat and enslavement of each other's peoples. Enslavement also included the integration for the most part of such persons within the social organization and cultural milieu of the tribe. It was not in their best interests to engage in wars of annihilation or genocide since these would eliminate trade partners and the desired commodities obtained through these partners. However, it should be noted, there are examples of complete devastation by raiders of pre-Hispanic pueblos such as Riano in the Chama Valley (Ebright and Hendricks 2006, 42).

In sum then, the region was a highly complex and multifaceted one where major language families, multitudes of languages, and hundreds of dialects were deeply embedded. It comprised a region of complex systems such as Paquimé, confederacies such as those in Sonora, and certainly homesteads and "Rancherias"—the temporary housing of hunters and gatherers in the midst of agriculturalists who themselves were influenced by Mesoamerican sources including maize agriculture, as has been described. How these various groupings carried out trading and warring was the consequence of multiple means of communication, including the use of a lingua franca like Pima, bilingual and trilingual capacities, sign languages, oral messages and knotted maguey, and certainly smoke signals for long-distance communication. But these systems were certainly strained and some were dissolved by the impact of the Spanish hegemonic process.

SPANISH HEGEMONIC PROCESSES AND THEIR FRAILTIES AND DISCONTENTS

Antonio de Nebrija, the humanist scholar, in the prologue of his *Castilian Grammar* published in 1492, described that when he presented his grammar to Queen Isabella, the then Bishop of Ávila interrupted the exchange by stating, "Soon Your Majesty will have placed her yoke upon many barbarians who speak outlandish tongues. By this, your victory, these people shall stand in a new need; the need for the laws the victor owes to the vanquished, and the need for the language we shall bring with us. My (Nebrija's) grammar shall serve to impart them the Castilian tongue, as we have used grammar to teach Latin to our young."[14]

This statement as a general principle has been followed by most empires or imposing nations, as Mary Pratt (1992, 5) suggests, to impose their "planetary consciousness" of the natural world in addition to other formats as those above. For postcolonial invading nation-states, however, such a process is not unilineal nor is it ever an easily accepted dictum. For the most part, the human populations upon which any type of hegemony is attempted are usually accommodated to some degree or the other, resisted to a finite conclusion, or negotiated in the favor, to some degree, of the population "culturally bumped" by the other.

No hegemony, whether ideological, linguistic, cultural, social, or economic, is ever complete. The most that hegemonic empires can hope for is that the seeds of their controls take hold strategically rather than only by coercion so that those seemingly controlled accept their lot based on some legitimate claims, such as religion or economic convenience, ideological parallels, and occasional breakthroughs and transformations such as by the use of middle-range brokers to interpret or ease various impositions. Strategically oriented empires and nations using methods to gain "legitimacy" rather than relying simply on coercion will result in a higher degree of control rather than those that rely on force or violence—though violence or force may be present in both methods and coercion remains into the present. And those upon which such impositions are impressed do not go gentle into the good night. For one, such populations may choose to negotiate from "positions of strength" with the interlopers in strategically viewing themselves to be able to maneuver into much better positions. Early in the conquest the Tlaxcalans negotiated their vassalage by petition to the crown and were carried by a delegation to the court in 1528 accompanied by Cortez himself (Sabes, 22–23). Seventy years later, Juan de Oñate y Salazar penetrated into New Mexico with a major component of his soldiery—Tlaxcalan warriors and probably their scribes—and established the area of Analco in Santa Fe, New Mexico, after Oñate y Salazar's conquest. Much earlier, Coronado's expedition (1539–1542) had a number of Indigenous contingents—that is, units of Mesoamerican troops of approximately 1,300 to 2,000 warriors who originated from "across present-day Mexico, from Veracruz to Puebla to Mexico City to Pazcuaro to Colima, with an additional five hundred or more *indios amgios* from what are now the Mexican states of Jalisco, Nayarit, and Sinaloa . . ." (Flint 2009, 65–66).

In the SWNAR, however, the Yaqui nation of Sonora is a prime example of resistance and negotiation. They long resisted Spanish and Mexican political subjugation but allowed Jesuits into the Yaqui Valley of Sonora in the seventeenth century after they had soundly defeated Spanish forces and their Indian allies and negotiated an alliance with the Spaniards as respectful allies rather than as subordinated populations, as Folsom (2014, 73–95) has noted in his recent work. Their strategic decisions would allow them to have the advantage of allowing linguistic and cultural influences only through the hands of the Jesuits until their expulsion in the eighteenth century and without the presence of a civil or military authority. In fact, Yaquis like the Pueblos in New Mexico retained territorial autonomy, not unlike the Tarascans of Central Mexico, who served the Spanish well and often. The Yaquis in fact did not allow the Jesuits or later Franciscans wholesale access to their environments, although the eighteenth century saw enormous seesaw relations of conflict and accommodation between Yaquis and Spanish authorities and religious missions established in their territorial confines.[15]

In addition, there were peoples like the Opata who not only were amenable to Jesuit and Imperial penetration but in fact became the poster examples of eventual strong acculturation, linguistic replacement by Spanish, the bearing of arms for the Spanish in the field of combat, and the formation of entire companies of presidial soldiers. They became highly Hispanicized in religion, dress, behaviors, social relations, language, religion, and economic and political institutions. The reasons for this included their dispersed spatial locations, disease and demographic reduction, encroachments of their territories, and absence from homelands by working in mines established by Spanish authorities nearby (Yetman and Shaul 2010, 223–59).

Yet there were others such as the Tarahumara of the lower and higher Sierra Madre of Chihuahua, with whom initial contact was made in the middle of the sixteenth century, though Franciscan and Jesuit missionaries did not begin to evangelize the area until the beginning of the seventeenth. However, Spanish mining encroachment stimulated a series of intense conflicts and wars by the Tarahumaras and numerous other Indigenous allies through most of the seventeenth century mostly in response to *"reducciones"*—reductions to mission settlements. Despite this, many of the Tarahumaras refused involuntary settlement and for two hundred years managed by fierce resistance and withdrawal to the upper Sierra Madre. Their exodus fostered an informal recognition of Tarahumaras as relatively independent peoples of the Sierras, where they adopted selected aspects of Spanish/Mexican culture. Relative independent ritual Catholicism and Tarahumara beliefs, language, and ritual became integrated especially after the Jesuit expulsion of 1767 so that the ceremonies, as will be discussed in chapter 3, of their matachines, not unlike the Pueblo versions of New Mexico, emerged as Indigenous syncretisms along with their modes of communication.[16]

In general, linguistic hegemony for the Spanish colonial periods was a hydra-headed enterprise dependent in part on the measure of resistance, the use or misuse of the Spanish narrative by the Indigenous populations themselves, the impact of schooling by the missionaries, and the capacity of Indigenous populations to maintain their cultural and linguistic resources. These dynamics created the impetus of continuing contradictions in which seemingly "settled" arrangements between imposed populations and their sources come to a final arrangement. Yet such seeming normalities would seldom not be contested. On the other hand, the cross, the sword, and the pen demanded unyielding acceptance of the Spanish colonial narrative to one degree or the other, and Spanish language policy and learning was entirely focused toward directing colonial subjects, Native or not, to fall under the aegis of the Crown and its agents by combining coercion and accommodation. These were the mechanisms of seeking to exchange the complex and diverse Indigenous narratives of selves, there's, spaces, and places with a seemingly homogeneous imperial version, itself beset with its internal contradictions, imperative adjustments, and the reality of a dynamic, often violent, and exceedingly fragile Spanish/Mexican presence as mostly unwanted interlopers.

SPANISH LITERACY, BOOKS, THE GOLDEN AGE, AND *DON QUIXOTE*: THE DESTRUCTION OF ONE LITERACY TRADITION FOR ANOTHER

Spanish colonial literacy was one of the main agents of transmitting the Spanish imperial megascript and the oral and written transmissions of that narrative. It was, to be sure, the key focus of the Crown. The teaching of Spanish was closely linked to religious conversion so that such catechism as Fray Alonso de Molinas's *Doctrina Cristiana* of 1546 ensured the memorization of doctrine and its written and read repetition (MacDonald 2004, 16), itself an earlier 1544 version by Fray Pedro de Cordoba (Medina 1987, 73). Yet early in the colonial imposition, the colonial authorities confronted the reality of Mesoamerican codices, records, literatures, and documents. Referred to by those who inscribed and knew the contents of these many forms of knowledge as *Tlamatinime*, or the "Aztec wise man," he was thus described: "He possesses writings; he owns books. [He is] the tradition, the road, a leader of men, a rower, a companion, a bearer of responsibility, a guide" (Boone 2010, ix). These idealized intellectuals described by Fray Bernardo de Sahagún fifty years after the conquest in fact became the sources for the reenscribers (Indigenous students trained by Sahagún) of the new narratives chartered by the Spanish religious and colonial authorities to reconstruct the histories and knowledge base in part of that which was destroyed by the initial penetration and destruction of Tenochtitlan. Most pre-Columbian codices were burned and many of the pictographic narratives that followed, including the Florentine Codex and the Codex Mendoza, were in fact written pictographically, in Nahuatl, in Spanish, and in Latin following the conquest. There are more than likely sixteen pre-Hispanic Codices, some of Mixtecan origin and others like the Borgia Group of manuscripts that are strictly pictographic, as well as the four Mayan codices (Glass 1975, 3–80; Glass and Robertson 1975, 81–252; Coe 1973). While Sahagún especially sought to reconstruct the preconquest periods, initiating a kind of "salvage anthropology" laying out the history, religion, beliefs, medicine, political organizations, and leading personages of the preconquest and as well of the impact of the conquest itself, these ethnographic and cosmic narratives were in fact very much also influenced by fifty years of Spanish colonial ideology and religion (Nicholson 2002, 25–39). Despite the enormous importance of Sahagún's works and those of his author-students, these were not preconquest documents but recreations including those of the grand poet-king, Netzahualcoyótl (1402–1472) and his equally productive son, Netzahualpilli (1464–1515) (Schwaller 2014, 40–41). These postconquest works then are the replacements in part of hundreds of years of literacy of ancient representations by reconstructed pictographs, and an alphabetized Nahuatl, in Spanish and in Latin. These were replacing some of that which was destroyed, but they also were used as the means by which the authorities could better understand the underlying ideological ethnography of the Nahuatl-speaking peoples to more efficiently approach their conversion and to stamp out this very knowledge and belief system (Nicholson 2002, 25). Even though Indigenous/mestizo intellectuals wrote of Indigenous people like Fernando Alva Ixtlilxochitl and his *Suaria relación*, which is a collection of narratives of the Texcoco region from A.D. 1000 until the conquest, these were all in Spanish (Schwaller 2014, 45).

There is, however, an interesting speculation that is also germane to this discussion and that is, given the prominence of the Tlaxcalans among Coronado early in his exploration, as well as Oñate y Salazar and their likely establishment of the Analco neighborhood in Santa Fe, New Mexico, during the latter's penetration, would they not have carried their knowledge of Mesoamerican pictography with them? There is no evidence that this was so but it would not be difficult to imagine their doing so since there were influences of their designs on Puebloan materials and especially so of the Saltillo diamond style of textiles (Lucero 2009, 16). More importantly, Taube (personal communication, 2016) has suggested that the "netted earth" or wavy line "web" motif, which is the way in which the earth is often depicted in Late Postclassic Central Mexico in the Codex Borbonicus and is itself traced to the Classic Maya, appears as a motif in the "retablo" of the nineteenth-century artist and *Santero*, Antonio Molleno. According to Montaño (2001, 35–36), he was probably a Genizaro,[17] a Hispanicized Indigenous painter from Chimayó, New Mexico, who was himself probably a student of an anonymously named "Laguna Santero," who painted between 1796 and 1808. Lastly, what is equally intriguing is that this "netted earth" motif appears in the murals of the pre-Hispanic Red Temple of Cacaxtla in the Tlaxcalan region (Swartz 2010, 149). None of these limited examples, however, would support the establishment of Mesoamerican pictography in New Mexico.

For some three hundred years, then, the empire established its cultural, linguistic, political, social, and economic dominance, fragile but persistent, through the continuous use of highly ritualized forms and presentations. For example, Imperial language policies between missionaries and the court were at times both contradictory and oppositional, depending on the colonial period, but nevertheless were important in establishing linguistic hegemony as a standard for the acculturation of Native peoples.

Written Spanish during the colonial empire had myriad functions, not the least of which was the central means of transatlantic communication to the crown relating civic, religious, extraction of gold and silver, and military information regarding the status of its various regions, political units, missions, and military forces. Literally thousands of letters, journals, reports, complaints, and accounts were written during the colonial and later the Mexican period. The Documentary Relations of the Southwest holdings of the Arizona State Museum at the University of Arizona number over one hundred thousand Spanish and Mexican colonial documents, largely in microfilm and gleaned from multiple sources and collections. But contained within such a collection are the nuggets of persuasion, cognitive restructuring, spatial redefinition, and ultimately the attempt to negotiate and impress alternative identities and relationships, and extract and exploit their physical and cultural contexts. Such a process in fact is an attempt, sometimes highly successful and sometimes less so, to redefine the "me's" and the "there's" and the not "me's" and the "not me's" and the "others" and the "not others" as I have discussed in chapter 1.

The colonial period was also an explosive era of creative works. It is most curious that one year after the Pueblo Revolt of 1680, Pedro Calderón de la Barca, the master dramatist and poet, seemed to have closed the "Golden Age" after succeeding the other Golden Age poet and dramatist Lope Felix de Vega Carpio (Lope de Vega) after his death in 1635 (born fifteen years after Cervantes in 1562). From the Picaresque novel through drama through art through poetry, Spanish letters emerged before and in the midst of the dreaded Inquisition and Spain's transatlantic inundation of Mexico and the Americas and its attempt to impose its language and most of all its religious scripts and the broader Spanish script of imagining, including witchcraft, magic, inexplicable bilocations,[18] and strange islands and many-limbed peoples, as depicted in so many maps of the period including the Spanish favorite of Cibola and the "Island" of California-based Amazons. Yet what else was being transported in terms of actual books despite the fact that what reading and writing taught to Indigenous persons, especially of the SWNAR region, did not include fanciful plays, Renaissance treatises of science and art, or Lope de Vega or Calderón de la Barca?

Yet what must be appreciated is that written materials were not just transatlantic religious works but commercial secular commodities controlled by booksellers and bookmakers. They were part of the urban landscape of Mexico and especially stimulated by the entrance of the printing press into Mexico City only thirty-nine years after its introduction into Sevilla in 1500.[19] Booksellers especially played an important role in the commercial trade of books to the Americas and were instrumental in staving off the heavy hand of the Inquisition from its commercial transactions. In fact, the Inquisition's most important focus was less on the lay booklist but rather on any treatise that was considered part of the Reformation. Especially targeted were enlightened treatises like Voltaire's *Social Contract* (Gallegos 1992, 69).

Booksellers in particular made sure that chivalric novels of Spain and translations from France and other languages were part of the transatlantic market. Many of these, because of the high cost of transporting heavy-bound volumes, were published in miniature sizes and in limited quantities, such as the Carolinian cycles of the *Tales of the Emperor Carlos Maynes and of the Empress of Seville* and the Arthurian cycles translations, and the short *Chronicle of the Very Noble Gentlemen: Tablante de Ricamonte y de Jofre*. Dozens of the *Caballero* titles found themselves shipped to Mexico and the Americas amidst hundreds of poems, histories, epistolaries, and many dozen religious treatises (Leonard 1953, 1992, 102–11). But among those books most critical of the entire chivalric mode and its imaginings, including mistaking windmills for giants, is Cervantes's singular *Don Quixote de la Mancha*, published in 1605, seven years after the founding of San Gabriel de los Caballeros in New Mexico by Juan de Oñate y Salazar and only two years prior to the founding of Santa Fe in 1608 by Governor Pedro de Peralta (Julyan 1996, 313, 324).[20] According to Leonard (270),

> Surviving records at Seville indicate that quantities dispatched in 1605 varied from "three books of *Don Quixote de la Mancha* printed at Madrid by Juan de la Cuesta" which a "Juan de Saragoza" sent on the *Nuestra Señora del Rosario* to Juan de Guevara at Cartagena,[1] to the 262 copies consigned to San Juan de Ulúa on the *Espíritu* Santo for Clemente de Valdés, a resident of Mexico City.[2] Another substantial shipment was Diego Correa's, who forwarded two cases of books, including 100 copies of Don Quixote, to Antonio de Toro, their owner, at Cartagena on the *Espíritu Santo*, probably another ship bearing the common pious name.

How many of these survived a trip north to the SWNAR, there is simply no way to know, since no commercial records from any of the regions between the seventeenth and nineteenth centuries in colonial Spain survived, nor is there a mention in any will or testament of any other lists of records of titles mentioned. We can say, however, that it would be improbable for either soldiers, colonists, or missionaries not to have read one or more of the hundreds of titles made available either through the printing presses of Spain or Mexico City, either in pamphlet form, abbreviated sizes and shapes, or as bound volumes, although the latter had a worse chance of surviving the rocky roads to the north. In fact, Gallegos (1992, 54–57) who has examined legal documents of the eighteenth century, including wills and settlement of estates, shows that booklets, books, volumes, and tomes of other than religious texts were distributed among the "*vecinos*" or "Españoles Mexicanos," as de Vargas described them. For example, the settlement of the estate in 1785 of Francisco Trebol Navarro of Santa Fe includes:

Three Volumes of Ordinances
One volume, entitled *Historia de Gibraltar*
One complete work of all of the sciences
A volume of *Castilian Orthography*

A volume of *Swiss Philosophy*
A Guide for Foreigners
Religious texts were also included (57)

From the hundreds of possible sources, from these mentioned to religious scripts of various sorts, including biblical, sacramental, and dogmatic treatises, and their performances in ritual or in public performances, at the bedside of the cross and the gun, the pen was to become the central means of establishing brittle but persistent Spanish hegemony over populations. As will be discussed both from the declarations of possession, obedience, and vassalages required of Native persons to the manner in which presidial soldier's service records were organized and the premises, categories, and concepts used to define their identities, the litany of imperial design was present and indefatigable. As discussed in more detail below, the actual numbers of schools and their influences is debatable. Debatable as well is the idea that they were important mediums of linguistic and cognitive hegemonies. But there were other linguistic and cultural means by which to impress hegemonic processes upon Indigenous populations, as the following illustration suggests.

UNPACKING THE NARRATIVE: THE ACTS OF POSSESSION AND OBEDIENCE AND OTHER PERFORMANCES OF IMPRESSION

The Act of Possession (*Requerimiento*) was part of the "seeing man" repertoire and it was a statement announced by the Spanish colonizing authorities and other European powers from the fifteenth to eighteenth centuries proclaiming complete control over an area of land for his/her sovereign (Servín 1978, 295).[21] It ironically was based on "rights of discovery"—that is, that the "discoverer" or the agent present had complete control of a section of the land, and that it was proclaimed for the monarch (ibid.); all this precluded the presence of the thousands-of-years-old settlements among Native peoples. This was in fact performed by a symbolic act of control or something equivalent from Columbus through Juan de Oñate y Salazar in New Mexico in 1598 (ibid., 303). In Oñate y Salazar's case, it was itself accompanied by a celebratory theater representation written by one of his lieutenants and the first theatrical piece written in the SWNAR region, among other more traditional performances.[22]

Thus upon crossing the Río Grande ("Del Norte" according to Oñate y Salazar) from what is now Juárez into El Paso del Norte on April 30, 1598, on the Feast of the Ascension,[23] Oñate y Salazar issued his proclamation, scribed by his notary and secretary of the expedition, in which are contained highly rationalized statements of legitimacy based on a series of celestial calls, including reference first to the Holy Trinity, the omnipresent and omniscient power of a godhead, and its direct lineage to all forms of human endeavor, including all imaginable political entities, a metaphor in which the godhead is the originator of all things, and invokes the Virgin Mary, who herself is the apogee of kindness as an arm of God, and, in a sort of chain of being, introduces Saint Francis, as well as an extended treatise into the resurrection, the life of Jesus, and the direct connectivity to St. Peter and all of his religious descendants and to the kings of Castile and all of their successors.

Finally, according to the notary, Governor Don Juan de Oñate y Salazar took possession "of these kingdoms and provinces" by tacking a cross on a tree and then uttering the following:

> . . . I take and seize tenancy and possession, real and actual civil and natural, one, two, and three times, one, two and three times, one, two and three times, and all the times that by right I can and should, at this said Río del Norte, without excepting anything and without limitations, including the mountains, rivers, valleys, meadows, pastures, and waters. In his name I also take possession of all the other lands, pueblos, cities, towns, castles, fortified and unfortified which are now established in the kingdoms of New Mexico, those neighboring and adjacent thereto, and those which may be established in the future. (Hammond and Rey, 1953, 335)

The litany continued so that all natural and human resources were included: from mountains to rivers, all wild life, and of course all minerals, and as importantly "together with the native Indians in each and every one of the provinces, with civil and criminal jurisdiction, power of life and death, over high and low, and from the leaves of the trees to the stones and sands of the river" (ibid., 335).

One wonders what Indigenous peoples could have possibly gleaned from such packed statements, symbolized by the nailed cross on a tree, and accompanied by actual theater production. What major meanings and mappings were divulged other than puzzlement from either not understanding the language or the ritualized performances such as that by the captain of the Guard Marcos Farfán de los Gados, who composed and produced the play? We do not know if any or all of these at this particular event and crossing treatises were translated by Nahuatl speakers, and if they were, were they able to communicate with the Jumanos, Mansos, and Sumas living in the vicinity of the crossing? These peoples' languages were in fact descended from a common linguistic source—the Jornada Mogollon, which was an Uto-Aztecan subfamily (Beckett and Corbett 1992, 32–48)—so that either bilingual Spaniards or accompanying Tlaxcalans may have provided sufficient equivalences to be understood.

Regardless, however, from the point of view of Oñate y Salazar, such an oration and reference was the lineal connection between himself, his sovereign, Christ, the Virgin Mary, and the Godhead. This created an unbroken rationalization for the hegemonic impression upon land, animals, minerals, rivers, and most importantly the rationalization for judgment, evaluation, sentencing, and legal legitimacy for a kind of control probably unknown to the Indigenous nations of the region. This was the "seeing man" at his most expressive role simultaneously bringing to bear the sacred with the profane.

Yet each Pueblo that comprised the Pueblos system from the south to the north of the Río Grande Valley had be to be informed of their new masters, the conditions of their "vassalage," and most importantly the advantages and extreme disadvantages accruing. Two notable examples provide insights into language use, translations, and interpretations, and the processes of the initial production of hegemonic impressions. In fact, only a few years before this colonial penetration, the 1573 Ordinances of Discovery, Law 15 described how interpreters should be used and license given to capture Indigenous persons for that function:

> 3. Having made, within the confines of the province, a discovery by land, pacified it, [and] subjected it to our obedience, find an appropriate site to be settled by Spaniards and if not, [arrange] for the vassal Indians so they be secure. 4. If the boundaries of the settlement are populated, utilizing commerce and ransom, go with vassal Indians and interpreters to discover those lands, and with churchmen and Spaniards, carrying offerings and ransoms and peace, try to learn about the place, the contents and quality of the land, the nation(s) to which the people there belong, who governs them, and carefully take note of all you can learn and understand, and always send these narratives to the Governor so that they reach the Council [Consejo de Indias]. Try to bring some Indians for interpreters to the places you go, where you think it will be the most fitting . . . Arid by way of said interpreters . . . speak with those from the land, and have chats and conversations with them, trying to understand their customs, the quality and way of life of the people of that land, and disperse yourselves, informing yourselves about the religion they have . . . if they have some kind of doctrine or form of writing; how they rule and govern themselves, if they have kings and if they are elected as in a republic or by lineage; what taxes and tribute they give and pay and in what way to which persons . . . And in this way you will know if there is any type of stones, precious things like those which are esteemed in our kingdom.[24]

I would term this "Fieldwork 101" for an anthropologist, and of course this approach to conquest and control certainly is found much earlier in the Greek Xenophon's *Aanabis, Up the Country* and afterward in the works of Roman Julius Caesar's *Gallic Wars*, in which both regard the use of initial inquiries using fieldwork techniques and interpreters and "native informants" to gain knowledge, information, and ease of entry and control of unknown populations and territories with minimum casualties.[25] The Spanish were no different than their military forebears and had learned hard lessons in the various expansions in Europe, the Americas, and earlier with the Islamic Empire. Perhaps also Vásquez de Coronado, Sanches "El Chamuscado," Oñate y Salazar, and later De Vargas of Reconquista may all have read both Xenophon and Caesar as part of their military and civic training for imperial expansion.

ENTERING THE PUEBLOS AND ACTS OF VASSALAGE: SETTING THE LINGUISTIC STAGE

Upon entering New Mexico, the first sizeable Pueblo Oñate y Salazar selected for his announcement as a "seeing man" that they were now to be vassals of the King of Spain and under the protection and instruction of the Roman Catholic Church was the Pueblo of Santo Domingo (Keres), where he assembled with his captains, soldiers, and allied Tlaxcalans. He also assembled the heads of the seven pueblos of the Cherechos under its Captain Pamo; Captain Poquia of five pueblos of the west; Pestaca captain of the Emmes and nine pueblos; Captain Atequita of the Tzios and of two pueblos; Paqui, captain of the pueblos of Tziati and Pequen; Cali, captain of the pueblos of Cachichi; and Poloco, captain of five pueblos. Here the title "captain" was the colonial term for head or ostensible battle chief of the Indigenous group in question.[26]

Arrayed before them, according to the scribe of the event, was "the presence of Don Juan de Oñate y Salazar, governor, captain general, and adelantado of the kingdoms and provinces of New Mexico, its discoverer, pacifier, and settler for his majesty, our lord, in the valley and pueblo of Santo Domingo, head of the province of the said kingdoms..." Then in sequential order were "in company with his lordship, the most reverend father, Fray Alonso Martínez, apostolic commissary of his Holiness and of the friars of the order of Saint Francis; the reverend father Fray Cristóbal de Salazar, preacher and teacher of theology in the said order; the beloved lay brother, Fray Pedro Vergara..." Following them were "Vicente de Zaldívar Mendoza, sergeant major of his majesty's army, and numerous other captains and soldiers; and there were likewise present a multitude of Indian chieftains and common people; natives of these kingdoms of New Mexico, and among them the captains and chieftains of the pueblos and people."

In gauging impression management, it is salient to understand that Oñate y Salazar was accompanied by an invading army. From the Spanish point of view, no expedition or colonization was considered as having a chance of success but except to resort to arms. Thus there were "numerous other captains and soldiers" and referring to their

Tlaxcalan allies "there were likewise present a multitude of Indian chieftains and common people." These were not the Indigenous persons from the Pueblos, for they were referred to "as natives of these kingdoms of New Mexico, and among them the captains and chieftains of the pueblos and people." The organization of weaponry, reliance on Indigenous allies, military tactics and strategies, use of translators and interpreters, and the majority of those enlisted to accompany his entrance were in fact military by training, by conviction, and like Francisco Vásquez de Coronado's earlier sojourn, they were organized along military lines. The fact that three "falconets"—small-bore artillery—were part of the weaponry provides a reasonable expectation that these would be handy to kill large numbers of persons in a fairly efficient manner for the period in question.[27]

Pueblo peoples had been subjected to cannons by Vázquez de Coronado's army fifty years previously and by other minor expeditions like the misnamed "Chumascado-Rodríguez" expedition of 1581 that occurred in the periods between Vázquez de Coronado and Oñate y Salazar.[28] The Pueblos were also familiar with the Spaniards' Mexican Indigenous allies, who were mostly Tlaxcalan infantry warriors including their servants. Their tactical and strategic lessons were learned much earlier in joining with the Spaniards against the Aztecs and seventy years later still allies with privileges and part of the conquering army.[29] In fact, the participation of these peoples against their northern brethren is underappreciated, and their contribution to the defeat of many peoples in the region extended from Durango, San Luis Potosí, Chihuahua, and the Presidio of San Juan Bautista near now Eagle Pass, Texas, and into New Mexico.[30]

The political stage was set within a militarized religious context represented by Oñate y Salazar himself, the dutiful friars, and of course his captains and soldiers, Spanish and Tlaxcalan. But importantly, three interpreters were present: one who spoke Nahuatl and two Indigenous persons left behind by the Chamuscado-Rodríguez expedition who were described as "Don Tomás" and "Don Cristóbal," Indian interpreters of the languages used by the Natives of these provinces. After having sworn in the interpreters and satisfied other necessary formalities, the governor spoke to the Indian captains, explaining the object of his coming (Hammond and Rey 1953, 338). The entire sequence of communication may have involved a three-way interpretation between Spanish to Nahuatl to Keres and then from Keres to Nahuatl to Spanish. Even a two-way interpretation, especially if directly from Spanish to Don Tomás and Don Cristóbal—who allegedly spoke Keres—and then back to Spanish, would be problematic given that much of Oñate y Salazar's request for vassalage could have left out critical and crucial understandings not easily translated from one to another and back from one to another or perhaps from one to the other, and then to the other and back again.

As described by Oñate y Salazar's scribe, Juan Gutiérrez Bocanegra, his Acts of Vassalage were as follows in the first Keres Pueblo and all others that he entered with some variation depending on the size of the Pueblo and the type of reception received. He and his troops entered "Santo Domingo," which they had renamed. Presenting himself within the main kiva of the Pueblo, he announced that he had been sent by the king, who sought to save their souls and to protect them, as he did worldwide, and that they had been sent to invite them to be the vassals of the King, as had all others, and named México, Guatemala, Tezcuco, Michoacán, and all others. All this was to be done of their own free will and in so doing they would benefit greatly by being protected from their enemies and free "to conduct their arts and trades and their crops and cattle."

According to Gutiérrez Bocanegra they responded to all this through the interpreters in "agreement and harmony and with great rejoicing. Following this they agreed to become vassals of the king and they would obey and submit to his will. They were then warned that not doing so would result in severe punishment and they still agree." Oñate y Salazar then proceeded to explain that the main reason for the Spanish and the king's willingness to travel so far to their lands was to save their souls. All this was witnessed by three of the Spanish principals and his secretary (ibid., 339–40).

Given the religious rationalizations noted in the Act of Possession, and the fact that their vassalage meant that any opposition could be met with swift and uncompromising punishments and staged before captains of the Spanish and Tlaxcalan armies and their captains, this would not seem to be efficacious to "free will" and freedom of choice. While the Crown and Oñate y Salazar sought to avoid confrontation, nevertheless, the presence of an armed army, the recollection of Vásquez de Coronado's bloodshed, and the impressive array of arms and potential violence would not seem to support a rational choice for becoming vassals of a system unknown to the Indigenous peoples present.

This potential became actualized later in the near unrestrained violence against the Acoma who killed thirteen Spaniards when a soldier named *Vivero* stole two turkeys, a bird sacred to the Pueblos, and violated a Pueblo woman (Trujillo 2008, 95). Because of their celestially and judicially declared authority as noted above, including life and death judicial proceedings, these ensued after Oñate y Salazar declared a "war by blood and fire" against the people of Acoma. According to Trujillo (96), the result was that in 1599 eight hundred Acomas were killed and five hundred survived and were taken prisoner, where they were then tried. Oñate y Salazar found them all guilty. He ruled that children under twelve were not to be harmed and dispersed the girls to a priest and the boys to the brother of one of the captains killed in the original conflict. Sixty of the girls were sent to convents in Mexico City, never to be seen again.

Trujillo observes:

All women over twelve and young men between twelve and twenty-five were sentenced to twenty years of personal servitude. Two Hopis captured in the fight were sentenced to have their right hands cut off and were set free to take home news of their punishment. Finally, men over the age of twenty-five were sentenced to twenty years of servitude and to have a foot cut off and twenty-four people suffered this punishment. For maximum effect and as an example of the dangers of rebellion, this sentence was carried out over several days in nearby pueblos. (97)

Yet within two years, most had escaped from servitude and rebuilt the Pueblo of Acoma, which stands together with its oversized casino in 2017, four hundred years later.

It would seem that whatever legitimacy was declared by Oñate y Salazar and his colonists was superseded by the willingness of the Acoma not only to resist the declarations of the empire but to rebuild what had been destroyed regardless of the imposed narrative and it justifications. Ultimately the sword was mightier than the pen but it was insufficient to establish the type of hegemony and defeat leading to either cultural or linguistic replacement. On the other hand, an important precedent had been set and that was the use of violence against any resistance to the alleged harmony established by the Crown. By 1570, that responsibility would fall primarily to a chain of small forts that ensured that the Spanish megascript of the Church, the Crown, and the military was adhered to and these were centered on the presidios as the basic line of defense, control, and subjugation of its often-restive population.[31]

Yet these presidios are instructive because they also establish what I would term "the military mindset" or script of hierarchy, obedience, rank, and warriorship, and importantly "individuation," markedly different from that of the Indigenous populations and from which can be gained an insight into one of the major hegemonic instruments in the region.

PRESIDIAL SERVICE RECORDS: INSIGHT INTO THE IMPORTANCE AND ESTABLISHMENT OF CATEGORIES OF IDENTITIES

The presidio system as the military arm of the Imperial design of the cross and the sword was the major mechanism of subjugation and control of Indigenous populations throughout the SWNAR. Comprised mostly of ill-equipped mestizos, mulattos, and *claimed* criollos (my italics)[32] (Moorehead 1975, 182–83),[33] they were often poorly armed, mostly underpaid, and often exploited by their own officers in tiny garrisons of no more than fifty and often much fewer due to frequent illnesses, death, and desertion, as further discussion will show. The presidial soldiers as combatants led a hard life, many times faced overwhelming odds against often skilled Native warriors, and often were far outnumbered during the three-hundred-year presence of the presidios.

Nevertheless, these soldiers were spread throughout the region in the earliest presidios established in 1600 from Parral, Chihuahua, to Santa Fe, New Mexico, and then later between east and west to Texas and Sonora, and one in Baja California.

But these very hardy soldiers were for the most part persons, as will be shown, accustomed to hard conditions, and their service records indicate not only their points of origins and their means of livelihood—they also represented categories of importance that identified each one and provided an insight into the cognitive mappings most important to their identity. These contrast to what Native persons might use for their identity markers as warriors or wives/mothers and these differences aid an understanding of the manner in which subtle but important linguistic and cultural hegemonic penetrations were established, and were the "natural" categories probably used as daily masked discourses.

It is not possible to contrast these categories directly with their warrior counterparts for two important reasons: first, there was no comparable record for Indigenous warriors kept by Native peoples; and second, the enormous heterogeneity of Indigenous populations of the region precludes easy generalizations and comparisons. Moreover, the even more limited information on the roles of women further complicates our understanding of how sex/gender shaped self-labeling and local classifications. However, we know that warrior societies among the Pueblos and the Plains peoples were prevalent and crosscut the divisions created by membership in other kin groupings such as lineages, clans, or moieties, as well as medicine societies and dancing groups. It is probable that, especially among Pueblo groups generally, they can be divided among the eastern and western groups, with the former emphasizing patrilineal lines of descent and the latter matrilineal with ownership of housing and unmovable property in the hands of each (Eggan 1979, 227). Yet it is also the case that, regardless of lineality, as Tracy L. Brown (2013, 60) has insightfully described, authority was in the hands of men in the precolonial period, so that the most important political leaders were men, and specifically in such peoples as the Hopi, land and communal labor were provided to balance the time that men would invest in their political offices. Yet women played key shamanic roles that provided the underlying cultural glue for these offices by lending their ritual power to such societies. Women were also the main agents of reproduction of the entire edifice of warriorship, whether genetically or domestically.

The point here is that the groups of most importance are kin related, warrior related, and also care related and are the primary principles of social organization and identity and not the individual. Even the naming of children did not fall into the hands of the parents but rather, such as among the Tanoan Pueblos, were baptized with corn water during the first solstice ceremony and named by the father's sister, emphasizing the patrilineal side of the group (Hawley Ellis, 1979, 356–57). While there was the individual recognition of differences, such differences were strongly embedded in group identities and how well each individual carried out their rights and obligations to the particular group event or activity. As suggested by Brown (2013, 39), stratification among the Pueblos was evident in their political spheres during the colonial period and was "divided by class and gender differences . . . [i.e.,] a ranking of people based on gender and power, [and] prestige and authority" (ibid., 39). Nevertheless, the general dictum required rendering onto the group and not the individual regardless of stratification.

PRESIDIAL SOLDIER'S SINGULAR IDENTITY

One way in which we may understand the manner in which the local group orientation was countered by the Spanish narrative and its focus on the individual is to follow the basic categories of identity for presidial soldiers. A document that followed a presidial soldier's career is known as a *filiación*, or origination of service and details, depending on when the snapshot was taken, other important events of multiple types, and noted sometimes in the margin of the document. My sample of 436 soldiers[34] spans the SWNAR except for New Mexico, which Bernardo P. Gallegos (1992) has most interestingly covered. These data are for dates mostly from 1769 to 1816, during which eighty-five did not finish their enlistments due to desertion, illness, death either natural or at the hands of Natives in combat, discharge by permission, in fifteen cases removal for being *inutil* (useless), and one release for being a minor.[35] Thus in examining enlistment and full-service *filiaciones*, most consist of two paragraphs marking individual identity within a single social organization—the military presidial company—and, as important, the order of presentation itself, giving an insight into the most important source of identities for the individual soldier. There are also full-service *filiaciones* containing the same type of information through the life course of the individual until his departure from the unit, or some are also created to note special awards and recognitions.

The *filiaciones* follow a standard format used in this type of document and are usually limited, and here are provided in English (my translation) and in *Script* of one example of the original in the appendix and the source in endnotes 36, 42, and 44. Variant spellings of words and names and surnames are original to the documents. That said, the three samples are selected to reveal different class, ethnic, and mobility factors that are part of the hegemonic narrative provided as "normalized" scripts by the imperial scribners and certainly followed the soldiers into their entire occupational history. They were among the main sources of identity not unlike the modern "DD214" archive that follows all contemporary members of the armed forces in the United States and composed of similar information. In the contemporary period, these are placed in "jackets" or envelopes denoting that the information is kept within but connoting also that it encompasses the serviceman. So too among the presidial soldiers the *filiaciones* had equivalent functions as the documents and were also probably placed in "jackets."

The first *filiación* discussed is from the company of Opatas of Bavispe, Sonora—an all-Indigenous company in 1803; the second, a criollo from the Province of San Carlos, Durango in 1792; and the third an example from a largely mestizo company of the Royal Presidio of San Juan Bautista of the Río Grande, Coahuila, in 1797. Each provides specificity to the general "megascripts" normalized by their intent, format, function, and impression.

Filiación

Company of Opatas of bavispe [*sic*]

Domingo Miranda, son of José and Guarda, natural son of the pueblo of Bacadeguachi, government of Sonora, occupation Laborer, his age twenty years old, religion Holy Apostolic Roman Catholic. His physical characteristics the following: Black hair and eyebrows, narrow nose, dark complexion, beardless, and his height 5 foot, 2 inches and 2 Linea (.0571348 per inch).

He enlisted voluntarily to serve for ten years in the Company of Opatas of Bavispe today on the 17th of August of 1803 without obfuscation and the penalties were read to him according to this order and because he did not know how to write he made the sign of the cross and was warned of its justification and there will be no excuse of any sort [to not understand it] and witnessed by Lieutenant Don Antonio León and Sergeant Juan Chumacero both of the same company. He said he was married in Bavispe on the 27 of March, 1803.[36]

Upon examination, the document begins with the individual's "Christian" name: "Domingo" and surname "Miranda," which rationalizes his individual identity and links him to a religious tradition of naming with the paternal surname. Immediately, this is followed by his parents' names and surname with father's first, "José," which cements his descent to him, but his mother is known only by her Christian name of "Guarda." Guarda means "to put away," perhaps denoting her occupation as a servant in a Spanish Mexican household, and her lack of surname indicates Indigenous status. That she does not have a surname would not be unusual, especially if she had been a slave but probably baptized since her son is listed as "Holy Apostolic Roman Catholic." Both define him as of legitimate birth. This is a crucial referent defining his legal "place," and being a "natural son" of the pueblo of Bacadeguachi defines his identity by virtue of a physical space itself ensconced within the government of Sonora. "*Natural*" in Spanish has a number of meanings, including "born in" but also indicates its semantic relation to the now Spanish "naturalness" of the place. The pueblo is "San Luis Bacadeguachi," founded in 1645 by the Jesuit missionary Cristóbal García on Opata

territories and part of the "reduction" process of concentrating Indigenous populations around a mission.[37] Both provide the religious contextualization of the named
places themselves and, coupled to his identity as a Roman Catholic, establish the religious cognitive mapping necessary especially for identity formation and amendment
to other identities. The central attention to only these categories, the overwhelming
"scripted" context for an individual is the legitimacy of the Church as the source of
individual and group identity. It also indexes the celestial rationalizations forming a
local version of the larger megascript. His former occupation as a "laborer" places him
specifically at the lower end of occupational statuses as well.

Additionally, the document outlines the importance of physical attributes classified
by color of eyes, hair (even its state), skin and height down to small increments, as well
as the shape of the nose, and, as the following will illustrate, any physical scars or marks.
The lack of facial hair would identify him as either a beardless youth or an Indigenous
male since most plucked their facial hair instead of growing a mustache or beard.
In this manner, internal racialized categories are accentuated, especially in relation
to color and composition of hair, nose, and skin tone. The marking of Indigenous
bodies provides an implicit contrast to more desired characteristics. Pigmentation
especially was utilized to locate and infer status with darker hues as lesser and their
opposite higher, as indicated by numerous commentaries made by Spanish/Mexican
authorities and their accompanying colonial *casta* labels like "coyote," "lobo," "torna
atrás," (literally, "turns back" but also backward buttock) and "tente en el aire" ("hold-
yourself-in-midair"), but these examples are connected with shades of melanin and
given either animal categories or physical or pejorative terms.[38] Certainly the broader
categories of *mestizo* or *mulattos* do not just refer to admixture of Indigenous and
Spanish or African and Spanish genetic patterns, but each has the underlying melanin
architecture of dark to lighter hue. Depending on sources, "caste" categories themselves vary in designation, but regardless of the specific differences in terminology
their differentiating functions by prestige, value, and privilege served the interests of
those claiming "purity of blood" despite the obvious genetic and social contradictions
inherent to such an imposed scaffolding of seeming differences.

However, within the present document the second paragraph also provides insights
into the most important categories concerning rank, chronology, and legal constraints
and responsibilities. The subject is admonished and constrained under legal penalty to
serve an allotted time period and such warnings are read and witnessed by an officer
and a Sergeant, the former probably either a criollo or mestizo since in some Opata
Companies only Spanish/Mexican officers could serve as such, and the latter at the
rank of sergeant as well since the surname "Chumacero" is Galician.[39]

Unlike the Indigenous populations who were recognized for their individual prowess and entitled to some degree of differentiation as war captain or war leader because
of proven capacities at war making, they did not follow a chronological system of

promotion and their participation as warriors was limited by age, sex/gender, and health. Male warriors were recognized by the military society, medicine clan, or tribal group they belonged to. However, this was not part of an institutionalized system of stratification. Presidial soldiers were part of a system of recognition that was highly stratified, with rights, duties, and obligations that were prescribed and not ascribed per se, although mastery of arms and leadership would have also been of importance, as well as the number of combat engagements in which they had participated. It is not surprising that the admonitions and warnings of his expected fulfillment of duties, as witnessed by two presidial soldiers, were never part of either the nomenclature or expectations of Native persons. Secular group expectations were the basis of not only recognition of value; they also sustained military efforts and the group's cohesion.

If the person was not literate in Spanish, which was the case for the great majority of the cases analyzed in my research of 381 records in which a "*no saber firmar o lo firmo*" (did not know how to sign or signed) was indicated, 309 could not sign their names except with a cross and 72 (19 percent) signed with their names and some with a rubric. Out of a total of 436 soldiers, 55 records did not indicate whether they could or could not sign. Signed documents are the few means of ascertaining probable literacy and have been used by the literature as a means to gauge writing and reading capacities in the Spanish colonial, English, and American periods.[40] This literacy rate was not quite as low for New Mexico as shown in Gallego's work but nevertheless he estimates a third of his sample of 424 enlistees were illiterate (1992, 53). As has been indicated, if illiterate, the person made the sign of the cross, as this example has shown, and none of the Opata *filiaciónes* in my sample indicate a signature. Yet, this does not mean, however, that Opatas were all nonliterate and military prowess was not appreciated and rewarded by rank. As the following muster rolls of the same company on January 1, 1816, reveals, two sets of officers appear in these rolls and signify a two-tiered structure as figure 5 illustrates.[41]

Partial Muster Roll of the Opata Company of the Pueblo of Bavispe, Sonora	
Classes	*Nombres*
Teniente Colonel (Lieutenant Colonel)	*Don Benito Espinosa*
Teniente Veterano (Veteran Lieutenant)	*Don Francisco Villaescuna*
Capellann (capetlan: Priest)	*Don Luis Fernandez*
Soldado (soldier)	*Juan Jose Arvizu*
Soldado (soldier)	*Bernardo Martinez*
Opatas	
Capitan De Naturales (Captain of the Naturals i.e. Indigenous Peoples)	*Don Gabriel Camacho*
Priimero Alfarez Teniente (First Lieutenant)	*Don Francisco Fernandez*
Segundo Alfarez (Second Lieutenant)	*Don Christobal Grijalba*

FIGURE 5. Partial muster roll of the Opata Company of the Pueblo of Bavispe, Sonora.

Opportunity or not, these were obviously segregated companies between officers but, as indicated by the use of the "Dons" of the Opatas, they were also a measure of upward mobility within the Spanish hierarchy both military and civil. Nevertheless, there is still the "Garden of Eden" effect in place in which they are regarded as "Naturales," and Indigenous populations were regarded as simple creatures of nature abounding in desire, corpulence, and innocence as well as simplicity of mind and soul. This point of view was not likely held by the soldiers themselves but does reveal the underlying contradictory colonial meganarrative of Native peoples to be cultivated and harvested or mined, not unlike flora, fauna, or minerals.

On the other hand, the next *filiación* is among the most telling of documents in revealing the deep caste and class divisions present in the region, as well as the fact that disease was no stranger to the elite, by the reference to the smallpox pits on his sixteen-year-old face in the following eighteenth-century text, translated by me:

Filiación

3rd Company of the Second Squadron
Company of Dragoons

Don Pedro Policarpo Alcue y Armendáris, son of Don Pedro Manuel Capitan of the Third Company of the Second Squadron of Dragoons and of Doña María Rita de Alcue y Armendaris, natural son of the Valley of San Bartolomé, Bishopric of Durango, Occupation "Campista" (Agricultural Worker), his height five feet, his age sixteen years, Apostolic Holy Roman Catholic, his physical signs are these, black hair, black eyes, ruddy white complexion, narrow nose, pockmarked smallpox pits with a birthmark close to the right side of the nose and beardless.

He presented himself before me the Commander in Chief of this named company Don Diego Santa María with superior dispatch of the Senior Brigadier and Commanding General Pedro Nava on this date of the 17th of June of 1791 and admitted in the rank of Cadet whose place was given in the said Company on the 10th of March of 1792 and was instructed on the obligations and penalties and signed it before the witnesses José Ignacio Pavia and José Trinidad Rodríguez Sargent and Corporal of the Company.[42]

Signature with Rubric:

This *filiacíon* is a cultural mother lode of colonial scripts of privileged standings, underlying formulas of stratification, and their religious sanctification. First, this sixteen-year-old is already addressed as "Don" as an honorific, marking him along a number of important dimensions, and such titles were part of the lineage inheritance from his father and mother. His father by his title was the captain of Dragoons and the mother was also from the Armendáris line of descent and merited the title of

"Doña," and both were the descendants of "fathers and grandfathers who were high ranking military officials and *hacenderos*, with land holdings as far back as the early 1700s in Chihuahua."[43] Second, the *filiación*, however, also cognitively and spatially places the individual within the medieval religious/military megascript mapping by reference to his birth in the Valley of San Bartolomé, Bishopric of Durango as place of birth, his Apostolic Roman Catholic affiliation, and the privileging of the individual by the presence and blessing of his father, the captain of the company and thus a direct lineage connection to the military. Third, his position, status, and privilege are further legitimized by the honorific presence of the Commanding Brigadier General Pedro Nava as further witness to Pedro's lineage rights, duties, and obligations and more importantly his "right" to be so inducted without necessarily being formally prepared for the military position as Cadet since for the most part non-criollos could not aspire to the officer corps except those in the segregated ranks, as was shown. It is also apparent that his ability to sign his name and with a rubric both indicate having learned to read and write from either mission sources or from his parents, which were for the colonial period mostly reserved for those categorized as criollos. When all of these aspects are combined with the physical characteristic present and especially that of melanin, then we have very much a corporally based system of cultural entitlement and responsibility created by inheritance within the Spanish megascript.

The following *filiación* is more than likely that of a mestizo and not either Indigenous or criollo since no honorific titles are included for either him or his parents. Secondly, he did not sign his enlistment and is uneducated but not belonging to an Indigenous military company. Indigenous persons joining a mestizo company in the Presidio system became mestizo as one of the means of removing their status as "Natural" (Natural) while Indigenous persons joining a Pima or Opata Company were designated as "Natural," which the following does not in the text translated by me.

Filiación

Royal Presidio of San Juan Bautista de Río Grande Coahuila

Pedro Lombraña son of Baltasar and Juana de los Santos natural of this Presidio and dependency of the Government of Coahuila and neighbor of the same with the occupation of agriculturalist and member of the noted government and his height is 5 foot 3 inches, his age is 22, his religion is Apostolic Roman Catholic. His physical signs are Black Hair, Hazel eyes, dark complexion. Eyebrows the color of the Hair, Regular Nose, and scant beard with pockmarks of smallpox.

He was enlisted for ten years in this Company on the 17th of August of 1797 and the ordinances and penalties were read to him and because he did not know how to write, he made the sign of the cross and was warned of the consequences and that there would be no excuse of any sort [not completing the enlistment]. Witnessed by Sergeant Antonio Aguilar and the Soldier Diego Mares.[44]

As in the preceding discussion, this *filiacíon* like most accentuates the individuation of the soldier. But as in many cases revealed in this research, smallpox pockmarks play an important role in the individual's identity as well give an indication of its wide spread character during the colonial period.[45] In a way, scars become naturalized not unlike eye or hair color and part of their "jacket." Since these were the survivors and possibly immune to further illness, it also indicates how deeply the disease impacted Spaniards but in particular Native peoples throughout the colonial period as early as 1593 and especially through 1625. Over 150 years before this *filiacíon* was written, the Jesuit missions of SWNAR early on suffered from smallpox, measles, and epidemics of various sorts (Reff 1991, 162–68). The diseases traveled north to Santa Fe from Zacatecas through mission and trade wagons on the Camino Real, and from missionizing, mining, and town sources to the northern areas in general. With reference to Sinaloa and Sonora, among the Yaqui, Pima Bajo, and Opata as well as New Mexico Pueblos, the Native population was reduced by 90 percent by the eighteenth century (ibid., 325). Other parts of the region were affected to different degrees, such as in the Arkansas and Texas region where Perttula (1992) estimated a major demographic reduction from European diseases of up to 95 percent in the Caddo culture area, which is contested by others (Widmer 1994, 478). Similarly, California's Indigenous population was decimated by attempts to "reduce" Indigenous populations to missions, which simultaneously acted as the laboratories for the spread of epidemics. These and associated civil and military settlements and forts created the perfect incubation combinations for smallpox, measles, syphilis, malaria, and influenza that reduced the populations by 85 percent according to Bauer (2014, 195).

Thus the *filiacíon* is a bureaucratic instrument that classified presidial soldiers within a racialized matrix of presidial soldiers and is a contrast to the group reference for most Native persons, but it is also a tool that reveals one of the most important sources of linguistic and cultural and class hegemonies—the demographic reduction of entire populations and the revealed tragedy imbedded within a simple category of visual markings of pockmarks among the soldiery itself and certainly among Native Presidial soldiers.

These *filiacíones* are an important tool to decipher the underlying message of privileging those who could write and its relationship to melanin. As stated before, of my total sample of 436 soldiers, of which 55 did not have a yes or no signature, 72 soldiers could sign their names, of which 18 were classified as *trigueños* (dark complexion), 2 classified as "pinkish or ruddy dark," and the rest as "blancos" (white). We can note that of all those who could sign their names, 75 percent, or 54, were classified as "white," which is beyond an accidental probability; therefore the relationship between "blanco" and literacy was positive and that between *trigueño* and literacy negative. Such complexity of distribution of privilege according to hue makes claims for the treatment of soldiers as a group in the same way along the lines of warriorship problematic. But this obviously differentiates and reduces the individual to a type and assembles the "me's" and "them's" along melanin/race dimensions not defined by any catechism or religious doctrine of equal treatment under a benevolent being for both the darker soldier and the darker Indigenous person.

SPANISH COLONIAL LANGUAGE POLICY AND PRACTICE: 1523–1821

While the *filiación* and the Acts of Possession and Obedience provide an "on the ground" glimpse of the characteristic use of "seeing man" rationales of Spanish and its contrast to Native persons' social and cultural premises to identity and sense of self, Spanish colonial language policy is an important area to understand in order to gauge policies over time and their impact on Native peoples in the region. For the Spanish colonial period between 1521 and 1821,[46] the Mendicant orders focused on the recovery of Mexican Indigenous Languages early to about 1580, but intermixed by changing Imperial Policy toward Indigenous languages and the learning of Spanish (Hidalgo 2006, 358–59).[47] Charles V's proclamation of 1550 stated specifically the official policy of the New World would be "Spanish Only," but in fact Mendicant orders and especially the Jesuits embarked in learning the language of the Americas through the sixteenth to eighteenth centuries until expelled in 1767. Yet Phillip II, who became king when Charles V abdicated in 1578, overturned the proclamation and emphasized the necessity for Nahuatl to be taught as the normative language because at the time it was the largest and most concentrated in New Spain. On the other hand, the same seemingly enlightened king confiscated the *Encyclopedia on Mexican Language and Civilization* in 1580 and interrupted the Crown's liberal policy on the Mexican language (ibid., 359–60). According to David J. Weber (1992, 401) "the law of March 8 1603 in the *Recopiliación de leyes, tomo I, lib. I tit. XV, ley v*, made it obligatory for *doctrineros* to learn Indian languages."

Yet for the missionaries of Central Mexico and SWNAR the practice of learning the Native language was crucial and in fact instituted a type of transitional bilingualism in order to spread their doctrines and the entire edifice of the missionizing megascript. In SWNAR, early language transmission was divided such that Franciscans worked mostly in Coahuila, Nuevo León, Nuevo Santander, New Mexico, and

Texas; the Jesuits mostly in Sinaloa, Sonora (including present-day Arizona), Chihua-
hua, and Baja California with their replacements by other orders, and in Baja Califor-
nia by Dominicans and in Alta California by the Franciscans (Kelly 1940, 349). The
Jesuits especially used a stepped bilingual approach in which missionaries like Eusebio
Kino first learned one or more Indigenous languages before embarking physically to
Sonora and then using this knowledge to write local dictionaries to communicate
Indigenous versions of the Catholic doctrines to Native peoples. In his *Memoir of
Pimeria Alta* previously cited, in describing his interactions with the Opas and Coco-
maricopas, Kino stated that, because of their common language, "I at once and with
ease made a vocabulary of the said tongue, and also a map of those lands, measuring
the sun with the astrolabe" (Bolton 1919, 128). Following Kino in 1756 in Sonora,
Friar Ygnacio Pfefferkorn states that he found learning Pima was difficult because of
the lack of dictionaries and grammars, so he remained with another missionary who
had learned the language: "I remained for a time with Father Gaspar Seiger . . . who
had supposedly mastered their language to learn . . . at least as much of the language
as would be indispensable to me for the necessary offices when I took my post" (Pfefferkorn 1989, 230).

While Pfefferkorn acknowledged the necessity for missionaries to learn Indigenous
languages, most if not all such approaches were designed to Hispanicize Native persons. It was basically a transitional method of both communication and proselytizing
and coercively organizing Indigenous populations around the mission. Yet it was also
likely that the further the mission or villa was from either central colonial authorities
or from Spanish Mexican towns, the greater probability of not only the retention of
the Native language but its necessity since obviously the demographics were such that
there was a greater number of Native language speakers than Spanish speakers. This
fostered the practicality of bilingual skills on the part of missionaries.

The use of Spanish by Native peoples varied according to their needs, necessities,
and objectives, and was certainly frustrating for missionaries like Ygnacio Pfefferkorn.
According to Pfefferkorn, Sonoran Pimas negotiated their bilinguality on call:

> Sonorans do not at all like to speak the Spanish language even though they may have
> learned it quite well by constant association with Spaniards living among them. When
> they are questioned in Spanish, they reply in their own language. They may rarely be
> persuaded to give an answer in Spanish, even though they know that the person who
> is speaking with them understands not a word of their language. On the other hand,
> those who are raised in the houses of the missionaries prefer Spanish . . . [and] . . . which
> they generally like to display by answering in Spanish if they are addressed in Sonoran
> [but] they seem to forget every Spanish word the moment they come into confessional
> (1989, 229).

SCHOOLING AND LEARNING IN
THE COLONIAL REGION

Given the diverse linguistic context, the crown sought to formalize "Spanish only" and announced its legal stricture "La Real Cedula" (Royal Proclamation) on May 10, 1770, in which it sought to teach Spanish systematically to all Indigenous children in schools and to persuade adults to send their children to school for instruction. This would promote their learning of the language in order to replace the numerous Indigenous languages to their extinction (Rospide 1995, 1416). Rospide informs us:

> The proclamation demanded that each town should have schools of Spanish with the provision that indigenous priests may fulfill the necessary sacraments but that finally Spanish would be the only and universal language in the colonial domains since it is the language of monarchs and conquistadores which together may lead to the extinction of the numerous indigenous vernaculars . . . The underlying rationales were that Spanish was part of a superior culture and the sole and ideal instrument of communication to evangelize and civilize the "naturales" (1995, 1417–18, my translation).

The reality, however, of all such "seeing man" proclamations is that they had to fit the ecological conditions of a region often beset with violence, struggles for survival, and a very long Royal Road to resources and assistance. Conflicts over scarce natural resources in arid environments in which rain-fed agriculture is primarily dependent on the control of riverine systems were inevitable. Spanish penchant for cattle and sheep led to extensive and severe soil erosion, and the creation of miles of arroyos with no or limited vegetation. Taken together, cattle, mining, and related Spanish introduced "development," straining the limits of fragile and frail subecologies. The climate was often not conducive to the physical or mental health of the intruding colonists, missionaries, or soldiers alike, and often their lives were interrupted by scant food supplies, especially at the onset of Spanish expansion. Such conditions continued in greater or lesser degrees throughout the colonial period. Within such an economic and social state of affairs, schooling as such was not the fallback position for most missions, pueblos, towns, and rural communities. Communication using multiple approaches was imperative. In the colonial project, the Spanish language was important and institutional, but in fact most colonists and Indigenous peoples, especially after the Pueblo Revolt in New Mexico and the necessity of communications in the mines of Sonora, Chihuahua, Coahuila, and Nuevo León, often brought Indigenous and Spanish Mexicans together. This was one of the major sources of language learning by each.

California was a special case in that the lower portion now known as Baja California was forcefully missionized by the Jesuits, but few permanent colonies on the peninsula were developed, although the Jesuits constructed seventeen missions and forty *visitas*. This represented the primary form of European presence until their expulsion in 1768. But by 1767 these missions were the carriers not only of religious indoctrination and language but also disease, which depopulated the lower part of the peninsula in less than one hundred years from 40,000 to 7,000 (Weber 1992, 241). The second important special characteristic is that after exploration, from as early as 1542 by both the Spanish and English, it was not until two hundred years later that Gaspar de Portola in 1769 moved with a colonization plan to Upper California with an entourage of soldiers, Franciscans, and equipment for supporting the expedition. This was followed by the better-known Junipero Serra, who created a chain of twenty-one missions from San Diego to Upper California and turned those to the south over to the Dominicans after the Jesuit expulsion. Serra established nine of the eventual twenty-one missions. But California had a third important characteristic in the development of hegemonic practices and impacts. Unlike much of the New Mexican and Sonoran and Chihuahuan areas, the focus of interaction between the Franciscans and Indigenous populations was a program of linguistic and cultural and territorial disassembly visited upon Indigenous children and their parents.

This focus was such that it was designed to "transform the population of pagan Native Californians into a peasant class of Hispanicized laborers" (Lightfoot 2006, 59). Mission Indigenous peoples' children were removed from their parents and grandparents; the aim of this was to eliminate continued interactions with their elders. According to Lightfoot (61), girls between seven and nine were removed from their homes into a dormitory until they were married. Some became domestics in Spanish households and learned to sew, among other tasks which would include washing, cooking, cutting, cleaning, and all other tasks associated with the household. Boys and unmarried men were placed in separate dormitories from which they were assigned laboring tasks as well as religious instruction. These seemed more like concentration camps with floggings, strict time and work schedules, hard work, and roll calls. Coupled with the usual visit by frequent mission epidemics, the linguistic and cultural aftermath appears to have been linguistically and culturally devastating (ibid., 53–55).

Certainly the Franciscans of New Mexico not only were coercive but also resorted to the lash to induce or force Pueblos to conform to Catholic dogma through ritualized and repetitive instruction; however, the urban and agricultural complexity of the Pueblos were not amenable to such "directed cultural change." In the aftermath of the Pueblo Revolt this would have clearly disrupted the agricultural rain-fed and irrigated food-production processes. Spanish control also had to contend with the fact that Pueblos had "reduced" themselves by living in compact urban pueblos much before the arrival of Spanish controls. In Sonora, "reductions" were certainly employed among the Mayo, Opatas, Yaquis, and Pimas. Through a combination of the carrot and the stick, missions emerged, especially through the production-based approach of Friar Eusebio Kino. He developed most of the "reductions" by using cattle and sheep as attractive incentives to coerce Indigenous populations to settle close to missions (Spicer 1962, 126). The response of Indigenous communities was not always positive. In the case of Yaquis, they resisted fiercely the undue influence of missionaries, and as noted before, invited missionaries along their own terms and not that of either the Jesuits or Franciscans who followed them.

In California, such forced cultural change was coupled, however, with massive forced relocation of thousands of coastal peoples through the policy of "reduction." In the aftermath, however, one unplanned impact was the rape of Native women by Spanish soldiers when these were stationed around the mission or in mission pueblos. As a result, large numbers of linguistically divergent tribes and bands were forced to live as "neophytes" in multiethnic villages. Such relocations resulted in conditions as Lightfoot so eloquently describes in the following manner: "By removing the neophytes from the territories of the birth, the fathers alienated them from their mythical landscapes, the graves of their ancestors, and the named rocks and landmarks so central to the construction of native identity" (2006, 65). On the other hand, Lightfoot remarks that instead of destruction, "[A] widespread re-creation of Indian identities and cultural practices throughout colonial California . . . [and] new kinds of Indian identities, social forms, and tribal relationships emerged" (ibid., 208). This was dependent on the specific ecological and political context—that is, the result of negotiations and strong reactions by Indigenous peoples with specific missions as to how much reduction took place. The result was that many Indigenous peoples conserved their cultural and linguistic frameworks. Others expanded into larger unsegmented tribal organizations from formerly acephalous political units and in fact provided the basis for the continued instruction of Indigenous children in their own languages, such as among the Kashaya Pomo (ibid., 209). Regardless of Franciscan intrusions "on the ground," the fact that Indigenous peoples managed to surpass the capacity of these hegemonic processes to eradicate or eliminate Indigenous language and culture is remarkable, and not often acknowledged in popular histories of the region.

In New Mexico, Franciscan friars very early in the seventeenth century worked in twenty-five missions among 60,000 Indigenous peoples in ninety pueblos in which each allegedly was placed with a school. Each mission was responsible, with various degrees of success and continuity, to teach reading, writing, manual arts, singing and instrumental music, according to Spell (1927, 31). Fray Alonos Benavides's *Memorial of 1630*, describes his inspection tour as Third Custodian of Missions and the First Commissary of the Inquisition between 1626 and 1629 in which he visited many of the missions.[48] His first inspection was of the province of the Piros, which he describes as having fourteen Pueb-los and 6,000 persons on both sides of the Río Grande River (Río del Norte). He noted that the three Franciscans had not only taught Catholic doctrine but also "singing, writ-ing, crafts, and trades in their schools, as well as how to live in polite society" (17).

In each of the missions that he visited, he concluded with almost the same stock answer, and it would seem to be less of a conviction and more of necessity to please his superiors. Yet there are two of note that seem to be more genuine and that con-cern his comments of the Keres (where Oñate y Salazar made his first vassalage pronouncement). First, he says that for ten leagues there are seven Pueblos with 4,000 persons, and "Indians are quite clever at reading, writing, and playing all musical instruments—good hands at all trades" (Spell 1927, 13). The second, which seems more efficacious, is his resettlement of the Jemez, who had been scattered by hunger and war. He gathered them in two pueblos, San José and San Diego de la Congregación, and proudly announced that all of them have homes and concluded, "And so today that congregation constitutes one of the best towns in the Indies, with its church, friary, and schools teaching all the trades that may be found elsewhere [including reading and writing]. And although half of this nation died, Your majesty [Felipe IV] may still count here on more than three thousand newly assembled taxpay-ers" (Spell 1927, 29). Such demographic decline may have been more important than the efficacy of Franciscan pedagogy to spread their divine teachings, writing, reading, and performances to half of the remaining living population.

In these two examples, Benavides observes that the Franciscans in at least two of the missions did establish schools and seemed to have operated them well in spite of the drastic decline in population—at least until the Pueblo Revolt, in which all books, documents, letters, pamphlets, broadsides, archives, and all other written materials of the period were burned. On the other hand, the blissful manner in which Benavides mentions the loss of half of the population to war and epidemics does indicate that mortality rates were less impressive to report than successful hegemonic practices. Yet, with the Pueblo Revolt, language hegemony was certainly not only struck down but its documentary trail turned to ashes by a people sick of cultural, linguistic, and human oppression and among the greatest of expressions of discontent. In fact, among the many dictums established by its leader Popé was the abolition of Spanish. The Pueblos were directed to discard their baptismal names, never utter Christian deities, and "... were ordered likewise not to teach the Castilian language in any pueblo and to burn the seeds which the Spaniards sowed and to plant only maize and beans, which were the crops of their ancestors" (Hackett 1942, 235). This of course was overturned by their reconquest by De Vargas by 1693.

Despite best efforts by Spaniards, we do know that literacy was acquired especially by Indigenous officials of the mission, such as cantors, and they were used after the

Pueblo Revolt during and after the reconquest of New Mexico in 1692–1693. Former missionized literate Native persons were used by the reconqueror Captain General Diego de Vargas Zapata Lujan Ponce de León. In his report of Sunday, February 28, 1693, he writes: "I sent from the pueblo of the Pecos on 26 September of this present year (1692), with the letter, cross, and a rosary, so that it might be taken and given to Antonio Malacate, captain and leader of the Keres Indians who left Zia Pueblos and live in Santa Ana Pueblo, to whom it was given. He was ill and sent in his place to see me the Spanish-speaking Indian cantor, named Francisco, who was from the Pueblo and knows how to read and write."[49]

In fact, literate Bartolome de Ojeda, who had been a Zia war captain (and probably had been a cantor as well) against the Spanish in 1680, was captured by the Spanish in that year and returned with them in 1692 as an ally. He was instrumental in initially influencing Pueblos not to resist de Vargas's new invasion by carrying a cross in front of him. He reports, for example, to de Vargas by letter and informs him of the resistance and strategies of some of the Pueblos:

Bartolome de Ojeda to Diego de Vargas, [Zia, 1 July 1696] L.S.
Lord governor and captain general [*sic*].

My soul will be glad if this letter finds your lordship very well, as I am, thanks be to God. I remain at your lordship's order for whatever you may wish to command me. I am informing your lordship about what has happened to us around here.

The soldiers left with the rest of the people from the pueblo. They went to attack the mesa where those enemies were. Then we tried to go out, because there were many tracks going back and forth to San Juan Pueblo. As we were approaching, they came at us, taunting, and we withdrew to level ground, which caused them to come out. The men fell upon them, and forty died, with the prisoners that makes forty-two. I say this because the Indians, who were curious about this, counted them, and they never say there are more than there are.

So as to inform our lordship, that entire gathering was made up of Acomas, Zunis, Moquinos, Navajo Apaches, Cochitis, Tewas, Tanos, and Jemes of San Juan. That young man who is going is from San Juan, and the other younger one is from Acoma. They reported how many there were and how the gathering, as I say, was ready to lay waste to Santa Ana Pueblo and the people who were in the milpas and carried the horses and livestock. All this, as they acknowledged, had already been arranged among them. Nothing more occurs to me. May God Our Lord keep your lordship in that villa of Santa Fe.

From your lordship's servant and compadre, who kisses your lordship's hand.
Bartolome de Ojeda (Kessell, Hendricks, and Dodge 1994, 740)

This particular letter also reveals in the closing that de Ojeda, who was appointed by de Vargas as governor of Zia, also had established a co-godparenthood relation (compadre) with de Vargas by referring to their relationship not only as his vassal (servant) but also his fictive kin and thus placing de Ojeda in the upper caste of the system of hierarchy in part through his literacy capacity.

Yet, the acquisition of literacy by Indigenous peoples was spotty throughout the region, and there had been no consistent efforts at establishing schools or teaching reading and writing, except by the Jesuits in Sonora, Chihuahua, and lower California until their expulsion, and by the Franciscans in New Mexico, which no longer supported schools after 1700 (Spicer 1962, 429–50). Spicer concludes that the Jesuits left a small number of Mayos, Yaquis, and Opatas in Sonora who were literate—especially the Yaqui, who integrated a literate Catholic ceremonialism—and he concludes that "any other type of knowledge beside the sacred no literate tradition had been created in the course of 250 years of contact, anywhere in northwestern New Spain [Southwest North America]" (430). Texas was a little different in its constant hostility toward the Spanish colony, and even though the first mission school was established in 1690, the scarcity of mission and the lack of an educational system all mitigated the acquisition of literacy by Native peoples and colonists alike (Berger and Wilborn 2017).

Although Spanish was an immersion language for Native persons, and depending on the Spanish governor in power, Indigenous residents were also subjected to proclamations of many sorts, such as those issued to Pueblo communities "concerning marriage in the eighteen century" and for illegal cohabitation (Brown 2013, 12). Brown observes that the end point for all such communications and legal interventions was ultimately that "Spanish authorities—be they civil or religious—sought to remake Pueblo identities and communities" (ibid.). The hegemonic success of Spanish is an artifact of how well and how often Native peoples declared their own autonomy and how well they managed to impress Spanish authorities that they were needed more by them than by the Spanish, especially so in relation to their defense against other Indigenous populations. On the other hand, the Spanish also had to provide the legal means and space for their allied populations to have a degree of cultural and linguistic autonomy "on the ground," without which their own survival was in jeopardy. In fact, the postreconquest governance model for Pueblos especially was structured around a type of "indirect rule" model, in which Puebloan governors were selected by the ritual societies within each Pueblo but anointed by the Spanish civil authorities with the caveat of each knowing the Spanish language and Spanish institutions (Gutiérrez 1991, 158). As Gallegos points out for New Mexico, publicly read village announcements, or *bandos*, were not only translated to the Indigenous languages but were in fact read also by Indigenous individuals, who were termed

Ladinos, who could read them in Spanish (78–81). Gallegos, citing original sources, asserts that "the royal bando . . . was published in the voice of Antonio Jojola of the Tigua Nation and a Ladino, in the Castilian language" (81).

In the following chapters, I discuss literacy and language discourses as part of the synthesis of Spanish/Mexican forms within traditional conflict dance reenactments such as the matachines—a highly ritualized drama of dancers that was integrated within both Indigenous and Spanish/Mexican Pueblos and spread from Chihuahua and Zacatecas to the Taos Pueblos and beyond.[50] The discussion in chapter 3 examines the syncretic forms involving principle players such as Moctezuma, of Aztec origin, and La Malinche converted to a child virgin from her traditional translator and cultural broker roles, as well as the presence of bulls, clowns, and mayordomos (foremen), together with an array of dancers dressed in combinations of stylized Spanish and Indigenous dress topped by bishopric miters.[51]

The aforementioned practices and hegemonic processes from the pre-Hispanic period to today are embedded in continuous exploitive and extractive platforms in which aridity, minerals, valley oases, high and low deserts, huge mountain ranges—the sources of networks of riverine systems—and coastal regions constrain as well as permit human use. All serve as the sources for the formation of human settlements, transhumance, and migrations and penetrations whose political systems varied according to their historical mode of production, distribution, and consumption, as many of Eric R. Wolf's works have shown.[52] From these material limitations and potentials, a continuous struggle has emerged among Indigenous populations in addition to the continuous exchange of trade and commerce between Indigenous populations and European—and much later American colonial—regimes, depending on the period in question. Such limitations, for example, the advent of the Little Ice Age of the sixteenth and seventeenth centuries, probably contributed to the drought and freezing temperatures that greeted the entrance of the Spanish Empire into the northern region and in turn played important if not crucial roles in the failures of the conquerors and colonists leading to the Pueblo Revolt of 1680 (White 2014, 428).

THE DYNAMICS OF INTRUSION AND DISCONTENTED GENES

What must be considered among the persistent and consistent dynamics of this Spanish/Mexican and Indigenous interaction of the SWNAR is that before the establishment of the border, moving alliances, conflictive relations, slavery, trade, multifaceted acculturation—two and three ways, and exploitive and cooperative relations—were the consistent hallmarks of the region set within the limits of the ecological limitations and constraints noted. Of central importance to the region is that among the primary identification markers, given the human dynamics, before the imposition of the region by the border, Spanish/Mexican and Indigenous populations vied for control of the limited natural resources of the region, not only material property, land, and flora and fauna but also, most importantly, human beings as slaves of a system that antedates the arrival of Western Europeans.

Brooks (2003, 14) describes the "great captive exchange complex" of pre-European Indigenous populations like the Pawnees who served as middlemen "that operated throughout the continent, stretching from the Southwest Borderlands northward to the Great Lakes and beyond." Once connected to the European version of a market-oriented process, thousands of Indian captives, including Pawnees, were "transported" to French Canada and British America and some even to the Spanish Caribbean" (ibid.). As will be seen, with the introduction of American hegemony, in the northern side of the region this process ceased but started again as African slavery was extended into Texas. With the rise of the Mexican Republic as well, such processes were interrupted but not terminated until the Mexican Revolution.

With European intrusion prior to the American presence, the SWNAR can be characterized as a region in which dynamic exchange, conflict, and cooperation bounded by ecological constraints and potentials ranged from Tamaulipas and Coahuilla through Nuevo León through Chihuahua, Tejas, Sonora, Nuevo Mejico, and California. These contending populations sometimes were friends of friends, enemies of enemies, friends of enemies, and enemies of friends. From the Caddo and Comanche of Tejas to the Apache and Upper and Lower Pimas and Opatas, Mayos, and Yaquis of Sonora, to the Pueblos and Navajos, Apaches and Utes of New Mexico, to the Indigenous California peoples like the Kumeyaay whose revolts in San Diego lasted longer than any other area from 1775 through the Mexican period, Spanish/Mexican-Indigenous relations were in constant flux. These encompassed a range of social interactions, from exchange through compadrazgo, intermarriage, and raiding for each other's peoples for slavery and labor but asymmetrically since the power of the Imperial state always trumped local versions. Such consistent dynamics created the necessity of developing highly contingent and contiguous cultural and economic boundaries, so new categorical terms and their local variations popped in and out to identify newly forming populations with varying local versions of casta nomenclature—such as coyote, *pardo*, Genizaro, mestizo, mulatto, and *vecinos*—associated with such terms as *pelo quemado* (burnt hair) or *color bueno* (good color, i.e., fair or white skin), and all variations in between. Missionaries like Jesuit Ygnacio Pfefferkorn complained in 1765 or so that there was hardly a "true Spaniard in Sonora and there is scarcely one who could trace his origin to a Spanish family of pure blood" in any of the former Sonora (now Arizona) presidios, towns, and missions (Pfefferkorn 1989, 284).

DISCONTENTED GENES

The genetic history of the region exemplifies the intermixture and boundary creat-ing processes simultaneously with many of those affected seeking new cultural and social fits and localized terms. Not surprisingly, this makes social and cultural discus-sion about claims of biological purity and cultural ethnicity much more problematic between those forgetting an unforgiving history, and those seeking renewal in claims of noncontamination and nativism. Gabriela Martínez-Cortés et al. (2012), shows that in examining maternal ancestry of Mexican mestizos, they "confirm a strong gender-biased admixture history between European males and Native American females that gave rise to Mexican mestizos." This pattern for the SWNAR to different degrees holds true, as indicated by Bryc et al. (2015, 43), who observe that "[c]onsistent with previous studies that show a sex bias in admixture in Latino populations, we estimate 13% less European ancestry on the X chromosome than genome wide, show[ing] pro-portionally greater European ancestry contributions from males."

Genetic admixture of Mexican-origin populations varies in general but seems to clump regionally so that according to Martínez-Cortés et al. (2012), in Mexico, "In the total population sample, paternal ancestry was predominately European (64.9%), followed by Native American (30.8%) and African (4.2%). However, the European ancestry was prevalent in the north and west (66.7–95%) and, conversely, Native American ancestry increased in the center and southeast (37–50%), whereas the African ancestry was low and relatively homogeneous (0–8.8%)." An earlier study by Long suggested a similar percentage for Arizona to that of the Mexican north, with the "following estimates: Amerindian, 0.29 +/- 0.04; Spaniard, 0.68 +/- 0.05; and African, 0.03 +/- 0.02. The interpretation of these results with respect to Amerindian and Spanish ancestry is straightforward. African ancestry is strongly supported by the presence of a marker of African descent, Fy" (1991, 427). Texas and California have similar genetic admixture rates, except that depending on the study for Texas, for example, the European ancestry in San Antonio, Texas, is gauged at 50 percent, Native American 46 percent, and 3.1 percent West African to almost 58 percent European, Native American 38 percent, and almost 3 percent African (Beuten et al. 2011). Cal-ifornia studies, like studies of all other regions, will vary in admixture depending on the historical period analyzed, but the percentage admixture according to modeling done by Price et al. (2007) is a distribution of 50 percent European, 45 percent Native American, and 5 percent African.

A very sophisticated analysis of Mexico and Sonora by Silva-Zolezzi et al. (2009) states that Sonora had the highest estimates of mean European ancestry, with a range of 0.616 to 0.085 for Sonora, and as well the lowest of American Indian contribution of .0362 to 0.089 (8612). Similarly, for a sample studied by Klimentidis, Miller, and

Africa	4%
America	23%
Asia	< 1%
Europe	70%
West Asia	2%
Trace Regions	
North Africa	3%
Senegal	1%
Native American	23%
Italy/Greece	28%
Iberian Peninsula	26%
European Jewish	7%

FIGURE 6. Ethnicity estimate for Carlos Vélez-Ibáñez: DNA tests for ethnicity and genealogical DNA Testing at Ancestry DNA (2014b).

Shriver (2009, 378) of Hispanics and Native Americans in New Mexico, an unhappy surprise awaited some who self-identified as either one, so that self-identified Hispanics had Native American admixtures of 32.7 percent while for self-identified Native Americans the average Native American admixture was 71.8 percent. West African admixture was low for both, at 5.7 percent and 2.9 percent, respectively. The study concluded that both groups underestimated their degree of admixture with other groups (379). As well, there are subgroups such as within Spanish/Mexicans in Southern Colorado who carry the genetic mutation of 185delAG inherited through their Ashkenazi forbearers that selects for both breast and ovarian carcinomas.[53] There is no doubt that Jewish genetic forbearers, along with thousands of other genetic materials, were transatlantically transmitted, and are found in the SWNAR.

Figure 6 shows my DNA mapping; my ancestors are primarily from Sonora (including Arizona) and Sinaloa and are, to varying degrees, representative of the region. The results are from two different sources but apparently with almost the same results, except that the second analysis includes examinations from between thirty thousand and sixty thousand years ago to reveal Neanderthal and Denisovan traces, which were 2.3 percent and 2.6 percent, respectively, like most European populations. The data from six generations ago to ten thousand years ago tallies as 60 percent Mediterranean and northern European, 21 percent Native American, 15 percent southwest Asian, and 3 percent sub-Saharan African.[54] This second analysis seems to indicate an ancient Greek relationship, which seems to reinforce the ancient saying of accepting gifts from this genetic population.

Like most populations from the region, I reflect the genetic admixture of those of the "seeing man" and "those seen," of the conquerors and the conquered, of the Islamic conquest of Spain through the conquest of Mexico and to the expansion of the various versions of the mestizo to the present in this region of Southwest North America. The irony of course is that, as for many of us, mine is the world of mestizaje, given the indication of hominins that began at least sixty thousand years before.

Regardless of shared genes, always present in this region was the Imperial presence to Mexican Independence, whose policies sometimes favored the Indigenous population through its missionaries against civil and military authorities. However, the social control imposed limited their independence of movement, trade, and exchange among and between tribal peoples and established its racialist hierarchy no matter how frivolous or simply dysfunctional in reality the caste system was, and many times at the end of the lash. Hanging on by their toenails in Texas, Coahuila, Sonora, and certainly in Nuevo México, the constant thematic for the Spanish/Mexican was the use of force and the unconstrained use of alliances and sometimes persuasion to reduce, missionize, and Hispanicize Indigenous populations. Yet there were subtler means of language impression, and we take up the important roles of cultural production and especially ritual performances as crucial conveyers of the colonial "megascript" and the attempt to homogenize a complexity of diverse populations, but not without their discontents from the Spanish/Mexican colonial period to the present.

3

COLONIAL AND BIFURCATED
LANGUAGE PERFORMANCE

᷒

The Processual Analysis of the Matachine Complex
of Chihuahua and New Mexico

In some places the Indians are practiced and play other [beside the flute and drum]
instruments such as violins, harps, and a kind of zither, which is called guitarra
by the Spaniards, from whom they have learned to play all these instruments. The
Moctezuma dance is solemn and majestic and originated with the Mexicans, after
whose last monarch, Moctezuma, the dance is named. . . . This performance they
execute in time with the music in the most beautiful order.

YGNACIO PFEFFERKORN ON STATION IN SONORA
BETWEEN 1756 AND 1767.[1]

THIS ANNOTATED DESCRIPTION OF PFEFFERKORN'S longer description of the matachines, alias Moctezuma performance, and instruments will be discussed fully below, but it should be noted that it provides a telling and pointed reference to the manner in which both dance and music were syncretized—in this case, within the Opata and Eudebes peoples of Sonora. He continues, "They carry on the orderly and rhythmic manner which they observed in the dances of the Spaniards, many of whom live among them" (1989, 181). But what is also shown is that Indigenous peoples not only incorporated Spanish/Mexican linguistic and cultural forms, but made them "theirs" and therefore changed and continued the practice to the present. In part, such innovations were specific.

We will be taking up the manner in which hegemonic language and culture mechanisms become "owned" by those upon whom they may have been employed, according to the political ecology of the context and the manner in which unexpected factors contribute to this ownership. This ownership is not of a cultural artifact adopted sui generis by populations, but rather, is transformed and integrated powerfully within their capacity to innovate and move concepts, practices, and performances along their own assumptions, needs, and desired functions. My initial discussion will focus on an Indigenous version harkening back to the eighteenth century among the "Rarámuri," commonly known as the Tarahumara of Chihuahua, and the second on the Hispanic/ Mexicano complex from the same century forward and especially that practiced after the imposition on the region by the American colonial project. How best to understand this process is by looking at the manner in which one important symbolic and processual anthropologist experimented with different concepts, which will enlighten the examples of Pfefferkorn and others.

PROCESSUAL ANALYSIS

In 1971, as a graduate student at the University of California, San Diego, I had the envy-inducing experience of attending seminars held by the great British anthropologist Victor W. Turner, who then had been experimenting and formulating novel concepts about the idea that "human social life is the producer and product of time, which becomes its measure . . . so that the social world is a world in becoming, not a world in being . . ." (Turner 1974, 23–24). This emergence is continuous regardless of impediments, oppressions, subjugations, and all of their opposites, including the hidden dimensions of human events that are not seen, not "front stage," and often obscured by claims of ideological purity, celestial references, or seemingly meta values. They are accepted by some who have the power and resources to make them seem universal. That approach in fact guided much of my work for the next forty years so that this book is very much influenced by what may be termed "the processual" approach, which is open to all sorts of acceptances of temporary structures, temporary influences, temporary ideologies, temporary controls and oppressions, temporary hegemonies, and temporary responses, adjustments, and agreements. As humans we are in constant temporal fluxes but always trying to find a place to land or to establish some sort of fixed position to give our emotions, psyche, and relations time to settle down a bit. However, because we are creating the very time and space in which we engage with others and ourselves we can never "finish."

We try to think so by our inventions, narratives, and megascripts, and we also create many different mechanisms by which to attempt such "fixity," including claims to being a *gente de razon* (people of reason), as the Spanish/Mexicans referred to themselves in comparison to lower castes, slaves, and Indigenous peoples. This is what the colonial project sought to do for the last five hundred years and it certainly tried to do so with hundreds of different sorts of imaginings, including performances of many sorts, dramas of many kinds, and musical compositions—all repeated, imposed, made temporal, and pushed for their acceptance without negative feedback among those being affected. In simple and traditional types of "impression management" performances, such as the drama of the "Moros y Cristianos" (Moors/Muslims and

Christians), one can discern the reenactment of the defeat of the Islamic state in Spain, but it also serves as an object lesson accentuated by the promise of violence to Native Pueblo peoples, as Perez de Villagra (1992) describes it:

> A jolly drama, well composed, Playing a Moors and Christians, With much artillery, whose roar Did cause notable fear and marveling To many bold barbarians who had Come there as spies to spy on us, To see the strength and arms possessed by the Spaniards, whose manliness Was by no nation noted more, As we shall see here further on, Than by the folk of Acoma, who had There in the midst a mighty spy. (150)

One can observe that the Spanish/Mexican megascript, which never was monolithic, could never be a whole one, but also those affected could not be either what they were or what they were becoming and to this moment still are. When protests ensued they were met many times with violent reactions, which created violent reactions and developed an emergent cycle. Such protests continued beyond the colonial project and into the nation states, until only a few short years ago when the notable confrontation occurred in 1973 at Wounded Knee, South Dakota, and in Mexico in 1994 by the Zapatistas in Chiapas and even more recently in Sonora by Yaqui peoples intercepting traffic of a major highway to protest governmental encroachments on their water rights (Barry 2014).[2] Similarly, the Rarámuris of Chihuahua continue their battles with land encroachments of their natural reserves by mestizo politicians.[3] But the fact is that in the daily discourse of populations on both sides of the region protest continues on a daily basis, in myriad settings, and in untold covert and overt ways often "off-stage" to the consciousness of one or more of the participants.

Such reactions so late in time in the twenty-first century have their genesis in the processes of impositions five hundred years before. From the moment that Vásquez de Coronado, Oñate y Salazar, de Vargas Zapata, and so many others entered the SWNAR, multiple methods were utilized to impress, coerce, convince, and enculturate, and simultaneously sought to erase, dilute, and "whiten" the entire sociocultural and economic basis of living of hundreds of thousands of Indigenous peoples. Yet they did not succeed. Hegemonic processes are, as I have mentioned above, so prone to the limitations of their internal contradictions that not only are there spatial and temporal fields to be filled, contested, or changed, but also, as will be seen, they will be incorporated and made part of "theirs" such that except for specialists, few would notice that these are not, as would those arguing an essentialist position think the outcomes to be, anything but Indigenous. Yet the Spanish hegemonic process used multiple linguistic and dramatic media by which to seek to gain control of bodies, ecology, and minds. These are among the myriad representations that emphasized the "seeing man" approach, but what is of interest is the manner in which these became appropriated and in some instances removed the "seeing man" to be replaced without its presence and reconfigured and synthesized as something celebratory of themselves.

But these performative mechanisms need to be examined by their processual dynamics that even today unfold according to ritual cycles established by a potpourri of missionaries, administrators, and the military, which once performed were also changed, negotiated, resisted, and confirmed as from the outside but now "theirs." As will be seen, what was "theirs" in fact became a different type of "theirs," and the "me's" and "they's" became sometimes like "them," sometimes like "us," and sometimes not recognizable by either but made part of the liminal quality inherent in the manner in which humans unfold in the ritual dramas of everyday life but acutely so in the dramas concerning the processes of "cultural bumping."

Sometimes, the bumping process is so onerous that it eliminates much of the "bumped" population by a combination of disease, famine, and war. In other instances, combinations of repression, accommodation, and integration within specific class groups unfold and reshape the structure of relations within the impacted population. At other times even the conqueror changes, and the local versions of culture become refreshed and enhanced by the conquering population [so that] human populations often may become more distinct but sometimes more similar after bumping into another (Vélez-Ibáñez 1996, 6–7). We can apply similar understanding to the impact of American hegemony on those who remained and moved to the northern region after its imposition. We will take up more specifically the language and cultural measures utilized by the new colonial entry of the American state on both the Indigenous and Spanish/Mexican populations in the next chapter.

However, for our purposes of the performative aspects, here it is sufficient to state that for the Spanish/Mexican versions theirs is largely a ritual complex of linguistic and cultural reaffirmation and projection in spite of a long tradition in the northern region of cultural and linguistic erasure and assimilation by the American state of both Indigenous and Spanish/Mexican populations. For the Rarámuri, in the present, theirs have similar functions in relation to the Mexican state as well.

We turn then to these next by examining the Matachines Complex among the Rarámuri of Chihuahua, and second, among the Hispano/Mexicanos of Bernalillo, New Mexico. Each will consist of dramatic representations of "selves" and claims to righteousness, conversion, and oppression and escape. Each provides the opportunity to fundamentally understand that there arose throughout the region myriad "liminal" identities, multiplex identities, and also claims of the opposite by those affecting others and those being affected. The underlying dynamic to these ritualized processes is that in fact these are "social dramas" in various forms, whether kinetic or harmonial, so that to Turner these are "units of aharmonic or disharmonic process, arising in conflict situations" (1974, 37). These are for heuristic purposes emergent stages that are never complete—they may be useful to recognize the rough outlines of the "bumping process." Turner nicely divides these into, first, "the Breach" of a seeming regularity in which, in our case, are the explosive breaches infusing the Amerindian worlds by the colonial projects; and second, the crisis drama in which the breach widens and envelops most of those involved—both those who are breached and those breaching—so that the crisis continues until someone yells "uncle." Third, some kind of redressive action emerges in which at least one party calls upon the other for legitimate actions such as judicial redress or appeals to a celestial broker, or those breaching decide on a change of strategy such as giving beads, or bibles, or symbols and artifacts of reconciliation such as crosses, blankets, and perhaps food. And last, this I would term a temporary reconciliation and recognition of authority or power, or simply being in their "best interests" to find a modus vivendi for a short time until the next breach occurs. The only difference is that I contend that all "reconciliations," especially of bordering populations, eventually unravel because of the built-in dialectical contradictions created and developed over historical processes that must eventually unravel to some degree or other.

THE TRANSBORDER MATACHINES

The Matachines Complex, and I use "complex" rather than "dance," is a deeply embedded performance ritual situated within the life and ritual cycle of an Indigenous and/or Mexican/Spanish community to the present. Its SWNAR versions extend since pre-imposition periods from tiny Rancherias in the upper folds of the Sierra Madre among the Tarahumaras (Rarámuri) and west to the Mayo, Opata, and Yaqui (Yoéme) towns of Sonora and on to the north to Taos, New Mexico, and all along the Río Grande Valley south to El Paso and certainly into Chihuahua, Nuevo León, and Zacatecas. Members of these communities have moved to the northern segment of the SWNAR, as twentieth- and twenty-first-century migrations to Guadalupe, Arizona, to California, and to the Midwest and southern United States. Its origin has been examined by Spicer 1962; Dozier 1970, 187; Acuña Delgado 2008, 98; and among the most recently accomplished summaries of origin are that of Rodríguez (2009, 6–7) who cites sources of their distribution among the Tarahumara, Yaqui, Otomi, Ocoroni, Hichol, and Cora Indigenous peoples and deftly provides a thorough review of the differences of opinion as to whether the complex emerges from Arabic or Italian sources of European pagan or Moorish sources.

Rodríguez also indicates that the complex should not be confused with the dance of the *Moros y Cristianos*, which she regards as a separate innovation (2009, 7).

Warman (1972, 156–57) is emphatic that the two developed independently but that the matachine ritual played an important role in the colonization of the northern areas (SWNAR). Velasco Rivero (1987, 207) has the opposite position and states that the performance derives from the seven-hundred-year conflict between Muslims and Christians on the Iberian Peninsula. The ritualized climax of this conflict was the performance of the matachine, and the word itself was a synonym of *Matamoros* (Moors' killers), in which the Moors' chief is Pontius Pilate. The Christian chief is Santiago (a.k.a. Saint James, San Diego), who leads the battle ending with the conquest and conversion of the Moors by the conquering Christians.[4] "Santiago" in fact became part of the battle cry shouted by Spanish soldiers in their attacks on Native peoples throughout the American continents.

However, there is a very rich analysis by Treviño and Gilles (1994), who have traced similar performances back to the Aztec period to Moctezuma-centered complexes like those of the *toncontin* that was danced before the king of Spain as described by a seventeenth-century commentator and *netaltiliztli* by Francisco López de Gormara in 1620, both types part of broader calendric cycles (112–13). In addition, there is an acrobatic dance mentioned by early commentators who use the word *Matachines* for a dance as a favorite of Moctezuma II (Treviño and Gilles 1994, 117).

On the other hand, Rodríguez asserts unequivocally, citing Dozier (1970, 188), that "the syncretic complex was transmitted to Indians further north, including the Río Grande Pueblos via Mexican Indians who accompanied the Spanish colonizers." I concur but also suggest that the impetus to Chihuahua farther south was the Jesuit missionaries: even though Indigenous dancing in church buildings had by 1555 been prohibited in central Mexico by the First Mexican Provincial Council, "Conquest" dances and rituals were in fact held in churchyards in their schools and colleges, including the famous Jesuit Colegio de San Gregorio in Mexico, which was founded to educate the sons of the Indigenous nobility in the sixteenth century (Dutcher Mann 2010, 110–11).

It is notable that by the seventeenth century, Catholic choirboys known as *seises* danced "a dance of Montezuma in the Cathedral of Seville," according to Treviño and Gilles (1994, 109–10). This was intensively described by an important ecclesiastic of the period, Andres Perez de Ribas, who states:

> I shall tell here of a particular festival which is most attractive, as well as novel for persons coming from Spain or other countries, which is called the Dance of the Emperor Moctezuma. This dance, once performed for the pagan people, now is dedicated to the King of Kings, Christ our Lord: The most singular feature of this festival is the manner of dress and adornment of the dancers, this dress being in the style worn by the ancient Aztec Princes... On the heads of the dancers are placed pyramid shaped diadems covered with

gold and precious stones, in the manner of those worn by their Emperors . . . In the right hand they carry what is called by them an *ayacaztli*, which is a small brightly painted gourd filled with pebbles, which when shaken produces an agreeable sound. A small drum which in their language is called *Teponoztli* guides all the music and dance . . . To the instruments above described the Spaniards have added some of their own . . . Those participating in the central dance are usually fourteen in number, besides the dancer who impersonates the Emperor Moctezuma . . . The appearance of the Emperor is heralded by music and singing. The song translated runs somewhat like this: "Appear, Mexicans; dance Tocontin, for we now have with us the King of Glory." The three syllables of the word To-con-tin are sung to the rhythm of the beating of the drum. For this reason, the entire dance is sometimes given the name of Tocontin. The remaining dancers appear in two rows. . . . The movement of their dance is always slow and dignified, including not only the feet, but arms and hands, always waving in the same motion the long clusters of plumes and shaking their ceremonial gourds with rattles. The objects which they wave may be either of feathers, or of branches covered with aromatic flowers. At the end of this group dance each dancer takes his position to await the coming of the Emperor. The person representing the Emperor then advances with majestic dignity to take his place on the throne, while all others maintain the rhythm of the dance. (Treviño and Gilles, 1994, 109)

Consequently, the Mexican version of the complex was danced by Spanish choirboys who may have learned it from Tlaxcalan Indians, many of whom were taken to Spain in the sixteenth and seventeenth century.

As Jesuits moved their missions into the southern part of the SWNAR and especially into Chihuahua in the early seventeenth century, they were also accompanied probably by Tlaxcalan, Christianized Native matachines who introduced their versions into the Indigenous communities like the Tarahumara and Tepehuanes. Mexican Native peoples more than likely did the same into New Mexico, not as part of a Jesuit entry but perhaps with Oñate y Salazar and certainly with De Vargas, both of whom were accompanied by Tlaxcalans and probably other Mexica.

The matachines, regardless of origin and migration, stem from enactments of conflict, negotiation, separation, process, and eventual semiresolution—most of which are embedded into much broader cycles of ritual processes. They extend in different forms from Peru to New Mexico. Many of these are Indigenously formulated calendric cycles in form and function, venerations of earth mother figures like the Virgin Mary, and sometimes double presentations of two different groups such as the Turquoise and Pumpkin Moieties among the Jemez in New Mexico, as I have observed, representing an Indigenous presentation of selves in relation to the Spanish "other" and the Spanish/Mexican representation in relation to the Indigenous "other." Both of these can occur in the same place and space separated by a small time lapse, and both performed by Indigenous peoples except for the borrowed violin and guitar players from Spanish/Mexican groups.[5] Both are ensconced within a broader calendric cycle of emergence, in this case part of the Virgen de Guadalupe ritual, which itself is part of a series of punctuated ritual celebrations throughout the year. Even this temporal reference does not capture the much broader intent and functions of Indigenous ritual complexes that are less aligned to a European calendric time-space construct but rather to an Indigenous time-space of growth, renewal, and emergence that overlays the European ritual chronology. It must also be said at this juncture that the Indigenous version (as will be discussed), and especially that of the Rarámuri, is embedded within the larger crop production and harvest cycle during the year. The Bernalillo version of New Mexico is calendric but not tied to agricultural production. Most participants are urban dwellers. It is strongly associated with cultural and linguistic stability and maintenance in largely a politically dangerous situation because of demographic changes brought on by large-scale Midwestern Anglo populations.

Yet it is important to draw attention to the fact that the Matachine Complex is Indigenous/Spanish/Mexican and Spanish/Mexican/Indigenous. Both provide a sense of their origins, complexity, function, and insights into the limits of hegemonic impositions as part of the linguistic and cultural attempts promulgated by the Spanish colonial process. However, the Matachine Complex at its core is a recapitulation of what may have been a type of conquest and rejection narrative and one of subjugation and opposition, with a type of emergent but never completed denouement, as further discussion will illustrate. These elements changed over time so that once incorporated into the ritual cycle of their respective populations, the conquering aspect became less salient than did the "ownership" aspect. That is, as will be seen in both the northern and southern ends of the region, the Indigenous Tarahumara in the south took over the complex and created a process of initiation, control, and exhibition that became theirs and successfully created a platform of ritual self-determination in spite of all attempts to the contrary. Their "warriorship" of control is expressed with every performance. As will also be seen, in the north the Spanish/Mexican complex of Bernalillo serves the same function, but its self-determinacy lies in its continued performance against an encroaching Europeanized and Anglicized Catholic Church and the encroaching processes of urbanization and linguistic and cultural Anglo impositions. Their "warriorship" of control is expressed like their counterpart with every performance. More importantly, these examples provide us an insight into the wide possibilities distributed within the arcs of hegemony and discontents—from its origination five hundred years ago of a performance originally carried transatlantically to Spain to its return ensconced within the Catholic religious mythos designed for conversion but perhaps in the hands of Jesuits and of Tlaxcalans as well. Such amazing distributions

cannot follow binary models of neither imposition nor discontent but rather a processual, experimental, and emergence influenced and temporarily defined by context,
experience, and negotiations on the part of those performing and practiced to this
moment by Native peoples throughout the region and certainly from Veracruz to
Los Angeles.

Below I provide two ethnographic examples that represent different versions, but
both are part of the colonial and postcolonial periods of imposition and emergence
and each conditioned by their surrounding ecological, historical, and political contexts. Both emerge at about the same time frame—one in the south and the other in
the north of the greater region but from similar contested fields and arenas of action
of the seventeenth centuries to the present: the Tarahumara (Rarámuri) Indigenous/
Spanish/Mexican matachines of Chihuahua and the Hispano/Mexicano matachines
of Bernalillo, New Mexico, were selected from the literally hundreds of groups throughout South, Middle, and North America.

THE TARAHUMARA OF CHIHUAHUA
OF THE SOUTHERN REGION OF SWNAR

It is highly probable that the Tarahumara nation was a creation of the authorities of
Nueva Vizcaya in the beginning of the seventeenth century after an enormous rebellion by the Tepehuanes of that region between 1616 and 1619.[6] Missions, Spanish
settlements, and "reduced" Indigenous towns were completely eradicated by Native
peoples and became known as the "War of the Tepehuanes."[7] Bitterly fought, the
Spanish struck back with a vengeance on a war of extermination and exile, and created a categorical boundary to isolate and create a bounded group of persons termed
"Tepehuanes," who inhabited the northern Sierra Madre but were defined by the
Spanish military, civil, and missionary authorities as a regional entity "around which
they could put their arms," both figuratively and militarily, and created boundaries
between Indigenous peoples (Giudicelli 2006, 61). It was the very early Jesuit missionaries of the beginning of the seventeenth century who first differentiated between
Tepehuanes and Tarahumaras: the priest Joan Font states that ". . . with a war occurring
by the Tepeuanos and Tarahumara Indians on the one hand against others, and also
the interior nation of the Tarahumaros, almost on the section that they call the valley
of the Eagle, the Tepehuanos and Tarahumaros their friends to ask for help of the
Santa Barbara Tepeuanos that we call the valley of San Pablo, and those of Ocotlán
and Guansabi" (ibid., 63, my translation). Distinguishing between the two created the
impetus to imagine that these were different peoples and so that war visited upon the
"Tepehuanos" in fact spilled over on to the "Tarahumaras," who regarded themselves

as both (ibid., 68). The point of this exercise is that the matachines identified as Tarahumara are the outcome of a colonial definition based on its need to create a line of demarcation between Tepehuanes and Tarahumara based on the need to establish a "line of departure" against which total war was visited. Most of the major Indigenous rebellions of the seventeenth century were in the central corridor of the "Reign" (*Reino*) of Nueva Vizcaya, which was a huge geographical area that included Sonora and Sinaloa up to 1734 as well as the present states of Chihuahua, Durango Coahuila, part of Tamaulipas, Nuevo León, and New Mexico.

Revolts by different peoples were incessant from 1599 through 1650, including two by the Tarahumara in the 1640s and 1650s. The famous Pueblo Revolt of 1680 set off numerous revolts by seven other nations and a final Tarahumara rebellion from 1690 to 1698.[8] After the last revolt in 1761, however, the Tarahumara in fact served as auxiliary soldiers for the Spanish, and this can be noted from letters by the retiring Viceroy of Nueva Vizcaya Colonel Matheo Antonio Mendoza to the entering Viceroy Marques Cruillas, in which he recommended the recruitment of thirty auxiliary Rarámuri archers for each post as well as for their "value of auxiliaries as spies in broken terrain."[9] In this manner, the accommodating and resisting pattern of Rarámuri/ Spanish/Mexican relations came to be expressed in myriad ways.

It is then little wonder how the Matachine Complex became so importantly constituted in these aftermaths as part of their redefinition as Tarahumara; this stands in contrast to other Indigenous communities where it did not take root. Important is the fact that the matachine dance in the present probably does not recycle and recapitulate these ancient continuous conflicts but has adopted the complex as a means of creating crucial social networks across very difficult physical ecologies and distant communities. As Acuña Delgado's work shows, "In each zone of the Sierra Madre's mountains and canyons (these are huge like the Barranca de Cobre, which is longer and deeper than the Grand Canyon), each Rarámuri (self-reference by the Tarahumara) community have developed unique and different versions even though they share basically similar structures of operation but nevertheless may be identified by their localities" (ibid., 100–101; my translation).

The matachine is in reality not a retelling of the "Moros and Cristianos" narrative of the conquest of Catholic Spain over Islam and, by extension, the subjugation of the Rarámuri by the Crown, but rather the complex is crucially about whom they consider themselves to be and plays out their continuous resistance embedded within a complex ecological surrounding by their control and management of an imposed belief and performance system. This complexity is made even more salient when the Matachine Complex is regarded as conquest-oriented, calendric, and mythical, with multiple versions of localized observances and performances held within approximately thirty distinct Tarahumara communities (ibid., 99; my translation).

As will be described in the following section, as the agricultural cycle ends and they are about to collect their corn, they meet in some of the district towns from many isolated canyon and mountain hamlets to participate in one way or the other in their calendric celebrations and collective ceremonies. As importantly, the complex serves as a central functional mechanism that ties and crosscuts and "thickens" social relations necessary to maintain Rarámuri cultural identity in an ecological system in which they are dispersed in and to different parts of the mountainous regions of Chihuahua. Recruited from such outlying areas to central towns to practice and perform, Rarámuri identity is reinforced, roles and statuses defined, and declared authority established and reestablished. These practices represent the cultural "glue" necessary for Rarámuri "ownership" of the drama and are rearticulated and maintained, sticking as an overlay to the often fracturing canyons, declivities, arroyos, and towering mountainsides of the Sierra Madre.

The complex is embedded within the Winter Ritual Cycle and patron saints of each community, even though in other parts especially of Central Mexico in which the matachines were forbidden within the church, including among the Tarahumara, their performance took place in the evening in a church as part of honoring the patron saint of the day and without the presence of priests, who were forbidden by the 1555 edict mentioned.[10] With the Jesuits expelled in the late eighteenth century, for more than a hundred years the complex continued until the return of the Jesuits in the twentieth century. Its organizational structure remained basically the same except that in the twentieth century the Jesuit priest became a partner in the entire complex (Velasco Rivero 1987, 209). For the Rarámuri the most important ritual performances are in Holy Week, the Feast of the Patron Saint, the Feast of the Founding of the Church, La Purisima Concepcion (The Immaculate Conception), La Virgen De Guadalupe (the Virgin of Guadalupe), La Calendaria (Day of the Candles), Christmas, New Year, and Epiphany.[11]

Its cycle begins at dawn of Vespers on the 12th of October in the case of the Virgin of Pilar of the town of Norogachi, on the 12th of December of the Virgin of Guadalupe, on the 24th of December of Christmas Eve, on the 6th of January for the Feasts of the Kings, and on the 2nd of February on the Day of the Candles closing of the cycle. In between, the matachines may perform in other ritual contexts and festivals, or even a ceremonial curing, a wedding, or other important solemn occasion (Acuña Delgado 2008, 98–99; my translation). But all of these ritual expressions in fact are very much centered on the Marian cult and especially the Virgen de Guadalupe. I argue that they are deeply engrained within fertility beliefs that antedate the arrival of the colonial versions of mother earth. This is present despite the often commoditized association of the ritual and matachines as part of the more tourist-associated towns and communities in New Mexico and Chihuahua. It is important to note that commoditization does not erase the deep cultural and ideological commitment of its participants and its importance as a useful tool of discontent.

Directed by a *Fiestero* in Spanish and *Chapeyones* in Rarámuri and in other places also known as *Tenanches*, which is Nahautl, the Chapeyone is in charge of all economic and organizational activities and has been selected by Tarahumara authorities. While highly complex with a commensal ceremony tied into all other aspects of the ritual performance, the participants themselves are recruited weeks before by the Chapeyone, actually traveling to outlying rancherias and towns to recruit dancers, some of whom are already practiced matachines and have participated previously without pay. Tied together in the Rarámuri case is the local Catholic priest who is responsible for coordinating the mass, possible baptism, prayers, and blessings, and in fact is asked to dance with the group and sometimes does, according to Velasco Rivero (215). This will be a significant contrast to that of the matachines of New Mexico, as will be discussed. In addition, five older women carry images, icons, and crosses during any procession preceding or following the actual performance. They carry and wave religious banners as well as spread smoking incense in ceramic vases (ibid.).

The matachines in the Rarámuri in some areas are all men who themselves have passed through a kind of novitiate since they were children and at ten or twelve began to participate in small festivals. After they have been vetted and examined, they are then permitted to dance in larger festivals. However, along the great canyons women do participate with men, and there are also matachines made up entirely of women and girls who have passed through similar vetting processes (Acuña Delgado 2008, 99). There is no minimum or maximum number of participants, but most matachines consist of the young, mature, and novices (ibid.). Moreover, among the Rarámuri they may vary, with as few as two to more than one hundred arranged in double lines.

Their structure consists of the Chapeyon, the person in charge of the organization of the matachines, and between two and five dancers per group, depending on the number of participants. His/her task is to recruit and organize the dancers; prepare *tesguino*, which is an alcoholic drink made from fermented maize and taken at the end of the cycle of presentation; form the outside of the dance; direct the music, time lapses, and resting periods; and maintain high awareness among the dancers (ibid., 102).

In hierarchical importance, the Chapeyon is followed usually by two *monarcas*, who direct and lead the performance within the movements of the dance itself and who place themselves at the front and back of the double line of dancers. The *monarca* is distinguished by the kingly crown from which colored ribbons hang but is sometimes topped by four mirrors in the form of a cube inclined forward but not in the example in figure 7.

For the matachine, as well as for the *monarca*, the costuming is expensive, complicated, and highly syncretic of the origins of the complex itself, with boots,

FIGURE 7. Velasco Rivera: monarch with crown, rattle, and palm who directs the dance of the matachines, p. 320.

FIGURE 8. Velasco Rivera: matachine dancers executing their movements next to the violinists, p. 320.

huaraches, or knee socks, around which are wound bells or rattles, pants, or diaper-like loincloths, and a woolen coat. These are the Western accoutrements, which are then overwhelmed with a waistband, at the front and back of which are large squared cloths whose corners cover their front and rear parts of the loins. From the shoulders, two cloths in the form of capes reach to the ankles with various sashes with geometric designs surround the waist (ibid., 216). The head is topped with a headdress reminiscent of a tall fez, from which hang various highly complicated designed streamers. A brightly colored bandana covers the face from the nose down. The *monarca* carries a rattle in their right hand and a ribboned specter in their left, as seen in figure 8 (ibid.).

According to Acuña Delgado (2008, 99), the double lines of dancers are obligated in some towns to dance at particular places, such as in the town of Norogachi, and do so in six symbolically important sites: the *comerachi* (commensal site where the matachines gather initially to eat and end the performance as part of an exchange system), the atrium of the church, the cemetery, the priest's home, the exterior patio of interned student housing, and a small hill recognized as a community ritual gathering place. Each group dances six compositions at each one of these sites as well as in the interior of the church (ibid.).

The entire performance is accompanied by musicians of varying numbers but minimally a violinist and guitarist, as Pfefferkorn described in the opening paragraph of the chapter. In addition, there are auxiliary participants such as the governor of the town, who offers opening remarks having to do with expected comportment of all, as well as his officers and assistants, who provide the logistical and organizational support for the entire complex (ibid.).

THE PERFORMANCE OUTLINE AND PROCESS

Although there are variations in the actual movement and performance between towns and even subregions of the Tarahumara region, the basic schema is as follows from Acuña Delgado (2008, 104–5). The dance itself is done with a skipping two-step motion, with the body held erect, head upright, as well as a number of bowing actions and counter bows when matachines and *monarcas* meet during the weaving movements to the movement of their rattles.

The basic formation of movements 1–4 is illustrated in figure 9, as described by Acuña Delgado in Spanish and translated by me.

While it can be suggested that such a performance was induced by Jesuits, it is more likely that the Raráumuri adopted the performance as an incorporated ritual expression within the calendric cycles of their own version of performative meanings. It must be recalled that the Rarámuri did not by any means roll over either by violence or persuasion. Rather, in the process of interaction between them and Jesuits, civil authorities, and military authorities, they created a blended complex of multidimensional meanings and behaviors that they came to control. That the performance is a display of warriorship is highly likely. But it is not in the action itself; rather in the control of all processes themselves are acts of warriorship in the sense of a continued resistance to hegemony. They "own" and perform the Matachine Complex with or without priests and did so especially after the Jesuits were expelled, and for one hundred years they much controlled all aspects of the complex.

The entire complex, although rooted in the Marian and Catholic calendars, reveals the communal values of the Rarámuri themselves from the commensal activities, the all-night vigils, the recruitment and participation of matachines from surrounding communities, and their willingness to perform in a variety of settings and not just those of the winter calendric cycle. Such recruitment and performances crosscut ecological barriers and distances and create a subregional network of participants and believers who, in the activities comprising the complex, reinforce Rarámuri social identity. The "conquest" in this sense is in step for their social and cultural identity

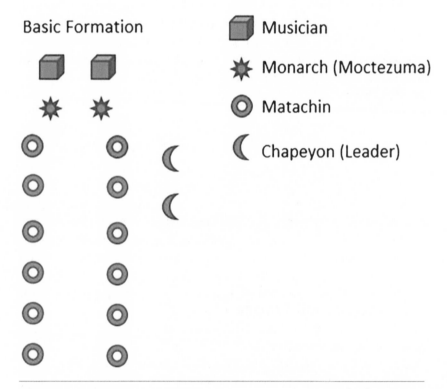

FIGURE 9. Rarámuri Matachine Choreography: Acuña Delgado with all reformatting by David Uzcanga (2015). Movement 1: The monarchs move between the matachines and displace themselves coming and going inside of the lines with turns of 360 degrees. Movement 2: The monarchs cross at 360 degrees, followed by a cross of the lines of matachines. Movement 3: Displacement of the monarchs forming a helix between the two lines of matachines, circling one and the other, while these march in place and move around 360 degrees with the monarch. Movement 4: Displacement like a wave of a complete line of matachines following the monarch in his trajectory, until they all finish in the same position. First one line and then the other. Variants: 1. Move around the space of the two lines. 2. Repeat it all. 3. Other alternative movements.

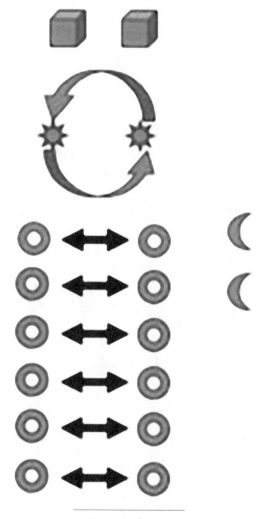

FIGURE 9. *(continued)*

and a defended cultural place and "peace" of selves—a denouement of sorts carried out in such a manner in which the central cores of community reciprocity win over the hegemony of ideology, language, and the physical presence of non-Rarámuri.

In fact, the entire cycle, as Acuña Delgado (2008, 107–8) points out, also coincides with the end of one agricultural cycle and the beginning of a new one because it is in October that the corn is harvested and between January and February that the land is tilled for the new planting. But as importantly, the complex is also marked in the day prior to its beginning, with animals sacrificed for its commensal activities and

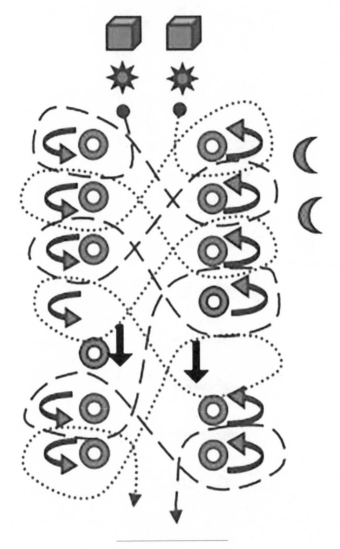

FIGURE 9. *(continued)*

their spirits offered to *Onaoruame* (God the Father) or *Eyerúame* ("the one that is Mother"). In this manner both the masculine and feminine are exemplified symbolically. This duality emerges from its embedded position within the calendric cycle and is manifested in multiple forms but ensconced within the great valleys, mountains, and canyons of the land of the Rarámuri. The great emphasis on the Virgen de Guadalupe complex throughout Mexico is reiterated here. As in other Indigenous communities, her veneration is coupled to a type of mother earth symbolic of fertility and growth not unlike the ancient Tonanaztín upon whose hill Guadalupe was asserted to have appeared.

But more importantly for our purposes in thinking about hegemonic processes and their discontents for the Rarámuri, "dance" is a type of language that sets forth their signifiers ensconced within a former European conquest performance. In fact, for the Rarámuri, Lumholtz (1894, 440–41) states that "to dance" means "those who are working," and its Rarámuri cognate is associated with the growth of plants and the growth of people, according to Acuña Delgado (2008, 97). But Luis Plascencia

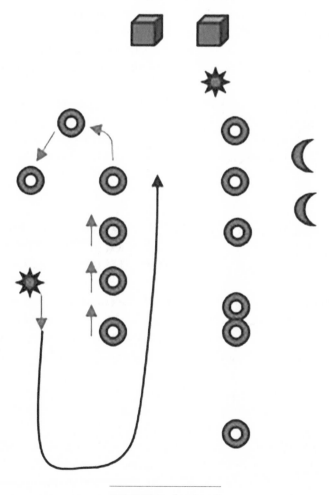

FIGURE 9. *(continued)*

(personal communication) reminds me that Lumholtz states this a bit differently: "Dancing is an essential party of the Tarahumari's worship; it is not for his pleasure; it is in order to secure rain and good crops and to ward off evil that he dances. The Tarahumari words for dancing are Nau-chi-li Ol-a-wa, meaning literally 'They are going to work.' An old man may say to a young buck who is idle at the feast: 'Why do you not go to work?' meaning 'why does [he] not dance'" (1894, 440–41).[12]

In this context, dance is a communication to the Catholic God, to the Rarámuri God, and probably to the Rarámuri Catholic Virgin and to the Rarámuri Earth Figure. But it also communicates in the language of performance a type of temporary resolution of five hundred years of attempted hegemony and the capacity of the Rarámuri to innovatively invent themselves and the "others" according to their premises about their connection to each other, to the earth around them, and to the non-Rarámuri. As well, and importantly for their purposes, these are rituals of connectivity to the past and the present, embedded physically and ritually in their canyons and mountains, situated in what became and is the Mexican state of Chihuahua, and still practiced to the present.

Yet, these performances and their underlying ritual and ideological necessities are not only taxed by historical and contemporary land encroachments, as has been noted, but Rarámuri youth have been recently detained in Texas, especially as mules serving the Sinaloa Cartel, carrying fifteen kilos of marijuana in exchange for a pair of tennis shoes.[13]

LOS MATACHINES DE BERNALILLO OF THE NORTHERN REGION OF SWNAR: CULTURE AND LANGUAGE AND THEIR DISCONTENTS

North along the Camino Real (the Royal Road) that extended in the colonial period from Mexico City through Chihuahua and then to Santa Fe is Bernalillo, located seventeen miles north of Albuquerque and forty-eight miles south of Santa Fe, through which the procession of the matachines parades (figure 10). Bernalillo is an old colonial settlement and now a small city surrounded by encroaching urbanization and changing ethnic demographics, and suffering the impact of land misuse, penetration of unwanted social issues, attempted institutional cultural and linguistic erasure, and modest incomes, like many equivalent small Hispano/Mexicano townships[14] in New Mexico.[15] Although in the present New Mexico has dual language programs for many of its students, their actual performance for the expansion of English/Spanish expansion is totally dependent on the expertise of the teacher and the pedagogical soundness of the program and school site. Except for this generation enjoying a modestly

FIGURE 10. Camino del Pueblo: Bernalillo. Photo by the author.

successful program, all previous generations were for the most part educationally subjected to language and cultural erasure by public schools, and even in the present, the emphasis is on English language acquisition rather than the development of functional bilingualism. Bernalillo was and is no exception.[16]

In the past, as discussed below, corporal and physical punishments were used as major means of language instruction throughout the northern end of the region, and New Mexico was no exception. Therefore, it is remarkable that in fact most of the rituals, prayers, and conduct of the complex are in Spanish and not English. I would suggest that in fact the Matachine Complex is a highly pertinent method for the retention of Spanish and its instruction to following generations. I would also consider the entire complex a cultural and linguistic method of resisting institutional and educational erasure of the three-hundred-year-plus presence of Hispano/Mexicanos and, as importantly, of a community-based identity and reference in light of massive economic, social, cultural, communication, and media representations very much opposite to the underlying values of community. Indigenous recognitions and historical identities exemplify the highly plural origins and syncretic cultural dynamics of Hispano/Mexicano/Indigenous interactions.

Simultaneously it also consists of populations of Hispano/Mexicanos for whom faith, religiosity, reciprocity, communal assistance, attention to lineal relations with the past, political wisdom, and unfettered reliance on their senses of identities balance to some degree the impacts suffered. Some work for the Indigenous casinos nearby, many work in the nearby city of Albuquerque, and many others work in the city itself, in construction, schools, farming, tourism-oriented service jobs, and as professionals in medicine, education, legal institutions, business and banking, and myriad other occupations and professions common to a town of 8,338 persons, of whom 72 percent are of Hispano/Mexicano origin.[17] Some are both professionals and in other occupations simultaneously. They work their acequias, or irrigated agricultural fields, some of which date to the seventeenth century, and still grow corn, beans, squash, and chiles, and perhaps raise a few farm animals for mostly home and ritual consumption.

For some, intermarriage with Indigenous peoples nearby has been a common practice for hundreds of years. They and their ancestors have lived in the area, including some who trace their lineages back to the time of De Vargas, who reconquered New Mexico in 1694 after the expulsion of the colonial empire in 1680. Some are the "new" Mexicanos from the nineteenth-, twentieth-, and twenty-first-century migrations north from the southern parts of the region, such as Chihuahua and many other parts south, who comprise about 18 percent of the Hispano/Mexicano populations in the present.[18] Some had married early French trappers, whose names appear as street names at present in the town, and many married among themselves and from other towns, hamlets, and small cities around the state of New Mexico and elsewhere. Some have married Anglo-Americans and their children speak only or mostly English, as do their spouses. However, if they grew up in the vicinity and went to their local schools together, it is more than likely that they will have a Spanish-language tilt to the English even though their own parents were from Missouri.

Just a few miles east of Bernalillo stands the even more ancient Pueblo town of Sandia, and adjoining Bernalillo lies Santa Ana Pueblo (made up of three Keresan-speaking villages: Rebahene, Ranchitos, and Chicale), and in this line of sight west-to-east and north-to-south from Bernalillo lie ancient histories of all the inhabitants. Some have carried on a tradition of reciprocity and exchange with Indigenous peoples of mutual help, assistance, and ritual respect. Theirs is a history of ancient enmities, of ancient friendships, of ancient conflicts, of ancient genetic exchanges, and of ancient cooperation, including the Matachine Complex, with their accompanying meanings, rejections, and accommodations.

Unlike the Tarahumara complex, the Bernalillo version was probably established during the De Vargas period. It is among the oldest Spanish colonial–influenced traditions whose origins can be located in Bernalillo. Its performance has been carried on for more than three hundred years consistently and, according to Rodríguez (2009), local peoples trace the origins of the dance to De Vargas's reconquest in 1694 as an expression of gratitude and as "a survival myth [that] this community has evolved about itself since the late seventeenth century" (116–17). According to knowledgeable local informants, the complex emerges from two Hispano populations of that period:

FIGURE 11. Matachine mural complex at San Lorenzo Church parking lot. Photo by the author, September 10, 2014.

first, those who were hidden by tribal peoples during the Pueblo Revolt and survived, and the matachines perform that "miracle," and second, those who returned to be reintegrated as a community into the newly established town of Bernalillo, where De Vargas died.[19] Yet there are other levels of meaning that we will take up at the end of this discussion that have not generally been considered. And from the historical "miracle" perspective, this thematic thread is among the central social and cultural dynamics that not only were responsible for its origination but also, from the perspective adopted here, allowed this important segment of the population to continue to emerge, expressing not only their Catholicity but as importantly their uncommon commitment to community involvement, autonomous decision-making, strong political influences, and a crucial cultural and social phenomenon closely associated with resistance to institutional, cultural, and linguistic hegemony of the nineteenth-century colonization of the northern region by the United States and other agents.[20]

Theirs is an ancient recurring ritual space, like those of the Rarámuri, very much influenced by the physical ecology they occupy. A notable aspect of the present is that the Rarámuri occupy disparate physical spaces within huge canyon walls, while the Hispano/Mexicanos occupy disparate cultural and social spaces with huge institutional walls, which they crosscut with their Matachine Complex. Yet each has visited the other in Chihuahua and New Mexico for special celebrations either organized by their respective states or arranged informally by the major religious and civic figures who are associated with the complex itself.

Its importance in Bernalillo is expressed by the murals appearing in various spaces in the town, as shown in figure 11 of the matachine mural at the north wall of a school gym directly connected to the San Lorenzo Church parking lot. The mural is an emblematic and representational narrative of the complex itself. Although the wall on which the mural is painted is on school district property, it formerly belonged to the church but was not physically connected to it. It is symbolic of the relationship between the church and the complex itself, and as the Spanish saying goes, "Juntos pero no revueltos" (Together but not mixed); one *monarca* mentioned this is significantly different from the Chihuahua model.

This complex is legitimized not by the church itself but rather by a smaller sanctuary built earlier in the nineteenth century, in which various *monarcas* served as mayordomos, situated behind the church itself and shown behind the sign represented in figure 12.

Notable is that the sign itself has the prominently displayed representation not of a cross but of a palm in the shape of a trident, which represents the Holy Trinity and is one of the instruments carried by the matachines and *monarcas* themselves, as seen in figure 13 and in figure 8 in the mural with multiple prongs.

It should be noted that this independence and association with the church is an expression of a constructed religious and cultural space between themselves and the

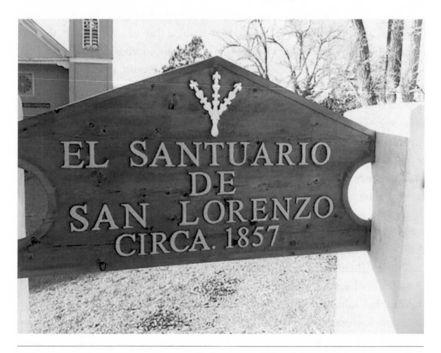

FIGURE 12. Sanctuary sign fronting the Sanctuary of San Lorenzo. Photo by the author, Fiesta de San Lorenzo, August 9, 2014.

FIGURE 13. *Monarca* and *danzantes* with palm and Malinche, Fiesta de San Lorenzo, August 9, 2014. Photo by the author.

control of the church as an institution. Like the Indigenous tradition, theirs is a type of declaration generated through changes of their historical contexts. This important ritual is in fact a performance whose central significance has changed over the three hundred years, but it is still very much associated with its origins and its relationship to Indigenous populations. It is also linked to its origins from Spanish/Mexican sources, and more recently to the hegemonic processes of language and culture from American sources after the imposition of the region.

THE RITUAL AND CALENDRIC CYCLE: CHRONOLOGY, DENSITY, ORGANIZATION, AND PERFORMANCE

The central cultural glue of the Matachine Complex is the organizational density that is maintained through a network and group of persons willing to engage, support, and carry out the performances, rituals, and obligations entailed in the complex itself. By organizational density I mean that first, the vertically arranged age cohorts of those participating range in ages between eighteen and sixty or more, and represent at any one time at least three generations of participants: from novices to *monarcas* and mayordomos, many of whom are descendants of matachines, mayordomas/os, and violinists, guitarists, or *rezadores*, who will be described shortly. Many will have started their preparatory processes earlier by attending mandatory catechism classes in the Sanctuary of San Lorenzo before the age of eighteen, and many begin as early as fourteen, according to Moreno (2008).

From this cohort, depending on the number of persons needed to replace those leaving, a selection is made usually through an interactive discussion between the mothers and fathers of the children with *monarcas*, other matachines, and the mayordomos and mayordomas of the complex. Participation from then on is voluntary but very much associated with another part of that density: the combination of the promise made to participate, plus the kinship and cohort relations comprising the total network of participants and associates, coupled with the ability of the persons to fulfill their promise at the year in question. While the promise to participate is paramount, there is also no doubt that kinship, friendship, and cohort relationships create the social basis for participation. These relationships emerge from having been born in Bernalillo, having a previous ancestor born there, or marrying into these networks, but are also cemented especially through adolescence by attending the same schools, recreational activities, and religious ceremonies, and the great attention paid to children's calendric celebrations as well as Catholic rituals of baptism, confirmation, and quinceñeras.

Occasionally a non-Hispana/Mexicana Malinche will serve in that role but primarily due to her mother's commitment to the complex itself and the *confianza* (mutual trust) that she has established among the mayordomas/os or other major figures like the *rezador* (prayer leader). As such, however, the organizational complex does have corporate functions that are hierarchically age-organized and extend beyond the life of its membership and are reminiscent of the Mexican tradition of the *cofradias* or *cargos*, which became widespread in central Mexico during the seventeenth century (Treviño and Gillis 1994, 121; Rodríguez 2009, 114). These were and are organized religious groups "responsible for organizing the observances of saint's days and other Catholic holy days" and are similar to the dance cofradias of southern Mexico and most similar to the "*danzas chichimecas*," according to Treviño and Gilles (121). The importance of the spiritual guide—the *rezador* (prayer leader)—has not been given its due for its cultural and ritual roles in any of the extant academic literature even mentioning its existence. From my point of view, it functions as the cultural glue of the entire complex. Although Moreno (2008) in his unpublished thesis recognizes the crucial roles of the *rezadores* during the fiestas and throughout the entire year, and does so by outlining their participation in the monthly rosaries that are the punctuating observances during the year as well as the nine-day novena prior to August 10 of every year (which is the actual beginning of the three-day performance), the broader rabbinical functions do not seem to be as well recognized.[21] From observation, the most senior *rezador* of three available, one of whom is a well-known woman, has a rabbinical function that encompasses the entire community and transcends the matachines themselves.

The *rezador* is the person who not only serves as the spiritual guide of the matachines but is called upon to recite the ancient prayers in wakes, special occasions, and informal blessings of land, events, and persons. He is the keeper of the holy script and knowledge that guides and contains the specific prayers, ablutions, blessings, and spiritual directions to the entire complex. He has been known as well to provide direction and the prayers to the *Hermanos Penitentes* and their *Moras* where these have been forgotten or displaced. The Mora is the organizational nomenclature as well as the physical site for the Penitente Brotherhood, where it holds its rituals and ceremonies. Like the matachines, the Penitentes, although a male confraternity, are of Spanish/ Mexican origin but from later in the late eighteenth century and probably stem from the Third Order of Saint Francis (Nieto-Phillips 2004, 45). They are completely outside of the purview of either the Catholic Church or nonmembers. One suspects that especially in the more northern areas of New Mexico, members of the Penitentes are also matachines and vice versa.

However, the *rezador*, because of his unique personality and developed capacities, also may very well also engage in community politics, and serve in elected state, county, city, and town offices or other important educational and institutional positions. But very important in many ways, he is the keeper of the totemic lineage knowledge of who is related to whom, who was married to whom, who owned the precious parcels of the acequias, who was responsible for the downfall of others, and, like in all communities, the knowledgeable keeper of those things that are not for public review and have to do with the tragedies of living and dying and failing and patrimony. The *rezador* is for many purposes of knowledge and spirituality much more crucial than the institutionalized roles of Church-sanctioned figures with which the Festival of San Lorenzo is held.

The matachines of Bernalillo center on two iconic figures: first, San Lorenzo, the patron saint of the poor, and second, the Virgin of Guadalupe or variations of her. There is a coupling and identification of San Lorenzo as a protector of the Hispano/ Mexicano families who survived the Pueblo Revolt in 1680, together with some indications that the nearby Sandia Pueblo harbored some of those fleeing their surrounding ranchos and villages. It can be concluded that these populations made a promise when they returned after the Pueblo Revolt that if their patron saint would keep them safe, they would dance in his honor each year on his feast day in the town of Bernalillo, founded by the reconqueror, Diego de Vargas in 1693. From this promise arose the rationale for persons becoming matachines by promising to faithfully participate in exchange for the fulfillment of a wish, desire, or need. Some others, although making a wish as part of the ritual process, also do participate primarily as part of a lineal duty passed down from previous generations. Not surprisingly, San Lorenzo is prominently displayed on webpages, tee shirts, prayer books, advertisements, and other media to announce the annual Festival of San Lorenzo held on August 10–12.

The Virgen de Guadalupe, and many of her Marian variations, is an equivalent or as importantly venerated a figure as that of San Lorenzo, even though Moreno would disagree (2008, 66). The Marian complex is of course a long-held belief system that stems from Spain, but the Guadalupe figure herself is much more associated with Mexico and certainly the SWNAR. The matachines themselves are considered to be her soldiers very much like the Tarahumaras previously discussed. She is exhibited in myriad ways throughout the year and in variations and is the centerpiece on the back of the *mantas* and even of the *toro* and *abuelo* (see figure 14).

She is especially present in the mayordomo's house, where, in different dresses, she is represented by pictures, paintings, and sculptures, and literally covers an entire wall adjacent to the large altar holding a number of religious icons, not the least of which is the Santo of San Lorenzo, also represented in different modalities from sculptures to paintings. But the central figure is his person represented by a prominent statue as shown in figure 15.

FIGURE 14. Malinche, *monarca*, *abuelo*, and *toro*: the latter two with visages of the Virgin Mary. Fiesta de San Lorenzo, August 9, 2014. Photo by the author.

FIGURE 15. San Lorenzo on the altar. Photo by the author, August 9, 2014.

ORGANIZATIONAL STRUCTURE

The Matachine Complex's organizational schema, like the Tarahumara example, has two main lines: the ritually responsible mayordomo, who is in charge of maintaining, manning, holding, and naming the monarchs, and directing all rituals associated with the complex that are held in their home, and the matachine ensemble. The mayordomos are the caretakers of the saint and are selected after years of preparation. An elaborate process of vetting and community agreement is described by Moreno (2008, 66) in the following:

> You have to ask the last person in the line actually. What we did the year that we decided, we went to the Mayordomo at the time who was Gloria García. She had the santo that year and we asked her if she knew who was at the end of the line and she told us who she thought it was. So it was just sort of like going from family to family you know 'so we heard that you asked for San Lorenzo. Did you promise him to someone?' and they said 'yes we did' and it just kept going until we got to the end of the line and what you do is . . . and at the time it was Mr. and Mrs. Santillanes, and you have to go to the house, you can't call on the phone or you can't see them on the street and ask them. You have to go to their house and ask for him and we set up a time, we went over there, my brother and I, and we asked them if we could receive San Lorenzo from them, so they agreed and offered him in return to us.

The selection process then is one based on following the chain of previous recipients and each recipient passing on their promise of whom the next selectees were to be so that by a process of elimination the couple in the example were able to place themselves in line to be eligible for housing the saint in their home. It is also a crucial means by which those seeking the honor are gauged by the previous mayordomos verbally, as has been pointed out in the example, so that the means of communication are of utmost importance in order to evaluate the seriousness of those in contention. As a most pertinent cultural practice, such promises and connections create a type of lineage scaffolding that is followed between and in succeeding generations. Since this process may take up to six years for any one couple (usually married or in the previous case brother and sister) it is during this period that they begin to save for the heavy cost of maintaining the altar, preparing food for the monthly rosaries and the novena, supporting visitors at any time of night or day during the twelve-month tenure of the offices, bearing all costs of the procession to and from the actual dance itself, and supporting the costs of food for the matachines themselves, which may cost up to $10,000. However, community persons have raffles and relatives all pitch in to help the family defray the cost. Some save for years in anticipation of becoming mayordomos. In this manner, this responsibility is very much like the *cargo* responsibilities of Middle American peoples and is very much aligned with the functions of the *Chapeyanes* among the Rarámuri.

The matachine ensemble is composed of two *monarcas*, two *toros*, two *abuelos*, six Malinches, and twenty-four *danzantes* (dancers), including eight *capitanes* (Moreno 2008, 51). The dance organization itself is along similar but not the same lines as the Rarámuri. It is divided along two axes: *corrida* or procession, which is performed along Camino del Pueblo Avenue shown in figure 10 and opens the festival itself and then the actual dance performance over the next three days. Accompanying the procession will be the violinist and guitarists who may have been or are matachines but are not dancing; but importantly, like many of the matachines, they are the grandchildren of former matachines and musicians. They will be responsible for the playing of the nine major songs that make up the actual scores used in the dance itself.

In this manner, through lineage relations, the corporate structure will be maintained and the age-stratified composition will also contribute to the matachines as a corporate institution. This age-heterogeneous principle is shown by children playing drums, who also participate by signaling the beginning of the procession itself. It is significant that the drums themselves are of Pueblo origin, as figure 16 illustrates. A number of young people wait in the wings to fill in when others tire or to participate in the procession, as figure 17 illustrates.

But it is the *abuelos* who are both participants and dance masters, and are responsible for the flow and rhythm of the dance itself and roam at will. They are not only disciplinarians of the dancers but also of El Toro, who symbolically represents evil, and use their whips to keep the *toro* especially away from the figure of the Malinche, who is a child dressed in white and represents both purity and the daughter of Montezuma. They are, however, also the instructors of the dancers and the overseers of the actual organization of the dance groups themselves. For the most part these are vigorous men in their early fifties or forties who must not only invest their time and energy in practice sessions with the dancers but also provide some religious instruction, especially to the Malinche.[22] As seen in figures 18 and 19, the white-hatted, whip-carrying *abuelo* keeps the *toro(s)* away and also acts as an escort for the *monarca* and Malinche during the dance, as well as maintaining the flow of the dance itself.

The eight *capitanes* are the fulcrums around which a complex of steps and turns are performed. They take their positions at each end of the file of dancers, four on the inside of the file closest to the *monarca*, who are referred to as *capitanes de adelante* (captains of the front), and four on the outside of the file, who are termed *capitanes de atras* (captains of the rear). These are persons who call out the next dance movement and like the *abuelos* also maintain line discipline. They are in line to replace the *monarca* when no longer able to be active (Moreno 2008, 62–63). The rest of the dancers will then move up as their experience and abilities improve and will become eligible to become *capitanes* over a period of years.

FIGURE 16. Tambores. Photo by the author, August 9, 2015.

FIGURE 17. Young women waiting their turns in the procession. Photo by the author, August 11, 2015.

FIGURE 18. The whipping of El Toro by the *abuelo*. Photo by the author, Fiesta de San Lorenzo, August 9, 2014.

FIGURE 19. Escorting the Malinche, Fiesta de San Lorenzo, August 9, 2014. Photo by the author.

The performances begin simply with deeply engrained rituals before community audiences each day, with persons numbering at times over a hundred taking up spaces of observation wherever available. Since much of the rituals take place at the mayordomos' residence, the street is the stage and chairs and tents are arranged for matachine-associated support of relatives, husbands, wives, and generations of former dancers as well. Persons, mostly Hispana/os from around the state, also attend and, from observation, many were dancers themselves, but most persons attending know or are related to the performers in the present or from the past. Attendance at the social drama rekindles relationships and associations and many conversations concern the major events in the life cycles of participants as well as retellings of school mischiefs and sports events. Many men in the audience wear veterans' caps, noting their service in Vietnam, while grandmothers and older aunts are surrounded by relatives.

Although rosaries and *novenas* are held each week, the initiating *novena* for the matachine performance begins on August 8 and is attended by most dancers and family. This sometimes coincides with practice dances that began a month earlier. Each *novena* is led by the *rezador* combining his narrative of San Lorenzo's miracles with the Marian-oriented rosary. During this period, retired dancers are presented and honored by the new dancers and those present so that during this period a generational connection is specifically made between those new and their lineal ancestors. A posted calendar of the event between August 9 and 11, 2015, is in appendix B. The following detailed schedule from Moreno provides a rich scheme (2008, 88, 90, 111) of his study in 2004, which began the three-day performance on August 9, 2004:

> August 9, 2004- "El día de las vísperas"
>> 2:00 p.m. *Danzantes* assemble at mayordomos Home (Montoya/Domínguez home)
>> 2:30 p.m. La Novena
>> 3:00 p.m. *La Danza* (matachines dance)
>> 3:50 p.m. *La Promesa* dance (Everyone welcome to participate)
>> 4:00 p.m. Supper (Hosted by the mayordomos)
>> 5:45 p.m. *Danzantes* assemble at Montoya/Dominguez home
>> 6:15 p.m. Procession to *Santuario* de San Lorenzo
>> 7:00 p.m. Visperas at *Santuario* de San Lorenzo

For the next three days, the complex continues with added events. On the second day a mass is performed in the morning, later a supper, then a *velorio* (all-night observance), and *Las Mañanitas* (a type of wake-up song) at midnight. The third day brings closure with variations, including a return to the mayordomo's home and the return of

FIGURE 20. Final dance of the community. Photo by the author, August 9, 2014.

the dancers back to their families with a late dance at 6 p.m., with a 9 p.m. ballroom invitation.

The dancers follow specific dance sequences in two parts, with each dance having its own musical score and each day varying somewhat slightly. The dance sequence itself consists of a series of intricate dance steps with constant movement and complex crossings, meetings, bowing, and resolutions, with the final sequence made up not only of the dancers but all who wish to join in its conclusion and who have made *promesas*, as shown in figure 20, with the entire sequences available in Moreno's matachine web page (90–104), but whose bare schema is presented below.[23]

The Dance

First part

1. La Marcha
2. La Cruzada / Trote del Coyote y El Gusano
3. La Cambiada
4. Cuadrilla de La Malinche
5. [La Vuelta]

6. La Toreada del Toro

Break

Second part

7. La Cruzada

8. La Tendida / La Cortesía

9. La Patadita / Bailada de las Promesas

THE RITUAL PROCESS

The most important rituals are in the first day, with the assembly of the dancers at the mayordomo's home and prayers that are said prior to their performance led by the *rezador*. Then the actual performance begins, ending in the late afternoon, followed by a procession to the Sanctuary of San Lorenzo. Most roles of the dance have multiple replacements, especially the Malinches, who are mostly young girls of seven to ten years old. Each dancer, as will be seen, is considered a "slave" of San Lorenzo, the meanings of which will be discussed, and of probably long-historical groundings and deep cultural processes. In this manner, the ritual community has announced its presence not in the church but in the mayordomo's home, representing the entire community assembled of the present and the past. At least one hundred persons assembled during the periods of fieldwork and these did so to participate and observe. Conversations are often carried on with commentary on how long they have been attending and how their grandparents, now deceased, also danced or participated in some way. Most know the others, and when they do not, a quick calculus is rendered to figure out the connections between families.

On the second day of the festival, the saint is carried into the church after the dancers have assembled at Our Lady of Sorrows Church. Many of the performers are seated lengthwise along the central foyer of the church so that each pew has one seated on the outside. Because of the large number of dancers who perform, as well as those who fill in when they tire, they either stand or find seating in the rear of the church. For the most part these are teenagers of both sexes and number thirty-three from observation. After mass they all file out and assemble, putting on their attire and conducting a procession from the church to the mayordomo's home about a mile and a half away, which is punctuated by the dancers performing and the matachines with the saint being carried by the mayordomos and flanked by *capitanes* to protect dancers and the saint itself. Two carry shotguns and fire them periodically, according to one *capitan* to ward off any attempts by someone trying to steal them, but more than likely as a means of warding off evil, according to the *rezador*. Regardless, this procession is community space and no one is allowed to pass the procession on either side, ensuring the ritual boundaries of those engaged. After arrival to the mayordomo's home, the matachines rest and have lunch with the youngest, first eating a homemade meal of tamales, beans, rice, and tortillas and a short time later once again resuming their performances for the next hour and a half, after which they have a processional around the neighborhood. This sequence ends by late afternoon; then participants have dinner together in the evening. Some stay and hold a vigil of the saint for part or all of the night. They in fact are "on stage" and the ritual space is maintained; their own liminal identities do not break what may be called the third space of ritual.

On the third day, the dancers assemble in the morning once again at the mayordomo's home, prayers are said by the *rezador*, and the performance begins. After three dances have been held, then the last, the *promesa*, the promise, is enacted. This involves those wishing to make a promise joining the dancers in the performance. After this, a ritual is conducted in which the saint is bidden farewell by the mayordomos, who are blessed by the *rezador*, and a procession is held carrying the saint to the new mayordomo's home for final rituals. The first turns over the saint to them, and then this is followed by all of the dancers taking turns dancing around a table with food to commemorate the completion of their performance and thus fulfilling their *promesa*. In the final ritual, the *rezador* sings farewell to each matachine, Malinche, monarch, captain, *tamborero*, *guardia*, and *abuelo* and calls each one by their given name. It is at this point that each person returns to their families, and each matachine donates a small amount of money (one dollar is the norm), which, as will be seen, may have more meaning as well. Thus each "slave" has been returned and the ritual space is given up with celebrations of food and beer and each becomes herself and himself again. Thus this entire ritual process follows the well-known steps of separation, liminality, and aggregation that Arnold van Gennep (1909) has called the "rites de passage"—rites that accompany every change of place, state, social position and age. And I would certainly include the movement from civil to ritual state. Yet in the Matachine Complex, each day participants reinforce and act these out, not in a linear manner but rather at times coterminous and parallel, yet culminating in the movement of their social identities to their final return among families and friends, accompanied by a small donation, as mentioned.

MEANINGS

For most observers it is clear that the entire complex is an intricate complex requiring enormous commitment, is of long duration, and must be practiced diligently beginning on the first Sunday in July and repeated on at least two to five more weeks, each following a prescribed ritual process according to Moreno (87–88). But what is crucial is that each participant, according to informants, became *un esclavo*—the slave of San Lorenzo—exactly at the initiation of liminal time when the *rezador* prays and intones their entry so that each person undergoes a social transformation, from daughter, son, father, mother, uncle, aunt, worker, teacher, student, or any other role imagined to become a "liminal" entity engaged in ritual space, time, and place, and belongs to San Lorenzo through their *promesas*. Her or his identity becomes part of the *communitas* (the suspended public and personal social identity) of the ritual identities of the matachines and moves into a liminal state between ingress and egress, and for these three days each was engaged in constant rituals and performances that removed each from kin and kith. They became "slaves" in more than one way in that they were totally committed to fulfill their *promesa* but were removed from their families by being taken into this ritual space. In fact, at almost every turn during their performances or during their downtime, their separation was monitored continuously by the *abuelos*, who directed them through and from all physical spaces so the dancers and nonperformers interact sparingly. Ritual space is well guarded by assigned guards at the end of the dancers and dressed in white with small whips held in hand, and they made sure such ritual spaces were adhered to even on the public street in the public processions to and from the church where mass was held in the saint's honor. No one was allowed to pass the ritual space but had to either remain in place if an onlooker or join the procession behind the saint.

The complex, as has been noted, also has deep historical cultural meanings that harken back to the four hundred colonists who escaped to El Paso during the 1680 Pueblo Revolt, with some families remaining but hidden by kin or kith, as among the Indigenous Tiwa-speaking Sandia Pueblo, according to some sources.[24] Forty or so of the separated families returned from El Paso after de Vargas's reconquest fourteen years later, as well as those who were hidden and another sixty-seven Españoles Mexicano families from Mexico City and the Valley of Mexico, who moved with de Vargas, as well as an unknown number from Zacatecas and others from Guadalupe del Paso, plus a hundred or so Spanish soldiers and groups of Indigenous warriors and their retainers.[25] Thus, the original Oñate y Salazar Hispanos "separated" from their villages and farms and missions lived "between and betwixt" until their return fourteen years later. For the many that did not, they settled in the El Paso area and founded the towns of Ysleta, Socorro, Senecu, and others and moved further south. A few families made a circular migration into Sonora. All of these places also celebrate the dance in the present and more than likely did so in the past. Thus the matachine "ritual space" may very well be representing the nongeographical territory of their liminal "in between and betwixt" identities after their separation, just as their ancestors were reincorporated once again in the reconquest. This is "acted out" in a performance filled with ancient movements, symbolic dress, the Spanish language, and role allocations of inclusion within ritual space.

But this removal may also include a layer of meaning of separation by slavery when hundreds of Indigenous and Hispano/Mexicanos were both slavers and slaves. While captured, many lived a liminal identity including those like the Genizaros previously discussed. However, simultaneous raids were conducted to recapture loved ones, which was an incessant process and their returns were celebrated with masses said and gratitude to possible holy intervention. And what is ritually noted in the Bernalillo Matachine Complex is that, at the end of the third day, the matachines *"se entregan"* — that is, handed people over and back to the families as described. A small "donation" is given to the *rezador*, which may be in fact a symbolic ransom that was often paid to various tribes for the recovery of the family members. Finally, according to Charles Aguilar, the rabbinical *rezador* and spiritual leader for all of the events, these various assertions are more than probable.[26]

DISCUSSION

Among those present who join in the final community dance and beyond the formal roles fulfilled, as I have already indicated, are many supporters who especially through kinship, cohort identification, and friendships participate as avid supporters. They participate in arranging the construction of the ritual attire, maintaining the altar at the mayordomo's home, cooking and helping clean up after the *novenas*, rosaries, and of course the actual procession and dance itself. They also support the entire edifice by assisting with food booths and selling tee shirts, rosaries, and other sundry items in order to help the mayordomos defray the heavy costs of their charge. Thus the Matachine Complex is composed of the many densities of relationships, interests, religious values, and commitments to the Bernalillo community. For three hundred years the core of the community rests on and also expresses these relationships in the yearly festival to San Lorenzo.

This Hispano/Mexicano/Indigenous complex served and continues to serve myriad functions, but the linguistic and cultural functions are crucial in light of two salient conditions. First, and we will take up a more in-depth discussion in chapter 4, are the regional linguistic impositions on entire generations of Hispanos/Mexicanos, who were and are being denuded of Spanish due to educational policies. This is in spite of the alleged bilingualism of the state constitution, in which it was never made a part, up to the present moment English has been the dominant language. Based on the census figures reported in Fernandez-Gibert (2010), 70 percent of the population of New Mexico could not speak English in 1890, a figure that decreased to 50 percent in 1900 and 33 percent in 1910, and in the present is 4.6 percent.[27] The introduction of the public school system and its English-only curriculum in the northern region were crucial to the acquisition of statehood and were factors in Congressional approval at the time, in order to deal with what was perceived of New Mexican populations as foreign.[28] This reduction of Spanish to 4.66 percent in the present is in spite of the historical reality of the large demographic presence of the Hispano/Mexicano population prior to 1900 and large-scale Mexican migration from the southern regions after the Mexican Revolution in 1910 and even into the 1970s. The unrestricted public education policy until the advent of bilingual education in the 1960s was to eradicate Spanish, and children were punished for speaking their native tongue at school (Espinosa 1975; Vélez-Ibáñez 1996, 101). Thus ethnocentrism, demographic fear, and monolingualism as primary beliefs played major roles in the loss of Spanish, which continues to the present in spite of language-immersion programs, which are voluntary for children and but still based on the movement from Spanish to English, with the former continuously placed as a secondary language.

The retention of New Mexican Spanish since its early introduction in the sixteenth century is primarily due to the insistence of many to speak, write, and read in Spanish, especially so through the religious rituals that they maintained and in private schools, and thus resisting cultural and linguistic erasure. All prayers are read in Spanish. Even though some of the attendees to the monthly rosaries and novenas may not speak Spanish, they understand and read the prayers. Since the attendees to these rituals are age heterogeneous, it is not unusual for children to attend them as well since some will be apprentice matachines, others Malinches, and others *tamboreros* or will simply accompany their parents or grandparents. From observation, some will read along with the prayers, others will recite and respond to the rosary process, and others will seem to mouth the words but not say them. When I enquired of some of the adults as to the Spanish proficiency of the children, some stated that they spoke, wrote, and read Spanish better than they did given the generational differences in Spanish and English instruction when they were students and the difference in approach their own children experienced through dual language programs.

For both the Rarámuri and Bernalillo matachines, these have been ancient and complex religious, ritual, social, economic, and cultural performances that have accentuated their control of the complex in widely different ecological circumstances, but ironically about the same time periods, and from very different political and social "positions." For the Rarámuri, they empowered themselves by taking over the complex in spite of the violence, warring, and suppression by Spanish colonial authorities and the absence of the Church, the latter of which was more than likely a benefit to this retention. Yet from the reintroduction of the Jesuit-led church in the eighteenth century to this day, they have managed to incorporate the Church into their complex and control its performance, functions, and outcomes of identity and senses of selves within a very complex ecology that guarantees group separation. Yet the

Matachine Complex, by insisting on recruiting participants far and wide, have developed a crosscutting process of cultural and ideational adhesion that guarantees they remain Rarámuri and not Tarahumara, as they were categorized by Spanish colonial authorities.

Like the Rarámuri, the Bernalillo complex emerges out of violence, warring, and nineteenth-century suppression by an invading and conquering American army. The initial *raison d'être* for the complex was initiated as a celebration of their reconquest of the Pueblo peoples and in gratitude for having their lives spared during the Pueblo Revolt, but more so for their continued protection against another possible uprising. The fact is that during the ensuing centuries they have become much more accommodating with the Pueblo peoples, with intermarriages, genetic mixing, close community relations—especially between themselves and the Sandia and Santa Anna Pueblos—and ritual exchanges; these guaranteed over the long run not only their survival but also their stability as a culturally vibrant people. The Matachine Complex for the Bernalillo community has been and continues to be a linguistic and cultural buttress in bright relief, in contrast to the assimilationist, language removing, educational hegemonic processes of the public policies and practices of the state and nation.

For the Bernalillo participants, as for the Rarámuri, their "I's" and "they's" and the "us's" and the "me's" are in continuous emergence with slices of identities and multiplicities seemingly homogeneous but in fact turned out from multiple histories, impositions, and ownerships, and as the following chapter shows vividly, unrelenting processes of conflict and emergence and discontent, as well as adaptation, negotiation, and types of temporary denouements.

4

AGAINST BIFURCATING THE REGION AND THE SEGMENTATION OF LANGUAGE HEGEMONIES

⁊⸱

The New American and Mexican Nations

Mexico never left the Southwest, it just learned English.
JOSE ANTONIO BURCIAGA, *DRINKING CULTURA*, 1992

T HE IMPOSITION OF THE POLITICAL BORDER in the region brought massive technological and economic changes, as has been discussed, including the impact of English on residing populations and those that were to follow across the new border line. Yet, from the very beginning of this penetration local populations were inventive on how they were to manage themselves in relation to this new language, maintain their linguistic capacity to communicate with others like themselves and others with whom they had established relations, and also attempt to negotiate the new language masters. Only shortly after the conquest of the region, one local farmer and probable trader had invented a trilingual dictionary that speaks to the manner in which, instead of allowing themselves to be erased linguistically, one response was not to join but to add to their linguistic repertoire.

HOMESPUN DICTIONARY

At the onset of the American period, a modest attempt was made to create a trilingual list of words—a kind of rudimentary but functional dictionary. It is perhaps symbolic of the way one member of a hegemonized population dealt with imposition by "slanting" his realities innovatively and incorporating a nonhistorical language as an added part of his repertoire without sanction or support, institutional permission, or the overarching military presence of a foreign army made legitimate by conquest. As well, this trilingual composition is a kind of "in your face" production that quietly and simply refuses to erase one language in the place of the other equally. This trilingual

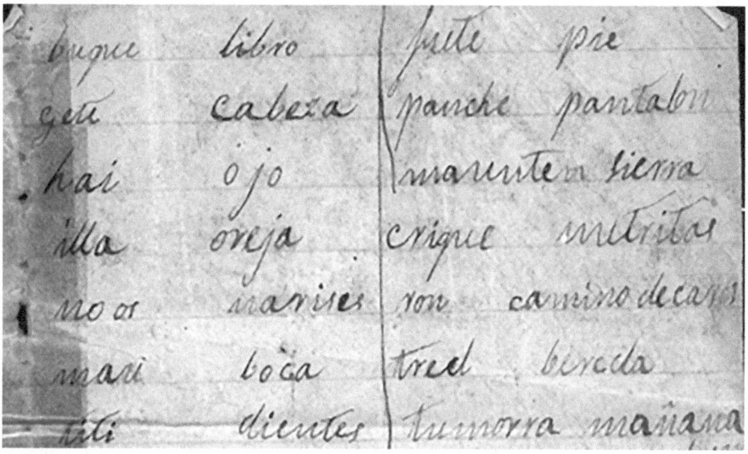

FIGURE 21. Sample copy of trilingual dictionary.

production was more than likely functional outside of mission auspices by a person dealing with traders, miners, sheepherders, and probably commercial agents. Trade in the mid-nineteenth century with Indigenous tribes like the Utes was an imperative for survival and access to needed natural resources such as bison, beaver, and other animal skins.

This example was brought to my attention by Samuel Sisneros. It consists now of five and a quarter loose pages, of breast-pocket size, approximately three by four inches written on line paper with no front or back hardcover. In its original circulation it was probably jacketed or slipped inside of another holder. It was written by José Agapito Olivas, who was born in Rio Arriba, New Mexico, in 1834. Although he is listed as a farmer in the 1870 Census, he was a man of some wealth, according to the land value listed in the census. Samuel Sisneros and I estimate that the work was written circa 1860, only twelve years after the conquest by the United States.[1] The translator was Spanish-speaking and has phonetically sounded out the translations from Spanish to English and from Spanish to Ute.[2]

A few samples of the Spanish-English are shown in figure 21 and in typeset in figure 22 and in figures 23 and 24 are the Spanish-Ute. The translator's inventiveness is notable, but the most informative aspect of this work is the necessary trilingualism needed for transactions of various sorts and the obvious care and curiosity with which this was accomplished. It is highly likely that, with the Ute speaker, the author was using Spanish/Ute to communicate with perhaps an equally bilingual Ute. With the English speaker, the author may have been using either language to communicate with

Buque (book)	libro	fute(foot)	pie
Gete (head)	cabeza	panche (pants)	pantalón
Hai(eye)	ojo	maunten (mountain)	sierra
Illa (ear)	oreja	crique(creek)	nutritas (Nuevo Mexicano)
No os (nose)	nariz	horse run	camino de caballos (sic)
Mau (mouth)	boca	treel (trail)	bereda (vereda)
Titi (teeth)	dientes	tumorra (tomorrow)	mañana

FIGURE 22. Typeset version of figure 21: Spanish-English.

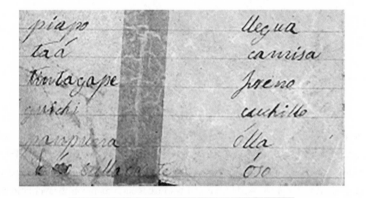

FIGURE 23. Sample copy of trilingual dictionary.

Piapo	llegua (yegua, mare)
Taá	camisa (shirt)
Tuitagape	freno (bit of a bridle)
Guichi	cuchillo (knife)
Panpuna	olla (jar, pot, or vase)

FIGURE 24. Typeset version of figure 23: Spanish-Ute.

the English/Spanish–speaking informant. It is also worth noting that the diminutive size of the dictionary indexes transferability as well as the need to quickly have available an invaluable tool for negotiations and transactions. José Agapito Olivas may very well have used the Santa Fe Trail to trade or sell sheep to the encroaching American traders from the east as well as to Utes who frequented the Old Spanish Trail moving southeast from Utah and Colorado.

Yet for many, the imposition of the border of the region also included in the twentieth century not only creative "slanting," in which impositions are deflected, but also cultural innovations and syncretisms with pain and discontent, as Gloria Anzaldúa (1987) has so painfully presented in her memorable work; this is somewhat analogous to the following discussion in which Anzaldúa's work is considered further.

WITNESS ONE: LEARNING ENGLISH AND ITS DISCONTENTS

I was almost six years old when I entered Government Heights Elementary School in Tucson, Arizona, in the second year of World War II. I had spoken both Spanish and English with most of the former at home, with relatives, and when visiting Sonora, which was fairly often, and when in turn family visited from Sonora, which was also fairly often. I spoke English mostly to my older sister at home, but always Spanish to my mother and father, the latter insisting that "English was for the streets" and Spanish for the home. I certainly did speak English in the streets, especially with kids who were not Mexican but Irish like Jackie Cox and Jewish like Leonard Zunin and Midwestern mixed breeds like Bruce Manners, all who moved into the partially Mexican neighborhood since the rents were cheaper and housing was at a premium during the war years. I also listened to *Let's Pretend*, which was a fantasy radio show on Saturdays, and during the week it was *The Shadow*, *Inner Sanctum*, *Fibber McGee and Molly*, Bob Hope, and *Your Hit Parade*—a musical show that my sister, who was eight years older than me, listened to diligently, where they played some jazz, lots of swing, and even more crooning by Frank Sinatra, Bing Crosby, and the Andrew Sisters—and too many others to recall. I also listened to Don Jacinto Orozco's gravelly voice on his early morning radio show, as well as the Mexican music of many sorts that my parents played, including Pedro Infanté, Mexican Swing by Luis Arcaráz, and *jarochos* from Veracruz as well. I also was used to going downtown with my parents to the Plaza Theater on Fridays, where they showed first-run Mexican movies, and I saw and heard Jorge Negrete and María Félix. I went to the Lyric Theater on Saturdays, across Congress Street, where they showed second-run American movies, and I saw and heard Humphrey Bogart and Ingrid Bergman, and (if I had the twenty-five cents for the bus and ticket) I went to the first-run films of the Fox Theater to join others in the Mickey Mouse Club to scream with joy at the antics of Donald Duck and Mickey Mouse.

Over the years, I learned to listen to old Tom Cox, Jackie's father, who had been gassed in World War I and still coughed up Flanders fields later in the midst of World War II and after. I got past his brogue by being attentive to his tales of the "Troubles" in Ireland, to which he had returned after the First World War to fight against the English, like many Irish who had migrated to or were born in the United States. But I had learned to listen to my father's unaccented Spanish narratives about how his brother and my Tío Lauro had shot a former revolutionary colonel as he was crossing into Nogales, Arizona, and whose body fell, straddling the yellow boundary line between the seeming bifurcated regions. The colonel had killed Tío Lauro's compadre when he would not step down as mayor of the town a few miles south of Nogales, Sonora. And of course my mother told, among many other narratives, of witnessing dying men in their courtyard in 1913 during the revolution while her own mother tended to their wounds and almost simultaneously while her father, as a colonel of cavalry, was being killed in the Battle of Parral, Chihuahua, by an explosive bullet to the stomach. Hers, she said, had been an extremely trying early childhood until she found refuge in Sonora with her married sister and children, where she later met Adalberto G. Vélez at a dance when he was visiting from Tucson.

Yet despite my knowledge of English and Spanish and their narratives and including getting used to the Irish brogue and its narratives, these did not place me in good stead in my elementary school and I was placed in that first year in "1C," in which all Mexican kids were placed regardless of ability in language. I stayed there for a few months until one of the bright teachers thought it ridiculous to keep me there and I was transferred to 1A and advanced rapidly to 1B in less than six months, despite what seems to be an illogical grade hierarchy.[3]

Moreover, I, along with the other Mexican kids was paddled, or had my hair pulled, or was merely scolded by towering figures when I was caught saying hellish words like "adios" or "como estas?" or "bien gracias" or anything that was of my language that had been spoken by my ancestors in this region when it was called Pimería Alta, then Sonora, and not Arizona. The principal, a well-regarded baseball coach, was a balding, red-faced, fat-nosed, and mostly scowling man who used his favorite toy for every devil word of Spanish in order to drive it out of his charges. The toy consisted of a baseball bat whose end was shaved thinly and pierced with holes and used for every satanic word spoken. Evidently the holes made the bat lighter for each stroke but the matter of fact is that it also pushed the skin up when the buttock was struck so when examined, the butt had portholes lined up, surrounded by puffed-up bruised skin.

The children also tried to go with the flow by creating a king and queen of the week for the person who received more "swats" than anyone else. They hated to count them, but like all things imperfect, they also constantly reminded them all of how little hope they had of escape. On the other hand, there were teachers that tried to protect them, and some of the teachers would move in front of them when the principal strode through the hallways before school when they were lined up ready to enter the classroom. Or at times they warned the children on the school grounds when he was roving about, but he also had an assistant with frizzy hair who was his alter ego and also made timely reports of those who uttered Beelzebub's tongue. For the protectors, respect and admiration were rendered, and they were the only reason for many not becoming early racists.

But the biggest anathema that was often struck was in the insistence on changing Christian names or anglicizing them beyond recognition. My sister Lucy's name was really Luz del Socorro, a deeply religious connotation but insufficient to counter the poorly devised pronunciation by so many, so, through daily use, it became Lucy. When my father was apprised that the school wanted to change his son's name to Charlie, that was the final insult for this Sonorense and he forbade them to do so, along with sending the promise of painful consequences to the same bulbous-nosed principal, even though my father had done nothing to prevent the paddling, the pulling of hair, or the standing in the corners for uttering the devilish Spanish because simply, he wasn't told by a muted son; I thought it was "natural" to be corrected in such a way.

OTHER WITNESSES

Lest this only be selective memory in which we all are encased, such practices were often taken to even greater lengths, as Ralph M. Flores (2004, 110) writes in his memoir of his family in Douglas, Arizona, in the early part of the twentieth century:

> And so it went [in describing the use of a riding crop by the principal for those speaking Spanish]. Those few Mexican kids who spoke some English would coach the rest of us during recess or the lunch hour. I don't remember the specific process of learning English, but I guess concern for my physical welfare motivated me strongly because I did learn it.

Or during her elementary school days in rural New Mexico, Gloria Zamora recounted her early brushes with the word-devil exorcist in the years 1958–1959 and a few years before the Age of Aquarius:

> One afternoon a blonde girl joins me on the steps of the cafeteria. She speaks only English and I Spanish. Somehow we have become good friends. We play and run with the other children. By the time of our Christmas performance, I have learned plenty of English, thanks to Hildegard. *And* Mrs. McCarthy beats the Spanish out of me by

pulling my braids and hitting my head face first on my desk. I learned pretty quickly to tip my face down into my chest and to use English words. (2004, 80)

Zamora concludes: "She is kind about everything except speaking Spanish at school" (ibid.).

Or turning to Elva Hart Treviño's autobiography of her life as part of the migrant stream in the late 1950s and in segregated Pearsall, Texas, which was her home base, she relates that her friend Dolores warned her not to speak any Spanish: "She told me that there was a pen on the playground labeled 'pigs.' She said that this was the word for *marranos* in English. This was where they put the kids who spoke Spanish in School. I was normally a quiet child, anyway, so I knew I could handle this" (1999, 75).

Yet it would seem that anyone undergoing such stresses continuing for the next many years in different ways and circumstances would be split up a bit, not unlike the border line that was imposed only a few generations before my father was born and almost a few before his grandfather was born. It was likely that a certain amount of shattering of the selves—and the "me's" and the "their's" and the "us's"—and the resulting configurations were, to say the least, challenging to figure out and to settle down. Our selves were, to say the least, in partial agony.

There developed in children caught up in such processes, and unlike Zamora, a "mute mutation" from personal experience and that of others (Flores 2004, 111), in which the fear of being embarrassed by a wrong accent, or a not quite well-structured sentence, or lilt on endings, or simply just not having learned a word or phrase trumped the necessity for communicating so that children often simply looked downward and shook their heads slightly or shrugged their shoulders while clenching their fists in their pockets or behind their backs. But worse for children, the necessity of asking to go the restroom could end in disaster, as Flores indicates, since permission could only be in English and an incorrect request would be punished. Children tried not to ask and too often urinated where they sat, only to be castigated for fouling the room (ibid.). This was a daily occurrence for many in the northern side so that learning was strongly connected with pain, embarrassment, or failure, and the "mute mutation" became the practice leading to certain academic failure and being stuck in the same grade for two years; or, when failure became too normative, they simply walked off and went home and were considered a "dropout."

Worse, some children never did learn English to their or anyone's satisfaction, nor the academic subjects that went along with it like mathematics, science, literature, and history. They also did not develop Spanish beyond the limits of a mostly working-class population's abilities to transmit the language. Some working-class families did teach their children to read and write and practice in Spanish, and some excelled in school despite the pain of linguistic repression, for they had a literate and stable foundation.

Some often spoke both languages together, filling in the blanks with one and often forgetting the other, known to some as "Spanglish" in the north and "Pocho" in the south—both are often derogatory appellations. But yet, José Antonio Burciaga so memorably referred to the words of our discontents as "compressed beyond their original meaning to say even more . . . These words enriched because they gave birth to a new world of ideas from a combination of cultures, ideas that were lacking a name until then" (1992, 4).

Gloria Anzaldúa's deeply incisive rendition of this process of creativity is articulated by noting the multifaceted capacities of this regional reality and of our creative discontents. She states of her and my generation and probably of those in the present (1987, 55):

Some of the languages we speak are
1. Standard English
2. Standard Spanish
3. Standard Mexican Spanish
4. North Mexican Spanish dialect
5. Chicano Spanish (Texas, New Mexico, Arizona, and California have regional variations)
6. Tex-Mex
7. Pachuco (called *caló*)

Yet there were great denials to these language capacities, to the experience of the transborder region, to the origination of Spanglish and its transborder people, and to being Mexican. Some also called themselves Spanish and not Mexican to please those who would acknowledge their connection to a now-foreign land recently divided, and this somehow would make Mexican children more legitimate as "Spanish." And in a deeply paradoxical and crazy-making way, non-Mexicans in the north promulgated the word "Spanish" for their version of what "they" thought the "others" were while rejecting the Spanish language itself or forbidding its use until taught as a foreign language in high school, sometimes by teachers who mispronounced words and who, when corrected, would become insulted and make the student pay one way or another. This had much earlier foundations, however.

For some "Mexican" children earlier in the late nineteenth century, theirs was an even more contradictory status when they were discharged from the Albuquerque Indian Boarding School for being "too Mexican." As previous chapters have already indicated, bilingualism and multiple identities were more normative than the essentialist "bloodline" conviction held by both Mexican and Indigenous populations. Some children enrolled in this boarding school were discharged, as indicated in

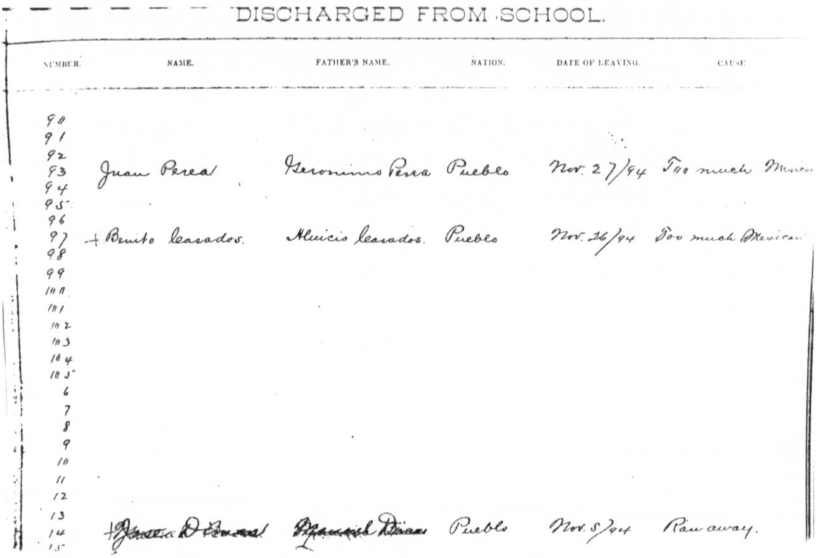

FIGURE 25. Sample of list showing children discharged from the Albuquerque Indian Boarding School. Photo by Samuel Cisneros, Found Archive, Zimmerman Library, without origination (2015).

figure 25, which shows, for example, that Juan Perea, the son of Geronimo Perea of the Pueblo nation, was sent home on November 27, 1894, because of "Too much Mexican," and Benito Casados, also Pueblo, was sent home for the same reason on November 26, 1894.

Other entries indicated degrees of Mexicanness as causes for discharge, including various rationales such as these:

> "Stayed for a month; upon his return sent for good. Half Mexican anyway."
> "Too much Mexican to be kept under orders from Dept."
> "Almost, if not entirely, Mexican."
> "Instructed by Dept. to get rid of Mexican blood."[4]

Yet, perhaps these "Mexican" children were done a favor in being discharged from the "Indian" boarding school, as that the system was not generally and not necessarily an agreeable experience.

For Indigenous peoples from the East Coast to the West, they faced a number of institutional and educational mechanisms for imposing linguistic and cultural hegemony. First were the Protestant and Catholic mission schools, subsidized by the federal government and established by the Indian Civilization Act of 1819, the primary objective of which was to turn Indigenous children into Catholic, Mormon, Presbyterian, Methodist, Baptist, Lutheran, Congregationalists, or any other denomination funded into the mission's ideology—and, of course, with English as the primary means of communication—many times in a boarding-school setting on the reservation itself, some of which are still in existence (Dejong 1993, 71–95).

Second, the American boarding school method, ensconced within a military-type organization, was a federally supported and funded enterprise designed to Christianize, acculturate, and decouple from original social relations; it was a cultural eradication that took place between 1870 and 1940 or so. Third were the public schools, the movement toward which began in 1891: "By 1909 . . . three thousand Indian students were enrolled in contract public schools in California, Nebraska, South Dakota, and Utah, and another 818 in twelve [other] states" (Dejong 1993: 177). None of these institutional mechanisms through the late 1970s were anything other than functions to obliterate the linguistic and cultural capital of children and to forcibly replace it.

WITNESSES OF A GENERATION

It is revealing that, for Indigenous children, the shocks of learning were not only corporal, cultural, linguistic, and familial, but also profoundly psychological and, as for Mexican children, filled with pain and disassembly of personality, but also resistance in their hegemonic confrontations.

In his memories of his service in the U.S. Marine Corps during World War II, Navajo code talker Chester Nez wrote of his experiences in boarding schools in old Fort Defiance, which had been a central fort established in 1851 in the middle of Navajo territory for Americans warring against Navajos and later reestablished as an Indian agency with the first government school for the Navajo in 1870. In between these periods, Navajos had been brutally expelled on the "Long Walk" of 450 miles and were later allowed to return to part of their land (Fort Defiance Chapter, ftdefiance.navajochapters.org).[5]

Before Nez passed away in 2015, he wrote of his early experiences as a child before World War II and the harsh disciplinary methods encountered in some of this first days in class; the experiences are very reminiscent of those of Flores:

> Questions began. The teacher wrote Yes and No on the board, instructing the students to choose one or the other for each answer. . . . We children listened, desperately trying to pull some meaning from what the teacher said. I clamped my lips together. As on

other days, I volunteered no answers. Anyone who answered incorrectly was punished. It was safer not to volunteer, not to stand out. But the teacher called on me. "Yes," I said, feeling sure that was the correct response. Her eyes squeezed into slits, and she slapped a ruler against her palm. "Chester Nez, the correct answer is 'No.' Come up here." Head hanging, I walked slowly to the front of the class. While the other students sat silent the teacher whacked me across the shoulders with the ruler. *It doesn't hurt that much*, I told myself, squeezing my eyes closed. But I knew it was wrong, trying to humiliate a person in front of his peers. (57)

Like Flores recounted in his work, Nez described asking permission to go to the bathroom, which entailed speaking in English. Errors were not countenanced ". . . so most tried to hold it until after class. We weren't allowed to fidget or to look around at each other. Eyes stared straight ahead. Feet were planted firmly on the floor. Hands and heads remained motionless. But in order to avoid being hit, we had to learn [English]" (ibid.).

Simultaneously, however, Chester Nez also learned that the harshest disciplinarians were the matrons, most of whom were Indigenous women and oversaw their care and who also enforced an English-only policy. He states: "I addressed a boy, using his Navajo name. The matron struck me on the back of the head with her open palm. 'English only.'" After they were given "English" names they were asked to pronounce them. "When asked for their new names by a teacher or matron, they struggled to remember. Punishment was immediate for those who forgot" (2011, 49).

Yet like all hegemonic attempts, these had mixed results, and while many children did lose their language capacity, others reacquired it upon returning to the reservation, especially in ritual participation, as Chester Nez did. Yet there were entire generations for whom language facility was markedly interrupted and their own children depended on the grandparental generation to learn the language or often not, depending on the period in question. For these children attending boarding schools or Mexican children attending public or parochial schools in the '20s, '30s, and '40s, they would also be the generations going to war. As a Marine, Chester Nez would in fact use the irrepressible Diné (Navajo) language to help create and use the Navajo code during combat in numerous landings and fighting in the Pacific where he was wounded.

Mexicans born either north or south who were drafted or enlisted often used Spanish to both urge and calm each other during combat in the Pacific and Europe and, very soon after World War II, in Korea. Ruben Moreno, a Marine veteran of the Korean War, narrates the tragedy of combat in Korea in which, after he saved a fellow Marine, Polaski, he and "El Bobby" (Roberto Moreno)[6] searched for more wounded on a hill under fire from Chinese troops (Vélez-Ibáñez 1996, 203–4):

Just about then I decided to see if there were any other guys down where Polaski had been and I asked some of the others that were around to go with me. Nobody volunteered but just then "El Bobby" was coming up the hill. He had been held up spraying foxholes. He said, "*Vamos*" and I said no, don't go with me. I wanted to protect him. His wife was expecting their first. But he said, "*Vamos, para que sepan que los Mexicanos saben como morir donde quiera*" (Let's go, so that they learn that Mexicans know how to die anywhere). So we went down, and Bobby covered me by keeping the Chinese down. I collected some weapons but there was nobody else around. We went up over the ridge again, when I looked back, Bobby was curled up on the ground shot in the chest. . . . I picked up Bobby in my arms and tried to shake him awake, but it did not do no good. Only years later did I find out [that our own machine gunner] had killed Bobby by mistake. I guess "El Bobby" and Polaski just traded souls.

In spite of all of the corporal and psychological methods used by educational institutions, individuals resisted, used, and retained a part, a portion, or a segment of the languages or their entirety. Ironically for the Diné, the code-talker necessity in war gave legitimacy to their language in spite of the fact that after they returned from war, their children would be faced with similar methods. These methods, however, were to change radically for ensuing generations, which will be discussed. For the descendants of Mexican-origin veterans, they would face much or many of the same approaches and those much subtler ones in the form of language labeling.

THE PROCESSES OF CULTURAL AND LINGUISTIC IMPOSITIONS AND THEIR DISCONTENTS: THE NORTHERN SIDE

An earlier discussion outlined the creation of the "Brittle Border" and its imposition on the regions after the American-Mexican War and the forced sale of remaining parts, such as southern Arizona and New Mexico and their discontents. As has been presented, wholesale economic changes accrued as the aftermath of the introduction of the industrial mode of production in the region. These, as will be recalled, led to the creation of the asymmetry between the north and south sections of the broader SWNAR. As importantly, it was emphasized that the movement of populations was an ancient one and that the Spanish empire moved from south to north, unlike the English colonization process, which was from east to west. Then the American imposition followed the same process. As will be discussed, the Mexican national state moved along the same axis as their colonial forbearers. Their population would move from south to north as well.

Both sought to impose their national identities in the north on Mexican and Indigenous populations and the latter on Indigenous populations using the mestizo and
citizen filter. Each differed in application, programs, and attention. Both ultimately
sought, especially among Mexicans in the north, the removal of Spanish and the
wholesale removal of the many Indigenous languages and their multitude of dialects.
The southern strategy, as will be seen, was quite different but with ideological nuances
not present in the northern side.

Behind the American version was a commitment to the eastern model of assimilation, Americanization, and linguistic removal and simultaneously its opposite Nativist rejection that is present in the ideological universe of language and culture in the
contemporary United States. This model had as its skewed and contradictory prism
from before the American-Mexican War to the present a strong Nativist rejectionist
penchant, especially against Irish Catholics, sometimes exhibited in riots such as in
Philadelphia and New York—these were based on the fear of the immigrant. This
had been coupled in a twisted manner to the idea of the melting pot of the early
twentieth century, in which immigrating populations entering Ellis Island would
change their names, learn English, rid themselves of their own devil tongues, and
become Americans. This rejectionist and assimilationist prism was promulgated by
different sectors of the American experiment. The assimilationist prism seemed to be
quite democratic so that schooling as described was not done for malicious reasons
but for ideological reasons having to do with a deeply held "megascript" that the only
good American was one using the East Coast prism of belonging and identity and
to whom the "theirs," the "I's," the "me's," were English speaking, preferably of light
melanin, of English/Scottish stock and preferably not Irish Catholic but Protestant.
Its sacred documentation providing guidance in values and beliefs was at one time or
the other biblical rationalizations and misinterpretations. This prism would entail
highly individualized notions of selves in which hard work, preferably at the mythic
farm, sacrifice, self-improvement, and success, were intricately tied to the Protestant
ethic and light melanin. This, bundled together with a mythical quest for Manifest
Destiny, rationalized all policies, whether of extermination of Indigenous persons,
war-making against Mexicans, and the erasure from public comment or acceptance of
that which did not fit the prism. Or to state it in more postmodern terms, this prism
and its megascript created the "others" in the opposite likeness of "themselves." This
took only a short time to implement.[7]

In her excellent work, Carol Schmid (2001, 14–15) lays out the historical American language prisms beginning in the eighteenth century and illustrates the contending points of view of the early intellectual and historical figures who were
concerned with "one nation under God." Even though there has never been a consti-
tutionally mandated official English, there were indeed contradictory positions held

by the early American thinkers such as Jefferson, who thought it appropriate to learn multiple languages, including Spanish since "this ancient part of American history is written chiefly in Spanish" (Schmid, 16 quoting Lipscomb, 1904, 167).[8] But the contention over language by the early thinkers was basically between the dominance of English or the dominance of German. Strong points of view prevailed with Benjamin Franklin, whom Schmid (15) quotes as saying, "Not being used to Liberty, (they) know not how to make modest use of it. . . . Few of their children in the Country learn English; they import many books from Germany. . . . Why should the Palatine boors [Germans] be suffered to swarm in our Settlements, and by herding together, establish their Language and Manners to the exclusion of ours?"

But yet not withstanding such points of view held by others, the Articles of Confederation were printed in German and English, with sundry other documents printed in French, German, Dutch, and Swedish (15), and there is no section of the U.S. Constitution requiring English. The eighteenth-century German schools proliferated, while generational loss of Dutch by the second generation was not unusual. German remained strongly in use, especially with the advent of German private and public schools, and in fact using German would easily transition children to English (19–21). This enlightened approach, however, fell very much by the wayside by the early twentieth century with the advent of World War I. As well, there is nothing in the Treaty of Guadalupe Hidalgo or the Treaty of the Mesilla requiring English of those in conquered territories. Both treaties protected the civil rights of Mexicans remaining in what became the northern part of the region.

These contradictory early language views took quite a different direction in regard to both Mexican origin and Indigenous populations. In both, war prevailed as the central mechanism for language and physical control of both, with the prevailing attitude toward Indigenous populations combining exterminating those resisting and "civilizing" those remaining, shunting others to reservations, and—in regard to language—eradicating Indigenous languages. From the heyday of the Indian wars and from the Iroquois of the east to the Apaches of the west, the latter of which finally succumbed in the late 1880s, "Indian" policy was to remove or "civilize" and to place them in boarding schools where there was to be no use of the Indigenous languages. For at least seventy years Indigenous populations were subjected to attempts at language erasure and cultural denuding through the boarding school mechanism, both by the hands of the federal schools and chartered mission schools. Corporal punishment and the cutting off of traditional hair practices that denoted age grades were both practiced, and use of Indigenous symbols and beliefs were systematically attacked by their exclusion and practice and substituted with dress, language, practices, and values that were considered "American." Taken from their parents, they were transported across the country to either alienating or distantly situated schools.

The model itself was created by Captain Richard H. Pratt, who in 1878 developed the famous Carlisle Indian School in a former Pennsylvania military structure not unlike the Fort Defiance model structured along military lines of obedience, discipline, and a nineteenth-century harshness. Students were to become farmers, Christians, and segregated, and had limited home visitations and interaction with elders, with an emphasis on spatial separation at least for the first forty years of these schools' operations (Dawson 2012, 81–82). Children were removed from parents at ages as early as four through their teens, although it was also the case that in the 1920s and 1930s many northern Indigenous students attended schools not far from the reservation, as was the case for Chester Nez (2011). Thus, as Dawson describes the demography and statistics of the system: "By 1926, two-fifths of all Indian students under the authority of the federal government (a total of 27,361) were being educated in 19 off-reservation schools. Over the course of a century more than 100,000 Indian children attended 500 boarding schools" (2012, 82).

But a change in schools from the boarding schools like Fort Defiance to public schools was a freedom that Chester and thousands like him had never enjoyed, so he recalls, "On my first day of public junior high school in Gallup New Mexico, I could hardly believe my ears. Navajo. Spoken in the hallways. Navajo! The classes were conducted in English [but] . . . [n]o one hit me across the shoulders with a ruler. I felt liberated!" (Nez 2011, 84). Nevertheless, English continued to be the primary method of instruction but, at least in his case, without the automatic corporal penalty.

For Indigenous populations, educational and linguistic policies changed and the atrocious militarized system was broadly denounced by the Merriam Report (a.k.a. *The Problem of Indian Administration*), published in 1928, which basically concluded that the entire system of boarding schools served to stunt the growth of children (Dejong 1993, 134).[9] More humane treatment of children ensued, but the system as a whole continued to not serve Indigenous students. Forty years later the Kennedy Report (a.k.a. *Indian Education: A National Tragedy—A National Challenge*) in 1969, which basically admonished federal and public schools, concluded that the tragedy "stemmed from the schools' curricula, attitudes, values and dogmas, all of which at times denigrated American Indians and Indian culture" (196). Yet as the next chapter will show, dramatic and positive changes developed in most Indigenous schools, but Indigenous language development remained a pedagogical and functional issue.

For both Indigenous and Mexican-origin populations, segregated and semisegregated schools were the norm, in part in the Indigenous case because of the reservation system and boarding schools, and for Mexicans in part because of the concentration of populations in neighborhoods but also because of internally developed segregation of children according to ethnicity within the same classroom. Separate classrooms in the same school were instituted where demographics did not dictate the ethnic composition of the classrooms, as in the "1C" example showed. Also, throughout the region segregated schools developed even though legally Mexican children could not be separated on the basis of language or culture in a separate school, as adjudicated by the lawsuit in California in 1931 of *Roberto Alvarez v. the Board of Trustees of the Lemon Grove School District*. Its decision concluded that "the separation was indeed deemed a segregation and the court ruled that the school board had no legal basis on which to segregate the children," but in fact de facto segregation cases were tried through the 1970s (Alvarez 1986). Similarly, *Méndez v. Westminster School District of Orange County California* in 1945 ruled that since there was no law that segregated Mexican-origin children, the attorney for Méndez charged that this was a violation of the 14th Amendment's equal protection clause. In neither Alvarez nor Mendez was the argument against racial segregation because Mexicans were classified as "white."[10] In both cases, the attorneys could not make a case based on race as being unconstitutional, since the U.S. Supreme Court in *Plessy v. Ferguson* in 1896 had upheld racial segregation—i.e., separate but equal stance. These cases that preceded *Brown v. Board of Education* in 1954 stimulated a series of lawsuits in Texas shortly after the Westminster case, since as Rivas-Rodríguez (2015, 28) so eloquently states ". . . then Texas attorney general Price Daniel issued an opinion on the segregation of Mexican American Children: 'Schools could not separate students . . . solely on race . . . But based solely on language deficiencies and other individual needs and aptitudes demonstrated by examination or properly conducted tests, a school district may maintain separate classes in separate buildings if necessary for any pupils with such deficiencies, needs or aptitudes through the first three grades.'"[11]

Thus local school districts used such language to allow broad discretion in the application of separating children along allegedly cultural differences and certainly linguistic ones, often categorized in the 1960s under the rubric of "special education," by using standardized tests to allegedly measure linguistic failings and the notion of cultural differences as the harbingers of academic and intellectual weaknesses among the Spanish-speaking populations of the northern part of the SWNAR. In Herschel T. Manuel's (1965, 51–72) highly influential work in synthesizing many of the known studies of the period in regard to Mexican-origin children's achievement and performance, a number of measures showed a strong relationship between performance and income so that the lower the income the lower scores on math and English achievement, intelligence, and other mostly English performance tests. What is important to note in this synthesis is the simultaneous employment in some of the studies of the liberal use of "retardation" as the condition suffered. This was especially the case of the study and publication of the Arizona *Investigation of Mental Retardation and Pseudo Mental Retardation in Relation to Bilingual and Sub-Cultural Factors* (McGrath and Abraham 1960, 155), in which it states unequivocally: "For [t]he children as a whole [Mexican and Indigenous in Arizona] . . . On achievement tests the apparent retardation varies from one subject to another, showing a progressive retardation in reading with advancing grade, but no clear trend in arithmetic or English language." This insertion of mental incapacity was to plague both Mexican and Indigenous children, who were tracked throughout their academic careers, resulting often in their being provided watered-down curriculum emphasizing "consumer math," "communication for living situations," or "everyday science."

This process of "dumbing down" simply led to even lower scores, reiteration of narratives of inability or incapacities, and to neither mastery of content nor language in either English or Spanish or in the Indigenous languages beyond the limits set up by such curricula. This set the stage for later discontent that would be part and parcel of the impetus of part of the educational reforms and cultural and linguistic revitalization of the late 1960s and early 1970s of the Chicano and Native American protests and civil rights complaints. Yet, segregation continued in its various formats. School boards often used language and culture as "special education" needs and their alleged "retardation" for the separation of Mexican children—a practice that seems to be at play with English-immersion programs up to the present.

For a short period of time during the epoch of the Civil Rights Movement of the 1960s, bilingual programs of instruction in various states were initiated; yet for neither population was bilingualism or native-language maintenance a standard practice to this moment. As the next chapter will discuss, the English-only movement dismantled many worthwhile programs of instruction and weakened others with the advent of large-scale Mexican migration in the 1970s to the present. Language maintenance and expansion among Indigenous peoples since that period have been both promising and disappointing. Generations of Indigenous populations in the north have remained culturally Indigenous, but consistent programs of Indigenous language instruction and development are not the norm. It is still the case that too many Indigenous persons of the most recent generations control little of their language, with generations of Mexican-origin adults unable to transmit their native language, as the next chapter will discuss.

THE PROCESSES OF CULTURAL AND LINGUISTIC IMPOSITIONS AND THEIR DISCONTENTS: THE SOUTHERN SIDE

The hegemonic colonial residue that placed *gente de razon*, i.e., Spanish/Mexicans, in competition for natural resources and land accentuated whatever real or imagined cultural differences existed between them and Indigenous peoples. These did not expire either with Mexican Independence in 1821 or with the Mexican Revolution almost one hundred years later. Often considered *naturales* or "barbarous," needing to be civilized and Christianized, this incessant process has never been reconciled or eliminated in the ethnic relations between mestizos and Indigenous populations, and especially is triggered by the mesitzo lust for Indigenous lands and natural resources like water. The notion of "whiteness" was an ideological imposition rationalizing the elimination of language and culture using educational institutions through the middle of the twentieth century and often coupled by multiple levels of physical violence, the history of which is long and sustained. This was often rationalized by characterizing Indigenous peoples as "indio," which was tantamount to being a "redskin" in American terms and largely derogatory and without humanity or rights of place, space, or language, especially throughout the late nineteenth and early twentieth centuries.

Under the iron hand of the dictator Porfirio Díaz, from the 1870s through the early 1900s, war raged between the Yoeme (Yaqui Nation) and the Mexican government. One result was that between 6,400 and 8,000 Yoeme who had fought against land and river expropriations were shipped to the henequen plantations in Veracruz by railcar, in which hundreds died and which is comparable to the Long Walk of the Navajo in the North, described earlier.[12] Leticia Acosta Briseño (1993, 411) in her work relays Doña Juana's description of her parents' deportations:

> My parents were taken in 1907, by force, and here they left their homes, their fields, their crops, not even a single grain of anything . . . well the federals came, surrounded all the homes and took out the families. First, they took the men, by force, and they took them all tied up as if they were delinquents . . . they slandered them, because they said they were from the mountains, but no, they planted next to the river and here they sold their crops all the way to Guaymas or Hermosillo, where they could sell their sustenance . . . but I don't know if they had done something wrong or not, but that is the way Porfirio Díaz slandered them, that they were rebels, against the pueblo, against the government but no, that was not the case, it is that they were just afraid that they would be killed because here they were hanged even in their homes, they were chased because the government never did like the Yaqui tribe, because they knew they were indigenous, they were Indians, that is why they did not like them . . . to appropriate all the Yaquis had, their lands, that is what they wanted. (my translation; punctuation and capitalization original)

My father, Adalberto Vélez García, born in 1900 and a child in this same period, recounted that between Magdalena and Imuris, Sonora, a distance of twenty miles, Yoeme men and women were hung from cottonwood trees for that distance along the

River Magdalena. When asked why this was done, he responded that the Yoeme were a brave people who resisted the "Yori" (white man) when they tried to take their lands and rivers.[13] Many Yoeme in this period began their exodus to Arizona, where they would found the Yoeme villages of Pascua Village in the west part of Tucson and Guadalupe Village south of Phoenix. Ironically, prior residents came to label Yoeme as Mexicans since they were not recognized by the U.S. federal government as "Natives" until late in the twentieth century.

Later pogroms by the revolutionary governors like Álvaro Obregón and Plutarco Elías Calles of Sonora during the 1920s led to the involuntary exodus of thousands of Yaquis to Arizona. Hundreds more were killed by the Mexican army in genocidal attacks on men, women, and children until a peace treaty was signed in 1929, and five years later eight of their towns and almost 500,000 hectares were guaranteed by the government of Lazaro Cárdenas.[14] This example of the Yoeme was repeated in different degrees throughout the regional south. The Rarámuri (Tarahumara) of matachine fame in the Mexican state of Chihuahua have been subjected to encroachment, especially during the nineteenth and twentieth centuries and to the present by mestizo ranchers and farmers, logging of pristine forests, as well as mining explorations and extraction for gold and other metals located in the Sierra Madre—all of which place into question their very existence as a people. Throughout the region, whether in Sonora, Chihuahua, Baja California, Nuevo León, or Coahuila, the encroachment by mestizo interests and governmental inaction and governmental permission, especially at the state and local levels, continue to the present.[15]

This conflict from the seventeenth century, as previously discussed in chapter 2 of this work, through the present especially has it manifestations in a constant turmoil between identity, materiality, natural resources, and language use, with the latter often important and crucial in both contradictory and complex ways. Alongside the hegemonic Spanish language, judicial cases could not be brought against such encroachments, the development of legal charters of association, incorporation by Indigenous entities like cooperatives, self-protection organizations, community action groups—all imperative to be organized under the hegemonic institutional structures of the Mexican state. At the same time such linguistic needs, however, were confronted simultaneously with language loss since such instruction at least to the 1960s was largely focused on Spanish and not the retention or expansion of the Indigenous languages.

To different degrees, Mexican language policies ranged from benign neglect to attempts to create language brokers by training cadres of Indigenous students to carry out instruction in their villages, but in most cases the use of the Indigenous language, if considered at all, was a means of learning Spanish as the primary language for educational achievement.

MEXICAN MODELS OF LANGUAGE
AND THEIR DISCONTENTS

The model for Indigenous education and language for the southern region and for the rest of Mexico after the Mexican Revolution of 1910 was the American Boarding School model of forced acculturation, technical education, uniformed militarization, monolingualism, gendering of occupations, and cultural assimilation.[16] In 1926, the government opened the Casa del Esudiante Indigena in Mexico City. Like the American model, it gathered Indigenous men from throughout the nation with the primary goal of turning agricultural peoples into working-class subjects bereft of all of the alleged disadvantages of culture and language. By the 1930s this had been changed to the establishment of a system of *internados indigenas*, which served about three thousand students, but this was a small proportion of the federal schools, which enrolled over six hundred thousand Indigenous students, according to Dawson (2012, 83). However, the acculturated *internados* did serve the "middle-man cultural broker role" and were important in the attempt at nationalizing Indigenous populations to become Mexicans of the Republic, rather than as members of their own nations with or without the state's permission.

Yet there was a deep shift and change in the use and teaching of Spanish and Indigenous languages, according to de Varennes (2012):

> Mexico was the scene of serious discussions during the 1950s suggesting that it was inappropriate to teach in Spanish in an environment where the mother tongue was an indigenous language. By the middle 1960s, the principle of early literacy in the native language plus the teaching of Spanish as a second language became the official policy of the Mexican government. In the 1970s, a growing demand appeared for the whole educational programme in the larger indigenous communities to be truly bilingual and bicultural.[17]

This impetus came strongly from the attempt to "integrate" the Indigenous populations by the formation of various institutions, not the least of which was the INI, Instituto Nacional Indigenista, founded in 1948. The INI approached Indigenous peoples from a highly functionalist perspective of imagining programs "to induce cultural changes in their communities and to promote the development and integration in the intercultural regions to the economic, social, and political life of the nation" (Sosa Suárez and Henríquez Bremer 2012, my translation). This well-meaning interventionist program in 1950 created the first Centro de Cooordinador Indigenista in San Cristobal de las Casas in Chiapas in order to carry out programs beneficial to Indigenous nations bordering Guatemala, and by 1976 it had established seventy-six centers throughout the Indigenous nations. Programs ranged from health programs, literacy initiatives, economic projects, and in 1961 some of the first intern programs for Indigenous students. But among its most important programming was the establishment of bilingual and bicultural programs in 1951 in Chiapas and then officially an entire system of bilingual and bicultural education in 1963 at its centers. In the southern part of the SWNAR, four centers were established in Chihuahua between 1952 and 1980 especially serving the far-flung Rarámuri peoples; one in Baja California in 1974 serving especially Seris; and seven in Sonora and Sinaloa between 1973 and 1998 concentrating on Mayo, Yoéme, and Pimas. In addition, Indigenous-language radio stations were instituted between 1982 and 2012 in Chihuahua and Sonora (ibid.).

This impetus by the then INI meant that, according to Rodolfo Stavenhagen,

> for the first time in the educational history of Mexico, the Indian languages and cultures were given due recognition in school programmes . . . that Spanish will be introduced from the beginning as a second language and that the Indian students will become fully bilingual . . . At the same time, at the national level, the curriculum should be organised in such a fashion that schoolchildren all over the country will become aware of the pluri-cultural makeup of their nation, and respect for and knowledge of the minority cultures should become a part of the national curriculum. Of course, the full hispanicization of all minority ethnic groups is still the stated objective, but no longer to the exclusion of the minority cultures as such.[18]

The INI was replaced by the Comisión Nacional para el Desarrollo de los Pueblos Indígenas (CDI) in 2003, with a limited mission and made part of the central government, especially after INI directors and personnel supported a number of issues in the protection of the people whom they served and especially the agenda of one of its directors, Dr. Salomón Nahmad, who strongly opposed the further encroachment on the water rights of the Yoeme people in 1983.[19] The new version continues to function in twenty-four states through ten Coordinating Centers for Indigenous Development; a Research, Information, and Documentation Centre; and twenty-eight Regional Indigenous Development Centers. It also supports a network of 1,085 school hostels that are used for students from long distances. It continues to operate a Cultural Indigenist Broadcasting System (SRCI), which runs twenty-seven multilingual radio stations.[20]

Yet in spite of the many laudatory efforts concerning the learning of Indigenous languages, most recently the general trends in language learning are described by Cortés Vargas et al. (2008) in the following (translated from the Spanish with a slight stylistic change):

The majority of the indigenous schools of the country's Hispanization predominates directly [with] only 63 percent of the indigenous teachers speaking an indigenous language. There is a linguistic disorientation [since the] teachers that speak an indigenous language work in a community that speaks another and only 20 percent use the indigenous language but used only as a means of students acquiring sufficient Spanish to go on in classes in that language. Bilingualism that is theoretically the main focus at the indigenous preschool and primary grades have not been forthcoming for indigenous students. For students who have had little contact in Spanish, the teaching is unintelligible. Learning is problematic without even considering the displacement and loss of linguistic diversity that these practices induce.

While there may be variances in this generalization with specific schools in specific areas that do not fit this characterization and where a dual language approach that emphasizes linguistic and content learning in both languages is operational, this does seem to be the exception. Direct communication in the Indigenous languages seems to be uncommon. For the most part teachers are spoken to in Spanish by students and responded to in Spanish, with the Indigenous languages regulated to translation functions by speakers of the specific languages in the school. This is especially the case where migrant Indigenous students have moved to an area like the San Quintín Valley in Baja California, in a school that has a variety of Mixe and a few other languages spoken. While there is cultural attention paid in the form of festivities, celebrations, and Indigenous rituals, the formalization process of language use is not the norm, according to academic presentations made recently.[21]

According to the *Catálogo de las lenguas indígenas nacionales: Variantes lingüísticas de México* (*National Catalogue of Indigenous Languages: Linguistic Variation of Mexico*), the Indigenous languages of Mexico consist of 11 families of languages, 68 subfamilies, and 300 language variants (2008). Yet of the 143 Indigenous languages of Mexico, 60 are at risk of extinction, with 21 in extreme danger (Dell'Amore 2014). As figure 26 shows, there are at least 3 languages crucially in danger of extinction, with 15 severely or definitely in danger, some with as few as 2 speakers in the northern edges of the southern part of the region.

Like the Purepechas mentioned above, Indigenous migration both within country and migration between the southern to the northern regions of southwestern North America certainly are not conducive to maintaining languages. In the present, there are no accurate figures of how many Mexican Indigenous persons there are in the northern regions. Although statistical information on the Mexican Indigenous presence in the north and in the United States is found wanting, the CDI estimates that in 2010 the total Mexican Indigenous population, using the Population Census of 2010 of the Institute of Statistics and Geography (INEGI), was 15.7 million,

Endangered languages of Mexico
- ● Critically endangered (21)
- ○ Definitely or severely endangered, or vulnerable (122)

500 mi
500 km

NGM STAFF
SOURCE: UNESCO

FIGURE 26. "Sixty Languages at Risk of Extinction in Mexico?" Source: Christine Dell'Amore (2014).

of which 11.1 million live in Indigenous households. Of the 15.7 million, 6.6 million speak an Indigenous language while of the other 9.1 million, 400,000 do not consider themselves Indigenous (*Diario Oficial* 2014). Moreover, of the total number, 2 million lived outside of Mexico; the majority of these reside in the United States. "Thus about 18 percent of the total Mexican Indigenous population may have migrated north" ("Migrantes indígenas, un tema pendiente," *Letras Libres* 2014; my translation).[22] When such loss of a large portion of the population to migration north occurs, then it would not be expected that any of the Indigenous languages would be retained at bilingual levels by their children, given the erasing processes of both American educational institutions unprepared for these students and the sheer 24-hour bombardment of the media through its multiple electronic channels. In fact, from personal observation of Purepecha children in the Coachella Valley, these students were placed in Spanish classes to learn Spanish to prepare them for English as Second Language classes that are not conducive to language maintenance. Or frankly, these children are doubly erased by Spanish and then compounded by English.

As for internal migration, in the example of the Purepechas in Ensenada provided above, even with "bilingual programs," even the best are not well executed since there are so few Indigenous speakers of the specific languages needed at any one time. Then given the mobility of the children and their parents, a consistent curriculum for children would be improbable. When the national migratory streams combine with the transborder avenues for some of the major migrating populations like the Mixteca of Oaxaca, then the dispersal routes for Indigenous speaking children mitigate strongly against them, as figure 27 shows clearly.

On the other hand, there is a national recognition for Mexico to revitalize, reinforce, and develop Mexican Indigenous languages that acts as a counterweight to these

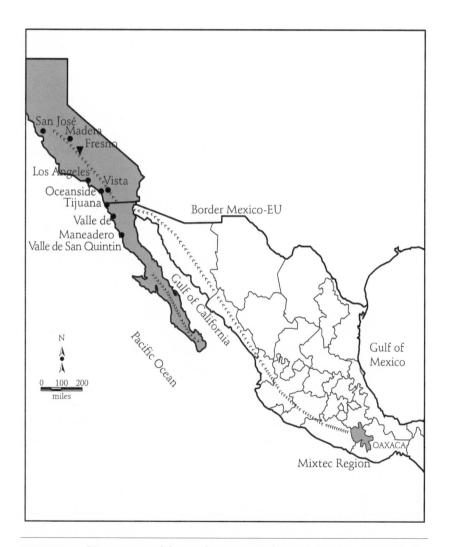

FIGURE 27. "Organización y liderazgo de migrantes indígenas en México y Estados Unidos. El caso del FIOB." Migracion y Desarrollo. Source: Laura Velasco Ortiz (2014). http://www .scielo.org.mx/scielo.php?script=sci_arttext&pid=S1870–75992014000200004.

processes of language loss due to migration, institutional incapacity, poor preparation of and lack of qualified teachers in the major languages, and lack of national integration of the languages in a functional manner.

COMMENTARY

The regional history of language use cannot be disassociated from the political ecology, economy, and conflict over resources by contending peoples and especially during the Spanish colonial, American, and Mexican periods. Hegemonic material processes are crucial to understanding the formations and stratifications of populations throughout the region, from the mission-oriented schools led by Franciscans and Jesuits to the results of the political restructuring of the region by contending national states, each with different versions of their educational obligations to their subordinated populations. In contrast to the pre-Hispanic period of bilingualism, lingua francas, sign, and long-distance communications, during the colonial period Spanish predominated but was often countered by acts of informed ignorance, choosing one language over the other as contexts dictated. Whether in the confessional, feigning ignorance of Spanish to the questioning of the priest in San Xavier del Bac in what is now Arizona, or appropriating the petition process by the Genizaros shown in appendix C, counterhegemonies emerged.[23] For the Mexican child being struck by a shaved baseball bat or riding crop, or being banged against the desk, there still emerged the adult who could tell the difference between these linguistic agents of language destruction from those who protected them simultaneously. For the Yaqui, for more than one hundred years, they have faced the modern nineteenth- and twentieth-century Mexican state in its various formulations and preferred war or exile to combat their cultural, linguistic, and spatial expropriation and extermination. Theirs is a tragic narrative of a courageous people who to this minute refuse to be defeated. For all of these peoples, the struggle for cultural, linguistic, and spatial security has and continues to be an engagement that does not cease. These struggles take multiple forms of communication and language expression, from newspapers to programs of instruction, from local attempts to retain language functions to university attempts to relocate the cultural functions of identity weakened but seldom lost, which we take up next. It is from these "me's" and "you's and "us's" and the "other," that we can come to understand how the seemingly powerless simply say "si se puede" and to a limited extent unhinge hegemonic processes.

5

THE RISE OF THE COCKROACH PEOPLE AND THEIR CULTURAL CITIZENSHIP

৵

The Making of an Unsiloed History

La cucaracha, la cucaracha,	*The cockroach, the cockroach,*
ya no puede caminar	*can't walk anymore*
porque le falta, porque no tiene	*because it's lacking, because it doesn't have*
marihuana pa' fumar.	*marijuana to smoke.*

THE REFRAIN OF THIS VERSION of the famous song from the Mexican Revolution was originally a song with different lyrics from medieval Spain belittling Moorish troops in comparison to Spanish infantry.[1] The Mexican revolutionary version is a caustic and damning narrative of the dictatorship and person of Victoriano Huerta, who murdered Francisco I. Madero, the revolutionary leader and first post-revolutionary president. Huerta selected himself president of Mexico with the help of the American ambassador and served for a year until he was exiled. He died in El Paso, Texas, after a circuitous route from the Caribbean to Europe to El Paso.[2] The song features marijuana centrally to denote Huerta as a drug-addicted sadist who wobbled when he walked under its influence and was unambulatory when he was not.[3] Many versions came out of the revolution and from different factions, such as Francisco Villa and Emiliano Zapata, and following them came more sedate versions to the present (Leal 1954,17).[4] But there is also a subtext to the revolutionary version in that also present is a call to arms of the downtrodden. In a turning twist of a Mexican *relajo* (joking quip) the cockroach of Huerta dies but the people arise, who Oscar Zeta Acosta in his autobiography[5] later referred to as the "Cockroach People"—that is, "Chicanos" in the northern region because of their endurance, capacity to survive, revolt, and excellence over adversity (ibid.).[6] This link between the revolution and the metaphorical revolutionary cockroach people was first made by Octavio I. Romano-V. (1969b) prior to Acosta's work, with his own essay, "Goodbye Revolution—Hello

Slum," which was among the first published, critical associations between "where we had been and where we were."[7] With a million Mexicans fleeing north and another million killed, the region as well as the country were convulsed by violence and radical changes of governments, peoples, and conditions. Both Acosta and Romano brought this relationship frontally and it clicked in the Chicano movement.

This was and is a historical and cultural referent for this population as a marker of extraordinary resistance at many levels of human endeavor—panoramic and transborder in scope and touching every locality, household, and family from prior to 1910 through the present, albeit somewhat dissipated by the 1990s. For many, the revolution was not a stranger and the connections were made by narratives from parents and grandparents of the region. At times stories were brutal and violent and at other times filled with the hopes and dreams of those who lived the transitions from revolution to barrios. It was often said in disbelief that in at least two past generations, every family had at least one revolutionary in each familial network, and grandparents especially were suspect of embellishments. But more than likely this disbelief proved itself to be wrong when their curious children looked into it much later, and sometimes in fact families had multiple participants on opposite sides of the conflict.[8] And certainly with much more than facts were children buttressed with layers of resistance to tyranny and a refusal to be given up or give up, as Hank López (1967, 81) recalls in his memorable early work:

> No doubt my chagrin [to being treated ahistorically] was accentuated by the fact that Pancho Villas's exploits were a constant topic of conversation in our household. My entire childhood seems to be shadowed by his presence. At our dinner table, almost every night, we would listen to endlessly repeated accounts of this battle, that stratagem, or some great act of Robin Hood kindness by "el centauro del norte . . ." As if to deepen our sense of Villismo, my parents also taught us "*Adelita*" and *Se llevaron el cañon para Bachimba* ("They took the canons to Bachimba") the two most famous songs of the Mexican revolution.

This narrative of participation also had another side—these were tales of memory of struggles, of opposition, of impossible odds, of overwhelming tragedy and triumphs, and not the least also was the fracturing of families by death, forced migrations, escapes, and "moving north." These dynamic narratives joined those narratives already present in the northern region of struggles to survive and contend with warring and raiding warriors, of intermarrying with the same, and dealing with droughts and long commercial roads between north and south, and with familial relations crosscutting political bifurcations and ethnicities. Those dynamic narratives moving north intermarried with those already present in Tucson, El Paso, San Diego, Douglas,

Laredo, Nogales, Las Cruces, Albuquerque, Los Angeles, San Antonio, and anywhere Mexicans resided both before and after the border imposition, such as Chicago. In many ways, the north become more Mexican, with a million Mexicans fleeing the revolution to be housed by cousins and brothers, and aunts and uncles in towns and cities like those just mentioned. These millions amply made up for the thousands who went voluntarily or were forced to go across the new border of a now fractured southern region after the American-Mexican War and the Treaty of the Mesilla and joined the eighty thousand who remained.[9]

But what also crossed over onto an un-strange land, like those who had been moving through rather than across for many centuries in Octavio Romano-V's version, was "not only an attenuated version of the Revolution [that] continue[d] in the north, with plot and counterplot, avoidance and memories of hate, but also [one that] continued the ideas, the intellectualizations, and the philosophies of the day" (1969b, 33–34). These were multiple arguments and multiple dimensions that may have been original to the now-crossed region to the south, but many also merged with what was here, and these will be taken up shortly.

Yet few of these multiple and layered narratives joined standard English-language periodicals and books, printed or published in any other form or medium. For the most part "the Cockroach People" were left out of the northern American narrative through much of the nineteenth and certainly most of the mid-twentieth-century narrative, except for typecast literary versions.[10] Willa Cather, for example, wrote of decadent Mexican priests and heroic French replacements in New Mexico in *Death Comes for the Archbishop*. Caricatures by John Steinbeck of lazy and mostly "Paisano" Mexican fishmongers enjoying limited mental capacities in Monterrey Bay, California, ruled *Cannery Row*. Frank Dobie's too many works expressed his condescending and patronizing Texas renditions of a Mexican vaquero's "loyalty" for their "amos" as equal to the "befo de wah'darky and as trustsworthy."[11] No comment is necessary from this last phrase.

The social sciences were not too far apart from these characterizations but relied, however, on "measures" ranging from IQ tests to performance tests in English for monolingual Spanish-speaking children. These tests set the tone, structure, and curriculum of language instruction for Mexican children and guaranteed the fracturing of valuable cultural resources—the Spanish language and as importantly the shared intellectual and historical presence untold in the erasing language. It was this revolutionary generation's children who suffered most in the process and often became the subject of eugenically premised tests of intelligence and mental capacities, manual dexterity, and naturalized assertions that Mexican bodies were able to withstand high temperatures in desert regions within the SWNAR. These premises were grounded on language, biology, and academic instruction of utility—not on reflection, remediation, or capacities for improvement. Simultaneously, they denied their historical experience and replaced it with a form of coerced acculturation. It was an early twentieth-century rendition of the "seeing man" rationale.

EUGENICS, LANGUAGE, CULTURE, AND THE MEXICAN "PROBLEM" AND THEIR DISCONTENTS

Thus especially the children of the revolution and Mexicans already present was visited upon them, as I have said elsewhere (Vélez-Ibáñez 1996), the eugenics social science paradigm of the 1920s that regarded Mexican children as intellectually inferior because of "blood" admixture, with an "emotional nature," and appearing "dull and stupid." This hegemonic imposition was singularly responsible, as was the adoption of scripted characterizations of Mexican-origin children. They "dehistoricized" and siloed generations of the population into a sort of national educational holding pen of inferiority and incapacity. Genetics aside in the modern sense, these analyses were presented as the defining paradigms for the "Mexican" educational problem until replaced by the paradigms of simplified and often simple-minded culture and language associations, although "retardation" seemed to have remained an underlying subtext even into the 1960s under the guise of the twentieth-century "seeing man" rationale.

It also simultaneously constructed a paradigmatic, ahistorical, linguistic, and cultural vacuum of the population reduced to these characteristics under the guise of a type of "seeing man" rationale. It was ensconced within the educational institutional narrative that influenced the manner in which the Mexican populations was perceived and defined largely as ahistorical beings tainted by language, custom, behavior, and these nascent erroneous biological characteristics.

Even though these have been replaced by a plethora of educational acronyms, typecasting children by language "ability" (addressed in the next chapter), from the epistemological premises, the labeling of "abilities" has as a reference and prism the hegemonic language without regard to the linguistic cultural capital of the children's own language. A subtext of inferiority undergirds all following meganarrative typifications and "treatments" of language instruction, including those in the present and their acronyms as an unintended but certain consequence. Removing the offending language is removing the historical cultural presence of its population and thus creates a people without a history, as Wolf has reminded us. Instead, history books for Mexican-origin students and their parents of this period and for many that followed were bereft of its many-layered narrative following in this chapter.

The underlying basis for exclusion and ahistoricism emerges from early eugenics movements without doubt and tied to immigration fears in the 1920s of Mexicans. The eugenics argument raises its serpentine head in the present almost one hundred years later so that the massive immigration expulsions, raids, arrests, fracturing of families, and the immense psychological and emotional costs in the present are directly associated with the long-standing nativist tradition discussed earlier and given substance by referring to the costs of educating Mexican-origin children especially.[12] Those in the present and last century are strongly associated with eugenics and racist-oriented associations and organizations, as will be discussed also in the next chapter.

Thus the typification of the intellectual and academic incapacities of Mexican children during the eugenics period was an essential part of the rationale for the expulsion of Mexicans in the 1930s when 500,000 Mexicans were expelled, of which 165,000 were American citizens (Vélez-Ibáñez 1996, n57, 288). Such actions in the past and in the present have been buttressed by the development of the "retardation" and "culturally different" paradigms still affecting directly and indirectly Mexican children and to this moment in regards to language development and pedagogy.

THE LINE OF DESCENT OF
THE EUGENICS PARADIGM[13]

In a brilliant unpublished essay by Ron López written in 1968, "*Los Repatriados*," he correctly connected the relationships between eugenics-oriented immigration narratives and racialist organizations and associations in the first half of the twentieth century.[14] He stated that among the first public expressions of that association as to the alleged effects of racial mixture and immigration was Kenneth L. Roberts in 1928 in a series of articles, among other pieces by Roberts and other writers.[15] Roberts ". . . became well known for his articles in the *Saturday Evening Post* on immigration and its danger to the Nordic people" (81). López states that Roberts expressed a concern for mixing with Mexicans by the following: "we'll have another mixed-race problem; and as soon as a race is mixed it is inferior. Those who think otherwise are merely uninstructed in biology" (81).

According to López, such racial premises were strongly buttressed by a series of organizations especially focused on "racial mixing" as the basis for deportation and expulsions. These included the following: the Immigration Study Commission of California, Immigration Restriction League, Order of White Citizens of America, National Society of Daughters of the American Revolution, and the National Society of Sons of the American Revolution (37). However, not only were obvious racist organizations involved but also organizations supported by well-known academicians (38).

One of these was the Allied Patriotic Societies Inc., whose vice president appeared before the Immigration and Naturalization Committee "with a memorial signed by 44 well known professors and scientists which 'expressed their fear that there could be no 'racial status quo' and, therefore, no 'reasonable degree of racial homogeneity'" (38). Basic racial homogeneity was necessary, they felt, for a civilization to have its best development (38). The list of those who signed the memorial included professors from Princeton, Harvard, the University of Wisconsin, Yale, New York University, the University of Michigan, and Columbia (8). More specifically, López mentions the following: C. C. Little, president of the University of Michigan; A. Lawrence Lowell, president of Harvard; Madison Grant, president of the New York Zoological Society; and Robert C. Ward, professor of climatology of Harvard (38). In addition, López points out that "the American Federation of Labor's position of immigration had long been restrictionist and in 1924 it had adopted the 'eugenics' argument" (39).

This eugenically laced argument seeped into the educational literature in sheep's clothing masked by reasonableness and logic and undergirded by the "seeing man" assumption. One of the first of the modern proposals that equates "Mexican" with inferiority and "American" with superiority is R. F. Dickerson, "Some Suggestive Problems in the Americanization of Mexicans," which appeared in the *Pedagogical Seminary* of September 1919. This periodical, primarily directed for the consumption of teachers, was by its very title designed to describe for educators the latest in methodological educational innovations and findings. The study, ironically written by the director of the YMCA in Tucson, begins with this description: "how large and difficult a part of our Americanization problem these people constitute" (283). His rationale of course is based on the eastern meganarrative of assimilation without regard to the last Mexican flag being lowered sixty-two years before across the street from the building that housed the YMCA.[16] He states, using the race terminology of the period: "Considerable numbers of this race are already well Americanized and are represented by many able, cultured and respected men and women" (288). Nevertheless, he states, "As a rule the Mexican boy is much retarded because he is instilled with . . . more or less primitive habits of living; illiterate, and devoid of American influences" (295). He is ". . . by an inclination to be more retiring than the American boy; temperamentally lack buoyancy and optimism of our own youth Anglo" (95).[17] He is not civilized or American. Thus retardation, although learned or "instilled," which by extension must be eliminated, is a consequence of being "Mexican" and must be snuffed out. The underlying premise for such elimination lies in the fact that others of the "race" are already well-rendered spotless, now cultured, and American, with the inferior Mexican "racial" characteristics erased. While an argument could be considered that this is not a "racist" argument but a "cultural" one—the former employing biological associations and the latter learned behavior—the cultural argument is glued to a necessary and sufficient premise that denotes inferiority to be eliminated or "whitened," to use more contemporary parlance, and is a replacement nomenclature for sheer biological terms. "Whiteness" is the privileged position denoting power and command and "civilization," certainly extending to language use and denotation of worth and value, as Hill (1993a, 1993b, 1995, and 1998) and others have developed. This will be discussed below.[18]

A year after Dickerson, Grace C. Stanley (1920) called for the formation of activity curricula especially designed for segregated schools. She totally opposed unsegregated schools for Mexicans because, as she points out, "in a mixed school certain features stand out for the casual onlooker . . . Mexicans . . . are handicapped by the lack of home training, by shyness, by an emotional nature, all of which interfere with their progress in the conventional course of study." (715). In addition, she states that "they appear dull, stupid, phlegmatic . . . restive in school and truant whenever possible." (ibid.). Because of this appearance, these children must be placed in separate schools where the results will show that her comments are valid. Her rationale for this comment: "We all know that Mexicans are different. . . . They have . . . native dexterity, penship [sic], drawing, handiwork, and stronger sense of rhythm" (ibid., 718). The Mexican then, is genetically strongest in the purely physical aspects of human activities because "[t]hey are primarily interested in action and emotion but grow listless under purely mental effort" (ibid.). Not surprisingly, the curriculum constructed for the Mexican at its core will be activity-centered tasks, for as can be judged from "the mental characteristics of the Mexican, our present course of study is entirely inadequate" (ibid.). Instead, the objectives of this type of curriculum should be the entrance into "skilled occupations . . . a new course of study with activities and occupations as the central thought" (ibid.). Intellectually inferior, she relegates Mexican children totally to a mechanical arts and crafts curriculum: "We need to cultivate the creative ability rather than the critical and analytical for the Mexican illustrates as he does in the large what is true only in a lesser degree of most of us" (ibid.).

Four years later one of the most important "empirical," studies done in the twenties is William H. Sheldon's "The Intelligence of Mexican Children" (1924). It is important because the effects of this study set the stage for the myriad number of pseudo-scientific projects; most of these had one primary objective: to empirically test the racial inferiority of the Mexican based on the differences of test scores. First a careful examination of Sheldon's basic premises will reveal a number of fallacious assumptions of the nature of tests and their reliability. His first premise is that "[s]ince it is now well established that intelligence tests enable us to compare one child with another . . . it seems probable that in the same way we can reliably compare the intelligence of different races by means of such tests" (139). This jump from the individual to a group for comparison using the same test violates rather strongly underlying test principles of any sort, and more critical is that these could reliably "test" for "intelligence."

That is, according to the author, test givers can reliably compare the intelligence of individual persons among the Iatmul people of New Guinea and the Eskimo of Baffin Island and make group comparisons from the then-constructed test results. If the comparison seems inordinately ludicrous to point out Sheldon's weaknesses, the next statement by the author may compensate for unnecessary exaggeration: "Moreover we can in this way by the use of intelligence tests get definite comparisons for each year of chronological age, in terms of mental age, and [at] last a picture of the development of intelligence year by year in the races studied" (139). However, within their descriptions of the study itself, he has included a very important piece of information that reinforces the basic theme that runs through the attitudes held by educators and test givers of the period. The author described the linguistic sampling area covered in testing one hundred Anglos and one hundred Mexicans in the spring of 1923 in Roswell, New Mexico: "In one school which had 100 of the Mexican population, teachers made themselves understood by the use of sort of a Spanish-English dialect colloquially called "'spic' or 'mongrel Spanish'" (140). Since the test was in English and since "spic" was the means of communication between teachers and children, there was a question of reliability in the responses of the children since their major means of communication was this "mongrel Spanish."

Following this, the author then described results of using the Cole and Vincent Test. Among other findings, Sheldon states, "While the I.Q. average for the Anglo was 104.8, it was 89 for the Mexican" (140), and considering the major medium of communication was "spic," the Mexican score was remarkable; it seemed to allow some transliteration to the English test. Moreover, he constructed an average IQ range description to reinforce the conclusions for a number of nationalities. The Mexican was fifth among nine nationalities cited, being five IQ points below the Chinese and two points above Indians (141). He states the following:

1. The average mental age reached its maximum [for the Mexican] at around nine years, while the curve representing white mental age continues to rise with chronological age (142);

2. Obviously as the children grow older, the superiority of the whites become greater ... the evidence points toward the probability that the difference will be found to increase constantly until the maximum is reached. The conclusion is in keeping with the results of investigations of Negro intelligence. For this race there occurs for a period of standstill at about the 10th year, beyond which mental development is continued only in exceptional cases (142);

3. Mexicans were equal in rote memory, visual, interest in numbers, including comprehension of time periods while whites were superior in comprehension, judgment, higher associative processes (142).

In summary, the author reiterates that first, Mexicans retained an average IQ of 85, and second, would perpetually show less mental development as chronological age increased (142). The conclusions then, supported by "empirical" evidence provided the type of support for "activity curriculums" that like-minded educators would insist upon for Mexican children throughout the Southwest. Shop classes for boys and home economics for girls were quite popular through the 1960s. Such special curricula would not include the "critical and analytical" alternatives necessary for development. One ramification of this study is that it was read before the American Association for the Advancement of Science in Nashville, Tennessee, and thus given the imprimatur of scientific legitimacy. One may pose the question: of the members of AAAS, how many scientists and educators were influenced by these conclusions about the inherent intellectual limitations of Mexicans?

Of significance is that a year before this study, T. R. Garth began using the National Intelligence Test on 1,004 Mexican children beginning in 1922 and ending in 1927. Garth (794) made the following conclusions:

1. Median NIT I.Q., 78.1
2. 1.1 years younger in mental age than Anglo
3. 80.5 of children were retarded

This last extraordinary finding, it would seem, was somehow not attentive to basic statistical rules about the distribution of characteristics in any normal curve of any sort and was skewed so badly that he did a retest a few years later. The retest of 683 Mexican children included 200 who could not speak English and the findings did not vary from the original (Garth 1934, 222). However, more pressing and contributing to the development of the eugenics-laden premises of Mexican inferiority was his review of race psychology research.[19] Garth (1925) identified forty-five studies of nineteen racial groups and concluded that "[t]hese studies taken all together seem to indicate the mental superiority of the white race" (359). He changed his position on racial inequality in IQ testing and supported the idea of equality in his 1930 article, even though he continued to give English tests to monolingual Spanish-dominant Mexican pupils.[20]

But, as in all things academic, the dynamic to study creates its own rationale. In 1924, using both anthropological and psychological techniques, a study was conducted in Tucson, Arizona, to test the effects of Indigenous blood and its melanin correlation on mental status.[21] The study by Franklin C. Paschal and Louis R. Sullivan (1925) was conducted with nine- and twelve-year-old Mexican children in Tucson, with the cooperation of the superintendent of schools, C. E. Rose (I may add that an elementary school three blocks from this writer's former home was named after this superintendent). The following is the stated "problem" Paschal and Sullivan set forth: "The problem is to analyze the group into its racial elements and to determine how these elements compare with each other physically and mentally" (2). By racial elements, they meant cranial size, physiology, differences, and shades in melanin, the most important element. It set forth the stated objective of finding empirical differences in mental ability according to physical differences among Mexican children. The investigators' correlations are described in their conclusions and remarkable findings:

1. That in studies of race psychology, the psychologist and the anthropologist should cooperate, because only when subjects of the psychologist are analyzed biologically into their racial elements can we really speak of race differences in mental ability.

2. Tucson Mexicans who are partially of Indian origin have a lower mental age than those Tucson Mexicans who are wholly of white origin.

3. That our results are in agreement with those investigators who have found a *definite* relationship between the proportion of Indian blood and mental status.

4. The correlation between mental score and individual race characters are very small in a group like this in which intermixture has taken place for so many generations. Of those chosen [in the study], skin color shows the highest correlation with mental scores.

5. Tucson Mexican children born in Mexico have an appreciably higher mental score than Tucson Mexican children born in Tucson. This indicates a more favorable selection of immigrants from Mexico in recent years. (73–74)

But significantly this work and especially T.R. Garth's findings were influential in Paul Popenoe and Roswell Hill Johnson's *Applied Eugenics* (1933). Citing Garth's remarks that Mexicans have attained an IQ of 70, Popenoe and Johnson state:

In the light of such facts as the foregoing, it seems premature . . . to argue that there are no fundamental differences of mentality between different races . . . [there is] . . . no evidence of equality . . . it is incumbent on all who are charged with framing national policies, to proceed on the assumption that there are marked differences between the various races of mankind and that, in some cases at least, these differences are so wide that one race may properly be spoken of as inferior to another in average endowment with a given characteristic. (1933, 284)

Regarding intermarriage the authors warn of the effect of "mongrelization" (to use their term):

> If one race is inferior to another, and if the partners in question are representative of their respective races, then the mating is between two persons, one of whom is inferior to the other germinally [sic], and the offspring will usually be inferior to those resulting from a better assorted mating. This result introduces no new idea. It is obvious and, in principle, not subject to dispute. (284)[22]

Contemporary social scientists may scoff at the inherent fallacy of these propositions as well as the melanin shade analysis, yet such studies did in fact create a layering to "whiteness" by associating intelligence among Mexicans with melanin so that expectations for children were very much influenced by how they looked. Thus if the child was *guero* (blonde), then more than likely teachers would pay more attention to the child. Signals were always displayed in school for the favorable treatment of blue-eyed Mexican children, who were considered exotic but were often showered with compliments of difference.[23]

However, studies concerning the mental capacity of Mexican children continued unabated, and O. K. Garretson's 1925 work in Tucson, Arizona (again), was his "A Study of Causes of Retardation in a Small Public School System" (1928). Again using English-standardized "mental" tests, his conclusions do not seem to differ from others in that "probably the principle factor governing retardation of the Mexican child is his mental ability as measured by the group test" (278).[24] However, Garretson's opinions did not deviate from his study in the ensuing years. He taught the history of education at the University of Arizona until his death in 1968. How much influence this study had on the instruction of language and academic subjects in Tucson is difficult to ascertain, but what is certain is that especially in high school, Mexican pupils were steered toward vocational subjects and often discouraged from seeking more academic instruction in mathematics and language, or were "tracked" in "slow classes where in such classes in unsegregated schools 100% of the pupils were Mexicans like those described previously."[25]

Studies focusing on manual and vocational strengths of Mexican children and their success contributed to the literature on mental ability and the forming of "special" curriculums. Merton E. Hill's work published in 1925 premised the following: "The Mexican children are actually making only 42% as satisfactory progress through the schools as are the children of other races. . . . The Mexican pupils have only 58% as good ability to do the work of the schools as have the American pupils; yet they have 90% as good ability as American pupils to do manual work, they show equal capacity in penmanship" (98).[26]

With this in mind, Hill proposed and recommended the following curriculum:

1. Simple arithmetic leading to a mastery of the four fundamental processes should be developed. This should be done for the mere protection of the adults in their small business relations.
2. Penmanship lessons should be developed, and the Mexican pupils and adults given an opportunity to written language for they appear to be adept in a certain manual dexterity that leads to proficiency in penmanship.
3. Lessons in hygiene and health.
4. As the Mexicans are lovers of music and art, lessons should be developed so that they may become trained along these lines wherein they show great proficiency.
5. As the Mexicans showed considerable aptitude for handwork of any kind, courses should be developed that will aid them in becoming skilled workers with their hands. Girls should be trained to become domestic servants, and to do various kinds of handwork for which they can be paid adequately. (101)

Further reinforcement for this proposition about the natural dexterity of Mexicans is the work by E. Lamb (1930), "Racial Differences in Bi-Manual Dexterity of Latin and American Children."

Lamb, after careful "empirical" study, concluded the following: "It does appear that a certain racial groups of stocks [including Mexicans] develop early skill in manipulation greater than the average of American children" (231).[27] Following these works, J. C. Merian in "Activity Curriculum in School of Program" (1933) quoted M. E. Hill's "The Development of the Americanization Programs," and concluded that, in general, "to date [the activity curriculum implemented] indicates a highly satisfactory achievement in . . . activities" (306).[28]

How directly such findings and contemporary attitudes and racialisms steeped into the works of analysis can be appreciated by attention to a large-scale analysis of teacher and pupil interaction in Texas. In 1934, Walter C. Coers published his "Comparative Achievement of White and Mexican Junior High School Pupils."[29] Coers initiated his studies with the following premises: "Since Mexicans, under school regulations of Texas are classed as white, children of these foreigners have open to them all the educational opportunities available to the children of other white races, and were brought to the schools by the compulsory laws present a problem which school authorities have to face" (157). Among the most pressing issues is that "[i]n attempting to bring about the assimilation of these Spanish-speaking children with the children for the school originally planned, teacher and administrators have come to realize the importance of knowing how the achievement of these foreign children compares with that of children of other white stock. As a contribution to that end the present study will attempt to determine the relative achievement of the white and Mexican children as found by standard tests" (157).

After extensive testing supported findings of the poor performance of Mexican children, Coers formulated a carefully thought-out conclusion:

1. In comparing the relative achievement of the two groups [Mexican and Anglo], the fact that the white children are superior to the Mexican children in mental ability must be kept in mind.

2. The Mexican groups in all three grades achieved more in proportion to their *mental* abilities than the whites on all parts except the language tests. (Italics mine: 162)

These conclusions, from whatever position is taken, not only reinforce the alleged inferiority of Mexican children but also provide a kind of "surprise" rationale to findings that may not quite coincide, since Mexican children achieved more in proportion to their alleged limits of mental capacity. But language, regardless of surprises, was the weakest in achievement and thus additional needs for "special" education would be indicated but very much defined by the premise of a limited mental capacity. Whatever instruction developed and followed had to be limited in quality in order to deal with limited inherent biological ability.

How these studies were reflected in the behavioral interaction between teachers and pupils is discussed in a study of the period. Guy West in "Race Attitudes among Teachers in the Southwest" (1936) compared Mexican-origin with Anglos teachers and reached these conclusions:

1. Mexican teachers had a tendency to pronounce no differences in superiority and inferiority among Anglo and Mexican students.

2. Anglo teachers were more strongly inclined than were the Mexican to claim superiority for Anglo students except in four areas: consideration, courtesy, tolerance, and discipline.

3. On the average, Anglo teachers appeared to claim superiority for Anglo students by more than twice as great.

4. Mexican teachers were more inclined to reflect attitudes of racial equality.

5. The existence of a superior attitude among Anglo teachers was obvious. (331)

It is interesting to note that in two classifications Anglo teachers preferred Anglo students over Mexicans in the highest percentage shown: 73.9 concerning intelligence and 69.5 concerning ambition.

How far the eugenics proposition had seeped into all aspects of instruction, and especially language for that period, is reflected in the work of L. W. Johnson in 1938, which appeared in the February issue of the *Journal of Educational Psychology*, enti-tled "A Comparison of the Vocabularies of Anglo-American and Spanish American High School Pupils."[30] He shows compassion and concern for the plight of the Mex-ican child who is tested by biased devices; he states: "There is general accord that, when measured by devices and standards used in the schools of the United States, the Spanish-American pupils are greatly handicapped" (135). But he states that this is "nat-ural because the Spanish American is a different race. His motives, his tendencies, his philosophy of life, and his customs are very different. . . . And since he uses a different language early in life, his idioms of thought are necessarily different. . . . He has a care-free attitude, is reckless of action . . . and dramatic" (135). This behavioral reflection, however, is offset by a return to a eugenics position: "While vocabulary study treats directly with the linguistic phase [in order to show the differences between Mexicans and Anglos], it is *almost* as closely related to environment and is *directly tied up with hereditary aspects of the problem*" (italics mine, 136).

Lest however one may think that many of these studies remained within the con-fines of the United States, by 1959 in Brazil a book was written by Oliveira Vianna and titled *Raça e assimilição* (Race and Assimilation).[31] The book for our purposes is particularly relevant, for as its major "empirical" evidence to illustrate the dangers and weakness of "mongrelization" are none other than Paschal and Sullivan, and T. R. Garth's works conducted in Tucson, Arizona. The author states that "there are no defi-nite conclusions [but] there appears certain psychological lines that appears along the morphological profiles of mestizos" (35). He states that the amount of blood (white) will pretty much determine the intellectual status of that individual as concluded by Paschal and Sullivan, and reinforced by the conclusions by Garth. The author also in his Brazilian treatise, however, misplaced place (and spelling of "Tucson") as being situated sixty miles south in Sonora.

DEMOGRAPHICS OF LITERACY AND SPANISH AND COUNTER HEGEMONY AND ITS CONTENTS[32]

For the generation of the children of revolutionaries, then, theirs was not to be largely a language instruction of stimulation but of utility. Theirs was a manufactured lin-guistic destiny of learning "shop" English for mechanics and carpentry, and theirs was a constructed linguistic destiny of learning "home economics" or English "for everyday use." Spanish was not only denied but discouraged. Only in high school could they begin to explore Cervantes and Azuela. In spite of all of these eugenically oriented curricula, many were able to transcend and in fact to become other than that predefined by a hegemonic ideology of language erasure and learning limitations. But this was only made possible by the linguistic resources germinated at home and by the sheer persistence of the children of the parents of the revolution and Spanish-language newspapers especially. They themselves revolted after World War II and in the 1960s to the present; this issue will be presented in the following discussion. But it must also be said that Indigenous peoples suffered through and continue to suffer through similar processes and revolted accordingly.[33]

But there were great structural and demographic changes occurring simultaneously that continued to unfold throughout the nineteenth and twentieth centuries. The structure of the economy of the SWNAR was developing radically and quickly. Mining, agriculture, ranching, construction, increasing urbanization, and the introduction of the railroad created the dynamic need for the importation of labor from what had become south of the border. Starting in the mid-nineteenth century, Mexican individuals and households moved in small- and large-scale migrations into California's gold and agricultural fields, the developing ranching and marketing in Texas, the mines and cotton of Arizona, the founding of numerous Homestead Act–based ranches and farms in central and southern Arizona, and emerging and intensifying trade and commercial activities in Albuquerque, Los Angeles, San Francisco, San Antonio, Tucson, and all along the border cities facing each other. Emulating their earlier migrating kin, these nineteenth- and twentieth-century men and women moved throughout the region—border or not—westward, northward, and eastward.

In the 1920s Mexican anthropologist Manuel Gamio documented their origins across Mexico and their spread across the United States. While the majority stayed in the U.S. states adjoining the border, El Paso's railroad node connected them to all of the United States.[34] They were recruited—albeit in some cases illegally—or attracted by farming, mining, and the railroad by recruiting agents to the Midwest, such as the packing plants of Chicago and the automobile factories of Michigan, as well as the agricultural fields of New Jersey, Florida, and Indiana.[35] Or they were pushed out of Mexico by one-sided development strategies of absentee U.S. investors, by the lack of Mexican elites' willingness to build a viable modernizing economy, by depressions, natural calamities, and political instability as much as the labor-exploiting stability of the Porfiriato, the migration of political refugees during the French intervention, and the enormous displacement of peoples during the Mexican Revolution. Thus a series of new entradas from the south to the north and back again became part of the "normal" dynamic of an increasingly integrated political and economic region. In this manner, in part, for the SWNAR from Texas to California, Spanish literacy and language practices expanded and increased as well.

Figure 28 shows that migration from south to north has not abated since 1850 after the Treaty of Guadalupe Hidalgo in 1848. It illustrates the formative, developmental,

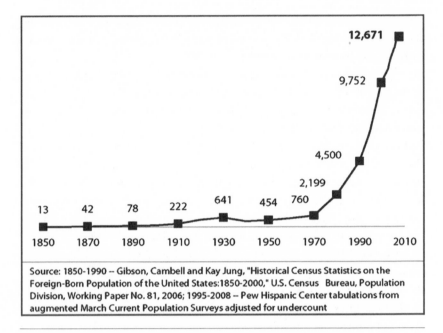

FIGURE 28. Original slide presentation by Douglas Massey for the Distinguished Wells Fargo Lecture, 2006, School of Transborder Studies, Arizona State University. Source: Massey 2006.

and structural process of an integrated regional economy.[36] It should be foregrounded that the 40 percent increase by 1870 was partially due to the exodus of parts of the Mexican intelligentsia during the French intervention, and the 1910 diaspora tripled the numbers of persons in part fleeing the Mexican Revolution.

THE EXPLOSION OF SPANISH LITERACY: COUNTERING THE "SEEING MAN"

Even though in 1808 *El Misisipí* became the first Spanish-language newspaper in the United States, published in New Orleans, a tradition of Hispanic American periodicals spread across the country and especially so in the SWNAR. We can illustrate from one period alone of the mid-nineteenth century to the early twentieth century how migrating Mexican populations developed numerous literacy practices that led to the formation of hundreds of Spanish-language newspapers. As such, newspapers may serve as a rough gauge of literacy in a language since there are no databases by which to determine levels or distribution of Spanish literacy for these periods, due to the fact that Mexican-origin populations were not asked for their literacy preferences in any U.S. census, nor were they separated from other "white" populations beginning in the 1860 census through 1880 in California, Texas, and the New Mexico Territory, which included Arizona.

Shortly after the French intervention in Mexico, hundreds of Mexicans moved across the new border in 1865, fleeing French political oppression. With them came a plethora of intellectuals to Tucson, Arizona, and El Paso, Laredo, and San Antonio, Texas, with their literary interests. They combined with residents already present to develop numerous newspapers and journals. Later, the Mexican Revolution and continued migration created even more audiences for literary works in the form of newspapers and cultural productions in theater. In Tucson, following the literary migration theme is that the Mexican community was largely literate and fairly well read in Mexican and Latin American literary classics. The people enjoyed reciting poetry, participating in declamation, and writing prose. Between about 1877 and 1921, literary works—including essays, poetry, short stories, and morality tales—were widely published in newspapers and sometimes in special supplements.

In spite of typecasting, language demolition, and mediocre curricula, Mexican communities in fact had vibrant Spanish-language media, performances, catechisms, and newspapers that served as the crucial means by which to retain and to develop Spanish beyond that taught in the household. As noted by Nick Kanellos (2000) in his pathbreaking work:

> Throughout the last two centuries, Hispanic communities from coast to coast have supported newspapers of varying sizes and missions, from the eight-page weekly printed in Spanish or bilingually to the highly entrepreneurial large-city daily published completely in Spanish. The periodicals have run the gamut from religious bulletins to international trade and scientific journals, as both the domestic and the international Hispanic readership have always been important targets for United States business and intellectual interests.[37]

These served the interests of those who were already in the northern region but also the million or more that moved north because of the Mexican Revolution, and forty-eight years before, in 1862, during the French intervention (as has been mentioned), and those migrating because of the structure of the developing industrial integrated economy. Spanish-language newspapers were not just read but became central mechanisms for providing platforms for not just a different narrative to that of the prevailing American megascript. They were vehicles for inspiring resistance, accommodation, adaptation, and protest, and they filled important social, political, cultural, and economic functions that their American counterparts could not and did not fulfill. As importantly, they were community links that supported myriad events like Cinco de Mayo, carnivals, and raffles for everything from helping the indigent to sponsoring lotteries for children's clothing or collecting monies for the remaining members of a family of someone killed by another or who died in the mines or on construction, or was bitten by a rattlesnake, kicked by a horse, run over by an automobile, or died of natural causes after surviving the revolution. Many were transborder in function and especially the exile newspapers, which many times represented both sides of political questions and sometimes only one, as Kanellos (2000, 26–28) has documented. They were the main defensive structures against housing, job, and accommodations discrimination but also emphasized citizenship and civil responsibility. They kept track of who lived and who died through the obituaries, which often were missing from their American counterparts. These guided relatives, friends, and neighbors to the right mortuary or church. Once there they closed the social hole made by a person's death with conversations, gossip, jokes, and men opening beer bottles outside in the parking lot. Special comments were made about those who were hypocrites or lived surreptitious lives, which had been mostly backstage and hidden until their lovers and children attended the funeral. Sometimes jokes on such things in sheep's clothing also appeared in special places in the newspapers for all to chortle at—but only in Spanish.

But beyond these deeply cultural, political, economic, and community functions, they were in fact the main source of literacy for many and a reminder of what needed to be kept, for they also advertised the latest plays and functions in Spanish. In Tucson alone between approximately 1877 and 1921, literary works—including essays, poetry, short stories, and morality tales—were published in thirty-two Spanish-language newspapers and magazines (Sheridan 1986).

The state of Arizona enjoyed the presence of ninety-two Spanish-language or bilingual newspapers and periodicals between 1877 and the middle of the twentieth century.[38] With few exceptions, all the journals in the 1870s were written either in Spanish alone, or half in Spanish and half in English.[39] Early writers included Francisco Dávila, Amado Cota-Robles, Carmen Celia Beltran, and Ramon Soto, with Beltran publishing through the 1940s. As well, dramatic arts, which intertwined the necessity of literate practices and oral skills, were exemplified in two theaters, Teatro Cervantes and Teatro Americano, which appeared in Tucson in the 1870s. They hosted traveling troupes like the *Compañia Dramatica Española*, whose director, Pedro C. de Pellón, founded the first group of amateur mostly Mexican-origin actors in the town, the Teatro Recreo in 1878. In the late nineteenth and early twentieth centuries, other theaters included El Principal, El Clifton, El Lirico, and El Royal, which was an important venue for La Nacional Dramatic Company. However, Carmen Soto Vásquez built Tucson's first theater explicitly for Spanish-language performances,

Teatro Carmen. The Sonoran-mission-style building was designed by renowned architect Manuel Flores, and its inaugural *Cerebro y Corazon* (Brains and Heart) was performed on May 20, 1915. Until 1923, Teatro Carmen performed Spanish-language literary productions, operas, musicals, and melodramas. Actors, plays, and play dates were featured in newspapers of the period (Sheridan 1986).[40]

Many persons of this generation continued writing in Spanish to relatives in California, Mexico City, and Sonora or wherever their relatives resided, as did many others throughout the region. While the context was Anglo-English, Mexican-origin populations used their knowledge to continue to keep and expand their cultural resource in novel and adaptive ways, as shown in this original example written in 1971 and represented in figure 29.[41]

Thus at a time in which there were no greeting cards in Spanish, the typeset language of the card is English, given that it was not until the 1980s that greeting cards were easily purchased in Spanish. This forced the writer to interject Spanish at two levels: first to integrate the written Spanish within the format of the message in English and then to unconsciously create the original phrase "Love *siempre*" as an ending platform in two languages, one by the writer and the other by the card maker. This is not Spanglish, which is oral expression, but rather the written language in English, which forced the writer to accommodate the document's written boundaries and structure but only to a point of linguistic comfort, which is largely unconscious and not deliberate. The English version of this would be "Love always" and this version, if it were Spanish, would be literally "*Amor siempre*," but in fact it is highly likely that the normative phrase would be "*siempre con mi amor or con mi amor siempre*" ("always with my love" in its literal translation but inverse in the last example).

Such capacities to linguistically manipulate both languages were very much associated with the availability of the hundreds of newspapers throughout the region. In New Mexico, Arturo Fernández-Gibert (2010) writes, "Nuevomexicanos managed to produce and sustain a booming Spanish-language press during the last two decades of the nineteenth century and the first decades of the twentieth century."[42] He supports his contention by stating that, in the 1880s, thirteen papers were published exclusively in Spanish, and in 1890 alone, forty-four followed suit (Meyer 1996: 8). Some of the most significant, according to Kanellos and Martell (2000), were *La Revista Catolica* of Las Vegas (1875–1918)—moved to El Paso in 1918 (to 1962)—*El tiempo* of Las Cruces (1882–1911), *EI boletín popular* of Santa Fe (1885–1908), *La voz del pueblo* (1888–1927) (founded in Santa Fe and moved to Las Vegas in 1890), *El nuevo mexicano* of Santa Fe (1890–1958), *El independiente* of Las Vegas (1894–1928), and *La bandera americana* of Albuquerque (1895–c. 1938), to name only a few (ibid.). Between 1844 and 1960, New Mexico had founded 357 Spanish-only and bilingual newspapers, with many concentrated in Albuquerque, Las Cruces, Las Vegas, Santa

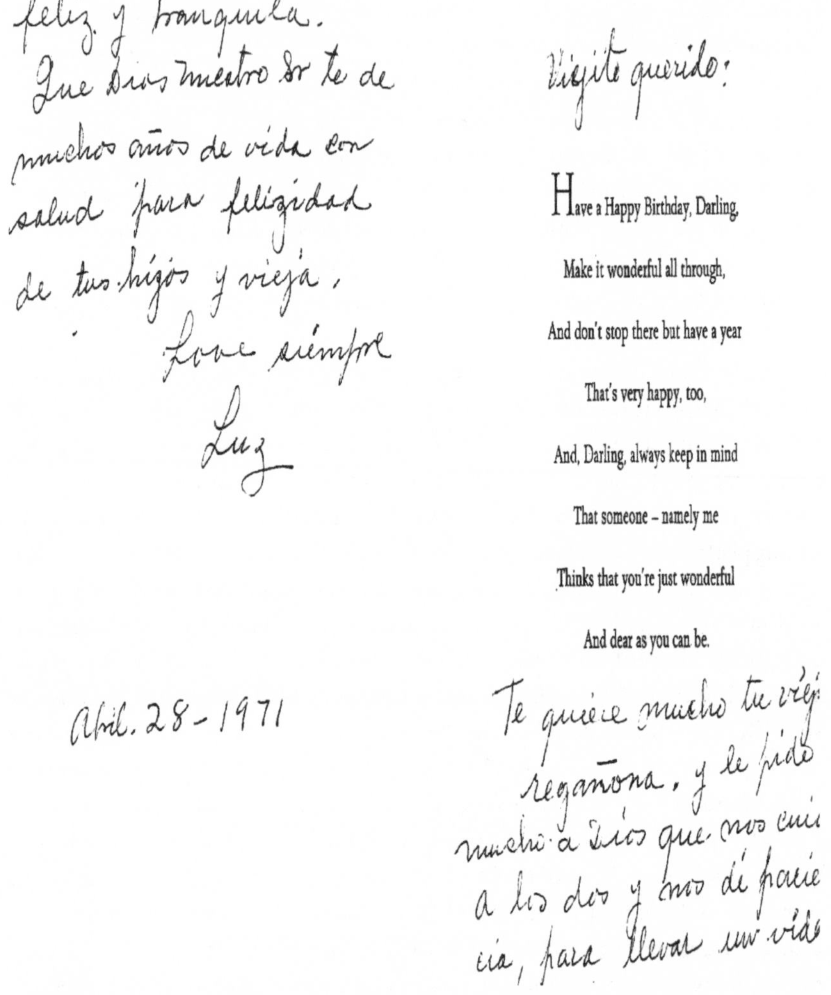

feliz y tranquila.
Que Dios nuestro Sr te de
muchos años de vida con
salud para felizidad
de tus hijos y vieja.
Love siempre
Luz

Viejito querido:

Have a Happy Birthday, Darling,

Make it wonderful all through,

And don't stop there but have a year

That's very happy, too,

And, Darling, always keep in mind

That someone – namely me

Thinks that you're just wonderful

And dear as you can be.

Abril. 28 – 1971

Te quiere mucho tu viej[i]
regañona, y le pide
mucho a Dios que nos cui[de]
a los dos y nos dé pacie[n]
cia, para llevar una vida

FIGURE 29. Birthday card by Luz de Vélez Ibáñez to her husband, Adalberto. Script: Viejito Querido: Te quiero mucho, tu vieja regañona. Y le pide [sic] mucho a Dios que nos cuide a los dos y nos de paciencia, para llevar una vida feliz y tranquila. Que Dios Nuestro Sr te de muchos años de vida con salud para felicidad de tus hijos y vieja. Love siempre; Abri1.28–1971.

Fe, and Taos and with a very large concentration in the 1880s (Kanellos and Martell, (2000, 289–95).

Similarly, in Texas, Conchita Hassell Winn (2010) enumerates the Spanish-language newspapers in Texas, which "numbered 150 in the nineteenth century and more than 300 in the twentieth." She traces the earliest to 1813, when the Gutierrez-McGee expedition attempted to forcibly remove the province of Texas from Spain, and the expedition evidently had a propaganda bulletin entitled the *Gaceta de Texas*.[43] The earliest newspaper published in Texas was the *Nacogdoches Mexican Advocate* (1829), which was printed bilingually, with opposite sides of the paper in English and Spanish. She states that "from the end of the Mexican War (1848) until well into Reconstruction (1866–1877), English-language journalists founding papers in South Texas employed the bilingual format employed during the Mexican campaign" (ibid.). However, monolingual Spanish news also dates from the post-American-Mexican War period, with *La Estrella de Corpus Christi*, or the *Corpus Christi Star* (1848–1849), as the first. This, she states, was followed by the Brownsville, Texas, *El Centinela* (1849) and morphed into the bilingual *Centinela del Río Grande*, or *Río Grande Sentinel*. Shortly after this shift followed the publications of *La Bandera Americana* (the American Flag), *El Río Bravo* (the Río Bravo), and *La Bandera* (ibid.).

Similarly, California had a spectacular growth in newspapers, beginning with *El Clamor Público* in Los Angeles in 1855 through the middle of the twentieth century, with no less than eighty-four in Los Angeles alone, and strong increases in the 1880s with the establishment of the railroad and the 1920s in the aftermath of the Mexican Revolution. For California alone, 192 Spanish-language newspapers were established during these "important migratory periods" (Kanellos and Martell 2000, 281–83). At the very moment that Mexican children were being stripped of their language, the counterpoint developed by Mexican newspapers in the northern region was helpful in having those same children at least observe if not read what their own parents were reading and commenting.

THE TRANSBORDER NARRATIVES OF THE COCKROACH PEOPLE: THE PEOPLE WITH HISTORY

These newspapers were also the main carriers of the transborder narratives, in contrast to those of the ongoing American scripts, by capturing the heterogeneity of community ideas and their accompanying intellectual frameworks. At any one time these narratives were explored and acted out in myriad ways, with persons sometimes holding more than one in mind in response to the life course of being Mexican and many times in unrewarding contexts. Sometimes those more partial to one narrative would temporarily encompass another or others, depending on context. It would blend so that a miner in the copper mines of Bisbee, Arizona, would become part of a general strike while simultaneously calling upon the dark Indigenous Virgin de Guadalupe as an icon, while feminist women formed the core of these strikes by using networks of women that walked the picket lines, assembled food banks, and were also beaten by thugs hired by the mining company. Among these narratives, some were long-held, practiced, and truly transborder in content and expectations.

Romano (1969b) articulates three in number: "Indianist Philosophy," "Historical Confrontation," and the philosophically transcendent idea of the mestizo in the form of "Cultural Nationalism." These, as will be discussed, are strong narratives to the American megascripts of the American Dream. But, I would suggest two other equally strong constructs that are seeming absolutely opposite one to the other. The fourth, the "Mexican Feminist Revolutionary" narrative, was carried, practiced, and integrated by women into the ideological premises of already existing Mexican populations in the very early twentieth century. The fifth was carried by about one hundred thousand men and women bringing their conservative Catholic beliefs as they fled from the Cristero Rebellion of the 1920s. The "Mexican Feminist Revolutionary" position articulated by pre- and postrevolutionary women is crucial because it serves as an integrating narrative that encompasses the first three, as I will show. The fifth narrative is made up of a profound religiosity exemplified by its very strong Catholic conservatism and was antithetical to the anticlerical and Church policies of the revolutionary government.

Romano-V's early version of the narratives must be understood within the limitations of the period (1970) but especially lacking is their inclusion of Mexican Revolutionary women and their intellectual and ideological critiques. Equally, the lack of attention to the thousands of Cristero men and women as well as around 2,500 priests, nuns, seminarians, bishops, and archbishops that were either exiled or left on their own with their accompanying narratives also were not included (Young 2015, 42).

Romano, nevertheless, does provide outlines of what he considered important intellectual and historical configurations articulated in the transborder region. I say transborder because in fact the ideological frameworks that he discussed did not disappear from their original roots and remained very much part of the discussions and arguments in and beyond the SWNAR. First, he cites the "Zapatista-Indianist philosophy," which is a quest to a return to origins and community rights and obligations. This I would suggest is the focus on land as the basis of community and individual identity and as well the notion of "lost lands." Like the Zapatistas and the Indigenous followers of that movement, populations in the north had undergone their own loss with the American-Mexican War and the Gadsden Purchase, having suffered their loss of lands in the new regime by taxes and questionable sales, even though there was continuous land ownership throughout the region by those who did not lose their lands, while others took advantage of the Homestead Act to homestead farms and ranches, for example in southern New Mexico and Arizona.[44] These combined with the influence of revolutionary experiences of lost lands and their quest for recovery and blended in community conversations in the home, and in public places like the barber shop, the local bar, or even at funerals.

Many were aware of their own Indigenous connections through familial relationships and the Indigenous communities next door, who had Spanish surnames and many times the same ones, so that a plethora of Garcías and Sotos and Lópezes and so on were members of the Yoéme Village of Pascua on the west side of Tucson next to Mexican barrios, where people intermarried, and each other's children were raised together, and young men and women went off to war together in all of America's wars. Families from both had fled the Mexican Revolution or the Sonoran pogroms previously discussed in chapter 3. However, both identified strongly with Emiliano Zapata's more Indigenous representations, and he was respected as the "good revolutionary," even by opponents.[45] As Romano-V. (1969b, 37–38) states,

> symbolically the Indian penetrates throughout, and permeates, major aspects of Mexican-American life, and hardly a barrio exists that does not have someone who is nicknamed "El Indio," or "Los Indios." For decades, Mexican-American youth have felt a particularly keen resentment at the depiction of Indians in American movies, while Indian themes consistently have been common subject matter in the neighborhoods' amateur artists, a fact that may be called an anachronism by some or the dislodging of history by others. On occasion *los Matachines* still make their Indian appearance in churches, and Aztec legends still pictorially tell and retell their stories in barrio living rooms, kitchens, in bars, in restaurants, tortillerias, and Chicano newspapers.

But beyond cultural representations, this ideological presence was always premised with the notion of returning to origins and back to that which was and can never be again unless it is struggled for and won again. For Mexicans in the northern part of the region, the "Indian is root and origin, past and present virtually timeless in his [*sic*] barrio manifestations—a timeless symbol of opposition to cultural imperialism" (ibid., 39). To be "indio" is to never give in, to never give up, and to never surrender for Mexicans, even when they were trying to exterminate the "indios" themselves. This thematic would be taken up strongly in the Chicano movement and would create an entire Indigenous complex of writing, longing, loss, and recapitulation in many works, such as the poetry of Alurista.[46] But this thematic also influenced a generation of Chicano anthropologists for whom a sense a "reconnectivity" initiated the necessity of broader narratives of Indigenous-Chicano relationships, so that Diego Vigil's *From Indians to Chicanos* (1980) set the stage for the discussion of north-to-south migrations connecting the regions of the cultural relations between Mesoamerica and the SWNAR (see the discussion by archeologists in chapter 2).

The second alternative narrative Romano-V. labels is "Historical Confrontation" (39). He relates that it is manifest in the hundreds of corridos sung throughout the region but more specifically one would suggest by the oral narratives of grandparents and grandmothers and attested to by Ron López's poignant rendering. For the author, the revolution was the great historical confrontation beyond the American-Mexican War, both not infrequently mentioned in the households of the region. This was made very present since his mother's father met his death by a spent dum-dum bullet, which struck his stomach and exploded as he was boarding the train leaving the scene of battle. This was retold along with the telling by his father of the death of the revolutionary colonel at the hands of his brother at the borderline of the Nogaleses. But the American-Mexican War had not been forgotten in many households and was told with the shaking of heads how "they" had stolen their lands. But this was also buttressed by the recognition of the San Patricio Brigade, which fought so valiantly for Mexico against the United States and was largely made up of Irish and a few German immigrants.[47]

But in fact, ideologically, "Historical Confrontation" was carried across the political bifurcation in the political stances of Ricardo Flores Magón and his brothers Enrique and Jesús, an anarchist-oriented ideology accompanied by its political organization, El Partido Liberal Mexicano, and whose newspaper *Regeneración* was first published in Mexico City in 1900 (Gómez-Quiñones 1973, 17). After exile to the United States from the dictatorship of Porfirio Díaz, they founded it again later in Los Angeles, with its underlying premise of revolutionary struggle, and tied the working conditions of Mexicans under Porfirio Díaz to the working conditions of Mexicans in the United States, thus attempting the organizing of an international workers union with common goals and objectives.[48] At a time of the infamous Red Scare (1919–1920) both the Magón brothers were imprisoned in the United States. Flores Magón died in Leavenworth and was probably murdered by prison guards (ibid.).

Yet the ideological anarchism espoused by Ricardo Flores Magón resonated with Mexican communities for its simplicity but also because of its lack of reliance on hierarchy and direction from the top. Many Mexican communities' accomplishments and failures emerged out of an engaged and attentive focus, as Gómez-Quiñones (1973, 5) so eloquently stated, to these basic outlines of belief:

> Immediate power was to be taken at the level of specific oppression, the work place, the neighborhood, the city. Overt action was to be constant. Work was carried out

individually, or through grupos de afinidad and sociedades de Resistencia, preferably in labor unions or in the community at large. Cooperation between groups was, at best, through loose confederations established at unruly large conferences where vague general strategy and tactics were hammered out . . . anarchists denied political action qua politics and rejected political deployment which Marxists hold as crucial. Covert activity directed against the state was emphasized, except by the pacifist or literary anarchists. A flamboyant tactic particularly associated with anarchists was the general strike.

This was a different narrative but it was attractive for a period of time until both oppression and imprisonment tested the foundations of the ideology.

Nevertheless, the general historical confrontation premise was very much part of the daily lived experiences of Mexicans, who were often engaged in strikes, labor disputes, and employment issues in the mines, construction, ranching, agriculture, and in the often hated laundries, where women worked in 120-degree heat without breaks or respite (Vélez-Ibáñez 1996, 120–21). Mexicans of the SWNAR in fact were among the first to create the phenomenon of organizing transborder worker's organizations, since the labor movement was normative across borders in both directions. Transborder industrial forms of union organizing were extensive, and when not suppressed by a combination of transborder police and military and use of extralegal methods, transborder unions had a profound impact on wages, but differentially applied (Devra Weber n.d.).

The notion of historical confrontation was also articulated intellectually with historical retellings of the past, often by grandparents who lived up the street or sometimes who also lived in or were visited in Sonora when the border was just a scar. Historical confrontations are often replicated by daily realities of miseducation, low wages, dangerous occupations, accommodation and housing discrimination, and crucially the continued and unabated suppression and attempted erasure of language. But the most present for the thematic of historical confrontation was of course that unhealed wound of the border itself, which was a constant reminder of lost possibilities, interrupted cultural affinity, and the often reduced, if not lost, capacity to communicate and create in the only language that was younger in existence in the region than Yoéme, Tohono O'odham, Keres, Tewa, Pima Maricopa, Diegueño, Caddo, or Rarámuri. Again, the Chicano movement, as part of its heterogeneous adherents, strongly confronted educational practices, the inequities of employment and housing, language loss, cultural subordination, and women's rights, and as importantly called forth a paradigm in which Mexican-origin peoples would be treated as historical beings and not simply as "immigrants" to be washed away in ahistorical assimilationist propositions. As importantly, bilingualism was to be cherished and fought for and implemented. Some of the first university-level courses were established in "Bilingual Systems," in the Mexican American Studies Department in 1970 and designed by the author.[49]

Romano-V.'s third philosophical trend is what he terms "Cultural Nationalism," but of a different sort. He reduces this narrative to the following very complex rendering:

> Generally, as a group, Mexican-Americans have been virtually the only ethnic group in the United States that still systematically proclaims its Mestizaje—multiple genetic and cultural origins exhibiting multiplicity rather than seeking purity. Philosophically and historically this has manifested itself in a trend toward Humanistic Universalism, Behavioral Relativism, and a recurrent form of Existentialism, this last of which is often naively and erroneously interpreted as fatalism. (Romano-V. 1969b, 41)

That is, these underlying concepts and expected behaviors have an important premise that is antiracist, even though Mexicans are often clouded by class-based racism of "whiteness," as grandmothers often ask "¿Como es?" (What is he like?) of a newborn. There is an underlying saving grace that many admit: "Somos como café con leche con un poco de uno a veces y un poco del otro" (We are like coffee and milk with a bit of the one and the bit of the other). While color is differentiated, there is also the recognition that it is not predictable in that the Yoéme ancestor of the grandfather will pop up seeming like a Pascola dancer but with blue eyes inherited from a grandmother, the progeny of her own grandfather's French-soldier origin in Mazatlán. And since familial networks have been quite useful in so many struggles of economy and certainly miseducation, relying on others makes it possible to have an expectation of acceptance of the weird, of the insane, of the malcontent, of the genius, of the builder, of the artist and the music maker, as well as the engineer and mechanic, the herb gatherer and the *curandera*. People marrying individuals who are not Mexicans have no choice but to become Mexicans in their social relations since the networks often function like black holes, in which the unsuspecting *huero* or *Chino* or *Negro* is sucked in to speak to the Yoéme grandmother. In part, it is also convenient to let others live their lives in tranquility without too much authority so that a kind of anarchistic approach to rules at times is called for in order not to be bothered with the bother. "Live and let live" is not to be confused with acquiescence but with respect for the other to be able to make decisions and, as important, to make mistakes and also to taste success. This is an existential basis for the notion of freedom and the Chicano Movement, especially through its created poetry, demonstrations, academic programs, and new fields of scholarly and historical potentials, and its courageous students, especially in their developed forms of literary expression and communication captured in song, performances, plays, and mural art. This process was best captured by Alurista's insistent refrain: "I do not ask for freedom/I am Freedom." I was there to hear it.

The fourth I have termed the "Mexican feminist revolutionary narrative."[50] It was strongly composed of an anarchist movement of women associated with the PLM that was strongly feminist, culturally nationalistic, democratic, and protective of Indigenous populations. It was strongly anticlerical and highly critical of the Church hierarchy and its relegation of women to secondary or tertiary roles within the Church and its penchant for subordinating women to the household and within it as well.[51] Sara Estela Ramírez took great physical risks at the hands of police and authorities to create "women's temporal and intellectual space." While supportive of radical men and a strong supporter of the Partido Liberal Mexicano (Mexican Liberal Party), she was no doubt an antecedent to the Chicana feminists of the 1960s. At an early age she moved to Laredo from Coahuila and was eminently anticlerical, anarchistic, and transborder, ideologically and in action. She published her work in Spanish-language newspapers and periodicals and founded some of her own as well.[52] Among these were *La Coregidora* and *Aurora*, published in Texas between 1904 and 1910 and comprising a variety of poet works, essays, and literary articles, according to Zamora (1980, 165).

His analysis characterizes her intellectual frameworks from a philosophical position as viewing moral behaviors as

> a dialectical process between two prominent forces in the universe—determinism and free will. This theme runs through most of her other political works. She believed that humans are inherently equipped by nature to actively care for the general welfare of others. However, we often exercise our free will and reject the determinants of nature. Those that reject the dictates of such a universal law disrupt the natural order of things. (ibid., 166)

But her philosophical position is expressed in her feminist position by attacking the patriarchal sources of women's oppression and their objectification, of which one expression is their definition "as glorified objects whose existence is dependent on forces external to the woman" (ibid.). These forces by implication are the patriarchal norms, mores, and standards in which women are made to be seen as virginal, pure, untouched, and to be protected by the hand of man. Theirs is a lofty position shredded of their humanity and made brainless on their pedestals to be adored unmovingly by men.

Also representative of this narrative, according to Macias (1980, 54), was

> Juana Belén Gutiérrez de Mendoza who was born in 1875 in Durango of an Indian mother and a mestizo father, and worked at such varied jobs as blacksmith, horse tamer, and farm worker. Trained as a typographer, in 1901 Juana joined the Precursors or early

critics of Don Porfirio who called for an anti-capitalist revolution by Mexico's peasants and workers against the Díaz regime. Angered by the foreign domination of Mexico's banks, insurance companies, mines, textile mills and railroads, aroused by the increasing impoverishment, exploitation, and debasement of the country's landless peasants and workers, and disturbed by the resurgence of the Catholic Church in Mexico, in May of 1901 Juana established an anti-Diaz newspaper, *Vesper*, in the extremely traditionalist provincial capital of Guanajuato.

A deep critic of the turmoil following the revolution and the ineptness of its leadership in transforming Mexico, as well as Mexico's weak and ineffective labor movement, Belén was also highly critical of the American AFL recruiting Mexican unions from the more uncompromising PLM, especially since she regarded the AFL as representing an extension of American influence that "exploited not only workers but whole nations" (ibid., 36). Numerous others, such as Hermila Galindo, a strong Carranzista supporter, considered that women were regarded as "a being without consciousness and without aspiration," sought the revision of the civil codes that subordinated women to the hierarchy of husbands, and, like other feminists, fought for women's suffrage (ibid., 66).

But among the most impressive revolutionary and critical feminist media was the role of the PLM-associated, *La Voz de la Mujer*, which was not only oriented to the rights of women but the rights of all peoples struggling either in Mexico or the United States. As Clara Lomas's (2003, 56) original research indicates, this was an effort run by women and espoused revolutionary action and behavior. She, for example, lists the staff who are primarily women to give an indication of the new spaces and temporal places created by Mexican women:

> Founded in El Paso, Texas, to function as a propaganda tool for the PLM, *La Voz de la Mujer* struggled against threats and harassment from President Díaz's secret agents, as did many other PLM periodicals. On its front page, *La Voz de la Mujer* identifies a staff consisting primarily of women: "Isidra T. de Cárdenas, *Directora* (Director); María Sánchez, *Redactora en Jefe* (Chief Editor); María P. García, *Administradora* (Manager); and León Cárdenas, Secretario de Redacción [Editor]."

Such feminist positions were not lost in the movement of women north during and after the revolution. The explosion of Chicana feminism of the 1960s owes its impetus not only to the American feminist movement but also to these Mexican women, many of whom had been imprisoned and exiled for their beliefs and actions and met similar fates in the northern part of the region. Some grandmothers did espouse these principles to their children and grandchildren by example with their own struggles and were part of that revolutionary generation.

There are myriad examples of non-PLM and PLM Mexican women joining labor strikes in the fields, the mines, in segregated department stores, and in the dreaded laundries early in the twentieth century.[53] Many such women joined others in the aftermath of being exposed not just to the feminist version of the anarchist Flores Magón brothers but to the available unions as the solution to working without surcease in 130-degree weather in laundries such as in Tucson (Vélez-Ibáñez 1996, 121). They acquired their feminist principles on the picket line, facing off police and thugs hired by the enterprise, and sacrificing home and hearth. As children, many Chicanas were told by grandmothers of these examples, or they recalled themselves as teenage girls on the picket lines and continued in dialogues and discourses until they could say no more. Sometimes sitting on grandmothers' beds they were told of surviving floods, thugs, and revolutionaries as well as bad bosses, of fighting off the hands of the unwanted, and most of all they told of the necessity of never, but never, giving up and showed this by example.[54] They were the thinkers, doers, and creators of a brand of revolutionary Mexican feminism that was transborder in direction, content, and action and taught early on that Mexican women were of unlimited potential to fight but also to win with strength and compassion. Their daughters and granddaughters of the Chicano era learned and made sure that men knew when they were acceptable as humans by insisting that those who were not were labeled as "Macho Pigs." I was a witness as well.

The fifth narrative was that of the largely conservative Catholic movement and proclerical program and revolt of the Cristeros. Between 1926 and 1929, Catholic men and women revolted by strength of arms against the Mexican revolutionary federal government that placed rigid restrictions of a multiple sort on the Catholic Church, clerics—including the shedding of Roman collars by priests and habits by nuns—worship, and training, and closed parochial schools. More than likely one hundred thousand persons fled from Mexico to the United States, but not necessarily all Cristeros, as figure 30 shows (Young 2012, 275). This movement is indicated in figure 30 in the period between 1924 (a low point in Mexican emigrants) and a peak in 1926 (which is at the most prominent part of the revolt itself). Continued migration through 1929 is indicated until the Depression strikes the entire region and the world.

Devastating west-central Mexico economically and materially, the methods used by the Mexican army are reminiscent of the much later Vietnam War and its search-and-destroy tactic and free-fire zones, which laid waste to the ecology, people, and land of regions. Thus thousands joined their northern brethren, and Young (277) described how many went to the Midwest to Chicago, Detroit, and to points west such as Los Angeles and El Paso. But a dramatic unintended consequence that occurred was the movement and deportation of Mexican priests and nuns and lay teachers who were Catholic and who refused to shed their Roman collars, habits, and beliefs. The nuns especially were strongly engaged as teachers in Mexican Catholic schools and when

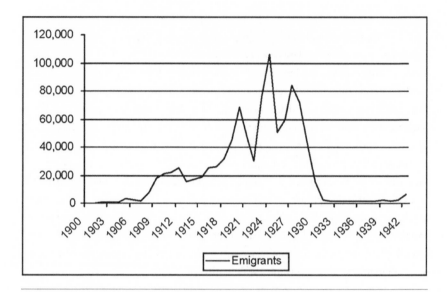

FIGURE 30. Number of legal Mexican emigrants to the United States by year. The Mexican Migration Project, Princeton University. Source: Jorge Durand and Douglas S. Massey, as cited in Young 2012 (as figure 2).

these closed down, Young (2015, 281) correctly points out that for nuns, "A more dependable source of income and stability—particularly for refugee nuns—was teaching, and this became the occupation of up to 50 percent of the refugee priests (and possibly a greater percentage of the nuns) in the United States. The unprecedented growth occurring in conjunction with the arrival of the refugees and the closing of Catholic schools in Mexico, generated a concurrent demand for Mexican Catholic schools in the United States, and religious refugees opened dozens of new schools within Mexican communities during the Cristero War years."

In this manner, the more conservative brand of Roman Catholicism took root and impacted strongly for many years in Mexican communities of the northern and Midwest regions: a more stringent "Jalisco/Michoacán" type of belief system with its rigid gender roles, patriarchy, Marianism, and a type of Catholic Protestant ethic concerning the abstinence of alcohol, prohibition of dancing, sexual repression, and very modest dress among women. As well, there was a strong inclination toward focused hard work, and a rigid corporate sort of social organization with a very conservative political outlook.[55]

Moreover, there were Mexican lay teachers in public schools. We do not know how many or of the overall influence they had, but within their own families we do get a sense of this from Tony Burciaga's description of the importance of his own mother, who had been one of those teachers, and her cultural and linguistic influence. She had fled the anti-Catholic hysteria in Mexico and with her husband had lived for many years in El Paso, raising six children and teaching them the intricacies of Spanish and Mexican culture, and most of all history. Her husband for many years had been the caretaker of a synagogue. He risked his life during a fire to save the precious artifacts of the Temple and, much later at his funeral, according to Tony, hundreds of believers of both faiths joined in remembrance.[56] Both raised highly disciplined adults and Tony became one of the founders of the infamous theater group of the Chicano movement, Culture Clash, as well as a highly regarded essayist and poet of things Mexican in both countries. He writes in his memorable *Drink Cultura*:

> The silence of our language, culture, and history was broken at home by our mother, a former school teacher in Mexico. She taught her six children to know, love, and respect our language our customs and our history. And this is one reason why I write—to express those beliefs to teach what was once a silent sin. These words etched in black ink are made not from individual letters but scars that perforate the paper-like open wounds of a young Chicano who sought the truth in his own reflection. (40)

Yet linguistically the schools and churches occupied by these priests and nuns and lay teachers who did teach were important mediums of language retention and strong academic foundations. They reveled in language learning and literacy and intellectual stimulation. For Mexican-origin children, expanding the knowledge of Spanish was a positive enterprise. The ability to read *Don Quixote* in the original had long-lasting implications.[57] For dissatisfied parents of children who had been in public schools and objects of erasure and cultural disassembly, and were tested out as retarded or spoken to in "Spic" Spanish or given mediocre curricula, the Mexican-oriented parochial schools trained thousands of children who went on to become leaders, doctors, engineers, nurses, writers, scientists, teachers, and even professors of anthropology, and many in fact would participate in that most discontent of narratives—the Chicano movement.[58]

Thus José Antonio Burciaga's laudatory essay of "El Cate" (El Paso's Cathedral Catholic Boys' High School) reveals that in this "barrio" school, which was the poorest high school economically in El Paso for one four-year period, 98 percent of its graduates were accepted to universities. In 1990 its eighty-two seniors earned fifty-five scholarships, with its students attending universities from UTEP to Harvard (Burciaga 1992, 88). The standard was simply one in which one of the brothers in charge quoted by Burciaga states, "I never listened to students who said, 'I can't do it.'" For Burciaga, who graduated thirty years before, "It hasn't changed since I graduated

thirty years ago" (89). Thus the Catholic parochial school did not expect less regardless of language, regardless of standing, regardless of class, regardless of being Mexican
or not, and no child was tested to death to determine his or her IQ or given language
categories that set them apart. Although it must be said that in parochial schools
in which the nuns and priests were English-speaking only, they applied some of the
same methods as their public-school colleagues to ferret out Spanish, as Burciaga also
admits. It would seem that the worthiness of the Spanish language was not valued
by parochial English-speaking schools as was success in all other things. From such
contexts many of us emerged self-disciplined, self-worthy, and also puzzled by the
avoidance of the maternal language. Such instruction was also filled with the mythic
narratives of the church that were often obfuscated by the courses in biology and
created puzzlement as to the violence and slaughter of the crusades, coupled with
pious indulgences for the broadsworded knights decapitating the heathen Muslims.

But for young Mexican-origin women, nuns served as contradictory models that
were filled with Marian expectations of purity and abstinence plus obedience to a
male hierarchical priesthood and church; but nevertheless, these nuns were women
who were accomplished teachers and bearers of knowledge as well as strong, determined, unabashedly tough, and instilled with a sense of achievement and success.
This was not lost on the young men who observed them as well and suffered at the
hands of a ruler or a Judo thumb hold, as used by Sister Saint Eleanor of Salpointe
High School in the fifties.[59] A layer of admiration and expectation beyond the *machito*
boundaries was established. There was something to be said for a corporate identity
that demanded nothing but the best of all, regardless of gender.

As well, the post–World War II "Little Schools of the 400" were developed by the
League of United Latin American Citizens (LULAC), which emphasized learning
the most important first four hundred words in English that a child should know,
using a very primitive style of "bilingual" education. This served as the precursor of
Head Start programs and for seven years, through the entire state of Texas, benefited
hundreds of children (Waters Yarsinske 2004).

The Chicano movement itself, then, with its array of multiple versions of those
narratives discussed, is the subject of an enormous literature written by the children,
grandchildren, and great-grandchildren of those who were tested, of those whose language and culture were rejected, of those who were spanked and whose heads struck the
desk, even though some had been treated the same way in their generation, according
to the thousands of accounts written between 1959 and 1990 by these progeny.[60] For
some, Spanish had become a hidden and unadmitted language so that in her poignant
and penetrating essay, Patricia Zavella (2001, 49) describes how Spanish had become
"the secret language" in her extended family. Only the preceding generations spoke it
in gatherings, and she and her generation were not taught the language since they had

learned of the penalties awaiting. But being attentive, she learned enough to understand the narratives of her grandmother and aunts and uncles, including those of exclusion in segregated swimming pools. But the impact on her and the following generations was such that "[t]here were never no overt lessons about how to confront such discrimination. We children were protected from such matters. It would take a nationalist political movement for me to feel the power of collective anger over such outrage."

But the "movement" was also about the movement of peoples for all the reasons mentioned here and across enormous expanses of space and to many places. This was and is the central tie from the past to the present and the future—the underpinning narrative framework for Mexicans of yesterday and today, binding them to a certain extent into a culture of crossroads and acceptance. This narrative strongly influenced the works, for example, of Roberto Alvarez's *Familia: Migration, and Adaptation in Alta and Baja California, 1850–1975* (1987), which was among the first to truly emphasize the transnationality of Mexican families and their long historical movement and presence. Gloria Anzaldúa's (1987) *Borderlands/La Frontera: The New Mestiza*—the poetic and magnificent south Texas journey—reconnected as well as revealed the multiple geographic and psychic borders within us all. As well, Vélez-Ibáñez's early work in Central Mexico, *Rituals of Marginality* (1983), was strongly influenced by this reality experienced by Mexican populations of the region. Later his *Border Visions* (1996) more specifically connected the dots using archeological materials to support broader contentions of multilineal migrations and multiple origins. All of the works mentioned, by Vigil (1980), Alvarez (1986, 1987), and Vélez-Ibáñez (1996), were strongly influenced by Romano's earlier work discussed here, while solitarily Anzaldúa (1987) exemplified the feminist position of Mexican revolutionary women. These works, as well as the much earlier pathbreaking work by Américo Paredes (1958) *With His Pistol in His Hand: A Border Ballad and its Hero*, served as the crucial connectivity tying politically bifurcated populations to the south-to-north migration and meetings of peoples trading, fighting, cooperating, intermarrying, settling, and recombining along crossroads of intensive "bumping."[61]

Teresa McKenna's literary marvel, *Migrant Song* (1997, ix), begins with her narrating her Grandmother Cruz's stories, songs, tales, and games. And what was most penetrating is that they served as the psychological frameworks for the "us's" and "her's" and "you's" and most importantly the "I's" that she came to understand thusly: "Later I understood that those nights connected me to a much larger story, one of revolution, from which my grandmothers, alone, had fled, bringing their small children over the border and into another land; one of struggle in which they had protected their families from hunger, drought, and influenza. But those nights at 821 Pioneer Avenue in Wilmington, California, commenced for me a song of migration that has since fueled my political and academic work."

McKenna was the descendant of those who came with the experiences and actions that carried the great narratives north to connect with those already present. And to that is the connection to those moving in the present. It is a continuation of humans moving across a vast region, leaving behind that in which they can no longer remain. And the language used for those in the past and those in the present was and is sometimes English, sometimes Spanish, sometimes both. But whatever means or media used, there continues to be the constant conflict with those who would erase and demand a kind of cultural homogeneity that a culturally heterogeneous population would prefer to layer and to add part of that homogeneity to much more layered cultural formations of the multiple "us's" and "me's" and "I's" in contradistinction to those who would have us all become English-only clones of a stripping process of language and culture. They continue to so insist in spite of the dynamic movement of peoples that harkens back to the pre-Hispanic periods.

They ignore the basic dynamics that have created and continue to create the population's heterogeneous "cultural citizenship," as espoused by Rosaldo (1989), in regarding culture theoretically and methodologically as a "busy intersection . . . where a number of distinct social processes intersect. The crossroads simply provides a space for distinct trajectories to traverse, rather than containing them in complete encapsulated forms" (17). From this follows his discussion of Latinos and a broader insistence for equity in education given the understood plurality of the cultural layers of the population who are the harbingers, change agents, and respondents to and within these intersections. Thus this dynamic has been stressed throughout this work to emphasize the hundreds of years of exchanges and conflicts and temporary adjustments and their contradictions and, more importantly, processes, as I have suggested in each of the preceding chapters. But the idea of "cultural citizenship" also includes the idea of differentiated group representation that would accommodate difference to compensate for past injustices (Del Castillo, 2005). For Rosaldo (1994, 402), "Cultural citizenship refers to the right to be different and to belong in a participatory democratic sense [so that] . . . [t]he notion of belonging means full membership in a group and the ability to influence one's destiny by having a significant voice in basic decisions."[62] But importantly for Rosaldo is that the national perspective of language is a "finite good—one citizen, one language, no more, no less." "What follows is a zero sum game in that the more Spanish is spoken, the less English is spoken, and the less English its opposite as well" (403).

It is exactly this perspective that also adjoins the eugenics argumentation of purity and the use of tests to ferret out the different and the languages spoken. That said, perhaps the notion of a differentiated cultural citizenship might be possible that leads to a greater democratization that would trump the nation-state's insistence, pragmatic formulas, and strategies of control, as well as their accompanying homogenous megascripts and plurality of languages and literacies. Yet the idea of "cultural citizenship" does have some problematic aspects such that citizenship in the nineteenth century and to the present has its central denotation of belonging to an institutionalized body, whether state or imperial, and of giving recognition to the identifying markers of the cultural population inhabiting the territorial boundaries of the legitimized citizenry. On the other hand, cultural membership may or may not coincide with that citizenry, and in the case of conquest this becomes even more highly problematic. The imposition of citizenry in all of its hegemonic functions—linguistic and cultural—may be culturally referent to the imposing group but have little to do with those upon whom such enforced citizenship is being visited.

COMMENTARY

Without doubt, the traditions of Spanish literacy and their narratives, which were established from the colonial through the Mexican periods, were ironically enhanced and expanded by its Mexican-origin population. This occurred especially so after the American-Mexican War and the Treaty of the Mesilla establishing the U.S.-Mexico border and because of the French intervention, the Mexican Revolution, and the Cristero Revolt. As important as these events were, Spanish literacy and language became much more prevalent as well because of the immense structural changes visited on the entire SWNAR. Its insatiable diet requiring skilled and unskilled Mexican workers as the new industrial formations in mining, agriculture, construction, and ranching took root in the region.

In spite of an early eugenically oriented and destructive process of typecasting, stereotyping, and trying to reduce Mexican children to hulks of themselves and at times succeeding, simply economy, migration, demography, and revolutions could not and did not eliminate the cultural and language presence of a highly heterogeneous Mexican population. These populations carried with them the counternarratives of origins, confrontations, cultural nationalism, revolutionary feminism, and conservative Catholicism and continue to do so to this day, along with a new breed of activist Evangelical Protestantism and the impact of the Mormon Church, especially in the state of Arizona. These were and are a multiplex people with layers of ideas and experiences that could simply not be erased and made into what the other demanded as the other and the "me's" and "I's" as "you's," and the "us's" as all of "them's."

To the present, these early developments fully blossomed into the late twentieth and twenty-first centuries and filled the Chicano movement with potentials and possibilities. At the same time, the underlying processes remained of the reality of an asymmetrical integrated political economy encompassing two nations, a common ecology, transborder production chains, and chains of labor and with them a constant replenishing of Spanish-speaking populations and their literary and linguistic capacities."[63] And it is these replenishing populations that English-only and destructive language policies and instruction confronted. These propositions are not unlike the "special education" classes for classified mentally retarded children and the culturally and linguistically "different" that were devised and supported by generations of test taking. Their parents had moved simply from one region to the other, pushed by economy, political disarray, drought, and untold human events but also recruited unabashedly by a constantly revamping of the SWNAR into a postindustrial model of production and chains of labor of the present. The region continues to be the platform for ever-expanding crossroads of people, culture, and language.

6

THE "ENGLISH-ONLY" PHENOMENON
AND ITS POLITICAL DEMOGRAPHY
OF THE NORTHERN REGION

જી

Bilingualism and Spanish as Secondary in a
"White" Context and English South

English is the spoken Language of the school and no other language will be toler-
ated in the school or on the school grounds.
WAKEFIELD JUNIOR HIGH SCHOOL STUDENT MANUAL,
TUCSON, ARIZONA CIRCA 1968 AND ONE OF THREE
FEEDER SCHOOLS TO PUEBLO HIGH SCHOOL

THIS NOW LONG-DISCARDED RULE was revealed to me during an English class at Pueblo High School in about 1968 when I was co-teaching a comparative cultures class, which had as its core function and focus stimulating mostly Mexican, Indigenous, and African American students to basically go beyond the limitations set by others, to become stimulated by works that showed them a bit of themselves in situ, and to have the opportunity to excel like no others. Part of our conversations so many years ago was the erasure of language that many in the class had suffered as a consequence of all those techniques discussed in the previous chapters. We lamented that loss until a student with a set of sparkling eyes and brighter brain — fourteen-year-old Isabel García — almost shouted, "Hey, they still do that at Wakefield! And they have a rule book that says so." Astonished, I asked for a copy and the quotes above are those crowded by other rules having to do with expected behaviors.[1] Not too long after that, school walkouts like those in Los Angeles filled the hallways, with exiting students led by Isabel and a few teachers following them.

Now in many states in the northern region this extreme has raised it ugly eugenics-laced head in response to a growing bilingualism and changing demography, and is legislated by persons who would not appreciate this book and would certainly would deny its contents. This narrative of bilingualism and English-only and the latter's eugenics lineage, its couplings to anti-immigration feelings and persons aghast at the reality and growth of bilingualism and its populations are analytically connected. At times the opposition is coupled to neo-Nazis and the old-time religion of extreme nativism. These are reminiscent of the nineteenth and twentieth century narratives of the Know-Nothings, the Ku Klux Klan of the Midwest, and the Posse Comitatus of recent vintage. It is also a very useful platform for the politically astute, like the former Maricopa County sheriff in Arizona, who proudly dons the mantle as "America's Toughest Sheriff." At eighty-three, his stature grew with each new rounding-up of defenseless women, men, and children and fractured families with aplomb while selling pink prison garb at local festivals.[2]

This chapter examines the dynamic and continuous asymmetry of the spread of English south in the region and the manner in which English has become a second but not secondary language, and finally to balance this process, it discusses the manner in which Indigenous peoples continue to struggle for their language rights. It will be observed that the region enjoys four processes simultaneously: the growth of bilingualism and the new demography, the English-only penchant, the penetrations of English south, and the current limits of bilingualism in the north, and the emergence of a new and profound legislative and language movement south. Each of these phenomena are closely associated with larger transborder and transnational projects that reach across the continent, but there are historical specificities that form the foundation of the processes.

POLITICAL PROCESS AND THE NATURALIZATION OF ENGLISH: THE CASE OF ARIZONA AND NEW MEXICO[3]

After 1848 and the loss of Mexican territory, English-language dominance north of the new border, now dividing the SWNAR, was established incrementally in some cases and forcefully in others. Yet, once the imposed border of the region was established, two contending dynamic processes became established: first, the practice of establishing English as the hegemonic language in the nineteenth century; and second, as has been discussed in the previous chapter, the continued movement of Mexicans to former Mexican territories due to changes in the structure of economy of the Southwest border region, as well as intensive networks of relations that crisscrossed the border through kinship, and the cataclysmic events of revolution and intervention, as well as the large-scale recruitment by U.S. employers seeking lower-cost labor, permanently or temporarily.

While newly imposed political control required that those Mexicans remaining in conquered territory were afforded the same protections as citizens, there is no provision in any treaty that such a choice required neither the erasure of Spanish nor the learning of the English language. Yet, except for New Mexico, all conquered or annexed territories eventually either under state or territorial control demanded that all of their residents learn to read and speak English, to the detriment of local cultural and linguistic capital; this also was mandated for émigrés. In this manner, English became naturalized as the only means of acceptable communication in the newly acquired territories so anyone crossing the newly imposed border also came under the aegis of mostly one-language preferences. Although, to different degrees, even Anglos became Mexicanized, especially in the workplace, where they learned Spanish or married Mexican women. The advent of the railroad in 1880 transported Anglo women from the Midwest and East Coast so that intermarriage between mostly Mexican women and Anglo men decreased by more than 50 percent. Afterward English became sealed as the hegemonic language through Anglo-only marriages.[4]

As examples, and basically the same pattern used throughout the SWNA region, Arizona and New Mexico provide the specific ways by which this was accomplished. First, public schools in Arizona accentuated English, to the detriment of Spanish in all forms. English instruction became the single most important means by which both Native Indigenous peoples and Spanish-speaking Mexicans in this new political regime were coerced to "Americanize," —i.e., to accept the eastern educational prism appropriate for immigrants migrating from Europe to the Eastern Seaboard. This prism includes a kind of megascript based on the notion of Founding Fathers, who espoused a variety of political positions based on the Enlightenment but which excluded slaves, conquered Indigenous populations, and to a lesser degree, Mexican populations of the new country. This megascript espousing equality did not extend to language and culture even though no treaty with either Native persons or Mexicans excluded their right to maintain their own language or even demanded that English would be the only means of legitimate communication, as in the Treaty of Guadalupe Hidalgo (1848) or the Treaty of the Mesilla (1853), or, as has been mentioned, guaranteed the same constitutional rights as American citizens who came to control the region.

Arizona was founded on the premise that the New Mexico Territory, of which it was not a part, was demographically and culturally "unbalanced" in favor of New Mexicans. When the U.S. Congress sought to give statehood status to the New Mexico Territory, which included the Territory of Arizona, a protest by the Arizona Territorial Legislature in 1906 stated that this "would subject us to the domination of another commonwealth of different traditions, customs, and aspirations" as if English and their newly arrived Anglo denizens had been perpetually present within their respective territories (U.S. Commission on Civil Rights 1972, 76–82). Similarly, the Arizona Territorial Teachers Association resolved that Arizona schools taught all classes in English while New Mexico schools used interpreters. Finally, it warned that the union of New Mexico and Arizona would disrupt the Arizona school system (ibid.).

"The Protest Against Union of Arizona with New Mexico," a territorial pressure group, presented to the U.S. Congress on February 12, 1906, the following:

> the decided racial difference between the people of New Mexico, who are not only different in race and largely in language, but have entirely different customs, laws and ideals and would have but little prospect of successful amalgamation ... [and] the objection of the people of Arizona, 95 percent of whom are Americans, to the probability of the control of public affairs by people of a different race, many of whom do not speak the English language, and who outnumber the people of Arizona two to one. (ibid.)

"The Protest" prophesied that New Mexico would control the constitutional convention and impose her dual language conditions on Arizona. Joint statehood won in New Mexico, 26,195–14,735, but it lost in Arizona, 16,265–3,141 (Vélez-Ibáñez 1996, 63–69). This made Arizona's Mexican population subject to the new state's language policy. New Mexico, however, followed a slightly divergent route.

In fact, the practices of the individual states rather than dictums by the new American republic's presence prevailed as the central means of eliminating Spanish literacy and language reduction or its retention. "States' rights" prevailed over the cultural and linguistic practices of those in both territories, to the detriment of one and the support for the other. For example, New Mexico's constitution provided for a bilingual instructional approach as stipulated in Article XII of the New Mexican constitution adopted in 1911, but there is also a contradictory section in another section. For the former it states,

> Education, Section 8 (Teachers to learn English and Spanish): "The legislature shall provide for the training of teachers in the normal schools (*schools that prepare teachers*) or otherwise so that they may become proficient in both the English and Spanish languages, to qualify them to teach Spanish-speaking pupils and students in the public schools and educational institutions of the state, and shall provide proper means and methods to facilitate the teaching of the English language and other branches of learning to such pupils and students." (U.S. Commission on Civil Rights 1972, 1–2)

Yet for the latter, Article XII, Section 8, in the Constitution as specified in Compact with the United States, Section 4 (Public Schools) states, "Provision shall be made for the establishment and maintenance of a system of public schools which shall be open to all the children of the state and free from sectarian control, and said schools shall always be conducted in English" (U.S. Commission on Civil Rights 1972, 1–2).

The second, however, partially prevailed after 1943, even though bilingualism (including Navajo and Spanish) became an important aspect of New Mexican instruction throughout the state. By the late nineteenth century, however, all other states established English as the hegemonic language of instruction so that early on English-only had its antecedents in instructional practice as early as the nineteenth century to the weakening of Spanish literacy and language use by Mexican-origin students. It also diminished the presence of Indigenous languages. Nevertheless, no state for that period in the SWNAR in fact established English-only on a constitutional basis, and New Mexico bilingualism was established only for a twenty-year period, according to its own constitution (ibid.).

Yet even New Mexico, which established bilingualism as more the practice than the norm, was often caught in the linguistic and culturally racialized politics of the time. David V. Holtby (2008) provides a sterling example of the manner in which Anglo sentiment for that period leading to statehood was expressed in the *Carlsbad Current*, an English newspaper of Eddy County. Not only did it seek to prevent New Mexicans the right to vote but characterized the rationale, according to Holtby (3), by stating that "there is but one race on the earth qualified by its nature to manage and govern man's destiny—the pure Anglo-Saxon." But its linguistic point of view was well expressed when it stated that it would be impossible for Nuevomexicanos to be citizens in a country "whose language they did not know." On the other hand, as Holtby (2008) shows, its Spanish-language counterpart, *La Voz del Pueblo*, countered by asking, "Can one imagine a greater crime that merits disqualification of the citizen than having preserved intact the cherished language of our fathers during three centuries of isolation?" The response was the sound of one hand clapping.

Nevertheless, the relationship between English, citizenship, and Eastern Seaboard Anglo culture became embossed as the natural state of things without question so that educational institutions, means of communication, public aspirations, and the only means of "achievement" economically were morphed into an assimilationist ideology. Like religious ideology, it became what was accepted as the raison d'être beyond question. In this manner an entirely ahistorical rendering of the Mexican-origin population became the narrative of much of North American history simply because that history was so ingrained with ideological premises that either dismissed, avoided, or simply excluded Mexican-origin populations from what in reality is the double tale of two empires expanding and meeting, their national independent versions locked in a war in which the loser and its populations became regulated to "foreignness" and stereotypes as only "cheap labor." Thus Mexicans became commoditized (as will be developed) by a highly naturalized "white racism" that became embedded in discourses of Mexican-origin populations, as postulated by Jane Hill (n.d.), and continued to be depicted, as Leo Chávez (2008) has so well presented in his *The Latino Threat:*

Constructing Immigrants, Citizens, and the Nation.[5] The historical consequences are that only when the prominent American historian Bolton wrote his primer in 1921—*The Spanish Borderlands*—did a Spanish and Mexican dimension begin to be added to the "Anglo-centric history of the United States" (Weber 2005, 1).[6] In the midst of all these cultural and hegemonic politics, as the late David Weber eloquently stated, "Mexicans became foreigners in their own land" in Arizona, as they did in Texas, New Mexico, and California, and Colorado (Weber 1973).

CONTINUED MOVEMENT OF MEXICAN POPULATIONS TO THE NEW NORTH AND THE EXPANSION OF SPANISH LITERACY AND PRACTICES

The above was accompanied by an opposite dynamic: the movement of Mexicans to former Mexican territories due to changes in the structure of economy of the Southwest North American Border Region as well as changing political conditions in Mexico and continued literary invigoration and the use of the Spanish language, as has been discussed in the previous chapter. Moreover, extensive commercial and kin relations augmented the crisscross pattern of transborder populations that in fact continued strongly up to the immigration-hysteria period of the late twentieth century and less so in the present.

Thus as shown in figure 28, migration from south to north did not abate since 1850 after the Treaty of Guadalupe Hidalgo in 1848, illustrating the formative and developmental economic and structural processes of an integrated regional economy.[7] As well, the 40 percent increase by 1870 was partially due to the exodus of parts of the Mexican intelligentsia during the French intervention, the 1910 diaspora tripling the numbers of persons in part fleeing the Mexican Revolution, and later the Cristero Revolt, as has been discussed as well.

SPANISH LANGUAGE, BILINGUALISM, AND THE RISE OF ENGLISH-ONLY: THE PRESENT STATE OF AFFAIRS

In order to understand the present state of Spanish literacy and language, we need to examine the formation of three contending processes: first, the continuing maintenance of some Spanish proficiency through the fourth generation in part explained by a twenty-year span of bilingual education; second, continued expansion of Spanish literacy through entering generations due to migration and immigration, and the counteraction of the English-only paradigm in response to demographic increases of Mexican-origin populations.

According to Fraga et al. (2006), the following illustrate the continuing maintenance of Spanish through the fourth generation. This work shows that their sample respondents had "strong English dominance and nearly universal English proficiency among the first-generation of U.S. born and generally strong Spanish retention, aided by refreshed populations of Spanish-speakers."[8] More specifically, this 2006 study showed that 91.3 percent of the fourth-generation Hispanics answered in English and 7.7 percent in Spanish; however, 60.5 percent retained proficiency in Spanish (ibid.).

Earlier works indicated that the replacement of Spanish, oral or written, was inevitable:

> With respect to immigrant children, 70 percent of those 5 to 9 years of age, after a stay of about 9 months, speak English on a regular basis. After 4 years, nearly all speak English regularly, and about 30 percent prefer English to Spanish. After 9 years, 60 percent have shifted to English; after 14 years—as young adults—70 percent have abandoned the use of Spanish as a daily language. By the time they have spent 15 years in the United States, some 75 percent of all Hispanic immigrants are using English every day.[9] (Veltman 1988, 44)

However, the question for both studies is not how much of the language is used on a daily basis per se but rather how literate are those populations in the ensuing generations in Spanish, thus indicating a level of proficiency in which communication in the language intersects with a field of use that goes beyond the familial circle. There is no doubt that the dominant language used within households greatly influences oral skills through generations, and mother's language in any household is a strong determinant of the use of language by progeny. As well, and for the most part, the dominant literate language used in most Mexican-origin communities in the school is English; children spend at least a majority of their day in literate English practice and none or little in Spanish. While newspapers, media, and advertisements in Spanish are common where a predominant population is either immigrant or first generation, these are not the major institutional avenues for literacy practice in Spanish. While there are banks, stores, churches, and other means of literate communications in Spanish, these are not systematic and continuing means of learning literate Spanish. It is in the schools where the erosion of literate and oral Spanish is almost guaranteed, even where children may have parents who read and write in Spanish. The exception to this process is the establishment of exceptional bilingual education programs that arise under great public stress, ignorance, and, worse, antipathies toward the population based on the changing demographics of the SWNAR.

BILINGUAL EDUCATION

For a period of twenty years between 1970 and 1990, as a result of the Elementary and Secondary Act (ESEA) Title VII Bilingual Education Act of 1968, the federal government was very much the initiator and designer of bilingual education. These programs had intellectual, empirical, political, and cultural justifications, some of which operated with great success while others floundered because of lack of institutional maturation, poor funding, inadequate instructional resources including ill-trained teachers, and poorly thought-out models of instruction with varying objectives and goals.

Nevertheless, its incipient format was in fact one in which the "heritage" language was used as a cultural buttress for identity and a very much needed method of expanding the intellectual and cultural capital of the Spanish-speaking student. These were the Spanish for Nativos programs of the 1960s, which were first introduced in the high schools in Tucson, Arizona, and specifically Pueblo High School under the impetus of educators Adalberto Guerrero, María Urquides, Rosita Cota, and Henry Oyama, who were longtime residents of Tucson.[10] Strongly influenced by Joshua Fishman's 1966 treatise, *Language Loyalty in the United States; The Maintenance and Perpetuation of Non-English Mother Tongues by American Ethnic and Religious Groups*, the genesis of Spanish for Nativos came as the result of their conviction that the intellectual and literacy skills of native speakers could not be met with the traditional approach of the learning of Spanish as a foreign language but rather as an enhanced curriculum that included the reading of Cervantes, Unamuno, Azuela, and a plethora of others, and the writing of university-level essays and poetry. They fought against the idea that Spanish was responsible for the lack of achievement by students. Instead they flipped the idea and supported a program of instruction in which Spanish was taught first; within the complexity of literacy, including prominent Spanish-language authors, this was the basis for intellectual development, so that intellectual development in Spanish was a necessary condition to the intellectual development in English leading to complex literacy and the reading of Shakespeare, Henry James, John Steinbeck, and many others. Guerrero and the others were crucial in developing the report *The Invisible Minority*, which led to congressional hearings, the aftermath of which was the development of the Bilingual Education Act in 1968.[11]

For the next twenty years, bilingual programs of varying quality spread throughout the United States but were especially concentrated in the Southwest. The literature from 1965 to the present has shown and supported the theoretical basis of this method and, in fact, according to David Ramírez (2000, 28), the empirical literature is sound in supporting the conclusion that "the best entry into literacy is through the use of a child's native language," referring to Clay (1993) and Snow, Burns, and Griffin (1998) as empirical support. Further, according to Ramírez (ibid.),

Literacy in a child's home language provides knowledge, concept and skills bases that transfer to reading in a second language (L2), e.g., English (Collier and Thomas, 1992; Cummins, 1989; Escamilla, 1987; Modiano, 1968; Rodríguez, 1988; Carter and Chatfield, 1986). This is supported by research showing that proficiency in L1 e.g. Spanish literacy skills is highly correlated with the development of literacy skills in L2. (Collier and Thomas, 1995; Greene, 1998; Krashen and Biber, 1987; Leshere-Madrid, and García, 1985; Ramírez, Yuen, and Ramey, 1991)

More recent meta-analysis has shown similar results, and Rolstad, MacSwann, and Mahoney (2012) concluded that programs utilizing the student's native language and English had much more positive learning and developmental results than only English instruction for nonnative English speakers. Their work found what the original developers of Spanish for Nativos and bilingual education had long known—that a well-planned and developed longitudinal program in both languages created the conditions for greater academic student success but were dependent as well on the availability of first-rate teachers able to offer the curriculum.[12]

The question arises: Why have not these findings been incorporated as part of a national policy of curriculum development and language instruction, which might lead to the development of even greater linguistic and educational capital and resource of Mexican-origin populations and other Spanish speakers? The answer lies in the continuation, at least in the Southwest, of historical prejudices, the reliance on a single linguistic and cultural prism of acculturation, the reinforcement of ahistorical ignorance especially in regards to Mexican-origin populations, the changing political demography of the region since 1970 forward, and the appropriation of Spanish by those espousing largely "natural" and pervasive "white" neoliberal theories. Last, but not least, as will be concluded in the last section of this work, there have never been any longitudinal studies of the impact of these programs on the development of adult literacy or language maintenance or their impact on following generations. This might have mitigated the more onerous effects of English-only projects.

THE ENGLISH-ONLY MOVEMENT: THE PRISM THROUGH "WHITE" NEOLIBERAL THEORIES

If we are to understand the very complex situation of Spanish literacy and language in the United States, there are also conflicting and contradictory pressures that are both historical and contemporary. The English-only movement is partially a function of historical state formations, attitudes carried over from different contexts, and the articulation of racialized scripts as a consequence of major changes in the political demography of the Southwest United States.[13] The various measures promulgated since the founding of English-only, as have already been discussed, have long historical antecedents in the early twentieth century and initiated largely in the SWNAR, especially in the states of California and Arizona. However, these cannot be understood apart from the entire question of legal and unauthorized immigration from 1970 to 2011, when in the latter period the growth of Mexican-origin undocumented migrants fell to zero. In the present, the basis of most English-only programs has been very importantly linked to those most concerned with the increase in the demography of this population and partially based on racialist premises.

"WHITE RACISM"

While it would be simple to reduce English-only propositions and measures to the revival of nativism and demographic changes, this would not explain how "reasonable" persons can join such propositions without reference either to history or deeply held "individual" racist positions. Jane Hill (2015, 235) has eloquently iterated that in part this is due to the phenomenon that she has termed "White racist Neo-liberal theories of language and culture," which transcend political positions and add further depth to understand the "state" of Spanish literacy and language.[14] She terms "White racism" as a cultural project in the United States in which most if not all "white" people and probably many minorities participate at one point or another, and the method used to ascertain participation in this project is through the systems of communication or "discourse" in which people participate (ibid.). As she shows in her discourse analysis of one of the major figures in the anti-ethnic studies measures in the state of Arizona, this figure has developed a rhetoric not of impassioned racist adjectives but rather one consisting of entirely rational commentaries in which "good faith" is the mechanism of discussion and entirely "reasonable," but whose premises are imbued with what have been termed "megascripts"—masked, hidden, and grey (Vélez-Ibáñez 2010). These include the case in which she analyzed profoundly attached essentialist and reductionist arguments in which the relationships between language and culture are simplified with simple "American" connections between language and economic opportunities. Such argumentations seep through many discourses on a daily basis and include academic, civil, economic, political, and certainly cultural systems of communication and behaviors.

Among the many intended and unintended consequences of such discourse are the reemphasis on the great American cultural prisms of acculturation, couched as the "melting pot," language replacement, cultural references, and accepted ritual and national symbols of representation. These in turn foster consequential educational categories of exclusion and inclusion of language proficiency in classrooms, such as SEI (Structured English Immersion), ELM (English Language Mainstream), and even an ALT (Alternative Classroom), each associated with a series of assessment tools that feed into these categories of instruction. Each has its own peculiarities, test-dependent practices, and segregating processes. In addition, even with the best of intentions, they very much mark the student throughout his/her educational journey.[15] The subtlety of this "white" process is entirely rational, supported by educational institutions, and the hallmark of English instruction for "ESLs," SSPs, and other like categories, but without regard to these underlying processes and subterfuges.

It can be safely asserted that the understanding between the retention, elimination, or expansion of Spanish, even by academics, is often imbued with both "white racism," whose characteristics for learning the English-language are reduced to opportunity, and "achievement." Spanish is subtly but consistently induced as the underlying causative factor of studies that accentuate the connection between Spanish-speaking children and their "failure" in achievement tests and low socioeconomic standing. This discourse is too often repeated as a mantra of causation or correlation, and continues to rationalize the "seeing man" syndrome.

POLITICAL DEMOGRAPHY AND ENGLISH-ONLY

Seeping in to the "white racism" construct is the actuality of the growth of Mexican-origin populations on the northern side of the region since the 1960s that seem to have been remarkable. Due to the combined growth in births and legal and unauthorized migration, the Mexican-origin population increased substantially. In 1960, the total Mexican-origin population was 2.9 million, and according to the 2010 Census, it counted "50.5 million Hispanics in the United States, making up 16.3% of the total population. The nation's Hispanic population, which was 35.3 million in 2000, grew 43% over the decade. The Hispanic population also accounted for most of the nation's growth—56%—from 2000 to 2010" (Passel, Cohn, and López 2011). From this total, 34.7 million were of Mexican origin and included U.S.-born, legal residents, and 6.2 million unauthorized persons (Passel and Cohn 2009). Importantly, "Among children ages 17 and younger, there were 17.1 million Latinos in 2010, or 23.1% of this age group, according to an analysis by the Pew Hispanic Center of which the majority are U.S. citizens. The number of Latino children grew 39% over the decade. In 2000, there were 12.3 million Hispanic children, who were 17.1% of the population under age 18" (Passel, Cohn, and López 2011).

In the state of Arizona, which has been at the center of anti-immigrant policies and English-only measures, the impact of demographic growth on school districts seems to have been dramatic, with Mexican-origin enrollment between 1998 and 2008 increasing from 268,098 to 416,705, accounting for 86 percent of the total student population growth in the state of Arizona, shown in figure 31 developed by García et al. (2012).

From larger growth patterns in other states such as California, Texas, and New Mexico and noticeable in states in the Midwest and the traditional South, anti-immigrant and English-only measures were pushed. The rationales of these included the increased costs of education, including intensive-English programs, use of social services, increase in penal populations, and alleged disease increases, which combined with nativist and racialized discourses, and importantly, the alleged destructive impact of job displacement on citizens. All of these rationales seep into the discourse concerning the Spanish language in one way or another and underpin the rationality of "white racism" discourses.

However, these rationales were based largely on the premise of the growth and impact of unauthorized Mexican-origin populations with total disregard to legal immigration and the natural childbirth patterns of documented, resident, and U.S.-born Mexican-origin citizens. This discourse avoided the fact that the Mexican-origin

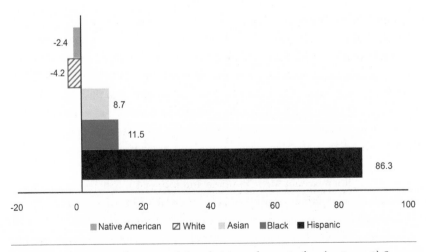

FIGURE 31. K–12 enrollment trends by ethnicity and net gain/loss (1998–2008) Source: Arizona Department of Education 1999, 2008, in Garcia et al. 2009.

	1970*	1980*	1990*	2000*	2010
Mexican	4532435	8678632	13495938	20640711	31798258
Puerto Rican	1429396	2004961	2727754	3406178	4623716
Cuban	544600	806223	1043932	1241685	1785547
Other Hispanic	n/a	3113867	5086435	10017244	12276073

FIGURE 32. U.S. Hispanic population by origin. Sources: U.S. Decennial Census 1970, 1980, 1990, 2000, 2010.

	1970-1980	1980-1990	1990-2000	2000-2010
Mexican	91.5%	55.5%	52.9%	54.1%
Puerto Rican	40.3%	36.1%	24.9%	35.7%
Cuban	48.0%	29.5%	18.9%	43.8%
Other Hispanic	n/a	63.3%	96.9%	22.5%

FIGURE 33. U.S. Hispanic population growth rates by origin. Sources: U.S. Decennial Census 1970, 1980, 1990, 2000, 2010.

population since the nineteenth century has been much younger than the general population, due to early marriage, more children who in turn have more children, and youthful immigration, both documented and unauthorized. Thus en toto the tally of this population in 2000, including all other Spanish-speaking populations, can be seen in figure 32, originally in the citation but expanded to include 2010.[16]

It would have been impossible for a total of 6.2 million Mexican unauthorized persons in 2000 to account for the reported total growth. The percentage growth in figure 33 is entirely misleading and too often misused as rationale for the legislative measures of English-only and anti-immigrant policies and legislation, as shown in figure 33, and migrated into discourses of Hill's concept of "white racism."

ENGLISH-ONLY RATIONALES AND FEARS AND ITS TOTEMIC FOUNDERS AND RELATIONS

In the present it can be observed that the total Mexican-origin population in the United States is made up of those who were born or migrated here and residents, of whom 20 percent are unauthorized. This growth, particularly for smaller rural communities in the United States, represents a radical demographic change in which the traditional eastern prisms are threatened by foreign populations so different culturally

	1899	1990	2000	2011
Arizona	28.2	1.1	2.3	5.9
California	8.3	2.9	3.6	8.4
New Mexico	65.1	0.1	1.6	4.6
Texas	5.9	1.5	2.7	8.9

FIGURE 34. Percentage of "foreign" language, non-English-speaking Spanish speakers. Source: Census Office 1897; 1990 Census of population, 2000 Census of population; Community Survey, 2013. Age ten and older in 1890; age five and older in 1990; age five and older in 2000; age five and older in 2011.

and linguistically and not "natural." When combined with fragile economic circumstances nationally, hysterical fevers, anxiety, and ethnocentric reactions give life to draconian immigration laws and regulations in many states, and there is no greater illustration than the English-only movements (Vélez-Ibáñez 2011, 27).

In an editorial column for the *Guardian* (UK), on March 8, 2001, James Crawford—a longtime critic of a monolingual United States—wrote that much of the English-only movement arose "because Americans who came of age before the 1970s had little experience of linguistic diversity. Growing up in a period of tight immigration quotas, they seldom encountered anyone speaking a language other than English except foreign tourists, who were usually white and European" (Crawford 2008, 6).

Yet the percentage of "foreign"-language, non-English-speaking Spanish speakers in the region does not reflect the overwhelming public perceptions of most Americans, as figure 34 shows.[17]

On the other hand, Crawford states that, regardless of these language demographics, there is an often-stated stereotype that "'[i]f you live in America, you need to speak English.' According to a *Los Angeles Times* poll (1998a), that was how three out of four voters explained their support for Proposition 227, the ballot initiative that dismantled most bilingual education programs in California. Many Arizonans cited the same reason for passing a similar measure [Proposition 203]" (Crawford, 2000).

Known as the Unz Initiative in California, Proposition 227 in 1998 required "that all students be taught exclusively in English and in structured English Immersion for immigrant students" without reference to either parental or student rights to decide to maintain, expand, or retain their native language and reduced language resources to just something to be removed.[18] Even though the 2003 Arizona measure was held unconstitutional, the state introduced a similar measure every year and only by the slightest of margins were these not approved, even though "[t]he most draconian official-English laws at the state level, in Alaska and Arizona, were struck down under the First and Fourteenth amendments. State and federal courts ruled that, while advancing no compelling public interest, these measures violated free-speech and equal-protection guarantees."[19] Thus while Crawford's is an appreciated hypothesis, the genesis of English-only emerges from the premises of the "rational" discourses just described but also lies in deeper nativists positions connected to extreme right wing opponents to Mexican-origin immigration and the possible loss of political influence and power due to the probability of these populations eventually becoming citizens and voting for non-right-wing candidates. This fear has spread to most states that have increased Mexican-origin populations and some for whom this is not even a possibility (Planas 2012). And these will probably be augmented by the 2016 election of Donald Trump, whose campaign was initiated not by a "seeing man" syndrome but by a blind, homogenizing, and ahistorical nativism.

It may be suggested that the initial fearful resistance to becoming part of New Mexico that founded the state of Arizona, as has already been described, is the twenty-first-century equivalent fear to that in the nineteenth century that Mexican-origin populations "would subject us to the domination of another commonwealth of different traditions, customs, and aspiration." Certainly, the seeming demise of Mexican American studies in Tucson is part and parcel of the continuing support of the ahistoricism mentioned. The Arizona legislature is very much a part of this enterprise. The fear of demographic replacement also holds true of losing one myth in exchange for other more accurate mythic explanations, but these are very much associated with "rational" discourses of a much larger scope. The Arizona legislature has led the nation in the late 1990s in promulgating English-only and anti-immigrant measures. It is therefore important to understand Arizona's push for such measures. However, this was preceded by Ronald Reagan, who signed into law a state employer sanctions law (Arizona passed its equivalent in 2007); other states followed California's lead in the 1970s. Arizona was not one of them. In 1994, California enacted Prop 187 with the Arizona version not enacted until 2004. Oklahoma enacted HB1804 in 2007; its equivalent is Arizona's SB1070 (2010).[20]

A simple scan can be rendered of the lineage of these various versions of anti-Mexican behavior in Arizona by linking the lineages and clans of the past to the present and between English-only, anti-immigration, and racialism. Former State Senator Russell Pearce of Arizona led and developed SB 1070 and English-only through a network of personalities that tie the opposition to immigration and unauthorized immigrants with English-only. Although he has been removed from office through a recall procedure by the Mormon community and others, which will described shortly, he is prominent in the Republican Party.

TOTEMIC FOUNDER

First, Dr. John Tanton, an ophthalmologist, is one of the apical ancestors whose totemic lodge is the source for the network of funders for much of the early English-only and anti-immigration initiatives. What is especially of note is his joining the board of Population-Environment Balance in 1973, founding and funding the Federation for American Immigration Reform (FAIR) in 1979, the Center for Immigration Studies (CIS) in 1985, a number of English-only associations, such as U.S. Inc., founded and funded 1982, and U.S. English, founded and funded in 1983. These include at least thirteen other such organizations, with some tied to neo-Nazis.[21] The inspiration for Dr. Tanton's ideological foundations is *The Camp of the Saints* (*Le Camp des saints*), a 1973 French novel by Jean Raspail that imagines Third World hordes destroying European civilization by their brown invasion.

It is important to note that these organizational connections are part of the structural and ideological foundations for English-only and SB 1070; key sections were upheld by the United States Supreme Court in 2012, and as importantly, for the funding of state legislative and executive offices. For example, Kris Kobach (in 2016 part of the Department of Homeland Security transition team to Donald Trump) was general counsel to Tanton's FAIR through the Immigration Reform Law Institute (IRLI) and was hired as a consultant by Sheriff Joe Arpaio of Arizona. Arpaio is the notorious Arizona sheriff who has honed anti-Mexican sweeps to a fine art and was found to have violated the civil rights of Mexican-origin populations. This support arose during Kobach's successful run for secretary of state of Kansas. Kobach had been hired as a legal consultant by Russell Pearce, who developed SB 1070 and other such measures throughout the United States. While Russell Pearce disavowed any connections to neo-Nazis, he in fact appeared in fundraising activities for J. T. Ready, whom he sponsored to the Mormon Church in Mesa, Arizona. Ready, expelled from the Marine Corps with a bad conduct discharge, is the neo-Nazi founder of an extremist organization, "America First," who, on May 2, 2012, murdered his girlfriend, her mother, and a small child, and then killed himself.

Finally, the last of the list of characters is the former superintendent of schools and later attorney general of the state of Arizona, Tom Horne, who initiated the legal and legislative restrictions on Mexican American studies and was an ardent devotee of Russell Pearce and strongly supported for office by Sheriff Joe Arpaio. Horne ran for attorney general of Arizona in 2010 and, with their support, won.[22] Many of these relationships then resulted in the passing of HB 1070, even though three parts have been declared unconstitutional, and they are directly linked to the Arizona English-only measures, as well as to other such measures throughout the United States.

However, since these activities, a new wind has been felt throughout the state in the form of coalitions between organizations like Arizona Promise in Action, which is a largely Chicano group, moderate Republicans, and especially businesses and various churches. Among the most important is the Mormon Church, which supported Pearce's Recall and ran the candidate in opposition to Pearce. What is of note is that between 2000 and 2006, the number of Spanish-speaking Mormon congregations grew from 389 to 639 in the United States, and the number of Mexican-origin congregations grew from 5 in 2002 to 13 in 2010 in Mesa, where Pearce currently resides. The Church itself estimates that 60 to 70 percent of their congregation members are undocumented.[23]

But Pearce ran in a newly created state-level legislative district, which, however, was contested, since once again the Mormon Church ran another Mormon candidate against Pearce (Bob Worsely, founder of SkyMall—a retailer for air travelers). Pearce once again was defeated on August 29, 2012, by strong Mormon support. His brother, who is of the same political stripe, was himself defeated simultaneously for another office. There are, however, many others in addition to those mentioned here (not the least of whom is Sheriff Arpaio, who was finally defeated for reelection in 2016), as well as many of the Republican legislators who represent equivalent ideological convictions. But Arpaio's term as sheriff finally ended, given various issues that have arisen, not the least of which are the *Ortega Melendres v. Arapio* class-action suit and the Department of Justice parallel suit regarding the racial profiling of Mexican-origin persons.[24] Federal District Court Judge G. Murray Snow (a Republican and Mormon) found Arpaio to be in civil contempt of court and issued his recommendation to the U.S. Attorney's Office related to the issuance of criminal contempt of court charges. Trump pardoned him on August 25, 2017 (Liptak 2017:1).

THE FUTURE OF SPANISH LITERACY AND LANGUAGE: THE RISE OF BILINGUALISM ONCE MORE AND TRANSLANGUALITY

There is one overwhelming linguistic process that has been overlooked in most discussions of the future of Spanish literacy and language in spite of the many legislative, attitudinal, and racialized measures designed to remove Spanish as either a cultural aspect of identity or its functionality as a cultural resource. That is the long-term impact of bilingualism. There is no longitudinal study of the effects of childhood bilingual programs on adulthood Spanish literacy and language retention or expansion. Most of the literature emphasizes bilingual elementary school programs, assessment and developmental techniques, and some attention to the teaching of "Heritage" students and the various methods and approaches used.[25] Yet there is no long-term research that speaks to the manner in which early bilingual programs that emphasize the expansion of the literacy and linguistic capacities of both Spanish and English and their efficacy in science, engineering, or mathematics are wanting. We have little in research that has focused on how bilingualism has functioned through adulthood that could provide the general public an indication of its efficacy and/or functions into maturity. In fact, a comprehensive analysis by Ramírez (2000, 28) states, "There are few studies on young children who are bilingual and beginning to develop literacy in one or both languages, and *none* documenting the development of bilingualism over time"[26] (my italics). Finally, there are no longitudinal studies that analyze the impact of bilingually trained persons on their children that might have given a much longer-term developmental gauge of Spanish language use and literacy practices.

Most of what can be stated is anecdotal at best but there are indications of such growth in the 2000 U.S. Census, according to the work of James Crawford (2002). He states that "[t]he number of minority language speakers who also speak English 'very well' increased at comparable rates: 44 percent in the 1990s, versus 39 percent in the 1980s. In other words, over the past 20 years, the population of fluent bilinguals has been increasing at about the same rate as the population that speaks languages other than English at home." On the other hand, there are no empirical studies to gauge the level of fluency, literacy, or functionality of that bilingualism among adults who were taught in elementary and secondary bilingual programs.

DISCUSSION ONE

The road of Spanish literacy and language in the SWNAR is one that begins in the sixteenth century and to varying degrees has expanded and constricted according to the political regimes in power, the functionality of the language institutionally, the presence of educational institutions supporting the language's learning, the repression of the language through war and conquest, the flow of Mexican-origin populations, and most recently, Central American populations (including individuals who speak an Indigenous language), but not the subject of this discourse, and legislative and administrative measures such as bilingual programs or English-only programs that supported or restricted the use of Spanish literacy and language practices.[27] The ebb and flow of literacy as reflected by the presence of newspapers and other literary practices are and continue to be a function of entering Spanish-speaking populations. From 1970 through 2012 the growth of these populations from Mexico has been impressive and also the object of restrictive, racialist, and institutional measures that seek to reduce its political impact on non-Mexican populations. These have a lineage of less than savory progenitors and activists, and align with rationalizations and reasonable argumentations and studies that eventually make correlational or causative associations between poverty and the Spanish language, Mexican culture, lack of educational achievement, and Mexicans as inherently suspect of being "illegal" migrants.

On the other hand, there are fresh winds of change in some parts of the country, which may lead to a reconsideration of the manner in which not only English is taught but how Spanish is recognized as a means of cognitive, linguistic, and academic development that leads to the highest levels of literary and linguistic achievement in both languages. Yet there are two important conditions that may increase the likelihood of Spanish literacy and language: first is the recognition that in a globalizing economy, the SWNAR is one of transborder populations, economy, polity, culture, and social relations. The integration of the transborder economy since the nineteenth century has given rise to myriad transborder initiatives, programs, associations, and connectivities in which bilingualism is a multifaceted resource for multiple levels of communication and culture with national origin of secondary importance.[28] Second, the academic literature on the mastery of multiple languages by bilingual development has reached a level of complexity and achievement, making it highly likely that the English-only paradigm will be replaced by something more akin to diverse, functionally developed bilingual programs. This would give all students the opportunity to become multiply educated and to continue that development through adulthood, fulfilling the economic, cultural, social, and political needs of the transborder region and a continuing global economy. On the other hand, these winds of change still must face the subtle, but always present discourses and megascripts that accentuate national acculturation, assimilation, regional ignorance, and essentialist single cultural identities based on less than adequate understandings of the complexity and situationality of cultures and languages, of the south-to-north movements and vice versa, of the changing political regimes, and of the integrated economic and ecological relations of the region. On the other hand, these winds may be interrupted by both the cognitive and physical walls that are proposed by the 2016 election of Donald Trump, whose educational supporters will more than likely reaccentuate the nativist monolingual tradition.

Herein lies the fact that from the nineteenth century to the present, myriad transborder connectivities have been created, including cross-border relations, visitations, kinship networks, educational stays, and hundreds of other rationales for transborder sorties. These include purchasing goods on both sides, working on one side and living in the other, and going to primary and secondary schools on one side while residing on the other. Many sought and seek medical care on one side less expensive than on the other, with communication links constantly reinforced through correspondence, telephone, and Spanish-language radio and television channels. In the

198 🏠 CHAPTER 6

present the use of many electronic communications, Internet sites such as Twitter, Google, Yahoo, DuckDuckGo, thousands of blogs, and texts multiply daily and many are in Spanish with networks in both English and Spanish. This has created and continues to create a very intensive transborder linguistic and cultural field of action, history, remembrance, and maintenance that belies easy political solutions or a national prism of identity that harkens back to the origins of the British colonies and is maintained as the central mythic reference in schools and in almost every possible means of human communication and is highly ritualized by national celebrations.

Yet the regional economy and its production needs for labor continue to this day, so that demographically, Spanish ebbs and flows according to the state of what is in reality a Southwest North American transborder economy and region, from which corresponding conflicts ensue over language, culture, identity, social relations, and political policies. In fact, the region has induced the travel of English south, bilingualism made necessary in specific business contexts north, and has created a number of processes that mirror the asymmetry of the region itself.

BILINGUALISM NORTH AND ENGLISH SOUTH AND THEIR CONTENTS AND DISCONTENTS

According to Krogstad and González-Barrera, a majority of English-speaking Hispanics in the United States are bilingual (62 percent).[29] Although diminishing by generation, the use of language is distributed in this manner: 36 percent are bilingual, 25 percent mainly use English and 38 percent mainly use Spanish, and among those who speak English, 59 percent are bilingual (ibid.). The retention of bilingualism, at least superficially, is generational, with 50 percent of children of immigrant parents doing so and diminishing to about 25 percent in the third generation, as shown in figure 35 (ibid.).

That said, however, it is curious that when bilinguality is examined, Mexicans have a smaller percentage of bilinguals than any of the other Spanish-speaking groups except for Puerto Ricans. Cubans, who are largely more recent arrivals (post-1959), seem to retain this capacity better than Mexicans in spite of the fact of being bombarded with the same set of media and communication in English-only venues. The more than likely reason for this is the very high-grade bilingual programs that Florida has maintained and especially those in the Miami-Dade area demanded by a very active political Cuban community. Very recently arrived, Salvadorans for the most part are among the most isolated and segregated of Spanish-speaking populations, concentrating in mostly Spanish-speaking areas with a very high proportion of Spanish-only households, and are in danger of being constituted as an "illegal class."[30]

Half of 2nd Generation Latinos Are Bilingual

% of Hispanic adults who mainly use English, Spanish or both

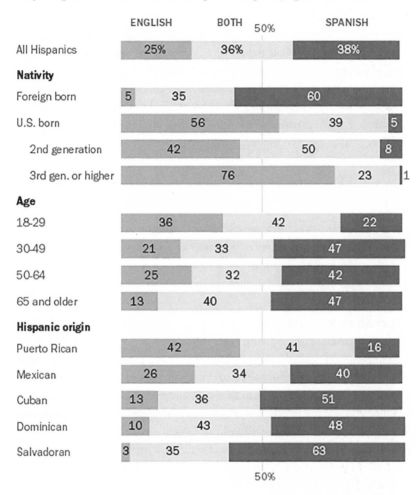

	ENGLISH	BOTH	50%	SPANISH
All Hispanics	25%	36%		38%
Nativity				
Foreign born	5	35		60
U.S. born	56		39	5
2nd generation	42		50	8
3rd gen. or higher	76		23	1
Age				
18-29	36	42		22
30-49	21	33		47
50-64	25	32		42
65 and older	13	40		47
Hispanic origin				
Puerto Rican	42	41		16
Mexican	26	34		40
Cuban	13	36		51
Dominican	10	43		48
Salvadoran	3	35		63

50%

Note: Foreign born includes persons born outside of the U.S. and those born in Puerto Rico even though those born in Puerto Rico are U.S. citizens. Second generation refers to those born in the U.S. to at least one parent who was born outside the U.S. or in Puerto Rico.
Source: Pew Research Center 2013 National Survey of Latinos

PEW RESEARCH CENTER

FIGURE 35. Jens Manuel Krogstad and Ana Gonzalez-Barrera (2015): "A majority of English-speaking Hispanics in the U.S. are bilingual," Fact Tank: News in the Numbers. Pew Research Center. March 24. http://www.pewresearch.org/fact-tank/2015/03/24/a-majority-of-english-speaking-hispanics-in-the-u-s-are-bilingual/.

What then accounts for the 40 percent capacity among Mexicans when the population numbers in the millions? In part, Mexicans have faced language discrimination longer than the other groups and have internalized all the spoken, activated, and unspoken erasing behaviors that have been primary in the educational systems of which they were and continue to be a part. Spanish, even in the best of educational settings, simply is not valued as a comparable or equivalent language to be expanded, explored, nor retained. The "white" syndrome, which has been suggested as the creeping element that seeps into the best of intentions, can be easily seen in the following "Facts about English Learners in California" of the California Department of Education (2015).[31] The objectives of the language development mission are the following:

> The CDE provides assistance to local schools and districts to achieve the following goals:
>
>> Ensure that English learners acquire full proficiency in English as rapidly and effectively as possible and attain parity with native speakers of English.
>> Ensure that English learners, within a reasonable period of time, achieve the same rigorous grade-level academic standards that are expected of all students.

The primary rationale is to "close the achievement gap that separates English learners from their native English-speaking peers" (ibid.). On the other hand, there would be no linguistically underdeveloped achievement gap if the most important cultural resource a child inherited could be enhanced and developed equivalently to English, and that is the language that she or he speaks and with which the child communicates. There would still be class-based issues, but the language platform upon which the child rests would not be one. But what is most compelling for the argument that Spanish is not valued is that in the state of California almost 85 percent of "English learners," ELLs to use the creeping nomenclature, are Spanish-speaking students, with the next largest group being Vietnamese (accounting for 2.3 percent), and for other groups, diminishing to 0.5 percent for Russian-speaking students. Thus, in California, of the 1,413,549 "English Learners," almost 85 percent are Spanish-speaking students and mostly in the elementary grades K–6, which is the perfect time in which children are like sponges and ready to expand their cognitive and linguistic capacities. Thus 1,201,516 Spanish-speaking students will be erased of their capacity to be bilingual and to read Unamuno, Cervantes, Azuela, as well as Shakespeare, or to be able to write essays in Spanish about self and others and about their multiple "I's." Simply, the statistical rendering of bilingualism does not tell the underlying narrative. A magical statistical creep replaces the erasing policies of educational institutions responsible for much of the shift in bilingualism through generations and expressed in daily discourses.

THE QUOTIDIAN LEVEL OF DISCOURSE

However, it is at the quotidian level of behavior that the secondary, sometimes tertiary, position that Spanish is rendered that provides a more behaviorally oriented understanding to this reality by this observed event. Most recently (2010) in a Scottsdale store in Arizona, a niece from Puerto Rico was buying clothes and she turned to her mother to ask for her advice in Spanish. Her mother is a graduate of the Pratt Institute of Art in New York and an artist and grade-school teacher in Puerto Rico. Before she could respond, a middle-aged Anglo woman standing nearby admonished both daughter and mother with the classic refrain of "You are now in the United States and you (the daughter) will never be successful if you don't learn and use English." The Puerto Rican mother, offended, responded in English and suggested that the woman was an "ignorant lout," with her response embedded in a rather haughty New York tone of voice with drawn consonants. The woman's physical response was one of perplexity. There is probably no Spanish speaker in the north that has not been subject to this sort of uninformed display, including myself and my entire family.

How then can we explain such behavior by seemingly rational people? One source we can turn to is Jane Hill's construct of "whiteness." She argues that the answer lies in that such rationality is a "normalized" action that has its own logic, structure, and space. Accent and pronunciation, for example, are the bane of many foreign-language speakers so that self-consciousness is even suffered by highly educated anthropologists. It is the case that from elementary school through the present, the devil Spanish accent had to be driven out. Other accents such as French or German are very acceptable and desirable but not any Asian or Latin American or African ones. Further, I spent countless nights as a child practicing the difference between *shoulder* and *soldier* in order to not again be embarrassed and mocked in elementary school for pronouncing one for the other. On the other hand, English speakers mispronouncing Spanish or speaking with fractured accents are perceived as rather quaint creatures but appreciated for their trying to speak it. The reverse is not valid for Spanish speakers.

Hill provides insight and analysis to this seeming quandary of exceptional treatment of the one and the acceptance of the other and the inherent contradictions that license loutish behavior. Hill (1998, 681) states that Spanish speakers are not allowed to utter English but with the most exact correctness in the "outer sphere": that is, the space and place that is a public sphere of officialdom, courts, and classrooms, and I would add recreational areas, churches in Anglo neighborhoods, in the streets in which Mexicans don't wander much, or in the malls, as the example showed—or frankly just about anywhere there are few of the "us's" and a lot of the "them's." This rigid division between the "sphere of comfort," where language reigns from monolingual Spanish to Spanglish to English, depending on the context, is rigidly separated from the "outer sphere," even when Spanish is used. Spanish in the public sphere, as Hill notes, quoting Urciuoli (1996, 35), is licensed and managed in events like "folklife festivals," as part of processes of "ethnification" that function to create differences that are "cultural, neat, and safe."[32] Perhaps the safest outer sphere in which Spanish is relatively savory is in the Mexican consulate but not without danger since the Spanish spoken may not be the Queen's Spanish. So what does this mean?

Hill states the following unequivocally, as she is wont to do:

> The main point of my argument is that Puerto Ricans [I would substitute Mexicans] experience the "outer sphere" as an important site of their racialization, since they are always found wanting by this sphere's standards of linguistic orderliness. My research suggests that precisely the opposite is true for Whites. Whites permit themselves a considerable amount of disorder precisely at the language boundary that is a site of discipline for . . . members of historically Spanish-speaking populations in the United States—that is, the boundary between Spanish and English in public discourse. (682)

The consequences for Spanish-speaking populations of this dynamic and the profound racialization that ensues is that the power dimension is maintained and permits the dynamic to exist, continue, and remain functionally useful, but not to the "other." Hill suggests that such a dynamic is maintained by Anglos using fractured Spanish, or mock as she terms it, or not one that creates "a desirable 'colloquial'" presence. But uses of Spanish by Spanish speakers are "disorderly and dangerous," and are some of the ways in which this arena of usage is constituted (682). She cites Page and Thomas (1994), who have identified "white public space," which she describes as a "morally significant set of contexts that are the most important sites of the practices of a racializing hegemony, in which Whites are invisibly normal, and in which racialized populations are visibly marginal and the objects of monitoring ranging for individual judgment to Official-English legislation" (ibid.). In this manner, the California Department of Education could maintain its invisibility while invisibly monitoring and judging the necessity of erasing the cultural basis of communication of over a million children and keeping their dangerous languages away from their most public sphere and neatly rationalized by an all-seeing educational man. Yet this situation was reversed by the passage of Proposition 58 in California in 2016, which removed all of the intervening regulations regarding requirements in creating bilingual programs and thus resulting in the destruction of the basis for the English-Only 227 Proposition previously in force.[33]

SECONDARY BILINGUALISM IN MOTION

This hegemonic secondary placement of Spanish is very much also influenced by, and is an artifact of, larger economically created structural relations between itself and English. Even with the widespread need for Spanish in business with the huge Spanish-speaking market, Spanish is too many times literally translated, culturally denuded, or made socially inept. There is little of the population represented in the television or film media except for Spanish-language media, itself obsessed with drugs, sex, and objectified women in its hundreds of novelas, commercials, and weather reporters. But, among the most telling of the manner in which Spanish is considered, in spite of the 35 million or so persons who are "Hispanic" and of whom 95 percent of adults would like to retain the language, is the function of bilingualism in the workplace (Taylor et al. 2012).

Title VII of the 1964 Civil Rights Act, Section 1606.7 governs what the Equal Employment Opportunity Commission refers to as "Speak English Only Rules." That section of the guidelines asserts that it "will presume that [an English-only rule that applies at all times] violates Title VII and closely scrutinize it." An English-only rule that applies only at certain times is permissible under Section 1606.7 only if it is "justified by business necessity" (U.S. Commission on Civil Rights 2011, 4). But while laudatory and protective in its intent, in the final analysis, the positioning of Spanish as a secondary language, while important to giving directions in the workplace—or "work Spanish" as some would designate it—is not a recognition of value but in reality a consideration for giving instruction toward a work goal rather than the language having a linguistic functional equivalence to English. Moreover, the general public's knowledge of the agency and the limited sources allocated by Congress limit the remedy that is available to workers who confronted violations of the law.

Even when Spanish is used as a functional work language, it remains secondary, as will be seen, or prohibited by ignorance, even in a university student's service office in which a former staff member was prohibited from communicating with Spanish-speaking students in the language by her supervisor, regardless of the functionality of communication and increased efficiency of sorting out student questions.[34]

ECONOMY AND HEGEMONIC PRIVILEGE AND ENGLISH SOUTH

But from the quotidian to the workplace, how are these dynamics played out and what are the structures of imposition and distribution of effects in the creation of economic "white spaces" and privileges? How do the structures of both vertical and horizontal relations within organized settings reveal the manner in which transborder "whiteness" becomes embedded? Recent works contribute strongly to this understanding in the SWNAR. First is Josiah Heyman and Amado Alarcón's "Spanish-English Bilingualism in Uneven and Combined Relations" (n.d.),[35] whose primary focus is on the way in which economic forces in the northern border region shape the manner in which bilinguals often "act [in] brokerage roles, transmitting power between English-dominant private and public sector institutions and Spanish dominant or bilingual workers, customers, and targets of control." Second is an unpublished manuscript by Heyman and Alarcón (2017), in which the authors detail the manner in which "market mechanisms and institutional constraints shape the valuation and social expansion of Spanish" (1). Both are based on firsthand fieldwork and provide an unusually deep look at how these processes function and contribute from the perspective applied here to "white" privilege created for and by both Anglos and Mexicans.

First is a glimpse of the manner in which bilingualism is used in what may be termed "vertical relations of power"—that is, unequal, dominant, hierarchical, subordinating, decision-imposing, and asymmetrical relations of control common to contexts of differentiated material and economic resources. Heyman and Alarcón sort out these in three settings: a Mexican maquiladora in Juárez, Chihuahua; second, an American call center in El Paso, Texas, where bilingualism is key for its function; and last, the role of bilingualism in health and public safety services on the American side of the region (127). They, however, pay great attention to the middle-course language of "Spanglish," part of the linguistic repertoire that combines Spanish and English and its focal mechanism, "code-switching," which requires, as the authors point out, "extensive capabilities in both languages, hence fluent bilingualism" (128), and is very important in the horizontal interaction one would surmise especially between persons of *confianza* (mutual trust).[36]

So how do vertical and horizontal relations in the maquiladora unfold to reveal both public and private domains of whiteness and nonwhiteness? First, both American and Canadian corporations, as the authors point out, need bilingual brokers to manage the complexities of finance and production to maintain the advantage of using lower-wage workers (128). These brokers range from U.S.-born non–Mexican-origin persons to Mexican-origin U.S. citizens to Mexico-born Mexicans, all of whom have the capacity to different degrees to travel through the hierarchies of the corporation. These may fill different roles such as plant management, technical functions, or top-level administrators. On the other hand, there are persons the authors point out that cannot communicate technical information so that interpreters are required to maintain the flow of information imperative to the factory system to function efficiently but also to maintain the hierarchy of production based on lower-wage labor

(129). In addition, Mexican nationals with fluency in English participate in important roles that required global communication with English as the lingua franca when "no one involved was a native speaker of English" (ibid.). They also point out, citing Melissa Wright (2006),[37]

> She observes that in the factories, English was a code for higher value and affiliation with (e.g., career paths into) U.S. corporate management. Spanish formed part of a set of signs (together with cheerful interpersonal interaction, showier clothing, etc.) of lower value, disposability, and a ceiling to career advancement. Her narrative focuses on the performance of these unequal valuations. Yet, at the same time, Spanish-English bilingualism, together with other forms of knowledge articulation, must surely have been part of this divided yet combined system of inequality at work . . . (ibid.).

In this manner, the privileging of English in this public sphere is provided greater legitimacy by its global functions. Its concomitant "whiteness" as a register of dominance becomes embedded as well with Spanish remaining as a means necessary for maintaining the stratification of production and low-wage labor.

Similarly, but taking place in the northern side of the region, are call centers utilizing Mexico-born bilingual operators who are key to maintaining a high-profit, low-wage production facility of information and communication. These fluent bilinguals, most of whom had attended schools in the United States, are paid less than English-dominant speakers and their Spanish-language skills are also unrewarded since it is "natural" for them to speak Spanish, and they are not part of the "white" public sphere (130). Within the call center analyzed by Heyman and Alarcón, Spanish and English operations were kept separate and operators could choose one or the other. But as they point out, the region is not easily divided linguistically, so when persons actually called, they often switched one for the other or communicated in "Spanglish" as well as using "relaxed, informal registers" rather than polysyllabic formal Spanish or English (130).

On the other hand, they point out that all corporate home officers were "English dominant, often English multilingual [but] at no extra cost, bilingual workers supply to English-dominant management [with] direct Spanish skills; Spanish-English flexibility; and customer service by means of communicating cues of solidarity," which I would term the means of developing *confianza* (ibid.). But it is crucially important to note that while workers utilize their cultural and linguistic skills, which are in fact part of their human capital utilized to enhance and make possible the communications necessary for such operations as a call center, there is no value attached to these capacities and in fact those workers are paid less for doing so if they are Spanish-only operators. In this manner, "whiteness," regardless of the ethnicity of the managers or workers involved, becomes embedded economically and is structurally and nicely "naturalized."

This process of "white" embeddedness, stratification, and reinforcing Spanish as a secondary language holds true to Heyman and Alarcón's field research in service occupations on the northern side of the region as well. What they found was that in health services and public safety services, fluent bilinguals occupied middle-range positions that interacted with a multilingual public while the managers were mostly monolingual English speakers. At the bottom of the hierarchy of service providers were lower-wage service workers and manual laborers who, in the main, were limited in English and spoke mostly Spanish (131).

The privileging process from the ethnographic data they discovered was that, for example, in health services in one doctor's office, the physician was dominant Spanish/English, but their patients were limited in their English skills. Yet a key university-trained, technical staff member crucial to acquiring patient information spoke little Spanish. When such information was needed, which was often, a medical assistant acquired the information, set the cultural stage for interaction, and established *confianza*. Similarly, the front office assistant was a fluent bilingual receptionist with similar roles (131).

The aforementioned example provides support for the phenomenon of the continued privileged position of English, especially in regard to the important functions of record keeping, input, and maintenance, while Spanish is reserved for the "affective" side of the treatment process. English becomes not the preferred language but rather the language of imperative necessity for the maintenance of the business side of the ledger, for which Spanish by implication is not suitable for institutional reasons like Medicare and insurance functions.

But Heyman and Alarcón (2017) find the same pattern in their studies of the cleaning services occupations and especially in a university they studied. While English is the dominant language of administration, teaching, and research, the institution maintains the structure of association "between low qualifications and low communication skill jobs with the Spanish language" (8). The sociolinguistic effect is the creation of a deep differentiation between Spanish-dominant Mexicans and bilingual Mexican-origin workers. Neither side crosses over to the other, with three-fifths of the seventy service workers the former, and not fluent in English, and the rest being bilingual, including the manager and the supervisor of the Mexican-origin group, an Anglo supervisor (8). This difference extends to communications when English-speaking Mexican-origin workers communicate with monolingual Spanish speakers by using English, knowing that the latter cannot understand the instructions, thereby undermining their competency, which in turn translates into possible negative technical evaluations of performance. The managerial response, because of their conviction that Mexican workers are more technically proficient, is to convert Spanish "into the language of control as a strategic move" (11). But as Alarcón and Heyman conclude: "This does not produce a discourse about Spanish as a technical competence, but rather as a social capital, recognized only tacitly, that has been integrated into the workforce in the pursuit of intensification and participation of work in a situation of growing competition" (ibid.). Spanish, in this context, remains a useful tool for communication for more intense work output but not a replacement as a language of prestige.

LANGUAGING AND TRANSLANGUAGING

Heyman and Alarcón do find a counterhegemonic process in the use of "Spanglish," which, from my point of view, also has, like "whiteness," moved into public domains and public institutions. Even in university settings, where clearly there is a penchant for separating English and Spanish, there are public spheres now that have been strongly influenced by the origination and development of centers and schools that utilize a variety of linguistic resources, including Spanish, English, and Spanglish as well as all three, treated to regionalisms, plays on words, *apodos* (nicknames), signage, art, and the presence of faculty, staff, and students of Mexican, Puerto Rican, Central American, and other "Latina/o" origins, as well as Irish-Columbians and assorted "others" of mixed cultural and linguistic origins. While instruction may be primarily in standard English, the move to Spanish or to Spanglish or in reality to "translanguaging," as discussed below, can also be an easy and preferred method of communicating more exact meanings that may be more closely associated with the cognitive and cultural resources used by students. Such contexts as entering an office with a greeting may range from "Hola," "How are you?" "¿Como estas?," "Hi," or "¡Muchacha!" to the utterances of nicknames such as "Lilliputian" (a combination of Liliana and the Jonathan Swift characters because of this person's diminutive height), or "Budweiser" for a staff member with the surname of "Corona," or "Bombera" (firewoman/man) for a staff member with recently acquired flaming red hair. This is the stuff that *relajo* is made of or the culturally constituted practice of verbal fun, puns, and nicknames used in horizontal relations to denote *confianza* (mutual trust) and functions to release the normal stresses involved in a hierarchical institution.

It is a kind of play that opens up a "zone at the boundaries of the community in which rules and conceptual schemata are dissected, reorganized and negotiated" (Briggs quoting Abrahams 1986, 4, in Briggs 1988, 172). This is a kind of "anti-formalism" means of moving relationships and exchanges to safer spaces and places in a "translanguaging" context and, I would suggest, a type of "third space," to use Anzaldúa's terminology (1987). Such discourses are in reality at the quotidian level of daily intercourse—"mixed," communicating multicultural and multihistorical renditions of the variety of selves in common concert and emerging from structures of commonality derived in practice and budding out from social relationships of exchange. So how can we gain insights into looking at translanguaging as normative rather than deviant, as creative rather than based on partial knowledge, and as imperative to the emergence of the selves of those who participate in their invention? By understanding that *relajo* in its translanguaging format may be enjoyed through multiple means like proverbs or joking phrases. Then its central linguistic sense or significance—or *sentido*—becomes valued and normalized. Like proverbs, from my point of view and agreeing and extending Briggs's characterization of their function and form, *relajos*—the command of relajo—are tested by the command of the range of their conveyers as well as by the number of themes that are performed (Briggs 1988, 3). *Relajo* in a translanguage context has similar dimensions of admiration for its quantity and range.

Beginning with the idea of "languaging" provides the foundation for "translanguaging," which is the basis for what I would regard as part of the psychosocial capacities Indigenous to linguistically diverse populations. Maturana and Varela (1987) state unequivocally that "it is in language that the self, the *I*, arises as the social singularity defined by the operational intersection in the human body of the recursive linguistic distinctions in which it is distinguished" (231). This is another way of stating that language, this "not there" phenomenon (to use Deacon's prior vocabulary), emerges and becomes a "there" scaffolding for the "not there" self but structured by the structures of commonality of multiple social domains as sources. This process *enables us to conserve our linguistic operational coherence and our adaptation in the domain of language* (Maturana and Varela 1987). Or more simply said, we become existent from language arising within and part of the many social domains of which we are a part. In the very processes of engagement, the shared structures of commonality develop over time—that is, "recursive" structures are "not there" but imperative for human consciousness. Very well generalized, Maturana and Varela conclude:

> At the same time, as a phenomenon of languaging in the network of social and linguistic coupling, the mind is not something that is within my brain. Consciousness and mind belong to the world of social coupling. That is the locus of their dynamics. And as part of human social dynamics, mind and consciousness operate as selectors of the paths which our ontogeny structural drift follows. Moreover, since we exist in language [the not there], the domains of discourse that we generate become part of our domain of existence and constitute part of the environment in which we construct identity and adaptation. (1987, 234)

The so-called external world cannot be revealed through language; so to use Gloria Anzaldúa's memorable phrase: "I am my language." González (2001) extends Anzaldúa and lends us a real conceptual hand to these more esoteric foundations by simply stating that in relation to her translanguage ethnography of Tucson, "I found something much more valuable [than regularized patterns of language socialization of children]: I found that what I knew about complexity and contradiction was not anomalous, but the very core of the borderland experience" (14).

But as well, languaging is much complicated if a broader sense of languaging is also enjoyed as that proposed by Shohamy (2006), who expands the construct to what anthropology would refer to as "expressive culture" by stating that languaging "refers to the multiple ways of representation that are not limited to words but rather include additional ways of expression consisting of a variety of creative devise of expression such as languaging through music, clothes, gestures, visuals, food, tears and laughter" (16). If attention were to be focused on the multiple syntheses emerging from the vast repertoire of expressive cultural behaviors just between two "translanguaging" persons and within the historical context of the region and locality, then the "translanguage" process is indeed one of complexity, contradictions, and variable pitches and registers not reflective of monocultural or monolingual assumptions.

The perspective adopted throughout this work is that this is the pattern of normalcy for most human beings. Given the complex and often contradictory grand metanarratives adopted from the Spanish period to the present in the SWNAR, ours is a linguistic and expressive cultural repertoire of emergent communicating negotiations having to deal with working through the layers of constructed selves and their very denials by powerful, traditionally oriented, one-language or two-language privileged institutions and their constant impositions and denials of our selves.

In reality the conversations in the SWNAR may switch to a variety of different registers of translanguaging based on ease and comfort and not a declared institutional preference, although non-Spanish speakers are spoken to in English with the courtesy that is deserved. As Heyman and Alarcón argue, skill is needed for such a linguistic and cultural capacity: "Only fluent bilinguals can produce sustained code-switching of this kind, and while one-language speakers can decode, that is challenging and imbalanced; a truly effective code-alternating dialogue requires multiple fluent bilinguals. . . . It is thus a core phenomenon in social relationships between bilinguals, though not obligatorily so" (133). From my point of view, this "linguistic dexterity," as Martínez (2006, 94) would describe it, is among one of many cultural resources that establishes *confianza* among bilinguals, especially from the northern side of the region. Such noninstitutional practices become "naturalized" over time and serve as a kind of "brown/black/white"(not in a melanin sense) space as opposed to "white" space in a limited but certain "public sphere."[38] This is "translanguaging" at its creative best and, with the advent of rap, hip-hop, and Reggaetón from bilingual Puerto Rico in translanguaged Spanglish for the millennial generation, this has even more acutely influenced the emergence of a combination of a three-faced mestizo/mulatto reper-toire, with artists' names like Alexis and Fido, Looney Tunes and Noriega, and "El Father."[39] As well, in the dual language presentation of the *Aladdin* musical in Los Angeles, in which both languages are woven in and out in a seamless manner (Gelt 2017), and the 2017 film *You're Killing Me Susana*, in which Spanish and English are used within this dark transborder love comedy, are portents of perhaps an expansion of the notion of translanguaging toward standardization (Cordova 2017, 3D).

Therefore, while institutions demand hierarchical control of language, in these "slanted" places, to use Campbell and Heyman's (2007) original term, translanguaging bilinguals take advantage of the "interstitial" spaces of hierarchies, as I have indicated elsewhere.[40] The way in which I choose to treat this concept is as slantwise behav-iors and strategies having much to do with borderlands populations "'going around,' underneath, sideways, or slipping by the structures of economy and power in order to access or to acquire needed resources and legitimacy in a context of alienation, marginalization, and racialization. Just as importantly, they maneuver between the spirals of the double helices of transborder racialism and gendered existence" (Vélez-Ibáñez 2010, 128).

Therefore, one way in which to move from a slantwise position to an integrated one, while keeping the dynamics of the other, is in fact to use Spanish, English and/or "Spanglish" and code-switching to our hearts' content in institutionalized settings such as universities, government, and commerce so that the presence of such usage becomes legitimized in the most important of institutions that continue beyond the life of the users of the language. Ethnic studies–oriented disciplines do exactly this and broaden the plurality of the institution itself in the north. Its opposite in the south is not the case, although English has become an important part of the educa-tional mission for all children in Mexico, but especially so on the Mexican side of the SWNAR. With enough practice and knowledge perhaps this inroad could be made as well. Yet it will be in more intensive discussions of the efficacy of dual language and bilingual programming that incorporates "translanguaging" that the reliance on the accidental as well as the "slanting" will shift. While counterhegemonic practices are welcome relief from the pressures of linguistic acquiescence, these are not the kinds of institutionally important developments that will change the secondary position of Spanish, the capacity to translanguage easily without recriminations, or deal with the reality of an asymmetrical regional economy. While historically Spanish has been a hegemonic language in relation to Indigenous peoples, English is hegemonic to not only Spanish and Indigenous languages but to those self-emergent "not there" versions of Hopi-English, Spanish-English, English-Spanish, and sundry other possible combinations in constant use and invention.

Much broader policy directions must be entertained that not only give support to the importance of Spanish in the region and its crucial efficacy in bringing about needed disassembly of "white" linguistic privilege, but also draw attention to the often contradictory and complex emergent renderings of ourselves. Institutions with all of their attending "seeing men" testing, educational and programmatic inventions, and institutions designed to label and erase the cultural and linguistic resources of populations should be able minimally to enhance and develop levels of bilingualism concomitant with the needs of an increasingly information-thick economy of a regional and global sort. In this vein, I will have more to say about "translanguaging" pedagogy in the last chapter.

ENGLISH SOUTH

The place of English in the SWNAR, regardless of the bifurcated political borderline, has been a presence and commonality due to the spread of American technology and power since the late nineteenth century. The necessity of English as a trade and commercial language for the region can be attested to by the willingness of parents to send their own children north to learn the language. This was the case of my father, previously described in chapter 2, in order for the Vélez family to move their carriage-making factory north to take advantage of the industrializing processes in southern Arizona, especially in copper mining. Most of my aunts and uncles and cousins from Magdalena, Sonora, knew English, ranging from high levels of literacy and oral skills to the limited capacity to ask where the "batroom" was located in an American department store in Tucson. It was not uncommon to observe magazines and books in English in middle-class homes in Sonora so that *Life* magazine was a favorite, and Spanish-English dictionaries occupied spaces in bookshelves next to an American novel or books on geography. The more affluent Mexican middle class, especially from the south, had sent children north to study, certainly from 1900 on. They traveled themselves, had business connections, or had been part of revolutionary activities in El Paso, Los Angeles, Tucson, Las Cruces, San Antonio, or Laredo, and by necessity and practice learned the same range of English. English then has been no stranger in the region to the present.

But there were hundreds if not thousands of especially young women, the children of Mexican elites in the southern region, who attended Catholic women's schools in the north as early as 1880 and especially so along the Texas/Coahuilla and Arizona/

Sonora borderline. For example, in Tucson in 1870, seven sisters of St. Joseph of Carondelet established the first boarding school academy for girls and a day school for boys, and instruction was in both Spanish and English.[41] Seventy years later in spacious new quarters and educational facilities, St. Joseph's Academy would serve as the center of instruction for the daughters of Sonoran families from the south. Our Lady of Lourdes Academy was founded in 1940 in Nogales, Arizona, and housed in a novitiate that had been built in 1926 by the Bishop of Sonora during the Cristero Revolt already discussed. On the first day of classes, the Minim Daughters of Mary Immaculate from León, Mexico, welcomed eight girls and ten boys as boarding students and 275 day pupils (ibid.). It is more than likely that in both schools the boarders were Sonoran women or young girls from Nogales south to Magdalena and further. Given the origin of the nuns, instruction was carried out in Spanish and English.

Equally, and almost in the same time period, in 1883, the Sisters of Charity of the Incarnate Word opened Our Lady of Refuge School as a private boarding school in Eagle Pass, Texas.[42] My aunts and mother attended this school in the early 1900s as children and learned to read, write, and speak English, and much later they communicated with me in excellent English. They in fact helped their own children learn English in Sonora and me in Tucson by reading to us all before going to sleep, each of us in our own respective regions. Later these same children attended Salpointe High School in Tucson in the 1950s, others attended the University of Arizona, and one other cousin whose mother learned English with my mother and her sister in the convent school in Eagle Pass, Texas, would graduate from the Imperial College London with a degree in mathematics.[43] These English-language linkages were not rare, nor were they the stuff of myth, but rather the regional dynamic was not just about the movement of Spanish north but also the movement of English south in myriad ways and continues to this day both formally and informally.

But what is of great import is that the asymmetry of the region extends to the asymmetry of the relationship between English and Spanish. Often this is missed in the discussion of the penetration of English worldwide and certainly south of the region. In fact, worldwide there is a tendency to uncritically regard the spread of English and its accompanying trade and technology as primarily a sound investment for the "development" of countries, as discussed by Hanson (1997), Crystal (1997), and Torres-Olave (2012). According to Torres-Olave, "monolingualism and cultural homogenization are presented as inevitable and desirable in a world where national barriers are becoming blurred by internationalization and transnationalization" (2012, 318). This may seem to be an overstated proposition given the most recent revolts in Oaxaca by Indigenous peoples specifically focused on the impact on NAFTA on their own livelihoods, culture, and language and the passing of national legislation protecting them. However, this occurs within the confines of the Mexican state's famous penchant for a yes—a yes and little implementation following. Nevertheless, it would not seem to be an inevitable washout, but yet real concerns for such homogenization are indicated in a most serious way. Torres-Olave's postcolonial position is much subtler in approach by taking a similar theoretical position as that taken here, and that is the manner in which impacted populations also interact in a multitude of ways with the presence of hegemonic transborder forces of economy, migration and movement, and political uncertainty.

In the southern region, English is handled in multiple ways, in some cases as a hopeful means of increasing the possible cultural resources available to overcome the effects of income disparities within the region by employment in enterprises such as the maquiladoras, as Heyman and Alarcón have indicated, in which English and Spanish are broker languages up and down the hierarchy of organizational structures. They also represent an added cultural resource to facilitate movement north to open a business or attend schools, or to simply get a job where English is a necessary condition of employment "north," and as long-term capital that may pay off in a number of years. For example, the Mexican state Tamaulipas has declared itself the first bilingual state in Mexico, and some of its children describe the opportunity in the following manner: "English is important to me because it means more opportunities and better communication when I grow up. Hopefully a better job, too, here or there in Texas" as eleven-year-old Silvia Alejandra Briseño stated (*Guardian*, 2009). From this vantage point, the reality of the transborder asymmetry is well expressed by the realization that English (not Spanish) is the imagined key to her future success. It would be an astounding contradiction for an eleven-year-old Anglo-American child to suggest its opposite and to pin her/his future on the learning of Spanish in order to have the option of a job here or there in Tamaulipas, or to pin their hopes on local varieties of language styles and a version of Spanglish. In this manner, even a child recognizes the incongruities of their future in the region, and their attempted solution for the future lies outside of their contexts, culture, or language. It is in fact not English per se that is the larger theoretical issue, but the reality of a dependent situation of economy relying on a corrupted political system, on the removal of its citizenry by the millions exported as commodities, on an opportunity structure dependent on the lowest of wages for the majority, and on the biggest accumulation of wealth by a tiny few. It relies on the construction of the frailest of social programs and scaffolding, of an educational system heavy with corruption and poorly paid and trained teachers, and finally on a culture of economic and political impunity saturated by the violence of drug trafficking, with the latter made possible by a long-standing voracious American market appetite. The penetration of English is multifaceted. Its service roles are equally so for Mexicans in order to enhance tourism or to serve increasing populations of elderly

Americans themselves marketed out of care in the U.S. English as a preparation for possible employment in the north is an artifact, not the cause, of its importance in the south. Sylvia Alejandra Briseño is only uttering an innocent's version of these masked truths shared by millions of persons in the urban barrios and ejidos of the region.

DISCUSSION

The discussion above has ranged from the northern regional perspective and the manner in which Spanish has been disregarded as a means of achievement and the eugenics-laden politics and opportunism of its adherents—much of it from circumstances directly arising from the fears traditionally used in the northern area toward "newcomers." It is also the case that such fears are directly associated with two important factors: first, the ahistorical ignorance of nineteenth- through twenty-first-century Americans moving from their points of origins to the region, regarding themselves arriving yesterday as "natural" inhabitants, and quickly locating themselves as "native" residents. Second, an entire educational system was set up to reinforce such ignorance, especially in regards to its unwavering historical support of monolingualism and assimilation. Its aftermath resulted in the destructive use of testing as a means of identifying the now dizzying lettered nomenclatures of children who could learn just about anything well done and taught, and without the banging of heads to desks or being typed throughout their academic careers as being faulted by the devil language and closely associated with supported lunch programs provided to children whose household income is below the poverty line. Except for the small historical occasion in the 1960s, bilingualism was generally unsupported, and Spanish was not perceived as the possible partner language. This took place despite the demographic and regional reality, and instead was placed within a context of "whiteness," with all of its contradictions and perverse privileging of sounds and sentences.

In the regional south of the SWNAR, Spanish is becoming increasingly a secondary commercial language and English is becoming dominant. This process is distributed by the structures of inequality of economy tied and integrated to a much broader regional economic platform. That said, however, the internal dynamics of the region of the south feed this dynamic by the insights that even an eleven-year-old realizes. In fact, on August 5, 2015, two hundred Mexican teachers of English as a second language visited my home institution, to whom I gave two lectures on the "hegemony of language" and its discontents and with which they were quite cognizant.

On the other hand, there are increasing possibilities of new ways of approaching language, at least on the northern end of the region, so that populations may better benefit by the recognition of methods and techniques that are not judgmental or culturally destructive. New approaches should not serve as the often-hackneyed suggestion of "serving the needs of the students"; rather, they should be simply for the region in the north to provide the best designed and taught, and the most stimulating and intellectually engaging program of instruction both strongly associated with the most respectful premise of the inherent right of children to learn from the most advantageous position that they bring with them. This should take into account the language they learn first and expand their creative use of a diverse translanguage reality. All must be ensconced within as unsegregated a school environment as possible, with the potential of all students to expand to as many other languages as they have the capacity for. We consider this in the next and final chapter.

7

BILINGUALITY, DUAL LANGUAGES, TRANSLANGUALITY, AND HERITAGE MAINTENANCE

༈

Contending Approaches and an Ethnographic Assembly of Funds of Knowledge and a Dual Language Translanguage Model

The silence of our language, culture, and history was broken by our Mother, a former school teacher in Mexico. She taught her six children to know, love, and respect our language, our customs and our history. And this is one reason why I write—to express those beliefs and to teach what was once a silent sin. These words etched in black ink are made not from individual letters but scars that perforate the paper-like open wounds to the soul of a young Chicano who sought the truth in his own reflection.

JOSÉ ANTONIO BURCIAGA, *DRINK CULTURA*, 1992

ON A DAILY BASIS, in parts of the region both north and south, scars continue to be created by approaches and methods that create generations of ill-educated and unprepared children. Children are tested, spindled, folded, and culturally and linguistically fractured in some regions by well-meaning but simply ignorant and uninformed and "rational" legislators and educational institutions. On the other hand, there are exceptional programs of instruction that give hope to the possibility of children being stimulated to grow beyond imposed limitations and labels. In this last chapter we turn to those exceptional programs for guidance and hopefully reproduction and implementation. We will look at the latest research and practices from the literature in Europe and the United States but also ethnographical information recounted through published fieldwork, the human dynamics that produce the most positive results beyond our penchant for measurable evidence. But this last chapter is also a rejoinder to the hydra-headed "seeing man" syndrome historically made up of so many facets, forms, representations, and claims of purity and reason to maintain the hegemonic position of languages through their multitudes of imperial, national, and regional authorities.

We need to begin the discussion with some basic parameters based on thoughtful reflections about bilingualism. This requires that we consider how this phenomenon functions, what its advantages and disadvantages are, and what the best possible nurturing and learning circumstances are that could allow children and later adults to flower as more fully emergent humans.

I have already briefly discussed some introductory elements in the last chapter and provided a précis of the rationale behind bilingual programs and their learning functions. But we need to foreground the cautionary suggestions made by Guadalupe Valdés (2003), who provided a convincing and insightful critique of the strengths and weaknesses of many methodological, technical, theoretical, and interpretive models utilized by a variety of researchers conducting bilingual research (50–61). Among these are class-specific biases of the samples, the yardsticks used as the basis of comparison as to what may constitute "balanced bilinguals," the tests used to determine level of bilingualism, the "fractional" view of bilingualism rendered from a monolingual premise, the measurement adequacy of instruments, and the complexity of the relation between bilinguality and cognition (59–60). Mindful of her carefully considered cautions, there are also other considerations, not the least of which are the theoretical assumptions and premises behind the construct of bilingualism. Conceptually for example, Bialystok (2010, 14) thinks about bilingualism as a phenomenon and not as a category, and as a process, for not doing so shears the concept of its multilayered nuances and of its delicacy as well as complexity. She states unequivocally: "Bilingualism is not like age, or gender, or grade, or any of the usual variables we use to classify children in developmental research. At best bilingualism is a scale, moving from virtually no awareness that other languages exist to complete fluency in two languages" (ibid.).

There are as well profound theoretical and historical concerns not unlike those raised through this volume that mark the work of others such as A. Suresh Canagarajah (1999) on "reconstituting" especially a dominant language like English by creating learning environments, freeing it from its privileged position as an imposition to one in which the language and "native" languages are negotiated in a concert of bilingual scales (126–46). Certainly, Sinfree Makoni and Alastair Pennycook (2006) go much further in almost removing the premises of questioning the theoretical efficacy of languages per se, since in one way or the other, given the primacy of national states with an identified dominant language, "bilingualism" is another version of the same privileging of "dual monolingualism," since all languages are inventions and most emerge from colonialism at some time and period (1). The creative contributions of Ofelia Garcia and Li Wei (2014) and the construct of "translanguaging" proffer a much more nuancedly edged concept and practice, as will be addressed, and provide viable options to those of Makoni and Pennycook (2006).[1]

Or, we may succinctly consider this behavior of bilingual languaging as a process not "out there" to be captured, but rather an emergent process that can unfold in the social exchange relations with others and in a very curious, perhaps species-specific, interaction with our various selves. But the latter could not have emerged solely from ourselves without others, which is both ironic and filled with pitfalls of differences and contradictions. This process doubles with emergent bilingualism and makes for complex operational maneuvering, as we shall see, of cognitive "executive functions."

Therefore, it follows that since bilingualism is processually phenomenological, Bialystok also notes that research on the concept is at best problematic and at worst filled with categorical and empirical pitfalls. For example, she states that controlled research on the impact that bilingualism has on children's development "requires that bilingual children are compared with equivalent monolinguals on specific aspects of performance" (ibid.). This assumes comparable testing devices that are not merely translations—a caution also voiced by Valdés. Given the complexity of neighborhoods, migration, immigration, class mobility, changing neighborhoods, catastrophic events, differentiated language policies, age-specific learning capacities, experimental programs, and more importantly an insistence on measuring performance and achievement based on norms appropriate for masked populations hidden under the convention as "normal"—all make for challenging approaches to an understanding of creative bilingual programs that in fact should not fit all and are sufficiently adaptive to shift when events and circumstances change as they must.

This discussion then begins by providing some of the bioneural literature, which importantly provides direction to understand some of the basics in keeping with the original tasks developed in the opening chapters. Hopefully this rationale and the methodological issues relating to the topic fundamentally provide intellectual and programmatic guidance to an occasionally bewildering literature that is often contradictory and incomplete and competes more rationally with the "seeing man" syndrome. The following provides a partial remedy to the very complex and often contradictory assumptions and approaches regarding bilingualism.

BIONEURAL PREMISES AND ASSUMPTIONS: THE BILINGUAL BRAIN

In order to begin the conversation to unhook the "naturalized white" renditions favoring monolinguality, especially in the United States, and in stark comparison to Canada, Mexico, and Europe, and certainly most of Asia as well as the Indian subcontinent, which has the largest populations of English speakers in the world, we need ask: what do we know about how multiple languages operate in favor of human emergence (rather than to its detriment, as would the English-only proponents propose)? The literature most pertinent is that conducted on the effect of environmental contexts, events, behaviors, practices, and multiple human and nonhuman experiences on the pathways of the brain and the neural connections that may enhance or impair cognitive performance. In other words, as far as possible we need to track down the specific ways in which bilingual neuropathways and associations are affected, made part of, and function as part of the neuroplasticity of the brain and the manner in which this is accomplished.

For example, we know that music, art, performances, and repeated actions like taxi driving stimulate strong neurobiological structural changes. The bane of many parents—video games—can enhance visual selective attention (Green and Bavelier 2003). Brain traumas have not been researched by neurobiological research examining the effects of practices already discussed in the previous chapter and their long-term impacts: the hair pulling, delayed and frustrated bathroom breaks, banging of heads to desks, the use of riding crops, and shaved baseball bats, or public-sector pressures for perfect performance monolingually.

That said, there is a high probability that PTSD contributes to verbal learning and memory deficits.[2] In this vein, Hill (1998, 684) has observed that the anxiety of Spanish speakers in the United States or Mexico in demanding contexts are often tongue-tied responses or muteness when called upon. For those traumatized early, and from personal experience, this is characterized by a rush of nervous anxiety passing from the diaphragm to the chest to the throat to the tongue coupled with the expiration of breath often expelled with grunts of frustration in fractured phrases. Martínez describes this process as undergoing a kind of "language panic" (2006, 12) while Burciaga (1992, 54) stated that in learning Spanish, for Chicanos, "there seems to be a barrier, a phobia that is more psychological than people realize. There is a resentment for past treatment. We have scars, and they appear when we talk in our mother tongue." As well, Anzaldúa (1987) considers that "Chicanas feel uncomfortable talking in Spanish to Latinas, afraid of the censure. Their language was not outlawed in their countries. . . . Even among Chicanas . . . we're afraid the other will think we're *agringadas* because we don't speak Chicano Spanish" (68).

But, we need to know how nontraumatic impacts operate in order to provide a rational approach of production to enhance the human capacities. How are the bilingual brains of the "I's" and "you's" and "they's" and "us's" developed in comparison to the monolingual versions of the same existential and cognitive layers of selves?

Interestingly, according to Bialystok (2009, 3),[3] "individuals who speak a second language have been shown to have increased density of grey matter in the left inferior parietal cortex, a change that is more pronounced in early bilinguals and those with greater proficiency in the second language" (citing Mechelli et al. 2004).[4] But its benefits seem to translate into old age in what is termed "cognitive reserve," which seems to be a sort of protective impact against cognitive decline, and she cites research in this area (Stern, 2002; Fratiglioni, Paillard-Borg, and Winblad 2004; Kramer et al. 2004; Staff et al. 2004; Valenzuela and Sachdev 2006).[5] The thickening of the gray matter, the denser packing of "information-processing nerve cells and fibers is an advantage especially in the brain's left hemisphere where most language and communication skills are controlled." Bilingual individuals in comparison to monolinguals have a thicker packing so that bilingual acquisition from an early age shapes the structure of the brain.[6]

But more basic are findings regarding attention, consistency, and control of learning for bilinguals. In their highly technical and informative work, Krizman et al. (2014) found that bilingualism increases neural response consistency and attentional control. Beginning with the hypothesis that "auditory processing is presumed to be influenced by cognitive processes—including attentional control in a top-down manner . . . in bilinguals, activation of both languages during daily communication hones inhibitory skills, which subsequently bolster attentional control" (35). That is, in comparison to monolinguals, which was the basis of their study, this research concluded that in fact bilinguals, contrary to the old hypotheses that bilingualism somehow inhibits or interferes with listening and learning, show greater proficiency: "In bilinguals, we demonstrate that better attentional control is coupled with greater consistency in the subcortical evoked response, which further relates to their proficiency in both languages. This relationship suggests that language experience influences automatic sensory encoding of auditory stimuli, likely through enhancement of top-down processing streams that act to refine bottom-up signal transmission" (38).

Such findings had been strengthened by Bialystok et al. (2005), who found similar results previously reported of the neural correlates for a "bilingual advantage." These were based on behavioral measures in conflict tasks in a sample of adults ages twenty-two to twenty-nine, composed of ten English monolinguals, ten French-English bilinguals, and ten Cantonese-English bilinguals who were treated to behavioral and magneto-encephalography (MEG) (40). This interpretation is based on the hypothesis that bilinguals are more proficient than monolinguals in tasks requiring inhibitory control. The neurological conclusions, however, are both interesting academically and by implications provide further support for providing the opportunities for enhanced bilingual experience and for strengthening the existing ones. That is, according to this research: "Many of the areas associated with faster responding in bilinguals were left hemisphere regions that bordered on language centers in the inferior frontal cortex. It is possible that bilingualism enhances those control processes in the left frontal lobe and makes them available for other inhibitory tasks, even nonverbal ones" (48).

For bilingual children, however, bilingualism seems to positively select for what is termed "executive functioning" of metalinguistic levels of cognition. As Ellen Bialystok and Michelle M. Martin (2004)[7] had found earlier, the later studies of the Toronto children show that "bilingualism slows vocabulary acquisition but accelerates executive function development across variations in SES and manipulations of task difficulty" (286). As Diamond (2010) describes this process, humans could become inebriated by external sensory stimulations, reflective musings, and "proprioceptive sensations (which make us aware of the relative positions of our own body parts)" (332). To be able to sort out the chaff from the wheat, it is necessary to suppress the great majority of stimulations to temporarily focus on the input to which attention is to be paid. Which input to select among the many—in an appropriate manner with the appropriate register—will be variable according to the context in which the input is being regarded. That capacity to select appropriately involves complex sorting processes, which are termed "executive functions" and have been located in the prefrontal cortex. They have special developmental importance during the first five years for all children (Diamond 2010, 332). Bilinguals from infancy have developed this capacity to greater degrees than monolinguals because of the necessity of switching syntactic, phonological, and semantic rules and thus expanding this "higher order" function. As Diamond concludes: "Evidently, shifting frequently and unpredictably between hearing two parental languages made 'bilingual' infants better able to cope with other unpredictable rule changes" (333). It is from this early practice and its continuance that perhaps forms the dynamic basis of "translanguaging" in which, as further discussion will develop, "is the process of making meaning, shaping experiences, gaining understanding and knowledge of two languages" (Baker 2011, 299), and perhaps simultaneously increasing the organism's capacity to increase its own capacity to learn to learn. This would be in keeping with Deacon's more "teleodyamics" complex-adaptive systems approach previously discussed (465).

Given these advantages, however, do these translate into what is still of high interest among researchers? That is, whether in spite of such findings, how are environmental contexts pertinent to cognitive and language functions? The work by Calvo and Bialystok (2014) purports to separate SES from bilingualism in order to test how each is pertinent to the cognitive and language outcomes of children in their sample of monolingual and bilingual children in Toronto, Canada. After an extensive review of the literature discussing the ins and outs of various measures and findings, they establish that SES is correlated with performance gauges on cognition and language, with the greater the SES, the better the performance, and its opposite holds as well.[8]

Overall, they found that SES played an extremely important role in working-class children (monolingual or bilingual) so that SES had a significant effect on children's language and cognitive development, irrespective of language background (279).

The Bialystok et al. (2010) study shows that bilingual children score lower than monolinguals in vocabulary, and this persists at every level between three and ten years old among the 1,700 bilingual children they examined; this is among the most thorough analysis illustrating these class-based phenomena. What is important to note is not that "bilingual education" is responsible for a slower vocabulary acquisition but that the home language, since it is of greater use in that context, will not accelerate the rate of vocabulary of the "non-home" language. Its opposite holds as well, with monolinguals' "home language" paralleling that of the prevailing institutions; monolinguals, of course—whose language is a single source—would have a tendency to use a greater range and compliment of vocabulary, dependent in part on class. Yet, there is more complexity to these findings, as elaborated by Collier and Thomas (Thomas and Collier 2003a and 2003b; Collier and Thomas 2004, 2005, 2010), who in their analysis of dual language programs unequivocally show that children who receive all of their instruction in English from kindergarten into grades three and four will outperform children who are taught using bilingual methods, but only up until grades three and four. What is most impressive is that the reverse is true from grades six and above.[9]

Thus the "bilingual brain" literature clearly has shown that bilingualism does in fact offer advantages of complexity while some have disadvantages in comparison to monolinguals in relation to smaller vocabulary ranges if the "home" language is other than that of the major institutions using the non-home language but only transitionally in bilingual programs. Yet class issues are clearly omnipresent but not determinant for bilinguals to develop important potentials for intellectual and cognitive capacities so that these advantages must be enhanced, with disadvantages treated with the proper interventions of program, teaching, and enhancement regardless of context, place, space, or country.

It is imperative to note that despite the commanding conclusion that bilingualism is a highly selective advantage biologically and cognitively, the question remains: Why has it not been adopted as a matter of course, especially in the northern portion of Southwest North America Region? Among other rationales is the one reiterated by Augusto Buchweitza and Chantel Prat (2013):

> Bilingual development gives rise to generalized improvements in the functioning of a brain circuit that supports perhaps the most essential and limited aspects of human cognition. These improvements include better executive function abilities and the benefit of

a cognitive reserve that seems to protect an individual from cognitive decline that occurs with aging. Given the preponderance of evidence to support these benefits of bilingualism, one might ask why all children aren't being raised bilingually? The answer to this is might be rooted in an out dated, and largely scientifically unsubstantiated notion that bilingual language development results in language delays. (439)

THE EUROPEAN EXPERIENCE:
TRANSLANGUAGING ACROSS BORDERS

In Europe, learning languages and the proximity of other languages than the national language in which a person was raised has been a commonality and not an exception. European "national" languages are of course all derived from subfamilies of Latin, Slavic, and Germanic languages interspersed with almost standalone "isolates" like Basque. In the present, according to the 2012 *Eurobarometer Report 386*, "Europeans and Their Languages," "there are 23 officially recognized languages and more than 60 Indigenous regional and minority languages, and many nonIndigenous languages spoken by migrant communities"(2).[10] Of these, 54 percent of Europeans have conversational knowledge of at least one additional language, 25 percent are able to converse in at least two additional languages, and 10 percent have conversational knowledge in at least three (12). Most European nations of course share multiple borders with other nations, such as Switzerland bordering France, Germany, Austria, and Italy, and then Belgium, bordered by Germany, the Netherlands, and France. Of course, Europe's present borders were not those of the nineteenth century, filled by empires and small and large kingdoms until their national periods. Yet multilingualisms of many sorts from the medieval periods were part of the historical traditions created by fairs, commercial relations, wars, and conquests and invasions so that, for example, Spanish soldiers spoke a patois consisting of Flemish, Spanish, and Italian, all developed during the seventeenth century of Spain's ascendency in Europe, as did all soldiers, especially to purchase items and to trade genes with the seemingly strange and exotic.[11]

Hundreds of years earlier, European merchants especially had been engaged in the "great fairs" complex of England in the eleventh through the fourteenth centuries to sell and buy goods and to communicate prices and to haggle back and forth in versions of English, French, Italian, and German and other languages of various sorts, as well as to fulfill contracts of sale and purchase previously negotiated.[12] Miller and Hatcher (2014, 172) describe how merchants selling their wares in England went to the "great fairs," with Spaniards taking merchandise to various fairs like Winchester, as well as German, Flemish, and Gascon merchants traveling to Boston (U.K.), while

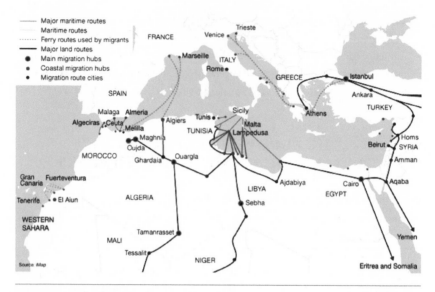

FIGURE 36. Mediterranean routes. From "Mapping Mediterranean migration," (September 15, 2014), BBC News.

Normans and Brabanters attended St. Yves and others. Cloth was traded by Italians from Lucca who purchased Meaux abbey's wool clip. In fact by the late thirteenth century, Italians were found in all the "great fairs" throughout England (ibid.).

The enormous impacts of wars on human expulsion from the Napoleonic through the two world wars in the twentieth century and to the present have been partially responsible for the movements and migrations of millions across borders—new and old. To this day thousands seek asylum and refuge—economic and political—across Europe, with migrants risking death boating across the Mediterranean to Italy and Spain, as well as Africans seeking entry into the U.K. through the under-Channel tunnel between Calais and England.[13] Figure 36 shows the Mediterranean routes.[14]

But these historical and contemporary dynamics of movements and language have also been given impetus by the European Common Market, with its regularized process of persons from a variety of countries crossing other borders in a circular work and return process of those between member countries. However, nonmember migrations and especially unauthorized ones became a "security" concern after the 1980s and complicated the regularized process instituted by Common Market (Huysmans 2000, 758). That said, the recent migration of peoples from former colonial territories, and the movement of refugees into Europe and the U.K. from war zones such as Syria, Afghanistan, Eritrea, Nigeria, Mali, Tunisia, and Iraq, as well as unauthorized workers from around the globe, all have increased the need for and use of bilingual and various immersion programs.[15]

Such a sketch of European historical language and population demographic changes and migrations (and its necessary linguistic shifts across time, space, and places) provides a mapping of the use and implementation of various language programs pertinent to the "state" of the needs of diverse populations and of the bilingual approaches to the instruction of children and youths in primary and secondary educational institutions.

EUROPEAN LANGUAGES AND THEIR CLIL DISCONTENTS

Excluding the United Kingdom and Ireland, at the national level, English is the most widely used foreign language in nineteen of the twenty-five member states. In the six remaining states, Russian is the most widely spoken (*Special Eurobarometer 386*). An outlier is Luxembourg, in which 80 percent mention French, followed by German at 69 percent, but both are official languages of the country, which makes perfect sense given its proximity and historical relationship to both and to Belgium as well as its French-speaking Walloons and Germanic, Dutch-speaking Flemings.[16]

Given these historical preferences, recent migrations of other peoples and their languages would require programmatic approaches that would need careful consideration. Among the most dynamic of programs are those referred to as "Content and Language Integrated Learning," or CLIL. Coined by the European Commission, it has two main features: linguistic flexibility and a strong stress on meaning and content learning.[17] It may include two-way immersion approaches in which half of the class is dominant-language speakers and the other half speakers of one other language, with two teachers, one of each language and culture, with the same curriculum. Lessons are in each language for the same percentage of time and based on locally spoken "community languages," not on "foreign languages" (ibid.). Thus for example, Germany is very specific in its model so that in Berlin, German is combined with English, French, Greek, Italian, Polish, Portuguese, Russian, Spanish, and Turkish. Hamburg combines German with Portuguese, Spanish, and Turkish, and Prana with Czech, and Gorlitz with Polish.

The U.K. has two-way immersion programs, for example, in two primary schools with an appreciable French demographic presence, while a number of primary schools have English-Spanish programs ranging from partial-early immersion to partial-late immersion to English-Spanish immersion through music and art and a variety of other complex models depending on the demography of the area (ibid.). Thus, the types of programs very much depend on the demographics of the local area and not a one-model-fits-all, except that there does seem to be an emphasis in the European case of dual immersion as the most applicable model, with great attention paid to local demographics.

The resulting research, as summarized by Gabriela Meier (2012), is that CLIL has succeeded in the following manner: (1) content and language-integrated approaches are more effective than isolated second language acquisition (Genesee 1994); (2) the attainment of language and content is increased; (3) it is for all learners with different outcomes; (4) it raises linguistic competence and confidence; (5) it improves literacy in the first language; and (6) it repositions languages in the curriculum. Using Germany as an example, the summary of research shows "that for both science and humanities subjects that the development of learners' subject matter competence is generally comparable to that of non-CLIL control-groups. In some cases, CLIL learners even seem to benefit from the CLIL situation with respect to certain aspects of subject matter competence" (e.g., Bonnet 2004; Lamsfuss-Schenk 2008; Bonnet 2013).[18]

If this is the case, then what has research found among the most efficacious of methods given the plurality of accepted languages as well and importantly the demographics of local conditions? What is most important among all of these findings, beside the important learning aspects, is the last finding in that the program "repositions languages in the curriculum." That is, the "foreign" language no longer become foreign, the second language no longer is second, the "ELL" is no longer a category, "ESL" is no longer a second banana, and "SS" (Speaker of Spanish or any other contextual label) becomes decategorized. The monolingual "seeing man" is blinded, as are their segregating linguistic categories. These become mute categories since the languages under the auspices of Content and Language Integrated Learning (CLIL) become the prevailing gestalt and not amenable to further reductions to a typology of less or to a labeling typification of rendering language use as either correlated or associated. Rather the focus is one of legitimization of equality and function to that of the "host" language, be it English or any other privileged language. Unsegregated, unprivileged, and with common linguistic, mathematical, scientific, and creative content for students, "whiteness" becomes transparent. At least within education institutions, equality of languages becomes part of its public sphere so that "rational" persons become rational in actuality and in policy.

On the other hand, there are institutional concerns in regards to this approach in that its application for some is directed toward "elite" students, parents, and institutions. Its efficacy is questioned by very recent research of the CLIL approach in Germany, with its triple-tiered primary through secondary school arrangement populated by students tested for entry. Breidbach and Viebrock's (2012, 5) review of the literature contextualizes the discussion with a historical setting in which "bilingual education" programs were established between France and Germany after World War II and promulgated by the Franco-German Treaty of 1963. The schools with the longest experience were those situated along the Rhine River and offered mostly in French, although English became important as well. By the 1990s a rapid expansion occurred with more than seven hundred schools modeled around the CLIL methods in various versions (ibid.).

According to their discussion, until grade four, most German states have children enrolled in comprehensive primary schools but then by examination tracked into three levels of intellectual development, each scaled to reflect less to more demanding curriculum, with the traditional gymnasium providing the general university entrance requirements with about 45 percent of all cohorts entering this type of school (6). Yet because of the popularity of the method, CLIL has been implemented at the primary levels in many schools. The authors point out that most of the experiences with the method have been in privileged middle-class schools of the gymnasium type (ibid.). However, this is complicated in that CLIL learners can be divided into two major groups: first, those who receive their content instruction through a foreign language such as English, French, Spanish, and other European languages, and a second much larger group who are speakers of German as a second language and are taught most of their content in German. Both suspiciously look like many bilingual and dual-immersion programs in the SWNAR. Nevertheless, the criticism by the authors is well taken since in fact elite students perform better than nonselected students in all materials, CLIL or not.

But the fact is that CLIL in Germany is oriented around social science-related subjects in the "other" language and is the stress of instruction. The natural sciences are largely in experimental stages of instruction at this point and mathematics is for the most part not existent in any CLIL oriented curricula. That said, the research comparing CLIL and non-CLIL schools concluded "that CLIL had a very positive influence on foreign language competence in general, which was most pronounced for reading comprehension and the ability to use elaborate strategies such as tolerance of ambiguity, appropriate strategies of inference etc." (Bredenbröker 2000). Yet, other work found:

> the relative absence of critical language awareness foreshadowed similar results by Bonnet (2004) or Lamsfuß-Schenk (2008), who both find little if any empirical evidence that CLIL learners—being in this very similar to their non-CLIL peers—develop reflective or critical competences all by themselves. In this, empirical research has certainly rocked the foundations of one of the chief arguments circulated in the German CLIL discourse in favour of CLIL, namely that the CLIL setting all by itself will cause learners to take a reflective perspective on content matter and the cultures behind the

working language. Such an inbuilt mechanism does not appear to exist in CLIL settings. (Breidbach and Viebrock 2012, 9)

Given the complexity of the attempts to create language programs for such a diverse and heterogeneous population of populations, perhaps Valdés's early warnings concerning research and application in the United States should be considered as important to ferret out the many layers of institutional and linguistic issues with learning and pedagogy in the CLIL approach.

THE FRENCH-CANADIAN PROCESS AND ITS CONTENTS

But if this is the case, what of a setting closer to the region and part of North America? That place is Canada, where English and French have been the proverbially "official" languages, depending on the area of the country. Thus, under Section 41 of the Official Languages Act, Allen states that "the Government of Canada is committed to (a) enhancing the vitality of the English and French linguistic minority communities in Canada and supporting and assisting their development; and (b) fostering the full recognition and use of both English and French in Canadian society" (Allen 2008).[19] This crucial statement provides an institutional context very different from the European case except for formally recognized national languages like in Belgium and certainly the U.S. case, in which English-only as an unofficial "official" language prevails. In contrast, Allen states that there is a plethora of schools that engage in a variety of language models depending on region and locality. Most students receive some form of French or English training for at least part of their educational career, but curiously she states that "some students participate in more enhanced language training such as immersion, extended, or intensive courses. These enhanced programs vary considerably and have been continually evolving with changes in policy and new approaches to language learning" (ibid.).

Among the most constructive of summaries concerning the Canadian programs and approaches are those summarized by Cummins (1998). He states that after thirty years of research on French-immersion programs, the following general programs beginning with early immersion programs starting in kindergarten have developed: first, early immersion involves 100 percent French in kindergarten and first grade with one period of English introduced in grades two, three, and some as late as grade four. By grades five and six, the languages are divided equally. The amount of time in French is reduced to 40 percent in grades seven through nine with more reduction at the secondary levels and more courses in English than in French (34).

The research findings resulting from such programs throughout Canada are that students become literate and fluent in French with no loss of English academic skills. Within a year of English introduction, students perform normatively in most English standardized tests except for spelling, but with more instruction, by the fifth grade, they perform the same as monolingually instructed students, including in writing and with no evidence of any lingering loss of performance in content areas "taught through French in early, middle or late immersion programs." (ibid.).

But as importantly, their receptive skills are superior in relation to native speakers but not as developed in their expressive capacities. In fact, by the end of the sixth grade students are only slightly below native speakers in comprehension and literacy but significantly below them in grammar, oral, and written French (35). Partly to blame, according to Cummins, is that, first, the curriculum is not learner-centered, but teacher-centered, with limited opportunities for the kind of problem solving and creative possibilities that a learner-centered approach would undertake to substitute to "directed" learning. Additionally, students did not engage in the types of writing assignments normative to programs in English or encounter the levels of literary quality associated with English programs (ibid.). What is significant, and still using the creeping (as opposed to creepy) nomenclature, is that neither L1 or L2 are given categorical "first" designations but rather are entirely dependent on locality rather than an a priori definition of the first or second, since, for example, French and English are both "official" languages.

However, these are not "minority" children ensconced in contexts in which the home language becomes a secondary one. In fact the startling conclusion of this review is that "[m]inority children who lack this educational support for literacy development again using creeping labels, L1 (home language) frequently develop a subtractive form of bilingualism in which L1 skills are replaced by L2 (ibid.)." That is, linguistic erasure coupled to cultural fracturing is the consequence of moving ahead of the research and supportive practices needed for "minority" students to fulfill their full human potential and very much like the general model of the U.S. assimilationist project.

TRENDS AND PRACTICES OF THE NORTHERN REGION OF SOUTHWEST NORTH AMERICA

The search for suitable language programs that somewhat mirror the Canadian and European models is an entangled one given that, first, there is no official language policy established in the northern region, but instead each state has developed its own. What must be considered is a regional approach rather than a national one in which contending state policies obfuscate and politicize rational decision-making in regard to the most efficacious approach for the human development of children. This work has established that economically, ecologically, historically, and demographically, the regions north and south are first of all characterized by intensive and dynamic relations between cultural populations, regardless and in spite of the politics of the region. The demographics and population concentration of Mexican-origin and other Spanish-speaking populations in the northern region have already been established in this discussion and demand a fresh approach to what we know to be fruitful learning directions established by both research and practice. The eastern American prism for assimilation and language replacement must be reconsidered in light of research that will be discussed that supports an intensive dual language approach of unsegregated classrooms in which the children's home language is fully developed with the home language of the partner language and funneled through intensive content material and developed in unison. "Immersion" in programs that segregate "minority" children for four or more hours in "stand-alone" instructional contexts has not proven to be educationally, linguistically, or culturally efficacious.[20] And in fact, the state of Arizona has reduced Spanish for native speakers to a modicum of attention because of its vaunted Proposition 203 English-only legislation but has been taken to task for its erroneous assumptions concerning "immersion" programs in the study by Rolstad, MacSwan, and Mahoney (2012). Using the state's own achievement data, they conclude that "[t]he Arizona English-only instruction policy has been advanced in a research context in which it can find no reasonable support . . . and suggest that the state has embarked on the wrong path. . . . Arizona's SEI program breaks down at its core" (203).

Robert Slavin et al. (2010) conducted a longitudinal study on fifth-year findings of three years of kindergarteners assigned to bilingual or English-only classes and then followed to grade four.[21] The programs were early exit transitional bilingual education and the English immersion approaches. And they concluded:

> The findings of the present study reinforce the frequently stated conclusion that what matters most in the education of English language learners is the quality of instruction, not the language of instruction (August & Shanahan, 2006; Cheung & Slavin, 2005). Schools may choose to teach English language learners in either their native language or in English for many reasons, including cultural, economic, or political rationales. Yet the claims that this choice is crucial for ultimate learning of English or Spanish reading are not supported by the data from this experiment. (17)

Now this may seem to be the death knell for those espousing bilingualism as a premise, but in fact what this study and the Arizona legislation and its criticized effects do show are the limitations of an English-only or "transitional" bilingual approach, both of which are based on the premise of removing Spanish as a parallel partner and as a means of instruction equivalent to English. What is interesting is that Slavin et al.'s conclusions seem to be in contradiction to Slavin's own previous research that shows that language of instruction, in fact, trumps quality of instruction (Slavin and Cheung 2005).

However, regardless of intention, methodology, techniques, or instructional approaches, like those of the Arizona legislative mandates, and those studied by Slavin of "transitional" programs, such programs are based on an inequivalent, subordinated, and unequal linguistic position. These programs reproduce language "whiteness" and accentuate the predominance and hegemony of English and its East Coast prism of unilineal assimilation as its final outcome coupled with a monolingual ahistorical insistence. There were never Native peoples creating grand cultural complexes, never any Spaniards inundating the land and genetically and culturally changing the human ecology of the region, and fewer Mexicans that were invaded all the way to Mexico City or Granduncles who saw the last Mexican flag come down in 1853 in Tucson, Arizona.

Yet we do know that there are cognitive, linguistic, and cultural advantages to early exposure to other languages that are part, as has been discussed, of associated development of the brain by putting together the tasks and solving the problem of assembling the languages and their knowledge for the various "I's," "selves," "me's," "you's," and "us's." We also know from the European CLIL model that this approach, where qualitatively coherent, functions admirably. The Canadian dual-immersion approaches also function for great benefit with programs designed to unfold over long duration rather than short-term "transitional" or shocked immersion programs like of Arizona and, until recently, California and elsewhere.

THE OPTIMAL CONDITIONS FOR SUCCESS

In part, demographics determine the efficacy of the model to be used optimally. The best model for the northern end would involve substantial numbers of "home"-language elementary school students, whether these be students speaking Spanish, Hopi, Navaho, or Tohono O'odham, and a concomitant representation of English-speaking partners of the same cultural group or not, beginning from preschool through high school. And what must be underscored is that it is not suggested that the partner population necessarily be from another ethnic group, but that the partners be speakers of English as the "home" language, although optimally for social and cultural reasons it would be desirable for multiple cultural groups to be represented. It is imperative that students not be segregated into "immersion" programs for multiple reasons, not the least of which is the certain decline in the home language, a lost cognitive development opportunity especially for preschool and first through third grades, and an attainment of less than positive results in English, as the Arizona case illustrated.

But the crucial evidence is found in the work by Collier and Thomas (2004). They report their analysis of fifty-six Houston school districts' one-way and two-way dual language programs for grades K–8, in which in the former, because some schools were not staffed to implement the dual language programs, a 90:10 ratio of "home" to "host" language was established for "transitional" classes as well as dual language classes in order to maintain consistency and then reduced to 50:50 as students moved from school to school (14).

The outcomes on national norm-referenced tests for reading in the first through fifth grades are as follows. Comparison schools, according to the study, were matched in terms of neighborhood and percentage of students with modest income, with the outcomes showing the Spanish-speaking students in the two-way dual language schools were at or above grade level in both languages in the first through the fifth grades. In English achievement, Spanish-speaking students in the two-way classes outscored the English language speakers in other types of bilingual programs so that "[t]his high achievement in Spanish significantly influenced their high achievement in English, in comparison to what we have seen in other school districts implementing little or no primary language support" (9). These findings have been further supported by the work of García-Vázquez et al. (2010) on midwestern Mexican-origin children, who assert that Spanish reading and written proficiency was strongly related to tests of academic achievement in English. They differentiated between oral and broad language use whose relations were small but had significant relations with composite, reading, and vocabulary achievement scores in English (403). Their general conclusions were that "these results . . . show that continued development of first language skills enhances scores in high school. In addition, these findings indirectly demonstrate that late-exit programs can lead to increased performance on standardized tests in English" (404).

But these findings are not just specific to Mexican-origin students and are supported not only by the European and Canadian examples but also by "Heritage" programs in Maine. Collier and Thomas (2004) researched a border region between Maine and Canada proximate to French- and English-speaking provinces probably not unlike many subregions of the SWNAR. In studying two school districts in which almost 100 percent of the students are culturally of Franco/Arcadian descent, they found their own grandparents, like the Mexican examples provided, were reprimanded for using French and, like Mexican Spanish, denigrated. About half of the students from both districts were schooled in dual language programs at a 50:50 ratio for grades K–12. The other half remained in English-only instruction. The researchers controlled for class and language. The outcomes, similar to those of Mexican-origin students in Houston and the Midwest, were such that French-speaking English learners who had ranked in the 31st percentile before the program ranked in the 72nd percentile four years later in English. Finally, in comparing the Texas and Maine examples, both one-way and two-way bilingual programs resulted in grade-level to above-grade-level performance in the second language without an achievement gap, and English, Spanish, or French speakers "in one-way bilingual classes reach grade level achievement in the second language by the 7th or 8th grade and score slightly above grade level for the rest of their schooling" (11). In dual language two-way classes, English learners reach grade-level performance in the second language by fifth or sixth grade, reaching an average at the 70th percentile by the eleventh grade (ibid.).

The social outcomes, however, were gauged to be impressive from the teachers' point of view, who expressed renewed investment in teaching, with staff and teacher development strongly accentuated and, as importantly for administrators, teachers, and staff, for whom student behavioral issues seemed to have abated, since students felt both valued for their "home" knowledge and for their ability to assist fellow students in reaching their learning goals (ibid.).

How do these programs, then, compare with the Arizona and the former California-type emphasis on English-immersion only—a.k.a., ESL—approaches? Collier and Thomas (2004) conclude that when the Houston and California Stanford 9 results are compared, what they found is that after twelve months of ESL barrages in California the results were almost the same as those of English-only students in Houston who were not treated by any program, so that this approach touted by Proposition 227 in California "is virtually the same as no special program at all" (16). The same would probably hold true if a comparison were made with the Arizona experiment.

In the present, according to the Center for Applied Linguistics, there are 248 two-way immersion programs in twenty-three states and the District of Columbia, and this includes all of the major states of the region. But many programs, like those in Arizona and California, are restricted to children who pass an English test prior to their admittance, or many are ensconced primarily in middle-class areas, so that this most advantageous methodology is not distributed equally by class.[22] In spite of this, dual language programs in minority schools have far-reaching implications so that students from minority schools with modest SES characteristics by high school develop high levels of academic "competence and motivation, ambition to go to college, knowledge about how to apply to and get into college, and pride in bilingualism."[23] Rather than regarding their "home" language as something to be discarded and useless together with the cultural underpinnings of such removal, such students have built-in cultural and linguistic integrity in both languages and in multiple cultural domains. Theirs are constructed forms of complexity of cultural levels and resources from which choice and outlooks lead to cognitively broad frames of reference and decision capacities, as indicated by the "brain" literature already discussed.

AN ETHNOGRAPHIC ASSEMBLY OF FUNDS OF KNOWLEDGE AS BALANCE TO DUAL-LANGUAGE SOCIAL INEQUITY WITH A BIT OF TRANSLANGUAGING

But dual language programs are not without their pitfalls and these must be avoided. Clearly the literature shows that in dual language programs and especially those populated by middle-class Anglo students, the English-dominant students not only supersede Spanish-speaking students, but teachers have a tendency to focus on the former's language needs to the detriment of the latter (Delgado-Larocco 1998; Moses 2000; and Valdés 1997). Valdés's (1997) early work clearly was concerned with exactly this process of class and cultural differentiation. In fact she was quite clear in suggesting that Spanish-dominant students' real linguistics advantage would be traded off to those not so situated. But this can be balanced by attention to spaces or zones that are "free" by student-directed, student-defined, and student-conducted exchanges with each other and with teachers as assistants in "translanguaging" experiments with the "students' own creative languaging, drawing from their entire linguistic 'repertoire'" (Garcia and Wei 2014, 61). Or, they could simply provide cultural and linguistic space to practice and "show off" their Spanglish proficiencies and their innovations such as hip-hop and the moves to go along with it. This must be practiced, encouraged, developed, and made integral to the language instruction of the classroom, with students encouraged and permitted to violate curricular conventions and practices. In fact, such experimentation can also be applied to providing "literacy spaces" not restricted by either language but rather writing in either, both in tandem or mixing, or transliterating from one to the other. Martínez (2010), as described by Garcia and Wei (2014, 62), specifically looks at the use of "Spanglish" as a literacy medium by sixth-grade students in Los Angeles. Students were able to take advantage of their own full range of language resources without repression, to more specifically detail and be able to communicate levels of meaning not apparent in either language — Spanish or English. As well, Escamilla et al. (2013) shows that for students from homes or environments in which both languages have been practiced, children will carry symbiotic systems and can in fact utilize them as resources to become literate.[24] In this manner, Spanglish may be spoken within and between different generations without stigmatization and is simply another cultural and linguistic resource "to be." But in general this may lead to a simple recognition in the SWNAR, and as we heard in chapter 4: "Mexico never left the Southwest, it just learned English" (55).

This unbalancing process can be further enhanced by teachers in the classroom and administrators in the office who are fully instructed, as will be discussed, in the "funds of knowledge" carried into the classroom by Spanish-dominant students and their parents. Spanish-dominant parents must be involved in substantive ways such as in the very construction of the cultural underpinnings of the classroom and become integrated through the mechanisms of training and development characterizing funds of knowledge processes. Then teachers and administrators will more than likely be able to counter the continued secondary stratification of Spanish-dominant students without denigrating the resources the children bring to the classroom and further alienating Spanish-dominant students from what could be an advantageous educational experience. It is simply insufficient for parental groups to become involved from the outside to a kind of an "in," even when engaged in the design of such programs. Even in those in which efforts are made to offset "unbalancing processes," such as those described by Freeman (1996), where Spanish-dominant parents were engaged in the design of programs for English-dominant students, their multiple cultural "selves" simply are not made a core element of the curriculum or of the recognition of those "selves" as pertinent to instruction or usefulness, unlike the presumptions and premises for English-dominant parents. It would be only "natural" for the power ladder to be so recognized.

Without having become involved at the level of the household, and without the knowledge of the wealth of cultural resources their Spanish-dominant children and their parents bring to the school, teachers and administrators will be responsible for the continuation of shifting even more of the advantage of a precious linguistic and cultural resource from those who live it to those whose advantages are already naturalized.

As will be discussed, there are remedies suggested by attention to the ethnographic "funds of knowledge" approaches that have been developed over a number of years.[25] From an anthropological point of view, there is a bias to focus on qualitative data and information in order to flesh out processes and to engage such programs as dual language programs at the quotidian level. Ethnography is at its best when it uncovers layers that others have missed or perhaps because the instructional data often are based on only quantitative approaches, as mostly presented in this review of bilingualism and dual language learning in this work. It is within such contexts that "translanguaging" expresses cultural behaviors unbeknown to monocultural and monolingual teachers and administrators. Uncovering layers provides a multiple dimension by which to gauge and measure, not in a quantitative sense but rather by observing on the ground, everyday processes of discovery not usually amenable to questionnaires or testing instruments. Ethnography and bilingualism go together if done right by trained observers and interrogators, and by listening and seeing carefully. The ethnographic method captures these processes that unfold in unexpected and unmeasurable ways and provides human dimensions that enhance our understandings that go beyond an ANOVA or chi-square analysis, although these are necessary but hardly ever sufficient to capture the emotive, the deeply personal dynamics of social relations and exchange in situ. The amazing manner in which what we think is "normal" is but another layer of rationalized permission to continue doing what we think we are doing and thinking what we think we are thinking and miss the often great differences between what we do and think.

Therefore, linguistic programs must recognize the importance of "home" cultural resources and translanguage expressive culture, integrate or make use of whatever program of instruction is developed, and ensure that home is not alienated from school. Their cultural contexts from whence children emerge and the linguistic resources they carry are generally made invisible by the institution, creating further alienation. As my colleague James B. Greenberg has so well stated, "the difficulty in educating our children begins in . . . industrial societies of the work place [separate] from the home" (1990, 37). Vélez-Ibáñez and Greenberg (1992) referred to these home cultural resources as "funds of knowledge," which they define as "those bodies of knowledge of strategic importance to households," and I would expand and include from our original research of course languages, lineage and historical oral knowledge, patterns and recognitions of social relationships, use and continuance of reciprocity and exchange, gender divisions and attitudes, and values toward selves and others. I would also include all implied and recognized computational, compositional, and literacy knowledge, patterns of organizing elements and data, ideological and religious principles including ritual processes and practices, internalized methods and practices of arrangement and organization, and the underlying orientation for the basis of physical and geographical spatial induction and deduction. Knowledge concerning the expression of physics and chemistry and biologics and botanies in congealed formats like mechanics, construction, homoeopathic medicine, grooming, plant use, herbal medicine, receipts, cooking, and repairing are also salient to local funds of knowledge. From figuring out "plumb" on a right-angled corner while constructing adjoining walls, computational knowledge is tapped and learned by children when in the proximity of the activity. Integral knowledge is that of the caretaking of children and expected social relations and their expressions and highly regarded emotive responses such as affection, love, tenderness, all of their opposites, and everything in between, to the emotional "gluing" and investments in these funds and their articulation and transmission between and among generations. We may refer to all of these as possible

which they are a part. Children internalize the calculus of these behaviors and relation-ships. Even if simply present and playing on the floor, children listen to the conversa-tion of adults and learn much about people and events within and outside the family, including gossip and criticism of family members that are deemed to belong only to members in the family. They will learn that these take a great deal of patience, practice, information, responsibility, and engagement in the social actions of reciprocity and exchange and their constituent cultural understandings of *confianza* (mutual trust).

But what is crucial to this concept of funds of knowledge is the inclusion of the actuality of local populations regardless of place, as a necessary and sufficient condi-tion for its utility to students, teachers, and administrators, and most importantly to the communities of which they are a part. Dual language programs, if stripped of the potential utility of these funds of knowledge as well as their contextual importance, treat language instruction as a mere medium rather than the message, which in the case proposed here is one of "culture" broadly conceived as processes of learning and discarding over time, place, and circumstances of such funds.

For our purposes here, we emphasize the broader regional reality of the SWNAR as crucial to the formation of these funds over time and how these are in actuality characterized is a matter of ethnographic knowledge not by assumed or presumed assumptions but gauged in probabilistic and distributional terms rather than finished products to be categorized and mined *a priori*. Thus, for example, in the original research conducted by Vélez-Ibáñez and Greenberg in the 1980s and subsequently published, we had no data in regard to digital information, computers, video games, or use of cell phones since these were either not noted or simply did not exist among the initial seventy-five households studied in Tucson, Arizona. Approaching equiv-alent households in the present would demand attention to these sources of funds of knowledge since almost every child in most neighborhoods has access to or uses digital devices as a matter of course regardless of context, class, and setting. On the other hand, in the region there will be commonalities and similarities no matter what new technical introductions have ensued between the two periods of time. There will be hundreds, if not thousands, of first-generation families, parents who work more than one job, parents struggling to raise their children in safe environments, children attending schools, some of which are more than ready and eager to accept them with-out qualification, while others use typecasting "low income, 100% lunch program eli-gible, English learners, and native speakers," many in abbreviated "seeing man" forms like LEPs, ELLs, SLLs, ESLs and all used as both premises and predictors of learning and learning capacities. But these latter labels will not include their actual experi-ences, potentials, achievements, skills, talents, and less of their home life but only that their "home" language is Spanish and a detriment. They could hardly predict that the fourth-grade boy in their class who hums and sings when no one is looking and seems distracted also knows how to play the guitar, violin, and accordion and can read sheet music like a professional and assists his father and uncles on the weekends by playing at weddings and local quinceñeras and knows more than one hundred songs by heart in Spanish and English.[29] So that a trained and learned teacher who really knew the student and home, as well as the literature on the benefits of bilingualism, would have not typed the student as only noisy by his humming in class but also would have known that these abilities contribute to the development of greater "executive function" like bilingualism and that musical practice and learning are strongly correlated with "cortical thickening and maturation," among other benefits.[30]

From our work in the 1980s and research in the 1990s with colleagues Luis Moll and Norma González, hundreds of such examples could be denoted and certainly in the present of many working-class and middle-class regional populations whose households contain funds of knowledge from airplane mechanics to architectural design, from home stores in which children learn to count and give change to customers, to young girls in junior high school participating in rotating savings and credit associations who are responsible for calculating the distribution of funds to participants (Vélez-Ibáñez 2010).[31] Present in these homes are practices in which both boys and girls early on learn to be independently skilled at repairing and fixing their toys and bicycles, to observing their own parents reading to them and their brothers and sisters, including Mexican fabulas and magical *cuentos*. But part of these funds are the linguistic, cultural, and social brokering roles many children will fulfill as translators and interpreters of their parent's realities, serving as intermediaries for them in difficult as well as daily events and necessities. Although stressful for the child and probably not enjoyed, nevertheless, such functions may increase the binguality of the child, and her/his attending neural implications can only be surmised.

From such circumstances, funds of knowledge in the region are developed and created. Too many times these are simply ignored or found useless in contributing to relational, instructive, or contextual functions.[32] But a great deal of literature has been generated since these early considerations by especially Moll and González (1997), who have expanded the usefulness and understanding of the original concept and applied it to the classroom.[33] It is not proposed that funds of knowledge are the same in all households, or that all such knowledge is immediately useful for school instruction. But what is imperative to know, especially for teachers and administrators of schools with large numbers of Mexican-origin students whose first language is Spanish, is that the ethnography of home is one important way in which the relations of *confianza* mutual trust between home and school become cemented. Once these are established, the discovery of the knowledge base of the child may be much richer than that assumed by the usual labels and categories used to understand the children of the region regardless of generation or status as a recent arrival. From such advantageous positions, programs such as dual language initiatives may perhaps be more congruent and relational to the home and made closely associated to the goals of excellence and unfettered achievement. Thus, the premise for the child, once such knowledge is learned by the teacher and administrators, is that she or he will not be treated as *tabula rasa* absent rich resources or that the content and ideas expressed by the child's home language are unsuited. Or worse, that the child is to be saved by yet another educational experiment, creating more uncertainty in the veracity of their own inherited funds of knowledge and the invaluable resource of their language as the means of communicating them. Finally, Cathy Amanti (1995), a former elementary school teacher who was among the first to be trained (and a pleasure to have helped in doing so) in the ethnographic method to capture the funds of knowledge of students, was amazed and surprised of the children's home base of information and experience and, just as an example, noted that many of these children are international travelers, which is neither seen nor recognized. Specifically, she states:

> Furthermore, because of these experiences [traveling] . . . many of my . . . students show a great deal of interest in economic issues, because they have seen the difference in the two countries, in immigration law, but also in laws in general; they would ask me why there are so many laws here that they don't have in Mexico. These children have had the background experiences to explore in-depth issues that tie in with a sixth grade curriculum, such as the study of other countries, different forms of government, economic systems, and so on. (137)

Thus these children had already acquired a comparative perspective rather than relying on monolingual, experientially limited single avenues of experience, not unlike those enjoyed by upper-middle- and upper-class children, who by privilege travel as a matter of course. Her surprise was the norm, not the exception, for teachers and administrators engaged in training, carrying out ethnographic research, and transforming the data gathered into useable learning modules for the classroom. Such conclusions are based on both observation and discourses with teachers and administrators supported by the multitude of studies carried out following those mentioned here[34] and supported by Torres-Guzmán for dual language programs (2002, 6).

The unbalancing processes that emerge from dominant "white" reservoirs in myriad contexts can only be offset by teachers in the classroom and administrators in the office who are fully instructed as to the funds of knowledge carried into the classroom by Spanish-dominant students. Unless Spanish-dominant parents are involved in substantive ways, such as in the very construction of the cultural underpinnings of the classroom, and are integrated through the mechanisms of training and development characterizing the funds of knowledge process, then teachers and administrators will more than likely contribute to the continued stratification of Spanish-dominant students, denigrate the resources the children bring to the classroom, and further alienate Spanish-dominant students from what could be an advantageous educational experience. It is simply insufficient for parental groups to become involved from the outside to a kind of an "in," even when engaged in the design of such programs. Even in those efforts made to offset "unbalancing processes" such as those described by Freeman (1996), where Spanish-dominant parents were engaged in the design of programs for English-dominant students, their multiple cultural "selves" simply are not made a core element of the curriculum or of the recognition of those "selves" as pertinent to instruction or usefulness, unlike the presumptions and premises for English-dominant parents. It would be only "natural" for the latter to be so recognized.

Without having become involved at the household level, and without the knowledge of the wealth of cultural resources their Spanish-dominant children and their parents bring to the school, teachers and administrators will be responsible for the continuation of shifting even more of the advantage of a precious linguistic and cultural resource from those who live it to those whose advantages are already naturalized.

A DUAL LANGUAGE EXAMPLE AND MODELS FOR DIRECTION

With the coupling of funds of knowledge training and development, or as will be seen, with highly congruent integration of general cultural knowledge or intense acceptance of valued parental cultural practices and modes of behavior like the calendric cycles of exchange, dual language programs could serve as models for direction for the present, often muddled state of instruction for Spanish-dominant students. And if we are informed by those dual language programs analyzed that used intensive ethnographic methods, these will also reveal the unfolding and mostly unpredictable processes in the areas of design, development, and implementation. These all-important processes are involved in developing trust with and commitment by parents who especially may not be familiar with these approaches and must become familiarized with programmatic goals, objectives, and expected outcomes. Not surprisingly, there will be many parents who have internalized the "white" ideological premises of homogeneity, monolingualism, and assimilation, all of which will be buttressed by the hope of their children achieving the "American Dream." These parents will be the most difficult to convince and many will opt out.

The works by Calderón and Carreón (2000) and Pérez (2004) provide opportunities to detail the linguistic, social, political, and cultural processes that are engaged when such programs are considered for implementation but without the discussed funds of knowledge. But these works, for the most part, seem to indicate that the programs they studied were integrated with an uncommon respect and acceptance of the students, families, and communities. These works examine the processes of design and operational management; the crucial involvement of parents; the engagement of students in their educational advancement and enhancement; and the profound attention to the cultural and social dynamics involved. These take a hard look at how entire programs of instruction were conducted and, with some, evaluated, assessed, outcomes communicated, and how these were used sometimes to enhance or change the enterprises. These works can function as primers on important issues of human linguistic and cultural development and emergence, giving those interested in policy and implementation all of the data and program efficacy needed for serious consideration.

A number of significant findings cut through these ethnographically oriented studies. First, Calderón and Carreón's (2000) analysis takes place in El Paso, Texas, is transborder in process, and interdependent with Juárez, Chihuahua, in structure, culture, economy, policy, and language. It is a local ecumene of the larger SWNAR in all of its characteristics, including enormous daily passage of persons north and south, of huge lines of trucks crossing bidirectionally transporting unfinished goods in one and finished in the other, and with thousands living on one side and working on the other, as has been done since the imposition of the border on the region to different degrees. But the underlying gestalt of the programs studied relied on quantitative data and ethnographic information collected over a three-year period, and focused on first, the language development of students; second, achieved student outcomes; and third, the professional outcome of the teachers involved (8). Their qualitative analysis focused on what the authors termed "activity settings" in daily interaction. The authors state that "[a]ctivity settings are analyzed through five elements: (1) participants, (2) tasks and activities, (3) scripts for conduct, (4) goals, and (5) beliefs. The separate functions are linked with one another in activity (Vygotsky 1987). Students and teachers are collaborators in the data gathering by co-constructing the ethnographies of their activity, goals, and beliefs in their teaching and in their collegial teams." Thus the stakeholders for creating and studying the daily interactive settings fell not to outside ethnographers, but to those strongly engaged in the process. This process orientation was the dynamic from the outset so that categorization was less likely, pigeonholing was weakened, and an open acceptance of differences and similarities commonplace.

But what was crucial in the design were three outstanding goals that were generated from the outset that were formed by the interactions between the major instructional stakeholders of principals, teachers, and bilingual coordinators. The first goal was to help students achieve academic excellence in Spanish and English; second, support of and enhancement of student self-esteem; and third, multicultural acceptance and interaction between parents, teachers, and students (14). Parental involvement stressed that the curriculum should be available to all students, and they obviously did not want their children segregated. The aftermath was that the first five grades had an equal representation of Spanish- and English-dominant children with a mix of children in levels of ability and buttressed by two teachers—one bilingual in charge of Spanish instruction and the other monolingual English—who teach two blocks in separated language instruction. Children were especially involved in cooperative learning based on an inquiry approach with a great deal of group interaction. All teachers had intensive professional development and training and formed into learning communities. Parental activities were school centered and stimulated interactions between parents of each dominant language group (Calderón and Carreón 2000, 27–28).

So what were the ultimate outcomes as measured by the English Texas Assessment of Academic Skills? First, at the end of the three years for third, fourth, and fifth grades, students made significant academic gains in comparison to those students in three distinct bilingual programs. Although Spanish-dominant students were still behind English-dominant students, they were statistically significantly above other Spanish-dominant students in other programs.

But among the most noticeable cracks in the program were those between a few bilingual teachers and monolingual English teachers in which the latter had not lost his/her presumption of linguistic and cultural superiority. Fortunately, these were in the minority and most of the teachers especially engaged in the daily ethnography of exchange moved much beyond their unfortunate attitudes (40).

The conclusions from this study were multifaceted:

1. Success emerged from those components carefully managed by the bilingual director and the teachers, but failures emerged from the lack of commitment and leadership by the principals and district administrators.
2. Success was achieved by the wholesale acceptance by teachers of a literature-based Bilingual Cooperative Reading and Composition model combined with mathematics, science, and the arts.
3. The impact on Mexican-origin student's roles changed from learning deficient to learning assets whose dominant language was valued and shared.
4. Achievement measures showed that both Spanish-dominant- and English-dominant students were significantly better than those students in other bilingual programs.
5. Spanish-dominant parents expressed pride in that their language was equally valued while English-dominant parents became strong supporters of the program. (41–43)

Yet there were failures in which there was a spiral-down impact on students' scores at the school in which the support by the administrator was tepid or nonexistent. This led to failure to implement the kind of curriculum imperative for the success of the dual language approach. Thus among the most crucial and telling of variables to program success, other than well trained-teachers, parental involvement, and student investment, was the direction and leadership that must be employed by administrators who must think outside of the box and outside of their upwardly mobile career ladders.[35]

The second example is from the intense ethnography by Pérez (2004) analyzing the major dynamics involved in creating, developing, assessing, and improving dual program operations and very carefully laying out flexible but patterned approaches. It too is an analysis from a Texas-based program in the San Antonio area, and very much associated with regional identity spatially and politically analogous but not quite the same as the El Paso/Ciudad Juárez-oriented example discussed. San Antonio has been heavily influenced by continuous Mexican replenishment since San Antonio's extraction from the Mexican Republic. San Antonio has always had a subregional identity associated with the bordering northern Mexican states of Chihuahua, Coahuila, Tamaulipas, and Nuevo León, all of which have been economically, culturally, and linguistically closely integrated and associated with especially San Antonio, including population movement from those states since the late nineteenth and early twentieth centuries, and certainly in the twenty-first. More culturally congruent institutions associated with Mexican-origin populations—like those of the Church, benevolent associations, parochial schools, private colleges, Mexican cultural centers, festivities, city-sponsored bilingual book fairs and public celebrations—and strong political presence have always been crucial to the resistance to the forces of acculturation and in contradiction and discontent to the San Antonio mythologized focus of the vaunted Anglo-Texan site of the Alamo.

The study was carried out in two K–5 elementary schools made up of 197 Mexican-origin students, 17 Anglo, and 2 African American, with variations in the number of Spanish- versus English-dominant students, but averaging 45 percent English to 55 percent Spanish-dominant students.[36] The structure of the program was similar to the El Paso version with an intensive effort for parental communication, interaction, meetings, informal visitations, and parent classes that not only explained the program, but in its entirety of the two-year study, reported that outreach to parents included reporting their children's progress, learning, and achievements (53).

The program itself was ultimately designed to start as 90:10 Spanish/English in the primary grades, moving to a 50:50 by the fifth grade, "integrating biliteracy and content throughout including Spanish language arts in science and math while the English teacher taught English literacy and language arts, and social studies" (117).

The study, which followed students, teachers, and parents from the initiation of the program to the study's conclusion two years later, was made up of a series of measures both mandated by the state of Texas and tests devised specially to measure levels of performance in both languages. Their results are both impressive and support the designed objectives of the program:

> The results demonstrated that literacy in Spanish was an influential predictor of English literacy at the .001 level of confidence. For students who entered the program as Spanish dominant, the findings showed that learning to read in Spanish assisted them to acquire reading skills in English. For students who entered the program as English dominant students and initially received literacy instruction in Spanish, were not deterred from acquiring literacy skills . . . Moreover the results showed that by the third grade, when instruction was 60% in Spanish and 40% in English, the two way bilingual program was beginning to accomplish its biliteracy goals . . . All of the testing showed that the students . . . were performing at or slightly above their peers in each of the schools . . . but they were also doing it in two languages. (161)

But the most important underlying premise that made these findings possible is that the program developed to ensure academic achievement for all students and not as "special education" students or labeled by levels of risk or reduced to language categories, but above all a program "that respected and valued the students' and community's linguistic and cultural experiences" (189). While it too did not have a conjoined program of funds of knowledge, it too would have contributed strongly to this most laudatory goal; but in spite of its absence, this also indicates that the program needs to be sufficiently fine-tuned, persistently guided by trained teachers, committed administrators, and intense parental involvement for it to work. Funds of knowledge as general cultural knowledge integrated within the daily instructional actions of the program and with "translanguage" spaces built in will lead to corresponding long-term affective and emotive impacts on social and cultural identity to correspond with the emphasized Mexican-centric patterns associated with San Antonio and most recently especially those of Mexican transnational entrepreneurs (MTNE).[37] Such patterns of course will vary with the actual demographics of the population and the distribution of their corresponding cultural groups.

DISCUSSION

From brain studies to comparative studies of European and Canadian examples to research accomplished with Mexican-origin and French-speaking children, the most pertinent conclusion that can be modestly suggested is that dual language immersion programs work quite well in closing so-called achievement gaps, create a healthy respect for and interest in language learning, develop complex cognitive structures, certainly replace the erasing well-intentioned but "white" approaches to cultural and linguistic removal, and provide the opportunity for removing the stigma of speaking the only language with which a child emerges as a human being. What is notable of course is that this approach is slowly but surely being accepted as a viable means by which children may expand and create the multiple levels of "I's" and "me's" and "us's" and "you's" and "we's" without being subjected to the narratives based on ahistorical renderings of the population in question. Coupled with rigorous programs of training and learning for teachers and administrators of "home funds of knowledge," as well as following models for dual language with "translanguaging" spaces and places as discussed, such a program of instruction and development is a win-win for children, parents, community, and the region as manifested in the measured outcomes in biliteracy and language and content. Simply, the demographic realities of the presence of such populations, coupled with the emergence of huge gaps of performance between children of different ethnicities and languages, with a full knowledge and appreciation of what does work and what does not, the fallback position must be one of instruction based on sound research and program success regardless of politics, regardless of ethnicity, regardless of tired narratives, and regardless of ideological convictions tied to ahistorical premises. The last gasps of hegemonic practices are being exhaled by the continued resistance, progress, and demand of not just "well-meaning" persons but also the inevitability of demographic and political processes working themselves out in favor of populations often unheard and ignored in place of mythic pretensions of homogeneity, monolingualism, and cultural erasure and removal of the underlying gestalt of privileged "whiteness." It is imperative that the cultural multiplicity of Mexican-origin and other Latino/a populations and Indigenous peoples are able to emerge fully as complex cultural beings with choices between their multiple "I's," multiple "me's," multiple "us's," worthy of respect and support for their wealth of their "other's"—all sometimes enhanced and sometimes repressed by long historical processes that continue to unfold in the present. From my point of view, this is the best response to the three "swats" that began this work and is a tribute to our discontents. Yet there are new dimensions of linguistic erasure in the modern southern region of the SWNAR.

LOS RETORNOS (RETORNADOS):
THE RETURNEES TO THE SOUTHERN REGION

Other phenomena exclusive to the southern region of the SWNAR and to other regions of Mexico that are most disturbing are that thousands of U.S.-born or U.S-raised

Mexican-origin children have left the United States in the past ten or more years, either because of their parents' deportation or their voluntary return, because of economic downturns, or of draconian laws like the reprehensible SB 1070 of the state of Arizona and their copycats in other states. These children and their families I refer to as the *retornos* (also *retornados*) even though strictly speaking the U.S.-born children are not returnees but rather are accompanying their parents. These children and Mexican-born children raised in the United States number five hundred thousand, according to one estimate (Matus 2016).

However, their accompaniment was stimulated at different periods by economic expulsion beginning in 2008. During that year, according to Rafael Alarcón (2008), the daily Mexican newspapers were filled with news of an imminent return of Mexican migrants because of the economic crisis in the United States and described how 1,500 persons returned daily to Sonora (*El Financiero*, October 25, 2008), of 4,000 migrants from Chicago to Mexico City (*El Semanario*, October 14, 2008), of 20,000 families from the United States returning to Michoacán for that year (*La Jornada Michoacán*, October 10, 2008). He reports as well that the National Institute of Migration stated that it had detected increasing number of Mexicans definitely returning from the United States because of the economic crisis in the United States. As well, the "Obama administrations deported more than 2.5 million people—up 23 percent from the George W. Bush years and is now on pace to deport more people than the sum of all 19 presidents who governed the United States from 1892–2000" (Rogers 2016). Between 2003 and 2013, the U.S. government formally removed 3.7 million immigrants to their home countries. According to the most reliable estimates, parents of U.S.-born children made up between one-fifth and one-quarter of this total, with the most deported to Mexico (Koball et al. 2016, vi).

The increase of returned Mexican-origin children, including many others who have lived an American civil life and are therefore primarily English dominant, reportedly impacted the population of primary school children along the Arizona-Sonora border cities, with increases of 30 percent in 2010 alone (*El Universal* 2010). For the state of Guerrero, it has had an estimated 950,000 Guerrero persons living in the United States, and in Chicago alone live 300,000, who are both authorized and unauthorized (the majority) (*Problematicas* 2016). Of those almost one million persons and their children, there is simply no way to determine how many families have been deported and/or returned voluntarily.

These children, once in Mexico, for the most part are not only discriminated against, but their linguistic and cultural skills are for the most part ignored by benign neglect, the subject of enforced erasure of English in favor of Spanish in a manner reminiscent to that of the Mexican-origin children in the United States during the heyday of such practices, or instructed in English classes teaching rudimentary English for first graders to high school students. According to Valencia Reyes (2009), almost forty thousand children had been returned in that period to face an uncertain future in schools. Evidence from intensive and extensive research carried out in the states of Morelos and Hidalgo by Valencia (32–43) states that education authorities, school administrators, teachers, and parents were not equipped to meet returning Mexican children's linguistic, literacy, and social needs or to take advantage of the cultural and linguistic resources of these children and their parents. In addition, children most often are given diagnostics in Spanish without English options, and school districts fundamentally fail to know or understand the curricular content and processes that these children have followed and mastered. Most distressing from this recent work is that none of the educational institutions could meet the cultural, educational, and linguistic needs of these "minority language learners," and even less recognize the social and cultural capital that these children utilize and carry with them. Such capital is not only not recognized but also may very well be that the first institutionalized response to these children is the attempt to erase that which is present with what is only partially a benefit, if at all.

In one of the few intensive studies done by Petron (2003), she concludes: "As students in their English classes in Mexican schools, they seem to have suffered a similar fate similar to that of Latino heritage language students of Spanish in the U.S. The linguistic and cultural skills they possess were not validated" (233). Their Spanish skills are often derided, stereotyped as "Pochos" or worse, and often ostracized, as supported by data from observations made during fieldwork explorations in Guerrero by myself and others in 2009.[38] In the *retonoros* case, the "seeing man" is indeed blind. This transborder dimension of hurting the innocent cannot continue on either side of the region.

CONCLUSION

⁂

Language is like life: I am energy—changing, evolving, weak at times, potent and powerful at others—merging with experiences, transforming from these mergers and their teaching and taking on a new meaning and form due to those mergers. But the light, energy, matter, unique, connected by sequence of history, experiences in a chain that define me and give me this ever so subtle unique distinction.

SHOHAMY 2006, 173

THIS BOOK STAGED ITS DISCUSSION along three main axes. The first is one from the literature on hegemony, which seeks to fundamentally understand how in the midst of all of those exploitations and extractions, peoples engaged with each other in war and cooperation in these regions and managed to insert their main means of communication (what we term "language") to become the mechanism and the messages of human conduct for all concerned. Within this axis is some theoretical attention from evolutionary anthropology of how peoples become what they become to form the "I's" and "we's" and "me's" and the "them's" and the "they's," and most importantly, the formation of the "other's" with language and culture, the means by which hegemony is transmitted, learned, opposed, folded, digested, changed, reinvented, and used. The second axis, along the long-traveled and immense region, was labeled as the Southwest North American Region (SWNAR)—a term generated by intense discussions from the literature from archeological to ecological, the political to the economic, and the social to the cultural. At its core are the contending dynamics of human populations in competition and cooperation for the plentiful and scarce resources it contains. The region itself ranges from arid lands to forested mountains spanning from the Sierra Madre to the Rocky Mountains, coastal marine ecologies, and transected by the ensuing great rivers of the Colorado and Rio Grande and their many kindred, as well as others crisscrossing east and west. But its highly sedentary and mobile populations—some for millenia and most recently by European intrusions of colonization—were all engaged in one way or the other in producing, exploiting, imposing, and extracting regional potentials and their constraining ecologies, as well as each other, to different degrees and intentions. These are the crucial political ecologies that contextualize our discussion of hegemonies and their discontents. Finally, the third axis is attention to the crucial necessity of removing the constraints due to disciplinary investments in siloed explanations and renditions of the cultural and linguistic historical and largely social-science approaches to human populations under severe pressures by colonial projects from the Spanish colonial period to the present and to fundamentally understand the various guises and masquerades the "seeing man" can assume and their unconscious and conscious believabilities. Wolf has eloquently phrased the necessity of eliminating the academic penchant for presenting colonial subjects as "people without histories" and thus unmasking the noblesse oblige of the "seeing man." This work has explored many facets of the academic enterprise to modestly contribute to this effort by attending to little-known colonial documents, biographies and ethnobiographies, ethnography, statistical treatments, as well as genetic and bioneurological materials of importance. These latter especially influence the polices toward language learning for the populations presented and seek better and more enhanced methods and approaches to provide maximum energies to novel ways of learning and teaching language. This is the next stage of creating the bilingual templates for peoples with histories, and the means by which to write and narrate them.

As was explained, hegemonic processes are usually never complete nor are they homogenous, but are distributed and filled with contradictions and errors of fact and fiction. They, nevertheless, are usually pretty terrible for the receiving end, no matter how reactive, adaptive, resistant, or seemingly "integrated." Their long-term effects, like PTSD, are many times masked by supervigilance of slights, hypersensitivity to correctness, overinvestment in perfect diction and communication, and the capacity to lie to oneself that "nothing much happened." But sooner or later, the masked symptoms must be expressed in sometimes weird ways by reinventing oneself in the images and likeness of the opposite of the "other," like Bartolome de Tejada, who became the governor of the Zia for the Spanish. He not only spied for his masters but also managed his Pueblo for them in spite of the fact that he had fought bravely against them earlier. He made it much easier for the "Act of Possession" after the return of the expelled Spanish Crown since he carried the cross before him as its symbol of celestial authority and connectivity to de Vargas to Carlos II and on high to the gods of the Catholic empire. Or four hundred years later, populations who opposed the entrance of the new American hegemonic power rationalized their becoming "Spanish" to differentiate themselves from the "Mexicans" in order to ensure their American-authorized privileged positions over the most recently arrived. This is in spite of the fact that only forty or so original families returned with de Vargas in 1594, and all the rest from Central Mexico or Zacatecas, or Chihuahua and among them many Tlaxcalan warriors. And all of the genetics of their descendants point to a preponderant admixture of

Indigenous and European and African genetic trading from numerous formal studies, including mine.

But in spite of their terribleness, hegemonic language and cultural processes can never be complete, homogenous, or one-sided. In fact, from precolonial periods Indigenous peoples were quite accustomed to contact with others, and for the entire SWNAR, multilingualisms, linguas francas, translations, interpretations, and long-distance communication by various means were normative. This was made possible by especially long-distance trade from south to north and west to east, especially of turquoise and other minerals at different periods of Indigenous history, between the monumental centers of La Quemada to Paquimé and to Mesa Verde and south as well.

Yet the Spanish entrance and colonial presence, initially brutal and later more benevolent, could not stamp out Indigenous languages regardless of missionary schooling efforts, Franciscan or Jesuit. For the most part, throughout the region from the Rarámuri of Chihuahua to the Pima peoples of Sonora and like the Tohono O'odham to the Hopi of now northern Arizona and to the Keresan-speaking peoples of New Mexico, these languages continued to be used strongly throughout the Spanish colony. In spite of the drastic demographic demise of these populations because of diseases and epidemics of measles, influenza, smallpox, and typhus that killed hundreds of thousands and many in the mines as well, these languages persisted, although impacted upon almost to decimation. Accustomed to bilingualism, these populations did in fact use the Spanish language for functional and ritual use and incorporated surnames within their cultural milieus because of the baptismal ritual. Yet it must be said that the Spanish colonial project, because of such widespread practices as slavery (which itself predated its existence to the colony), was very much responsible for the detribalization of many Indigenous peoples and transformed them into "Genizaros." These peoples, like many of their Indigenous associates, became adept at using the Spanish colonial legal system to seek redress. Under Governor Tomás Vélez Cachupín, they won numerous legal conflicts over land, slave rights, and individual cases seeking redress against Spanish overseers. But it was a different case under other governors, as in the denied case of the Genizaros, whose petition is illustrated in appendix C.

But there is also no doubt that the Spanish colonial introduction of entirely different cognitive maps concerning religion, group and individual identity, political and social identities, and cultural definitions of their "selves" impacted strongly but not without resistance and determined opposition, even while seeming to acquiesce to their newly defined senses of "selves." A brief examination, for example, of the hundreds of colonial presidio filiación (service records) revealed entirely highly individualized identities with special attention to personal and familial naming, titles, and religion.

Emphasized centrally were physical characteristics, including the high regard for melanin differences. This is in comparison to the Indigenous identification with moieties or clans, naming by lineage members, and a stress not on rank but on ability and successful passage of ritual requirements were indeed cognitive differences of importance. These differentiated the "individual" emphasis over "group" identity in spite of the fact that the soldiery was strongly identified by unit and military presidial location. However, it is in fact in the social location of each that the differences are acute—the soldiery part of the empire of conquest and colonization and the Indigenous warrior emphasizing protection, maintenance, and raiding for resources and people.

Yet even in that most impressive of colonial inventions, the Church—in spite of its contradictory roles of suppression, salvation, and protection, as well as lashings for noncompliance and fighting against the cruelties of settlers and soldiers—the Indigenous populations managed to incorporate as well as define those principles of most value. Inundated by political statements of "Acts of Possession" embossed and imprinted by references to celestial authority in a chain of being from a godhead to the terrestrial king to his representative to the incessant religious proselytizing by Jesuits and Franciscans, Indigenous populations listened, but responded differentially. A case in point is the priest in Sonora who complained of the confessed not responding in Spanish but in Pima while not seeming to comprehend Spanish except when they strategically decided to so do. At times rejecting and at times incorporating, Indigenous populations integrated the myths of the Church, the ritualized performances taught by Jesuits, or integrated those performed by Tlaxcalans such as the matachines of the Rarámuri of Chihuahua, or Pueblo peoples of almost all New Mexico, or of the Yoéme of Sonora. Thus Turquoise and Pumpkin Moieties among the Jemez to this day conduct parallel versions of the matachines: one Indigenous, the other "Spanish." Thus like these performances, language also was used and incorporated depending on circumstance, and playing the nonhearing role was a long-standing subterfuge, as was creating two renditions of what would seem to be a "conquest" performance of the matachines.

In totality, these processes of imposition are, as their counterpoints, arcs of hegemonies and discontents. Their distribution and impact are consequences of their levels of coercion and legitimacy and, for the latter, also part of the negotiated and strategic considerations adopted by Indigenous populations.

But the political bifurcation of the region introduced an overwhelming hegemonic dynamic in language, commerce, and relationships. Those who had been hegemonic in either spirit or practice became themselves the objects of these processes from the hands of the recently arrived. Many of these were newly learned English-speaking European migrants. Their governing, educational, and religious institutions and practices impacted doubly on the Indigenous populations, which were already impacted upon by the four-hundred-year presence of the Spanish colonial and Mexican Republic's policies. Simultaneously, the massive regional migration mirrored changes by industrial modes of organization in agriculture, mining, ranching, and urbanization that introduced the need for available labor. Without having to contract thousands from across the sea, the availability of Mexican brains and brawn were easily accessible. Thus the industrially stimulated migrations became a pattern of crossing and recrossing on both sides of the political bifurcation, and divided by what was only a sixty-meter difference in 1895 between countries as a border and without barriers, walls, fences, or impediments. These became a reality with the Great Depression of the 1930s and then only as a partial cyclone fence interspersed between two custom guardhouses. In many cases crossing populations went to live with or next to relatives who had already been part of the colonial and Mexican periods.

In a context of economic regionality of goods, services, labor, land, and kinship, but divided by a political line, these came under the linguistic and cultural hegemony of an East Coast prism of immigration, identity, monolinguality, and cultural singularity. It is from these sources that too many children of both Mexican and Indigenous parents on the northern side came to be often caught up in a vicious circle of becoming mutes of fear and oppression of the only languages they knew. Moreover, even when bilingual, they were often placed in separate and segregated classrooms in grades lower than the scaled hierarchy of the school, such as "1C" below 1A and 1B, as in my case. On the southern side, the prevailing prism was the new revolutionary mestizo construct of citizenship for all, which simultaneously paid lip service to indigeneity, with Spanish as the continued conquering language. Only after the Zapatista revolts of the late twentieth century were Indigenous languages given an official national status to be taught and developed. Serious attempts were made in spite of many pitfalls and inadequate programs.

Indeed, on the northern side of the region, the Mexican Revolution brought a million Mexican refugees of myriad classes and with them major narratives that were and are in contradistinction to the American monolingual and monocultural megascripts. These were the first completely multicultural ideologies as expressed by Indigenismo and cultural nationalism as mestizos and not as singularly cultural. Coupled to this was an underlying narrative of revolutionary and progressive ideologies, expressed by revolutionary feminism and influencing later Chicano movements. Certainly the very conservative Cristero movement, in which Mexican parochial schools were transplanted to Texas, Arizona, and California, gave the impetus to create part of the Mexican middle class in the region. Yet, the imposition of English continued unabated with the rationales primarily induced by the fear of demographic "imbalances" as expressed by the division of the states of Arizona and New Mexico, such that in the late twentieth century, English-only came to be the hallmark for political careers in many states, including California and Arizona, with the resulting tragedies of poor performance, poor graduation rates, and an overabundance of children simply walking away or "dropping out." This was in spite of the certain knowledge that such English-immersion programs resulted in the stunting of children and that in fact bilingualism was supported by an educational literature quite in contrast to the one often regurgitated by early testing studies showing Mexican and Indigenous children as mentally incapable of learning abstract knowledge.

On the other hand, this work has provided ample reviews of what can and does function to support the dominant home language of children and provides an understanding of the underlying cognitive and linguistic structures leading to achievement and intellectual parity—dual language instruction and the coupling of funds of knowledge methodology as necessary conditions for the acceptance of the cultural and linguistic value of language other than just English. From brain to achievement studies, dual language programs have been supported by careful quantitative and qualitative analysis in Europe, Canada, and the United States while funds of knowledge research has established not only its efficacy but its crucial role in equalizing the cultural narrative of the home with the school. Funds of knowledge and dual language programs spiced by spaces and places for experimental "translanguaging" are the "discontents" proposed here. These are counterpoints to the original monolingual, single-cultural model designed to erase, eliminate, and subtract invaluable cultural resources that, now legally possible in the state of California, will serve as the basic pedagogical platforms that contribute to the development of the totality of the complex humanity of children. In the twenty-first century the hegemony of language must give way to its discontents so that the multiplicity of the "I's" can be formed as a type of healthy self-regulatory individuation, as has been discussed. It is highly probable that social media and global communications will somewhat undermine the state-imposed narratives of what constitute "national languages," and more likely translanguaging will become the more normative means of communicating past the attempted political bifurcation of the border. Yet the tweeting languages distributions of the SWNAR are very much located almost totally within the respective bifurcated borders, except that Spanish becomes more popular the closer these are distributed to Mexico (Gayle 2012).

Finally, this work has allowed me to work out many issues of language and selves that were in my mind and that not only interrupted some "me's," but also created false expectations of self-worth and were based on the accepted normalized notion of homogeneity and language erasure. But like all things human, in which noise and emotion are paid much more attention than reasoned consideration, I now more than ever understand my first perplexed reaction to the principal using force seventy years ago. The reason was simple—I came to understand that it basically denied my ability to speak that which was nursed early on. It was reinforced daily by a Sonoran father insisting on speaking the language of affection and discipline, and of the oral history of Apache warriors and murdered compadres and given life by a mother who some-times spoke English in fractured phrases but who wrote in Spanish with the ease of a Cervantes or of an Unamuno and experimented with written language by simultane-ously incorporating Spanish affection to an English-language anniversary card. These are the now very much understood contrasts to the once-prohibited admonitions accompanied by violence, now thankfully mostly muted, but not for the *retornos* in the southern region of the SWNAR and perhaps restimulated by the new president elected in 2016 in the northern region. Now new energy may become invested in equivalent destructive propositions like English-only, working for the denial of birth rights, ethnic studies banishments, and the proposed forced removal of millions of persons by political demagogues from a region long inhabited in the past by versions of themselves bearing crosses across thousands of miles and meeting other versions of themselves bearing holy wands to create those like me and unlike me and all of the other "me's" and their multiple selves, languages, funds of knowledge, and genetic mutations. It is from the discontents to these propositions that innovation emerges; and it is from discontents where we first began this narrative that will, in the end, succeed in permitting this population and adjoining populations to emerge as whole human beings unfettered by shattering policies of culture and language. I would only amend Shohamy's delicate metaphor that language is like life to "language is life." It is what makes the present and absent "me's" and forms the basis of establishing enhanced representations of a people with histories and the unmasking of the "seeing man."

Appendix A

FILIACIÓN OF DON PEDRO POLICARPO ALCUE Y AREMENDARIS OF THE THIRD COMPANY OF THE SECOND SQUADRON OF COMPANY OF DRAGOONS

Filiacion

D.ⁿ Pedro Policarpo Mauc y Amendariz, hijo legᵐᵒ de D.ⁿ Pedro Manuel Cap.ⁿ de la 3.ª Comp.ª de dho. Cuerpo y de D.ª Maria Rita de Mauc y Amendariz: Natural el valle de S. Dieme. Obispado. de Durango; su off.º Camp.ᵗᵃ su estatura sinco pies, su edad diez, y seis años. S. R. C. R. R. sus señales estas pelo negro, ojos negros, Color blanco Rosado, nariz afilada, hoitoro de Viruelas, con Lunar junto a la nariz el lado derecho, Barvi lampiño

Se presentó ante mi el Comᵗᵉ en Gefe de los expresados cuerpos D.ⁿ Diego Santamaria con su Sᵘᵖ.ʳ despacho del Sor. Brig. y Comᵗᵉ Grᵃˡ D. Pedro de Nava, su fha 17 de Junio de 179?, y admitido en la plaza de Jadete, cuio asiento seledió en dha. Comp.ª en 10 de Marzo de 1792, y se le instruió en las ordenanzas y sus penas, y lo firma siendo testigos Jose Ygnacio Pavia, y Jose Trinidad Rodrigᶻ Sargᵗᵒ y Cavo del Cuerpo.

Pedro Mauc e Amendariz

Appendix B
TESTIMONIO DE DOÑA JUANITA

ORIGINAL OF DOÑA JUANITA in Leticia Acosta Briseño (1993, 211) *Testimonio orales: Del río Yaqui hacia el sur* (Oral Testimonies: *From the Rio Yaqui to the South*). Memoria del XVI Simposio de Historia y Antropología, Volumen 1, 403–20, 1993. Universidad de Sonora, Departamento de Historia y Antropología. © Derechos Reservados. Hermosillo, Sonora, México.

Mis padres fueron llevados en 1907, a fuerzas, aquí dejaron sus casas, sus fincas, sus cosechas, de no llevar de un grano de nada... pues vino la federación, rodearon todas las casas y sacaron a todas las familias. Primeramente se llevaron puros hombres, por la fuerza, a todos los llevaban amarrados como si fueran unos delincuentes... los calumniaron, porque dijeron que eran de la sierra, y no, ellos sembraban al margen del río y aquí ellos vendían sus cosechas hasta Guaymas o a Hermosillo, donde lo podían vender para su sustento... pues no se si tendrían algo malo o no lo tendrían, pero así los calumniaba Porfirio Díaz, que eran rebeldes, contrarios al pueblo pues, que estaban contra el gobierno, pero no, no era eso, es que tenían ellos el temor de que los fueran a matar aquí porque los colgaban hasta en sus casas, los perseguían porque el gobierno nunca ha querido a la tribu yaqui, porque sabían que son indígenas, son indios, por eso no los quieren... apropiarse de todo lo que tienen los yaquis, los terrenos, eso querían.

Appendix C

PETITION BY LOS GENIZAROS TO POPULATE THE OLD PUEBLO OF SANDIA, 1733, SANM I, ROLL 6, FRAMES 687–96. TRANSLITERATION BY SAMUEL SISNEROS. ORTHOGRAPHY IS OF THE ORIGINAL.

Señor Gobernador y Capitan General

Los hijos Genizaros de este Reino, los quales por la missericordia de Dios Nuestro Senor fuimos traidos al Gremio, y Abrigo de Nuestra Santa Madre Iglesia, rrecibiendo por Nra gran dicha el Agua de el Bautismo, y con el la fe de los misterios santos de el mui alto señor, favor tan excelente, y singular, a que nos hallamos obligados y rreconocidos; pues siendo tantas las Almas que sosobran en el mar immenso de la Gentilidad, a nossotros, por particular decreto, y Providiencia se digno de sacarnos, al Puerto Seguro de su Yglesia, en ella pues, gososos de tan crecida dicha, esperamos, mediante su divina gracia, darle colmados frutos de virtudes, y buenas obras, con las quales, llegado el Termino de la Temporal Vida, pasaremos alegres a dar la buena quenta de la distribución, que hizo en nossotros de sus Talentos; y esta supuesta, gosaremos el Prometido premio a los que fieles obserbaron su Ley, y mui Santos preceptos. mas porque para conseguir tanta Dicha, es prescisso, y Anexo, al servicio, y agrado de el Señor, dar el nessesario sustento al Cuerpo, como assi lo Dispusso, ordeno, y prebino, su infinita sabiduria y soberana Probidencia; para el qual, aunque en el Principio de nuestra Creacion, esto es, en Adan, y Eva, nos probeio de todo aquello que conducia, a nuestro Natural manteni[mi]ento, sin que para ello nessecitassemos de poner de nra parte algun trabajo, o medio; quisso Nra Desgracia que olvidados Nros primeros P<adr>es de tanto bien, y Beneficio, y soltando las Riendas a su desordenado deseo, quebrantando de Dios aquel tan santo, y saludable precepto, perdiendose ellos, y tanbien a Nosotros; en penitencia, de tan Atros Delitos salimos sentenciados, a la pena, y tormento, de cultivar la tierra, a fuerza de la fatiga, y propio trabajo de cada uno, Regandola con Prolijo sudor de Nuestro Rostro, como hasta aora, esperimentamos, y sabemos; y aunque en aquel entonces de Nuestra Pen[st]encia, era toda la Tierra Campo libre e immenzo para nra labranza, por ser Pocos los hombres e habitadores de ella, oi, por la probidencia, y disposicion de el señor esta tan llena, y Poblada de Gentes, que es nessessario, el avenirse todos a no pasar de aquellos limites, que por los superiores o Reies de la Tierra les son asignados en possecion a cada Uno, segun el fundamento, o motibo que se viere combenir para ello. por lo qual, y lo arriba supuesto, Paressemos ante la Grandeza de Vuestra Senoriya los Referidos hijos en la mejor via, y forma, que en Derecho Conbenga y decidimos que hallandonos Dispersos en las Villas, y Poblazones de este Reino, sin Abrigo, y forma de poder mantener N<uest>ras Personas y familias, pues no tenemos tierras proprias para ello, por lo qual pasamos la inconbeniencia y nessecidad que Dios sabe, y la Gracia de Vuestra senoria puede considerar, assi en el vestido, como la comida, y otros nessessarios de el cuerpo, sujetos a la Toleranzia de las estorciones, que la condicion humana de cada sujeto puede hacernos; y Arriesgados q<uan>do no todos, algunos de Nosotros que compelidos de sus grandes trabajos, y miserias, o otras estorciones que acaeser puedan en nuestro del abrigo, los incinte el Demonio, como nuestro enemigo, a que abrazando la abominable Apostacia Vaian a la Gentilidad, a buscar a sus trabajos el rremedio; esto prebenimos, en atención a que siendo, como son las inclinaciones, y Juicios de los hombres tan muchos y diversos, si Unos conociendo el maior bien que gosan en la Yglecia de Dios Nuestro Senor, sufren con humildad, y amor qualesquiera trabajos, e incombeniencias que en la Compania, y aiuntamiento de los demás se ofrecen, a trueque de no perder sus Almas, otros puede ser desatiendan todo esto, y olvidando lo principal, y puesto su cuidado en lo menos, como es lo Corporal, sugeridos de el Enemigo, (que embidiosso no sessa de Rodearnos) y instigados de sus nessecidades, executen lo dicho. y aunque pudiéramos pedir a la piedad, y grandeza de Vsa como a Nro. Sr y Padre. y que goso la Regia Authoridad para el Gobierno militar, y Politico de este Reino, el que nos agregase a los Pueblos de Yndios Christianos, que componen este distrito, no queremos pedirlo, considerando la Renuencia, y mala inclinación de dichos Yndios, pues despues de tantos anos de Doctrina, y predicacion Evangelica, en lugar de ir a mas, cada dia ban a menos, hallandose como se hallan, entre ello cada dia, mucho idolatras y hechizeros; y asi por no contaminarnos, con tan Pestilencia al [Docma], y costrumbres Perversas assi Nossotros, con Nuestros hijos, pedimos a la Grandeza de Vsa sea mui servido, de Asignarnos por Pueblo, para Nuestra manutención, y bien estar el

Pueblo, que llamando Sandia, puesto que al Pressente se halla, como se ve despoblado, y yermo; lo qual demas de ser conbeniencia para nossotros, lo es tanbien para el Reino pues siendo una frontera, y Puerta de los Enemigos Apaches, conseguirse ha con esto, el que se les estorbe la entrada, y assi mesmo que con las continuas Recorridurias de Tierra que nosotros haremos, esplorando sus huellas, no tan facil, y libre les sera el venir a sus hurtos, Asaltos, y homicidios; pues aiudados nossotros, de los Espanoles sercanos de Alburquerque, nos hacemos un muro fuerte, para Resistirse su deprabado intento. Y por que para la determinación de Vsa discurramos ser necesario, el que sepa el Numero de que dichos Genizaros nos componemos, decimos ser mas de siento las familias, que están dispersas por todo el reino. Assi en los Pueblos de Yndios, como en lugares de españoles. Y no es Nstra intención que en esto se intrometan los criados de Españoles, que por derecho de haverlo rescatado y tener como los hijos en sus casas deben servirles sino solos nossotros, los que como hemos dicho nos hallamos desacomodados, y dispersos.

Por todo lo qual a Vsa volvemos a suplicar con todo rrendimiento se ha mui servido de concedernos lo arriba dicho, pues allí conviene al servicio, y agrado de ambas majestades y de ser assi como esperamos de su fiel, y catholico pecho, agradeceremos, se nos de el despacho, o orden en esta ocasion, para que siendo, como es tan oportuno el tiempo de sembrar, y hacer casa, pasemos luego a hacerlo; y Juramos en debida forma este nuestro escrito no ser de malicia, si por el motivo tan justo arriba dicho, y en lo nessesario ettcetera.

Los Genizaros (rúbrica)

En la Villa de Santa Fe en viente y un dia del mes de Abril de mil sette sientos trenta y tres anos vista por mi el Coronel Dn. Gervacio Cruzat y Gongora Governador y Capitan General de este Reyno de la Nueva Mexico y sus Provincias por su Mag. la huve por presentada en lo que ha lugar en derecho y devía mandar y mande que los suplicantes presenten una nomina de los Yndios que pretenden poblarse con la distincion de sus Nombres y Naciones. Asi lo provey mande y firme con los testigos de mi asistensia a falta de escribano Público y Real que no lo ay en este Reyno

Don Gervasio Cruzat y Gongora
Witnesses: Gaspar Bitton Juan Antonio de Unanue

Nomina de los hijos Genizaros, que se hallan Dispersos en este Reino de la Nuevo Mexico: Primeramente en esta jurrisdiccion de el Rio abajo los casados son los sigientes:

"List of the Native Sons- Genizaros that are found scattered in this Kingdom of New Mexico. Firstly in this Rio Abajo Jurisdiction are the following married families:"

1. Antonio Gurule, casado, su mujer Theresa, sus hijos dos hombres, y una muger.
2. Sebastian Gallegos, Juman, casado con Quiteria, sus hijos –tres hombres.
3. Joseph Fernandes, Juman, su muger Angelina, his hijo tres: un hombre y dos mugeres.
4. Antonio Padilla, Panana, casado con Maria, su hijo un hombre.
5. Antonio Padilla, Panana, casado con Isabel, una hija.
6. Francisco Baca, Apache, casado con Maria, sus hijos: dos hombres y una muger.
7. Rafael Montoia (Montoya), Caigua, casado con Rosa, una hija.
8. Juan Antonio, Apache, casado con Maria, un hijo.
9. Pablo de Chaves, Caigua, casado con Rosa, dos hijos: un hijo y una muger.
10. Francisco de Chaves, Tano, casado con Mariana, sus hijos: dos hombres y dos mugeres.
11. Domingo Martines, de la Nacion A, casado con Antonia, sus hijos tres hombres y una muger.
12. Antonio Jaramillo, Caigua, casado con Pascuala, sus hijos: dos hombres y una muger.
13. Agustin Garcia, de la Nacion A, casado con Maria, sus hijos un hombre y una muger.
14. Joan Antonio Gurule, Panana, casado con Maria, sus hijos tres: dos hombres y una muger.
15. Joan Ulibarri, Apache, casado con Rosa, un hijo.
16. Cristobal Lujan, Panana, casado con Maria, sin hijos.
17. Cristobal Romero, Apache, casado con Antonia, sin hijos.

Solteros:

1. Francisco Sedillo, Panana.
2. Francisco Baca, Panana.
3. Andres Martin, Yuta,
4. Agustin Fernandes, Juman, viudo.
5. Antonio Tagle, Juman.
6. Francisco Garcia, Juman.
7. Bernardo, soltero.
8. Joseph, juman, soltero.

En la Villa de Santa Fee en viente y tres de Abril de mil sette sientos trenta y tres anos vista por mi el Coronel Dn. Gervasio Cruzat y Gongora Governador y Capitan General de este Reyno de la Nueva Mexico y sus provincias por su Mag. la nomina de los Indios que en ella se expresa como asi mismo lo que pretenden en su escripto, devía declarar y declaro no tener lugar la población que pretenden y solo se les permitira el ponerse en los Pueblos ya formados, para cuio efecto podía acudir el que quisiere a este superior

Gobierno para que se les segnale el Pueblo a donde debe ponerse. Asi lo provey y mande y firme con los testigos de mi asistencia a falta de escribano Público y Real que no lo ay en este Reyno

Don Gervasio Cruzat y Gongora

Witnesses: Gaspar Bitton Juan Antonio de Unanue

ENGLISH TRANSLATION OF PETITION BY SAMUEL SISNEROS:

Sir Governor and Captain General,

We the Genizaro Native Sons in this Kingdom, whom by the mercy of God our Lord were brought to the fold and protection of Our Holy Mother Church, and as a result of this great act were bestowed the water of baptism and with it the faith of the holy saints of the very high Lord, it being an excellent and singular favor of which we recognize and find ourselves obligated. Therefore being many the souls that suffer in the immense sea of paganism, but by decree and providence found it worthy to bring us into the security of the church, where, we are joyful of such a progressive act and we hope through your divine grace to return to you abundant fruits of virtue and good works and at the end of our temporal life, we would wish to perish happily voicing the good account of the blessings of your talents bequeathed us. Therefore it is apparent that we enjoy the promised reward anticipated for those who faithfully observe your law and very holy precepts. In order to acquire such fortune it is necessary that we give service to you and depend on the satisfaction of the Lord to provide us the necessary sustenance for the body that in your infinite wisdom and sovereign providence has mandated, ordered and prepared. For it is that in the beginning of our creation—that is of Adam and Eve—he gave us all that provides for our natural maintenance, for which we needed not employ any type of labor or means. Due to the disgrace of our first parents dismissal of all things good and beneficial and releasing the reins of its disordered actions, breaking God's holy and sound precepts which were lost by them and also by us. We are now sentenced by such cruel offenses and penanced with the punishment and torment to cultivate the land and each person working to the point of fatigue and watering the land with the sweat dripping down from our faces, of which we are still experiencing. And even though during the time of our penance, the lands were free and immense for our tillage, with just a few men and inhabitants on the land. But today by the provenance and disposition of the Lord it is now full, and populated by people; that it is known by all to accommodate and not cross those boundaries which the kings and owners of the land assigned to each person's possession according to the legal foundations or intentions that they were in agreement with.

For this reason and the above mentioned suppositions we the referred native sons present ourselves to your grandeur in the best manner, that asserting our rights we declare that we now find ourselves dispersed in the villages and populaces of this kingdom, without protection or without means to maintain our persons and families. In addition, because we do not have our own land we experience the discomfort and hardship that only God knows, and your magnificence can consider, that in our clothing and food and other necessities of the body are subject to tolerating the pressures that this condition can impart upon each one of us; and not all but some of us are at risk of getting trapped into such a plight, compelled by our hard work, misery and pressures which might incite the devil our enemy and then embrace the repugnant apostasy of the pagan world to find remedy and employment. This calls attention to the inclinations and judgments of the diverse populace some knowing the better good and enjoy the church of our God and Lord, but who suffer with humility and love for whatever chore and inconvenience but receive the company and council offered from others in exchange of not losing their souls; others might lose sight of this and put their care in the carnal world by the suggestions of the enemy (that its jealousy doesn't cease to surround us) and instigated by their own needs execute the aforementioned. And even though we can ask for pity from your splendor as our master and father with your royal authority over the political and military government of this kingdom who would include us with the Christian Indian Pueblos that are in this district but we will not do so because considering that the said Indians renounce you and have bad inclinations despite years of doctrine and evangelical teaching do each day find themselves going backward and involved with idolatry and witchcraft; and not to contaminate ourselves with such pestilence toward dogma and perverse customs so it is that we with our children ask that in your well served greatness assign us as a Pueblo for our care and well-being at the Pueblo called Sandia which presently appears to be unpopulated and gloomy; and also regardless of its convenience for us it would also be good for the kingdom since that it is at the border region and at the gateway to the enemy Apaches who disturb the entrance and in this way with our continued traversing of the land and exploring all its features we will be free and prepared for their future robberies, attacks and murders; but also with the help of the Spanish people from nearby Alburquerque, we will make a walled fortress to resist their vicious intentions. Thus for your determination we believe it necessary that you know the number of said Genizaros that we comprise of which we believe to be more than one hundred families dispersed throughout the kingdom in Indian Pueblos as well as in the territories of the Spanish. And it is not our intention to include the house servants of the Spanish because it is their right for they rescued them and brought them into their homes as their children to serve them, but rather this applies to only us whom, as we have explained, find ourselves discomfited and or scattered.

For all the above mentioned reasons we again request with our humility that it would be of great service and to the liking of Both Majesties and as we would expect from your faithful and catholic bosom, we would appreciate if you would give us the discharge or order in this case since it is such an opportune time to plant and build our homes which we would immediately proceed to do; and we swear that our writ is in due form and not of malice but rather motivated by a just and imperative cause.

Los Genizaros (rubric)

❧

Appendix D
LA CUCARACHA

La Cucaracha, la cucaracha,
ya no puede caminar,
porque no tiene, porque le falta,
marihuana que fumar.
Ya se van los carrancistas,
ya se van por el alambre,
porque dicen los villistas,
que se estarán muriendo de hambre.
Pobre de la Cucaracha,
se queja con decepción,
de no usar ropa planchada,
por la escasez de carbón.
(Coro)
Pobrecito de Madero,
casi todos le han fallado,
Huerta el ebrio bandolero,
es un buey para el arado.
La ropa sin almidón,
se pone todos los días;
y sin esas boberías,
se me figura melón.

From http://corridomexicano.com/letras/la-cucaracha.html.

(Coro)
Todos se pelean la silla
que les deja mucha plata;
en el Norte Pancho Villa,
y en el Sur Viva Zapata!
Una cosa me da risa:
Pancho Villa sin camisa,
otra cosa me da horror,
al vil Huerta en camisón.
(Coro)
Necesito algún "fortingo"
para hacer la caminata,
al lugar donde mandó
a la convención, Zapata.
Una guacamaya pinta
le dijo a una colorada,
quien se meta con mi patria,
se lo carga la . . .
(Coro)
Hay unos que roban mucho,
y luego huyen muy lejos,
validos de fuero y mando
y de que nos creen pen . . . itnetes.
(Coro)
Qué bonitas soldaderas
cuando bailan el fandango.
Viva Pánfilo Natera,
el orgullo de Durango.
Ya murió la Cucaracha
ya la llevan a enterrar,
entre cuatro zopilotes
y un ratón de sacristán.

NOTES

INTRODUCTION

1. As Flores Cano (2014, 173) states in his work and translated by me from the Spanish: "Thus, when the successive conquests by the *tlatoani Itzcoatl* provoked a political change and the *mexicas* (Nahuatl-speaking peoples) transformed themselves into one of the most powerful regimes of the Valley of Mexico, their leaders ordered the destruction of the ancient histories."

2. For example, Estevanico Dorantes—the famous Moroccan-born, African and multilingual explorer who with Cabeza de Vaca was the first to cross into Texas and northwest Mexico in 1535—had been captured and enslaved by Spain and became the personal servant of Andres Dorantes de Carranca. Estevanico is famous for being one of the four survivors of the Nevarez Expedition of 1528, whose disastrous end in Florida forced them to travel approximately from Galveston Island off the coast of Texas for the next eight years both separately and together, walking through Texas parts of New Mexico and down to Sinaloa. He returned with Fray Marcos de Niza later as the point person leading the Francisco Vásquez de Coronado expedition in 1539 seeking out the seven cities of Cibola. But in spite of his multilingual skills of a number of Indigenous languages of the region and cultural affinity, this exploration too resulted in disaster when Estevanico was killed by Zunis who regarded him as an evil Katsina. (http://biography.yourdictionary.com /estevanico).

    In his wonderful metaphorical and mythic description of Estevanico's arrival and demise as a "Black Katsina," Gutierrez (1991, 40) narrates the consequences of his killing in 1539:

The old men of the village huddled together in the Kiva, wondering the meaning of what had been said and done. Repeatedly they asked, Who was the black katsina? Whence had he come? What did he want? Would more katsina shortly arrive, as Estanico said? The old men were silent on these matters, as were the ancient myths. The answers to these questions would be found not in the Pueblo world but in a distant land across a sea in a place the black katsina called Castile.

To this day, however, the Zunis and their country cousins the Hopi make a Black Katsina (doll) named Chakwaina who, according to a Hopi priest and carver, represents Estevanico, "about whom Hopis are told since childhood." Different from the "Black Ogre Katsina (*Nata-aska*)," sometimes the major narrative does reiterate that Estevancio is killed by Zunis but sometimes he is expelled and "went to Hopi where he was accepted and lived. He was a real man" (personal communication, Delbert Silas, December 22, 2016).

As well, in his penetrating critique of the missing African-origins narrative in a recent publication (Vélez-Ibáñez and Heyman 2017), Álvarez in this same volume addresses the failure of any judicious treatment of these important populations:

> There is, however, a vestige of and reinforcement of the notion of the "Spanish borderlands." The border and even the SWNA are cast in the Spanish-Indigenous and (Mexican) mold of Spanish-Indigenous and to a lesser degree Mexican. The Southwest has always been marked as Spanish, Mexican, and Indigenous. What escapes the Spanish provincial view is that blacks (and in particular Spanish-speaking blacks) have been a central part of the Southwest. They were present when Hernán Cortes marched against the Aztecs in 1519 (and when Francisco Pizarro attacked the Incas twelve years later) (Wood 2010, 24). In 1598 the first contingent of five hundred colonists to New Mexico included persons of varied racial backgrounds and social ranks. The first Afro-Latino historical personage, immortalized in the memorable *Relación* of Alvaro Núñez Cabeza de Vaca, was the famed Estevanico El Negro, who in 1528 joined Cabeza de Vaca on the trek across the continent and in 1539 was with the Fray Marcos de Niza expedition to New Mexico and the legendary city of Cíbola (Román and Flores 2010, 5). Black soldiers, servants, and sailors were among the first settlers of the Southwest. They included black and mulatto men and women, both enslaved and "free" (Wood 2010, 25). A royal official asserted in 1774 that the Hispano population of northern Mexico were of Negro, Indian, and European ancestry and were so intermixed as to make it difficult for anyone to trace their ancestry (Forbes 2010, 28). The black-mulatto element reinforces the complexity, unevenness, and hegemonic perceptions of the region. But it is an element that has not received due attention. (172)

Finally, as chapter 2's "Discontented Genes" section also shows my own genetic mapping illustrates, there is no doubt of the strong presence of African genetic origins.

3. See Jovita Sabes (2010) who carefully lays out the successful method of incorporating Tlaxcalan sovereignty for Spanish vassalage and without the dreaded encomienda system.

CHAPTER 1

1. See Vélez-Ibáñez (2010, 123).

2. *Office of Immigration Statistics* 2014.

3. See Vélez-Ibáñez (1996, 5).

4. See this very long developmental "complex adaptive systems" approach by looking at Varela, Maturana, and Uribe 1974; and Varela, 1979, 1980, 1981, 1984, and 1989.

5. Marcel Mauss's *The Gift* is the seminal work on the basis of reciprocity and its iterations and has contributed to the creation of the foundation of theories and methods of human exchange systems.

6. In chapter 7, the notion of "translanguaging" in relation to the underlying emergent and active processes of language-use and transmission will be discussed, especially in relation to the works by Garcia and Wei 2014; and Canagarajah 2013.

7. Parts of this section appear in Vélez-Ibáñez and Heyman, eds. 2017.

8. View Beasley-Murray 2010.

9. For a statistical treatment of the social and economic manifestations of this concept, see Vélez-Ibáñez 1996. I would contend that if hegemony and their ensuing struggles and discontents were operationalized, these could be treated statistically to understand the diversity of impacts and their resulting oppositions and or adaptations and adjustments.

10. See Ilan Stavans (2003, 58) who states that "Spanglish is not a symmetrical two-way street. . . . Its speakers tend to adapt English words (mostly verbs and nouns) into the syntactical pattern of Spanish." On the other hand, the "barbarisms" that lexicographers point out as deformations of English into Spanish are, as Stavans states, "a borrowing and an error repeated today become linguistic rules tomorrow" (ibid.).

11. See, for example, Auer 1984; Galindo and Gonzales 1999; Martínez 2006; Myers-Scotton 1993; and Sánchez 1994.

12. Gramsci 1971.

13. See Swartz 1966. Political anthropology as well as political science has had a long traditional concern with the legitimacy-coercion axis in regards to local-level and national politics and the differentiated consequences of the use of power. As well, see Vélez-Ibáñez 1983.

14. See Harrington 1920.

15. Tinker Salas states that "prior to 1882, Sonora had no permanent settlement in the area of the border so that 'border settlements in Sonora developed as a direct consequence of economic exchange with the United States [and] new towns, such as Nogales, Sonora and Nogales, Arizona appeared along the once unpopulated border'" (Tinker Salas 1992, 437).

16. Parts of this section without the theoretical frames appears in Vélez-Ibáñez and Josiah Heyman, eds. (2017).

17. Ibid.

18. As a child I often visited the "factory," the remnants of which were still laying around in a building immediately connected to the living quarters of the Vélez family. The assembly and manufacturing was situated in a large rectangular room of approximately seven hundred square feet with a twenty-foot ceiling arranged such that the finished wagons could go out the front wooden gate not unlike the assembly arrangements in automobile plants. Equipment including thick hanging chains, a large blackened furnace, a tipped-over band saw, large and very thick wooden tables mostly upended, and a very large assortment of multiple sized hammers, tongs, wrenches, headless screwdrivers, pliers, and rings of many sorts laid all about. Unfinished mesquite wagon wheels, bands of Norwegian iron, thick nails, large flat-headed screws, and washers, and multitudes of axles were spread around the building. In the 1940s, this was the state of what had been a flourishing "factory," the livelihood for which was truly transborder in operation and from which, according to my father, also afforded my grandfather enough money to buy a Hupmobile automobile (circa 1910) and keep a half-filled chest of gold pesos. The Hupmobile was instrumental in the family's escape from revolutionaries a few years into the revolution and carried them to Tucson in a thrilling chase of horses trying to catch a twenty-mile-an-hour early twentieth century Hupmobile and of breaking axles. But this is another narrative.

19. Linda Ronstadt's great-grandfather was Federico José María Ronstadt. http://en.wiki pedia.org/wiki/Federico_Jos%C3%A9_Mar%C3%ADa_Ronstadt. Accessed 12 April 2015.

20. The Treaty of the Mesilla was the result of the Gadsden Purchase pursued by James Gadsden, the chief envoy for the United States and a South Carolinian railroad speculator, who threatened Mexican negotiators with American armed force if they did not agree to the $10 million purchase price of Mexican territory. During the negotiations Gadsden laid down an ultimatum by stating, "Gentlemen, is now time to recognize that the Valley of Mesilla must belong to the United States [either] for a stipulated indemnity, or because we shall take it." See Park 1961, 27.

21. See our work tracing the line of connections between hegemonic events and practices in Vélez-Ibáñez and Szecsy 2014, 4.

CHAPTER 2

1. See the seminal work by Hill 2001, as well see LeBlanc 2003, 357–65; LeBlanc 2008, 130–31; and finally Mabry and Doolittle 2008, 55–88.

2. See, for example, Mabry, Carpenter, and Sanches 2008, 172. They suggest that Hill's linguistic model of a Proto-Uto-Aztecan migration from central Mexico that brought Mesoamerican agriculture to the Southwest along with the familial languages does not "reconcile" neatly with current archaeological evidence; however, they state that a combination of "diffusion" and migration was responsible for the spread of maize agriculture and that irrigation technologies were independent inventions.

3. This work is a must read: Steven LeBlanc 2008, 130–31.

4. See a carefully crafted argument by Mabry, Carpenter, and Sánchez 2008, 155–83.

5. I have some disagreement as to the origins of the Genizaro document in the fine work by Ebright and Hendricks 2006. There is no empirical reason not to presuppose Indigenous authorship, given the rubric signed as "*Los Genizaros*." A Spanish intermediary would not sign "Genizaros" since it would conflate that person's identity with that of those for whom he would have allegedly written the document, which given the low social standing of Genizaros in this caste ridden system would seem less than probable.

6. Probably among the most single important contributions to an understanding of Españoles Mexicanos and Pueblo peoples, see Gutiérrez 1991.

7. See these most informative works by Fehrenbach 1974, 66–76; and Folsom 2014, 25, who summarizes the actuality of life and death and rhythms between exchange and war.

8. This is among the most important works filling a much-needed corrective to the lack of understanding of the originality and importance of sign as a major means of communication, see Davis and Supalla 1995, 80.

9. For Texas this work by Foster cannot be omitted: Foster 1995.

10. *Españoles Mexicanos* "was the term used by the reconqueror, Diego de Vargas to designate those returning to New Mexico after the Pueblo Revolt of 1680." As Campa (1997, 6) states its rationale: "Because they were all subjects of the Spanish crown at the time when Mexican nationality did not exist, it was natural for the old conquistador to use the national term 'Spanish' first and then indicate the province where these New World Spaniards originated." I use this term with a slash to indicate both cultural origin, colonial identity, and historical presence as well as where appropriate as a stand in for *mestizo*, which is a more racialized category.

11. Like Gutiérrez, the work by Brooks is among the most enlightening of treatises: Brooks 2003, 4–5.

12. Chávez 1995, 62. Chávez in his introduction states that for many Anglo historians, misidentification of Spanish surnames has become almost a cottage industry, misunderstanding the order of the patronym and matronym as well as silly surnames like that

of "Chamuscado," which was a nickname for Francisco Sanches of the Chamuscado-Rodríguez Expedition. As well, Chávez points out that in U.S. historical accounts the credit is often given to "Escalante" in spite of the fact that his true name is "Silvestre Vélez de Escalante" the latter meaning of Escalante, Spain and not a surname (xiv). Beyond this book, I may very well take up the task of correcting the repeated incorrect use of surnames for place names and important figures.

13. Quoted in Knaut 1997, 169.

14. Ferguson 2003, 33.

15. For a clear analysis of colonial impacts on the Yaqui nation, see Folsom 2014.

16. For the seminal work on Southwest North American colonial experiences, see Spicer 1962; and for a Mexican view, see Magallanes Castañeda 2001, 1–3; and Giudicelli 2006.

17. See Ebright and Hendricks 2006 for a very well-considered analysis of the Genizaro status.

18. Sor María de Jesús is an example of the idea of simultaneous appearances in more than one place is "bilocality," which was especially associated with religious figures like St. Catherine Dei Ricci and St. Martin De Porres (http://catholicmystics.blogspot.com/p/bilocation-bilocation-is-phenomenon-in.html). For this period Ágreda seems to have been the most adept. Sor María de Jesús Ágreda (1605–1665), the "Lady in Blue," who while still within her first three years of her sisterhood early in the seventeenth century experienced numerous bilocalities in which while in Spain she somehow appeared in Sonora, Nuevo México, and Tejas, in where she preached Catholicism to a variety of native peoples sometimes in sign language and in others in not-understood Castilian. Even in this mystical state she also intervened through her prayers during a series of battles between Indigenous and Spanish/Mexican populations resulting in the former's defeat. Evidently in the process of intervention and mystical appearance she was killed twice and managed to resurrect herself to continue her mission. Whether corporally, spiritually, or as she stated at times "intellectually," her appearances were part of the continuities of mythic, ideological, and corporeal conflict and persuasion between Indigenous and Spanish representations even at the noncorporeal plane. Her appearance is even recalled to this moment by some members of the Laguna peoples of New Mexico, who claimed recently to have seen a brilliant orb appearing during prayers in her honor. As well when having last appeared in the seventeenth century to the Jumano Indians in Texas, she left in her wake a countryside of blue flowers, which may have little to do with the Texas official state bluebonnet flower. But not only did she enjoy bilocality but she also dealt in the mystical matter of the Immaculate Conception, which her book *The Mystical City of God* was entirely narrated from the point of view of the Virgin Mary. It accentuated the Immaculate Conception and therefore denied the necessity for a male

presence in the birth of Christ—a position long opposed by "Maculaists" of the Church hierarchy but finally affirmed by Pope Pius IX in 1854 (Fedewa 2009, 257).

19. For a most fascinating account of the literacy preferences of the colonial Spanish era, see Leonard 1953, 7.

20. See Julyan 1996. There seems to be some confusion in the literature as to when and who founded Santa Fe and there has been a struggle for primacy rights to counter the "who was here first" claims between Jamestown (1605) and Santa Fe, with the latter probably a year or two older. Either way, both were colonial impressions on an otherwise Indigenous landscape.

21. A clear but somewhat Eurocentric focus, see Servín 1978.

22. According to *Texas Beyond History*, the act is known as "La Toma," marking the beginning of over two hundred years of Spanish rule in Texas. The celebration was concluded with a play written by Captain Marcos Farfán de los Gados. Although copies of the play have not survived, it is likely the first theatrical piece written in what is now the United States. As well, according to Lamadrid (2008, 427) more traditional performances were also given on April 30, 1598, of *Juegos de Moreos y Cristianos* (plays of Moors and Christians) upon the first crossing into New Mexico by Oñate y Salazar.

23. See Hammond and Rey 1953, 329–30.

24. See Ordinances for the Discovery, The Population and the Pacification of the Indies, The Laws of the Indies. http://codesproject.asu.edu/sites/default/files/THE%20LAWS%20OF%20THE%20INDIEStranslated.pdf.

25. See Brownson 1999; and Caesar 1869.

26. See Hammond and Rey 1953 cited above. All of the material is summarized from pp. 337–63.

27. Again see Hammond and Rey 1953, 226–85. Among many other weaponry, these "falconets" consisted of one small-caliber gun (*esmeril*), with chamber, and two small bronze pieces with chambers.

28. See Hutchins 2014, 121, 127, 187 for a description of arms and invasion composition and his contribution to the misnaming him, not Francisco Vasquez de Coronado, and continues the error of naming the expedition as such. This also reveals the misnamed Chamuscado-Rodríguez entry of 1581, misnamed because "Chamuscado" was his nickname meaning and referring to his singed beard because of its red color. His real name was Francisco Sanches "El Chamuscado." See the continuing contribution to his misnaming of Sanches and the name of the expedition by Mecham 1926, 266.

29. For the probability of Tlaxcalans and Tarascans being part of the Oñate y Salazar and Sánchez intrusions, see Hutchins 2014, 121, 127, 187; and Curtis 1927.

30. For an early rendition, see Simons 1964, 102–7.

31. See the seminal work by Moorhead 1975.

32. I use the term "claim" because although the category of criollo indicated a person born of Iberian-born parents, it is the case that such a category was loosely constructed and changes of identity were not only possible but also probable. Often such categories could be claimed without reference to records of authenticity of birth. Rather, the most important indicator was control and ownership of land and Native peoples as slaves. Even in Spain the genitor of attention to bloodlines was open to negotiation and as Nieto-Phillips (2004, 19) writes: "For a fee, families of dubious origins could produce documents that, effectively, purified their bloodlines by the mere assertion of blood purity." This practice was rather commonplace among the nobility, who, despite claims to the contrary "had been impregnated with Jewish blood."

33. See Moorhead 1975; he states that "[o]f the 911 officers and men of the sixteen garrisons ... between 1773 and 1781, only ... 49.6 percent were listed as ... europeos, españoles, or criollos; 37 percent as ... mestizos, castizos, mulattos, moriscos, coyotes, lobos and less specifically castas ... [and] ... 13.3 percent were Indians" (182–83).

34. In Vélez-Ibáñez (2017, 111), I analyzed the records of only 291 filiaciónes, which accounts for the difference in cases between that rendition and the number provided here.

35. These are arranged in order of use and all provided by the Arizona State Museum, Documentary Relations of the Southwest (DRSW). See Arizona State Museum n.d. a–e.

36. From the Arizona State Museum n.d., Document Number 041–04833, 197.

37. The town has 1,380 inhabitants and lies in the foothills of the Sierra Madre Occidental whose main river is the Bavispe and with a very low population density of 0.88 persons per square kilometer. See Bacadéhuachi n.d.

38. See Native Heritage Project 2013.

39. See, Chumacero 2013.

40. See Gallegos 1992, and especially his discussion of the efficacy of military records as a reliable source of consistency and accuracy (8) and uses Shofield 1968, 319 to support the use of signatures as a normative measure and as well agrees with Lockridge 1974, 7, whom he cites that although literacy runs a bit under reading skills they nevertheless are analogous indications of writing abilities.

41. Arizona State Museum n.d.c, 70.

42. Arizona State Museum n.d.d, 199.

43. Samuel E. Sisneros (2013, 2).

44. Arizona State Museum n.d.e, 477.

45. See Arizona State Museum n.d.a. Archives, Documentary: Microfilm records of 401 presidial soldiers. In this research, of soldiers, seventy-one were described as with "pozos de viruelas"; i.e., pockmarks from smallpox represent 18 percent of the sample.

46. The seminal work on language from the pre-Hispanic through 1970 is Heath 1972. Her historical and anthropological analysis is the basic for the changing language policies from the Colony through emergence of bilingualism as a viable option in the modern

period. Her work is especially crucial on how we think about the political ecology of language policy of Mexico.

47. Hidalgo 2006, 357–69.

48. See Benavides 1996.

49. See Kessell, Hendricks, and Dodge 1992, 513.

50. See Rodríguez 1996.

51. I conducted systematic participant observations of the Bernalillo, New Mexico, matachine Dances of the Festival of San Lorenzo on August 9–11, 2014, and for the same period in 2015 and the matachine dances at Picuris Pueblo on November 12, 2014. As well, fieldwork was conducted where ever dances were held, meetings were conducted, and novenas and rosaries held in homes of the dancers, mayordomos, and *rezadores* for a period of six months.

52. Eric R. Wolf's work is the central source of influence of my own work beginning with his early *Sons of the Shaking Earth*.

53. See Wheelwright 2012.

54. These data may be corroborated by contacting me. See Vélez-Ibáñez 2014b, 2015.

CHAPTER 3

1. See this early Austrian Jesuit who followed close on the heels of Eusebio Kino, Ignatz [Ignaz, Ignacio] Pfefferkorn 1989, 180.

2. According to Barry, "The Yaqui water war erupted when the state government pushed through the construction of a 155-kilometer aqueduct that transfers water from the Yaqui River west to Hermosillo, the state's capital and most populous city. The two main protagonists are the state's executive branch and the Yaqui Indigenous communities of the Yaqui River delta. Standing behind them are two rival coalitions of citizens, political parties, municipal governments, agribusiness sectors, and irrigation districts" (Barry 2014, 1). The Yaquis are seen to block major highways with their tractors and farm implements, as seen in a picture taken by Barry.

3. See "Tarahumaras protestan contra Javier Corral en el Senado," 2016.

4. See de Velasco Rivero 1987; my translation.

5. I observed both in Jemez Pueblo on December 12, 2014, and was struck by the parallel performances with the turquoise first, followed by the pumpkin and especially the pumpkin version, which was particularly brilliant in its presentation of force, energy, movement, and costuming as Sylvia Rodríguez would agree from her own work (1996, 111).

6. See Hadley and Schuetz-Miller, 1997, 12–13.

7. See Giudicelli 2006, 59.

8. See Spicer 1962, 26–35; and Magallanes Castañeda 2001, 1–13.

9. Letter of Coronel Mendoza to Virrey Cruillas in the Summary description of AZTM, AGN, Vol. 069 ff. 057–069.

10. De Velasco Rivero 1987, 209–12; my translation.

11. Fiestas De Los Raramuris: El Calendario Festivo Tarahumara Esta Estrechamente Relacionado Con El Ciclo Agricola. http://miradademujerespinosa.blogspot.com/2011/12/fiestas-de-los-raramuris.html.

12. Dr. Luis Plascencia pointed out this important and subtle difference in a personal communication.

13. See "Se duplica arresto de raramuris en EU," 2016.

14. The town's median resident age is 38.8, a year older than for New Mexico, with a per capita income of $19,567, and an estimated median house or condo value of a little over $110,000, which is about $60,000 than that of New Mexico and with a gross rent of $581 per month (city-data.com). Its crime rate is rated "high," according to city-data.com, with a violent crime rate of 902.1 compared to 214.1 in the United States. (Crime rates are generally given in ratio to population—e.g., annual 57 murders per 100,000 population.)

15. In a personal communication, Dr. Luis Plascencia pointed out the following interesting historical ecologically driven argument and an important sociopolitical-economic issue. He states that these "have shaped the wealth and social dynamic of the state: (a) the simple fact that such a large portion of the state is not under the jurisdiction of the state (i.e., federal land; over a third, including 3.5 million acres under DOD); and (b) the low rate of Mexican migration to the state. Economically motivated migrants are rational actors who generally migrate where there are jobs and job growth, not to economically depressed areas. Thus the 'Mexicanization' of such communities is low."

16. See Pelayo Cervantes et al. 2013. An examination of this manual is extraordinarily focused on ESL and ELL instruction, testing, mechanisms, and requirements but very short on actual bilingual programming following the same train of information.

17. City-data.com, Bernalillo, New Mexico.

18. Foreign born in Bernalillo are 1,068 of 5,804 Hispanics. Bureau of the Census 2010.

19. Both of these interviews substantiated my interpretations: Sisneros, interview (October 15, 2014, and Aguilar, interview (August 13–14, 2015).

20. I refer here to the Catholic Church in the middle of the nineteenth century led by Bishop Jose Antonio Laureano de Zubiria and Bishop Jean-Baptiste Lamay, both of whom had a penchant for suppressing local versions of Catholic ritual such as the Penitentes and the matachines.

21. I use the term "rabbinical" to emphasize the multiple functions of this role since it includes the "keeper of the knowledge" function, its teaching and recitation roles, its locus of center of control for the entire complex, its secular aspects including providing direction and actual participation in community issues, problems, and politics, and in fact is the "go-to

guy" for advice from legal to health and spiritual advice. The *rezador* leads by example in spite of major public roles he or she may enjoy and lives modestly in the areas of Bernalillo most associated with the older families and outside of the more urbanized areas.

22. I did not observe female *abuelos* while conducting fieldwork in 2014 or 2015.

23. See the entire sequence in Moreno 2008.

24. Both interviews provided important insights and support for interpretations: Sisneros, interview (October 15, 2014) and Aguilar, interview (August 13–14, 2015).

25. Crucial to balancing both misunderstood "Mexican" contributions and American misstatements: Chávez 1992, xvi–xvii.

26. Charles Aguilar fulfills the rabbinical role of the community spiritual leader and teacher of the past and meanings to the present. After numerous conversations the hypotheses of these various meanings he agreed were probable (August 13–14, 2015).

27. While in 2011, 36.5 percent spoke a language other than English at home, 72.5 percent spoke English very well, 13.9 percent spoke well, and 9.1 percent not well, and 4.6 percent spoke not at all, according to table 4. "Language Spoken at Home and English-Speaking Ability by State: 2011" (Bureau of the Census 2011).

28. See Vélez-Ibáñez 2014b, 60. Vélez-Ibáñez quotes from "The Protest Against Union of Arizona with New Mexico," a territorial pressure group, presented to the U.S. Congress on February 12, 1906:

> the decided racial difference between the people of New Mexico, who are not only different in race and largely in language, but have entirely different customs, laws and ideals and would have but little prospect of successful amalgamation . . . [and] the objection of the people of Arizona, 95 percent of whom are Americans, to the probability of the control of public affairs by people of a different race, many of whom do not speak the English language, and who outnumber the people of Arizona two to one. (U.S. Commission on Civil Rights 1972, 78–82)

CHAPTER 4

1. This information was obtained by comparing the Spanish calligraphy of letters and religious texts written by Olivas in that time period. Three documents were found and compared from the Sabino Olivas Family Papers, Box 2, Folder 7, 24903.

2. See Sabino Olivas Family Papers.

3. See especially Vélez-Ibáñez (1996, 298, n114), in which this program and its psychological implications are discussed briefly. As well see Combs (2014) for an important discussion of the absurdity of many programs in the state of Arizona.

4. From Sisneros, "Found Archive" (2015).

5. See Bial 2002; and Denetdale 2007.

6. Mexicans of the northern end of the SWNAR often attached a Spanish pronoun to first names, whether in Spanish or English, and nicknames as well so that *ranflas* (old car) became *el ranflas*.

7. See Horsman's *Race and Manifest Destiny*, which is a primer and crucial source developing how racialism and racialization were the foundations for the formation of Manifest Destiny.

8. Among the earliest associations made between the Spanish presence and the American absence: see Lipscomb 1904.

9. An important contribution, see Dejong 1993.

10. For the period in question see, Blanco 2010, 1–5.

11. A major new contribution by a scholar long associated with righting the unwritten record, see Rivas-Rodríguez 2015.

12. For scholars, it is crucial to read the Mexican literature too often ignored, such as López, Villanueva, and Ramos 2013, 122.

13. The narrative of this event occurred numerous times during conversations from my early teens through adulthood in addition to many others that accentuated "Yaqui-Yori" (Indigenous—"hombre blanco") relations that were tragic and reciprocal at different times. I was given a *pascola* mask by my father, who in turn had received it from his own and he from his father from a Yoéme shaman for protecting a young Yoéme boy who had been enslaved by a rancher but who was released after a pistol fight between my great-grandfather and the rancher, the latter of whom lost the altercation. The *pascola* is associated with the formula of the "one to the left of god," which refers to the Indigenous relationships to the world (*yoanina*) and is a type of necessary devil but also buffoon according to Olavarría 1995, 75. This event in the nineteenth century was connected to the demise of the revolutionary colonel mentioned earlier in the chapter in the twentieth century by my uncle at the Nogales border. The connection between the two is that Tio Lauro had been forewarned by Yaquis that the colonel was descending from the mountainous Yaqui area and going to Arizona through Nogales, where my uncle found him while crossing the yellow line between the two Nogaleses, as has been described, with the colonel meeting his end with a pistol shot through the mouth; the colonel's body fell straddling the yellow line with red spreading north and south, according to my father. The Yaquis returned the nineteenth-century favor with twentieth-century information.

14. See Secretaría de Gobernación 1940, 372.

15. See "Mexican Group Denounces Rights Violations against Yaqui Tribe Tomas Rojo," 2015.

16. Another crucial work important to understanding language impact is Dawson 2012, 83.

17. Probably with Stavenhagen the leading proponent for Indigenous language rights, see de Varennes 2012.

18. Like de Varennes, a champion of Indigenous rights and language, see Stavenhagen 1990, 60–61.

19. I had the privilege of hosting Dr. Salomon Nahamad at the Bureau of Applied Research in Anthropology of the University of Arizona in 1983 after a long judicial case in Mexico in which Dr. Nahamad faced trumped-up charges that were in retaliation for his unswerving support of the Yoéme. Twenty years later the central government tired of mostly anthropologists protecting the cultural, material, and linguistic rights of the peoples with whom they worked and created what is known as a revamped institution directed by politicians.

20. See INALI (Instituto Nacional de Lenguas Indígenas) 2008. See Pellicer, Cifuentes, and Herrera 2006.

21. This was an important conference that brought together both Mexican and American applied anthropologists: Programa del Encuentro Binacional de Investigadores 2014.

22. See "Migrantes indígenas, un tema pendiente," *Letras Libres* 2014. http://www.letras libres.com/blogs/frontera-adentro/migrantes-indigenas-un-tema-pendiente. Accessed July 10, 2016.

23. The Spanish legal and political system had a means for Indigenous peoples seeking redress or to seek a "place" in the structure of relations with the Spanish, which was utilized by Pueblo nations and displaced Indigenous peoples, especially of those known as "Genizaros," who either because of slavery, capture, purchase, or independent agreement were largely dislocated from their tribal origins and in some cases together sought redress, according to one petition most recently translated and shared with me by Sisneros (n.d.) and represented in appendix C: Complete Genizaro Petition by Los Genizaros to populate the old Pueblo of Sandia, 1733, SANM I, Roll 6, Frames 687–96. Transliterated and translated by Samuel Cisneros, archivist, and Zimmerman Library: Albuquerque, New Mexico, November 2014. For a full discussion of the petition and it implications for identity issues and the counterhegemonic use of Spanish by Genizaros, see Vélez-Ibáñez 2017b.

CHAPTER 5

1. "La Cucaracha" n.d.; Rodríguez 1883. Álvarez y Ca. 1883 has a number of refrains dealing with the Reconquista in 1492, when the Moors surrendered the southern half of Iberia to Spain. There are hundreds following this one and usually omitting the mention of cannabis and replacing it with dinero (money), *pata* (back leg), and many others.

Spanish	English
De las patillas de un moro	*From the sideburns of a Moor*
tengo que hacer una escoba,	*I must make a broom*
para barrer el cuartel	*to sweep the quarters*
de la infantería española.	*of the Spanish infantry.*

2. A key work that contextualizes the song is Rausch Jr. 1962.

3. See the stanzas from "El Corrido Mexicano" n.d.

Pobrecito de Madero,	Poor Madero,
casi todos le han fallado,	almost all have failed him,
Huerta el ebrio bandolero,	Huerta the drunken bandit
es un buey para el arado.	is an ox for the plow.
La ropa sin almidón,	He wears clothes without starch
se pone todos los días;	that he puts on every day;
y sin esas boberías,	and without those silly things,
se me figura melón.	he looks like a melon. (my translation)

4. An amazing scholar of all things literary is Leal 1954, 17.

5. Zeta Acosta 1973.

6. Huerta dies in the following refrain:

Ya murió la Cucaracha	The Cockroach is now dead
ya la llevan a enterrar,	they now take him to bury,
entre cuatro zopilotes	between four buzzards
y un ratón de sacristán	a rat as a sacistran.

See appendix D for the complete version.

7. The seminal intellectual statement for the Chicano movement is Romano 1969a.

8. For example, my grandfather, Colonel Julio Ibañez Camarillo, began his career as a military officer during the war against the French at the age of fourteen and fought in hand-to-hand combat in Puebla in the famous Cinco de Mayo battle and against "Moros Franceses," according to his military archive. He was killed during the revolution in Las Vacas, Coahuila, by *bala perdida* (spent bullet) in 1913 on the Federal side by Pancho Villa's forces as he boarded a train leaving the battlefield. My children's mother's grandfather was a train engineer for Villa. Perhaps he had taken Villa's troops to the area where in turn my own grandfather was killed but that would only be speculation and the earmarks for a novel or movie.

9. See McKay 2010.

The departures began soon after Texas declared its independence from Mexico. Much of this cross-border migration was associated with the seasonal return of

Mexican labor to Mexico each fall. However, exceptionally large numbers of Mexicans were compelled to return to Mexico periodically. Perhaps the first large-scale repatriation occurred at the conclusion of the Mexican War in 1848. San Antonio, for example, was practically abandoned by Mexicans after 1848, and a number of Mexicans were repatriated under the sponsorship of the Mexican government in the late 1840s. The precise number of Mexicans returned to Mexico from Texas during this period is unknown, although they probably numbered several thousand. During the remainder of the nineteenth century, harassment against Mexicans by Anglo-Americans was occasionally so severe that many were forced to abandon their homes in Texas and return to Mexico. In the 1850s a number of Mexicans were driven from their homes in Central Texas, and in 1856 the entire Mexican population of Colorado County was reportedly ordered to leave the county. Conflict between Anglo-Americans and Mexicans in the 1870s reportedly resulted in the expulsion of Mexicans from various locations in South Texas. (McKay 2010)

10. Among the earliest of Chicano creative literary artists: Suarez 2004. He often mentioned that it had been almost impossible for him to publish his early writings because of English-language and Americans'-only interpretations of Mexican life. He was not given real recognition for his early works until the rise of the Chicano movement. Mario was my brother-in-law's brother—Eugene Suarez.

11. Quoted in David Montejano 1987.

12. The massive immigration expulsions, raids, arrests, fracturing of families, and the immense psychological and emotional costs in the present are directly associated with the long-standing nativist tradition discussed earlier and given substance by referring to the costs of educating Mexican-origin children especially.

13. Much of the research for this section was done in 1970 and written as an unpublished paper, see Vélez-Ibáñez 1970. Later works by Gonzalez 2013, San Miguel Jr. 1987, and Valencia 2002 all discuss thoroughly these early racialized discourses, especially Valencia. However, none of the discussions directly associate their discussions with the American eugenics movement of the period, while connecting the ideological foundations of segregation, the differential treatment of Mexican children, the following unintended "cultural" rationalizations, and the myriad labels concerning language "readiness" as if they were speechless.

14. Ronald López n.d. Mr. López was a graduate student at UCLA at the time of his writing this work in 1968. It was used widely in incipient Chicano Studies classes since little had been published up to that time written by Mexican-origin scholars outside of the works by George I. Sánchez in opposition to the eugenics-oriented diatribes but in part replaced with a culturological category of deprivation. See Sánchez 1967.

15. In the *Saturday Evening Post* these included Roberts 1928a and 1928b; and Garis 1930.

16. The "Y" was in downtown Tucson across from what had been the old Presidio walls and more than likely the site of its flag pole.

17. See Dickerson 1919; and Meriam 1933.

18. See Hill 1993a, 1993b, and 1995. See also Urciuoli 1996.

19. See Garth 1925.

20. See Garth 1930.

21. Paschal and Sullivan 1925.

22. Among the most pernicious and racist of figures of embedded "white racism" are Popenoe and Johnson 1933.

23. The racialism behind this phenomenon was not limited to teacher-pupil interaction; however, in many Mexican families, part of the racialized identities that are considered a capital resource that might prevent discrimination also could provide an advantage. Nonetheless, such persons are often privileged even within Mexican families and the "Spanish" designation is used as part of the racial nomenclature especially in the southern region of Southwest North America.

   This racialized discourse takes many shapes and avenues, not the least of which was in segregated swimming pools that allowed Mexican children in some days and in others not. I was turned away from one swimming pool in Tucson, Arizona, for my darker hue while my fair-hair, blue-eyed sister was quickly permitted. But within Mexican households, concern for the color hue of newborn children was often expressed and the question "Como es?" (What's he/she like?) was asked and its subtext was very much a question about melanin and not about character.

24. See University of Arizona former professor of education, Garretson 1928.

25. See Carter 1970. This is a thorough rendering of much of the most serious educational issues facing Mexican children in the past and certainly in the present.

26. An important work that reemphasized Mexican inferiority is Hill 1925.

27. Like those cited, an important segment to understand is Lamb 1930.

28. This is a nail to be struck that penetrated Americanized curriculum for Mexican children for many decades is Meriam 1933.

29. Among the most pernicious of works is Coers 1934.

30. Like the rest and as misinformed is Johnson 1938.

31. This basically racist treatise is totally dependent on the early American educational racialist literature: Vianna 1959.

32. Portions of this section were published in Vélez-Ibáñez 2014a, 64–72.

33. Native peoples and Mexicans but not African Americans escaped the eugenics knife of sterilizations during the early twentieth century in the northern region of Southwest North America. Linguistically as well, Indigenous peoples were also subjected to the usual eugenically oriented intelligence tests as were Mexicans. They did not escape from

the recycling of the same inferiority paradigm to which Mexicans and certainly African Americans were also subjected. But for the latter, this is an entire history to itself. In 1984, Dana published a review article of intelligence testing of Indigenous children, in which he makes the following introductory statement: "Intellectual assessment of American Indian children has been carried out utilizing tests that have not been standardized on these populations and are generally inappropriate for description of their intellectual functions or for prediction of their educational outcomes . . . the continued use of verbal measures . . . perpetuates the erroneous belief that these children have limited intellectual endowment and can anticipate only nominal educational achievement." Yet between that year of publication and sixty years before, some form of intelligence and language assessments were commonly administered continuously and their impacts on language and academic development reflected the very quality of the warning Dana issued. But this is another book. On the other hand, rebellion against miseducation, poor health, poverty, dismal education rates, differential treatment, and cultural and linguistic fracturing became front and center in the Indigenous cultural renaissance of the 1960s through the present and were expressed particularly against the manner in which Indigenous children were typecast. Such typecasting was not an accident and very much a consequence of sixty years of "educational" achievement and intelligence testing results rationalized by the "seeing man" syndrome and accentuated by "whiteness" underlying its reasonableness.

34. See Weber, Melville, and Palerm 2002, 55–83.

35. The Alien Contract Labor law enacted on February 26, 1885, prohibited ALL recruitment of foreign labor for work in the United States and prohibited all contracts between employers and employees not of the United States. See the Forty-Eighth Congress, Session II, chapters 161–64. http://library.uwb.edu/static/USimmigration/23%20stat %20332.pdf.

36. See Massey 2006.

37. Among the most important works on Chicano letters is Kanellos 2000. http://docs .newsbank.com/bibs/KanellosNicolas/Hispanic_history.pdf.

38. The most important guide to sources is Kanellos and Martell 2000, 281–83.

39. See Bourke 2010, 92.

40. See Vélez-Ibáñez et al., 2009.

41. In Spanish: *Viejito Querido: Te quiero mucho, tu vieja regañiona. Y le pide* [sic] *mucho a Dios que nos cuide a los dos y nos de paciencia, para llevar una vida feliz y tranquila. Que Dios Nuestro Sr te de muchos años de vida con salud para felicidad de tus hijos y vieja. Love siempre, Abril 28, 1971.* The card was part of my memorabilia from my mother, Luz Ibañez Maxemin.

42. An important historical work of language politics is Fernández-Gibert 2012.

43. This site is a very revealing one if read carefully: Winn 2010.

44. For example, the family of Asuncion Bustamante. He was born in 1935 in Hatch, New Mexico, and was a Vietnam veteran who inherited 160 acres of land northeast of Hatch that was originally homesteaded by his paternal grandfather who was a native of Chihuahua and grew feed for cattle as well as chiles (personal interview, September 20, 2014). Similarly, Emilio Carillo of the third generation, who was the owner of the Cactus Cleaners of Tucson, was the grandson of Emilio Carrillo, born in Santa Cruz, Sonora, Mexico, who moved his family to Tucson in 1856, shortly after the Gadsden Purchase of 1853. He started ranching on his homestead in the Tanque Verde Valley in southern Arizona. http://www.tanqueverderanch.com/the-ranch/history/. Accessed July 25, 2016. The historian Armando Alonzo (*Tejano Legacy: Rancheros and Settles in South Texas, 1734–1900*) discusses the continuous Spanish/Mexicano land ownership in sections of south Texas. The same families still own the land their ancestors were granted by Spain or Mexico.

45. My mother (whose father was a colonel of cavalry fighting against the revolution) recalled that different revolutionary groups would enter towns with some breaking down doors and ransacking. Zapata's troops, according to Luz Vélez Ibáñez, politely knocked on the door to ask for food or care for wounded soldiers. A version of this appears in a short story, see Vélez-Ibáñez 1969.

46. Alberto Baltazar Urista Heredia (a.k.a. Alurista) was among the most prominent of Indigenista-oriented poets of the Chicano literary explosion of the 1960s through the present and a great admirer of the poetry of Netzahualcóyotl, the fifteenth-century poet-king of the city-state of Texcoco (1402–1472).

47. And at times the American-Mexican War had a different trope, especially concerning the San Patricio Brigade made up of Irish Catholics who had deserted the American army, fought for Mexico, and to which a shrine and monument still stands in Mexico City. My older sister in Tucson was to be visited by young Brendan Flannery (one of the neighborhood Irish young men whose families had moved into the neighborhood in the early fifties), which was protested by her Sonoran father who wanted only replicates of himself *pretendiendo* (courting) his daughter. When he was questioned by my mother, "No te acuerdas que pelyaron por nosotros?" ("Do you not remember that they fought for us?"), his reply after a few pensive and quizzical moments was "Ah, si dile que venga el muchacho," ("Oh, yes tell the young man to come")—a memory etched in my head for sixty years for its history and the use of rational argumentation and response.

48. This most important work on Flores Magón of the period is Gómez-Quiñones 1973.

49. The courses designed last appeared in a brochure published by the Mexican American Studies Department in 1969. The brochure itself unfortunately has been misplaced but it was distinctive for its cover featuring a three-headed logo mestizo used as the departmental symbol and commonly in that period by newspapers. The notion of "bilingual systems" had as its premises the idea of two equal languages being compared from "deep"

structures à la Chomsky to transformational grammars and phonology and syntax. Among the first to teach six parallel courses was a sociolinguist in 1970. Nevertheless, it required good command of both languages by students.

50. For a pre-1980 survey of Chicana literature and its strong feminist underpinnings, see Loeb 1980.

51. See Macias 1980, 53–82.

52. See Zamora 1980.

53. See for example Perales 2006, who analyzes the 1919 strike by women laundry workers in El Paso.

54. As a six-year-old I often marveled of my mother's *cuentos*, among them the story of her own mother taking a kitchen knife to the throat of my mother's older sister (Rosalina), who was going to be kidnapped by revolutionaries, but stopping when the knife began to cut the side of her daughter's neck. Or of my mother's *comadre* who, in conversations in Tucson with my mother and sister and female cousins while I played on the kitchen floor, related how her own mother and others had ambushed a group of *pelones* (Federal troops) and killed them all and took their weapons. Of such stuff these women were and are, but also the accompanying violence scarred them for life, and they were doubly cut when their own sons were wounded and killed and psychologically scarred for life beginning in the twentieth century, World War I, World War II, Korea, and their grandchildren in Vietnam and great-grandchildren in later war follies. *De eso venimos.*

55. I had the opportunity to observe the patterns of familial and community organization of two "Cristero" towns founded in Sinaloa in the 1940s: Cristo Rey and Isla del Mar as well as interviews with María Luz Cruz Torres who conducted intensive field work in both ejidos.

56. I spent 1994–1995 as a fellow of the Center for Advanced Studies in the Behavioral Sciences at Stanford, where Tony Burciaga and Cecilia Burciaga (his wife), who was an administrator and he the resident head of Casa Zapata at Stanford, painted the famous *Chicano Last Supper* mural. He narrated this historical event of his father's funeral during one of the evening sessions of *platica* at their apartment at Casa Zapata.

57. I had been introduced to *Don Quixote* in Spanish by an older sister as well as by the hundreds of representations of the character in wooden figures, oils, and metal forms when crisscrossing the region. I had learned early on about the foolish chivalric dreams of *Don Quixote* as well as his pragmatic sidekick—*Sancho Panza*. However, in my first humanities class at the University of Arizona as a seventeen-year-old, besides reading the *Illiad* and others, *Don Quixote de la Mancha* was read in English, with the instructor pronouncing the hero's name as "Dawn" as in the opening shot of the sun, "day" for the hard "de," "la" like in la la land, "mancha" as in" man" in English, and the surname as "Quicksot" and not the silent Arabically induced guttural sound. I corrected his

pronunciation but to no avail since he said that this was the way it was pronounced in English.

58. The literature is very large in comparing private to public school achievement and at times totally contradictory, especially that composed of works generated by the private schools themselves or associated with them. On the other hand, it is more than likely that for Hispano/Mexicanos and African Americans, Catholic schools especially have a positive effect on achievement across the board and controlling for low SES. See Sander's careful analysis in Sander 2001, 21–23. He states,

> Although Catholic schools are probably not better than public schools on the average, some Catholic schools are probably superior to the public schools in a community. This is probably the case for blacks and Hispanics in big cities. Catholic schools in inner-city areas that disproportionately serve a low-income population are probably more efficient than public schools, at least at the high school level. It is less clear whether Catholic grade schools are superior to public school grade schools in big cities. The results above suggest that blacks and Hispanics in inner-city areas gain from Catholic schooling. They have substantially higher high school graduation rates and do more homework if they attend Catholic schools. In results not shown, I also found that test scores were higher for minority students in Catholic schools . . . I could not show significant gains for white students in Catholic schools.

59. Witnessed by me but never enjoyed on numerous occasions in her homeroom and class on religion at Salpointe High School in Tucson, Arizona. Sister Saint Eleanor was a BVM nun who even with slightly raised black heeled shoes stood at no more than five feet but could bring down the biggest of the boys to their knees with a thumb lock. It was hilarious to watch some of the bigger bullies beg for release.

60. For an excellent discussion of literature of that period of 1959–1990 but without reference to the social sciences, see Lomeli 1993.

61. See Alvarez 1987; Vélez-Ibáñez 1983, 1996, 2010.

62. A key work by one of the most important anthropologists in the region is Rosaldo 1994.

63. Vélez-Ibáñez 2011, 25.

CHAPTER 6

1. Unfortunately, like all academic migrants, many old sources and papers have been lost. This manual had been protected from loss for as many years past until an office move within the campus at Arizona State University, and it's been lost or misplaced. That

said, the quotation was indelibly etched, since after bringing this matter up with school authorities I was accused of trying to destroy the school. I left a year later for San Diego State. Isabel García the daughter of a prominent union mine organizer, became a first-rate immigration lawyer and community activist. She is still brightly brained with no compunction to let people know the errors of their ways.

2. Sheriff Joseph Arpaio, the Maricopa County Sheriff had a tent that was placed in the middle of the Fountain Hills Festival biannually and prior to his defeat in the 2016 election. The sheriff sold pink underwear that is forced upon his inmates in the county jail. He was surrounded by his deputies and persons purchasing were vetted as they near his person. Occasionally, an unseen voice shouted a loud "boo" at the mention of his name over loudspeakers.

3. This section was published in Vélez-Ibáñez 2014a, 79–92.

4. See Vélez-Ibáñez 1996, 68. Between 1870 and 1890, 23 percent of all marriages were Anglo-Mexican, which dropped to 9.1 percent 1900–1910. See Sheridan 1986 for the original source.

5. Chávez's pathbreaking book deeply interrogates the multiplicity of media narratives and pictorial representations about the experiences of immigrants, unpacks their underlying prejudicial premises and ethnocentrism that impact an entire immigrant population— and reveals simultaneously, the broad cultural outlines of a deeply struck American cord of rejection of the "others" and insights into the highly-defended frailties of too many Americans.

6. See Weber 2005.

7. See Massey 2006.

8. The counterargument to the language loss premise is Luis Fraga et al. 2006.

9. An important scholarly work is Santiestevan 1991.

10. I was an observer of the program as a high school English teacher in this period who interacted with many of the students of the program. Although my conclusions were not developed as a formal analysis, I was constantly amazed at the breadth and depth of the literary skills of these students that carried over to their English classes and who were among the best of the author's honors English classes. In fact, I was introduced to Fishman by those who developed the Spanish for Nativos program.

11. This reminder of how history is viewed differently by commentators and participants is Cole Brousseau 1993. The original reference for "The Invisible Minority," was a National Education Association (NEA) report (NEA 1966).

12. See Rodríguez 2007. See also Eugene García 2005, who strongly advocates the "dual language" approach, and who reviews this model extensively and supports the efficacy of the approach.

13. See Ao and Lai 2003, 4.

14. Among the most important works on the topic of white racism is Hill 2015. As important are her insights and analysis found in her work: Hill 1998, 680–89, to which will be referred in the section on bilingualism in this chapter.

15. Observations of bilingual classes in New Mexico, California, and New Mexico utilize standardized tests to "locate" Spanish-speaking students and such assessments are "jacketed" in each student's record and carried through their educational career. What was most disconcerting is that in one case, the "bilingual" supervisor could not speak Spanish!

16. A pioneer commentator is James Crawford (2008, 17), "Monolingual and Proud of It," originally in the *Guardian* (UK), March 8, 2001, Reprinted in *Advocating for English Learners, Selected Essays,* Toronto: Multilingual Matters LTD.

17. See Crawford 2002.

18. Among the most important in reviewing the English-only approach are Salvador Gabaldon and Carlos Ovando 2011.

19. See Crawford 2006.

20. Luis Plascencia suggested these additional layers to the historical record.

21. See Gordon 2012 for brief backgrounds to anti-migrant and -migration organizations.

22. The 2010 state elections for office featured roadside signs emphasizing Horne's strong support by Pearce and Arpaio and especially in removing Mexican unauthorized migrants (examples upon request provided).

23. See Lynch 2007.

24. See Horwitz 2011. More recently Arpaio was found in contempt of violating a Federal court order against racial profiling, see Cassidy 2016.

25. A key work of "metanalysis" is Ramírez 2000.

26. See Ramírez 2000, 28.

27. Ovando divides the acceptance and rejection of bilingualism into four periods: The Permissive Period (1700s–1880s), the Restrictive Period (1880s–1890s) the Opportunist Period (1960s–1980s), and the Dismissive Period (1980s–present). This last is marked by its initiation by President Ronald Reagan and carried through the English-only blitzes. See Ovando 2014, 110–22.

28. For example, the School of Transborder Studies of Arizona State University, founded in 2011 and directed by me until 2015, has a central educational function of providing doctoral, master's, and undergraduate curricula focusing on Transborder Health and Community Development, Immigration and Urban Policy, Media and Expressive Culture, and Culture, Language, and Learning and demands levels of functionality in both languages in written and oral communication. As a school, it also houses other units devoted to the maintenance and development of widespread transborder institutional networks as well as a program devoted exclusively devoted to comparative border study and production in addition to community based applied research and educational programs

emphasizing language and learning research—all of which demand well-developed mastery of literate and oral Spanish.

29. An informative short piece is Krogstad and González-Barrera 2015.

30. See Menjívar and Abrego 2012. They quote the latest literature in concluding their fine work detailing the creation of legal illegal Salvadorans: "As Jiménez and López-Sanders (2011) argue, current immigration policies are detrimental for immigrants' long term social and economic incorporation across multiple generations and risk creating an 'illegal class'" (1414).

31. A recurring assessment in California, see California Department of Education 2015.

32. An innovative ethnographically informed work is Urciuoli 1996.

33. Proposition 58 repealed the English-only immersion requirement and waiver provisions required by Proposition 227 of 1998. In English-only programs, students learn subjects from teachers who speak only in English. Proposition 227 required English learners to take one year of intensive English instruction before transitioning to English-only classes. See https://ballotpedia.org/California_Proposition_58,_Non-English_Languages_Allowed _in_Public_Education_(2016). Accessed November 19, 2016.

34. This was related to me by one of his own staff members in 2015 at the School of Transborder Studies of Arizona State University. Evidently the supervisor is now retired.

35. These are among the first works on the penetration of English south by Heyman and Alarcón (2017).

36. In his excellent discussion of code-switching, Martínez (2006, 94) considers this phenomenon not as a detriment but rather as kind of linguistic dexterity and "multiplied several times over. Bilingual speakers may choose to switch between languages or between varieties and styles within each language. This linguistic dexterity, however, is often misunderstood and at times even maligned."

37. Wright 2006 is a crucial work.

38. I am not completely comfortable with using melanin designations to denote cultural phenomenon since it is too easy to fall into a racialist construction of position.

39. See "Reggaeton Music," 2016. Don Quijote Language School. http://www.donquijote .org/culture/puerto-rico/music/reggaeton-music.

40. See Campbell and Heyman 2007. As well, see Vélez-Ibañez 2010, 128–29.

41. See McMahon 1952.

42. My grandfather Colonel Julio Ibáñez Camarillo was the father of the aunts mentioned and was an officer of the Mexican army in Piedras Negras, Coahilla, just across the bifurcated line before he was killed in 1913. For details of Our Lady of Refuge Catholic School, see its website at http://www.olorschoolep.org. The school continues to teach children from Eagle Pass, Seco Mines, Quemado, El Indio, and Piedras Negras, Mexico.

43. Dr. José Luis Farah Ibáñez, Chair of the Department of Applied Mathematics of the Instituto Tecnologico Autónomo de México in Mexico City.

CHAPTER 7

1. Both Garcia and Wei push very decidedly toward paying pedagogical attention to the dynamic aspects of bilingualism in which "translanguaging" is integrated as a viable learning space in all classrooms and has the "potential to transform educational practices, as well as the lives of bilingual children" (62).

2. See Scheiner 2014. The study describes its hypothesis, sample, and findings:

> Verbal learning and memory deficits are frequently reported in posttraumatic stress disorder (PTSD), but may be a product of its psychiatric comorbidities, especially major depressive disorder (MDD). To evaluate this hypothesis, 25 medication-free patients with PTSD and comorbid MDD were compared to 148 medication-free patients with equally severe MDD alone and to 96 non-patients on a measure of verbal learning and memory. Additional measures of attention, working memory, and executive function were administered to evaluate their contribution to verbal memory impairment. Patients with comorbid PTSD and MDD demonstrated the greatest deficit in verbal learning compared to both MDD patients and nonpatients (omnibus effect sizes ranged d = 0.41 to 0.50), one that was not accounted for by other cognitive deficits. Findings suggest that a current diagnosis of PTSD makes a contribution to verbal learning deficits beyond the effect of depression alone.

3. See Bialystok 2009.

4. See Mechelli et al. 2004.

5. See Fratiglioni, Paillard-Borg and Winblad, 2004. See as well Perani et al. 2003; Kramer et al. 2004. Also in line with this hypothesis, Staff et al. 2004. As well and very well supported are Valenzuela and Sachdev 2006.

6. An important and concise work is "The Bilingual Brain" (2008), *Society for Neuroscience*, September 1, Review Date: January 15, 2013. http://www.brainfacts.org/sensing-thinking -behaving/language/articles/2008/the-bilingual-brain/. Accessed August 8, 2015.

7. A key work to understand the dual language process is Bialystok and Martin 2004.

8. A critical but balanced approach is Calvo and Bialystok 2014.

9. Personal communication from Robert T. Jiménez, who alerted me to the Thomas and Collier literature.

10. For a recurring analysis see the series under "Special Eurobarometer 386," 2012.

11. Invading fraternizations always include various degrees of linguistic exchanges so that the word "gringo" in Mexican Spanish probably develops out of the songs sung by American

soldiers, such as the "Green Grass of Home," during the invasion of Mexico by the United States in the nineteenth century.

12. A thorough scholarly analysis of this period is Miller and Hatcher 2014.

13. One of the initial works on this important process is Castle and Breeden 2015. http://www.nytimes.com/2015/07/30/world/europe/britain-and-france-scramble-as-channel-crossing-attempts-by-migrants-continue.html. Accessed July 30, 2015.

14. For an important series of representations see "Mapping Mediterranean migration," BBC News 2014.

15. See Frontex 2014:34.

16. See "Belgium," *The World Factbook*, 2015.

17. See Meier 2012.

18. See Meier 2010; Genesee 1994; Bonnet 2004, 2012; and Lamsfuss-Schenk 2008.

19. See Allen 2008.

20. See the important work by Rolstad, MacSwan, and Mahoney 2012. Yet the state of Arizona in 2004, to rationalize the effects of its English-only Arizona legislation, carried out a comparative analysis of the effects of bilingual education programs and structured English programs on student achievement and concluded, "The results show that students in SEI programs outperformed those in bilingual programs. This evidence lends support to endorsing SEI programs in favor of bilingual programs" (Arizona Department of Education 2004, 10).

21. See Slavin et al. 2010.

22. Two-Way Bilingual Immersion Programs in the U.S., n.d.

23. See Lindholm-Leary and Borsato 2002, 2.

24. As a high school English teacher at Pueblo High School in Tucson, Arizona, during the 1960s, I would "reverse engineer" passages from the Shakespeare's *Othello* and Achebe's *Things Fall Apart* by asking students from different linguistic groups to transliterate these to "Spanglish," Black English, and O'odom, with some measure of success and a great deal of fun and respect.

25. See Vélez-Ibáñez et al. 1992. This was the initial work that posited the construct of "funds of knowledge" developed during a discussion between the authors of the data that was being analyzed within the "Tucson Project," which was an NSF research investigation of Mexican-origin households in which Greenberg noted circa 1988 that these data were like "funds of rent" and followed by a suggestion by Vélez-Ibáñez that these were more like "funds of knowledge."

26. See Vélez-Ibáñez et al. 1992.

27. This most important work that sets the applied stage for the notion of funds of knowledge is in Moll et al. 1992, 133.

28. This is one version of the Cycle but best rendered in Vélez-Ibáñez 1993, 126.

29. This case description is of an elementary schoolboy of Mexican parents who during ethnographic research was discovered to be a child prodigy by learning to play and sing by

the time he was three and unbeknownst to his teacher who found him "noisy" with his humming and almost silent signing was considered a disruptive person, since his attention to the tasks at hand seemed to bore him. The field research was carried out by a team of researchers in 1990 made up of Luis Moll, James B. Greenberg, Kathy Amanti, Norma González and myself of seventy-five households.

30. A crucial study is Hudzia et al. 2014.

31. See Vélez-Ibáñez 2010. Basically, Rotating Savings and Credit Associations (ROSCAS) are savings and credit associations at the informal level in which ten persons would pool $10 a week and over a period of ten weeks each participant would receive $90 (excluding the recipient's own contribution) without putting in any more than pulling out. *Tandas* or *cundinas* are distributed from southern Chiapas to Washington State.

32. These are part of a very long list of skills, knowledge, practices, and beliefs found within the original research funded by the National Science Foundation and buttressed by the second research supported by the Kellogg Foundation.

33. See especially Moll and González 1997, and as well as González, Moll, and Amanti 2005.

34. One of the key works in the applied and formative development of the concept of funds of knowledge is González, Moll, and Amanti 2005. Other work using this concept may be found in González 2000 and González and Amanti 1997.

35. See Calderón and Carreón 2000.

36. See Perez 2004.

37. See Rangel-Ortiz 2008.

38. Data were collected from a sample of secondary school practice teacher's interviews in the state of Guerrero in 2009 by me and my colleague, Dr. Carlos J. Ovando.

BIBLIOGRAPHY

Abrahams, Roger D. 1986. "The Play of Play: The Human Encounter." Paper presented at the Annual Meeting of the American Anthropological Association, Philadelphia.

Acosta Briseño, Leticia. 1993. *Testimonio orales: Del río Yaqui hacia el sur* (Oral Testimonies: From the Rio Yaqui to the South). *Memoria del XVI Simposio de Historia y Antropología.* Vol. 1, 403–20. Hermosillo, Sonora: Universidad de Sonora, Departamento de Historia y Antropología. See appendix B for the original.

Acuña Delgado, Angel. 2008. "Danza de matachines: Estructura y Función Entre Los Rarámuri de la Sierra Tarahumara." http://alojamientos.us.es/bibemp/ulises/tarahumaras.htm. Accessed April 28, 2015.

Aguilar, Charles. Interviews. August 25, 2014; September 9, 2014; September 21, 2014; October 22, 2014; November 23, 2014; January 12, 2015; February 4, 2015; March 25, 2015; August 13–14, 2015.

Aguilar-Barajas, Ismael, Nicholas P. Sisto, Edgardo Ayala Gaytán, Joana Chapa Cantú, and Benjamín Hidalgo López. 2014. "Trade Flows Between the United States and Mexico: NAFTA and the Border Region," *Journal of Urban Research* 10: 2–19.

Alarcón, Amado, and Josiah McC. Heyman. 2014. "'Spanish Only' Cheap Labor to Stratified Bilingualism: Language, Markets and Institutions at the USA-Mexico Border." Unpublished manuscript.

Alarcón, Rafael. 2008. "El retorno de los migrantes mexicanos," *La Jornada*. http://www.jornada.unam.mx/2008/10/28/index.php?section=opinion&article=016a1pol. Accessed November 5, 2009.

Allen, Mary. 2008. "Youth Bilingualism in Canada," *Statistics Canada*. http://www.statcan.gc.ca/pub/81-004-x/2008004/info-eng.htm. Accessed August 3, 2015.

Álvarez, Robert R. 1986. "The Lemon Grove Incident: The Nation's First Successful Desegrega-
tion Court," *Journal of San Diego History San Diego Historical Society Quarterly* 32(2): 116–35.
http://www.sandiegohistory.org/journal/86spring/lemongrove.htm. Accessed June 12, 2015.
———. 1987. *Familia: Migration, and Adaptation in Alta and Baja California, 1850–1975.*
Berkeley: University of California Press.
———. 2017. "Southwest North American Language Dynamics and the Creation of Bordering:
A Commentary." In *The U.S. Mexico Transborder Region: Cultural Dynamics and Histor-
ical Interactions*, edited by Carlos G Vélez-Ibáñez and Josiah Heyman, 169–74. Tucson:
University of Arizona Press.
Amanti, Cathy. 2005. "Beyond a Beads and Feathers Approach." In *Funds of Knowledge: The-
orizing Practices in Households, Communities, and Classrooms*, edited by Norma González,
Luis Moll, and Cathy Amanti. Mahwah, NJ: Lawrence Erlbaum Associates.
Anzaldúa, Gloria. 1987. *Borderlands/La Frontera: The New Mestiza.* San Francisco: Aunt Lute
Books.
Ao, Terry M., and Stephanie Lai. 2003. *The Politics of Language: Your Handbook to English-
Only Laws and Policies.* 2nd ed. Los Angeles: Asian Law Caucus, Asian Pacific American
Legal Center of Southern California.
Arias López, José Manuel, Rafael Burgos Villanueva, and Raquel Padilla Ramos. 2013. "Recon-
sideraciones en torno a Uaymitún, Yucatán. Los yaquis y las condiciones laborales en el
exilio," *Ciencia Ergo-Sum* 20(2): 121–29.
Arizona Department of Education. 2004. The Effects of Bilingual Education Programs and
Structured English Immersion Programs on Student. Achievement: A Large-Scale Compar-
ison: Report, Phoenix: State Department of Education. http://epsl.asu.edu/epru/articles
/EPRU-0408-66-OWI.pdf.
Arizona State Museum. n.d.a. Documentary Relations of the Southwest (DRSW). Archives:
Archivos General de la Nacíon: Microfilm records of 436 presidial soldiers from the fol-
lowing: 1a Compañía del 7mo Escuadrón; 2nda Compañía De Volantes De La Colonia
Del Nuevo Santander; 2nda Compañía Del 1° Escuadrón Del Cuerpo De Dragones Pro-
vinciales Del Presidio De San Carlos; 3ra Compañía De 1° Escuadrón; 3ra Compañía De
2ndo Escuadrón; 7ma Compañía De Alternación; Compañía Presidial De Bexar; Com-
pañía De Caballería Y Voluntarios De Monclava; 1a Compañía De Volantes De La Nueva
Santander; 2nda Compañía Del Real Presidio De Aguave; Compañía De Caballería Del
Real Presidio De Río Grande, Coahuilla, Compañía de Opatas de San Miguel de Bavispe.
Microfilm references available for each upon request.
Arizona State Museum. n.d.b. Documentary Relations of the Southwest (DRSW) Archives. *Archi-
vos General de la Nacíon: Company of Opatas of bavisp* [sic]. Document Number 041–04833.
Arizona State Museum. n.d.c. Documentary Relations of the Southwest (DRSW) Archives.
Archivos General de la Nacíon: Compañía De Opatas Bavispe, Provincia De Sonora. January 1,
1816. Document Number 041–04833.

Arizona State Museum. n.d.d. Documentary Relations of the Southwest (DRSW) Archives. *Archivos General de la Nación: 3rd Company of the 2nd Squadron, Platoon of Dragoons, Provincial Troops of the Presidio of San Carlos de Cerrogordo.* Document Number 041–05697.

Arizona State Museum. n.d.e. Documentary Relations of the Southwest (DRSW) Archives. *Archivos General de la Nación: Presidio of San Juan Bautista of Río Grande,* Government of Coahuila. Document Number 041–02864.

Auer, Peter. 1984. *Bilingual Conversation.* Philadelphia: John Benjamins.

Baker, Colin. 2011. *Foundations of Bilingual Education and Bilingualism,* 3rd ed. Clevedon, U.K.: Multilingual Matters.

Barry, Tom. 2014. "The Yaqui Water War." Center for International Policy, *Americas Program.* November 13, 2014. http://www.cipamericas.org/archives/13463. Accessed November 13, 2014.

Bauer, William, Jr. 2014. "Native Californians in the Nineteenth Century." In *A Companion to California History,* edited by William Deverell and David Igler. Oxford: John Wiley and Sons, Ltd.

Beasley-Murray, Jon. 2010. *Posthegemony: Political Theory and Latin America.* Minneapolis: University of Minnesota Press.

Beckett, Patrick H., and Terry L. Corbettt. 1992. *The Manso Indians.* Las Cruces, NM: Coas Publishing and Research.

Benavides, Alonso de. 1996. *A Harvest of Reluctant Souls, the Memorial of Fray Alonso de Benavides, 1630.* Translated and edited by Baker H. Morrow. Boulder: University Press of Colorado.

Berger, Max, and Lee Wilborn. 2017. "Education," *Handbook of Texas Online.* https://tshaonline.org/handbook/online/articles/kheo1. Accessed July 14, 2017.

Beuten, Joke, Indrani Halder, Sharon P. Fowler, Harald H. H. Göring, Ravindranath Duggirala, Rector Arya, Ian M. Thompson, Robin J. Leach, and Donna M. Lehman. 2011. "Wide Disparity in Genetic Admixture Among Mexican Americans from San Antonio, TX," *Annals of Human Genetics* 75(4): 529–38.

Bial, Raymond. 2002. *The Long Walk: The Story of Navajo Captivity.* Buffalo, NY: Cavendish Square Publishing.

Bialystok, Ellen. 2009. "Bilingualism: 'The Good, the Bad, and the Indifferent in Bilingualism,'" *Bilingualism: Language and Cognition* 12(1): 3–11. https://www.cambridge.org/core/journals/bilingualism-language-and-cognition/article/bilingualism-the-good-the-bad-and-the-indifferent/36BAEB01D08C92D992254A6B89C22BB0. Accessed July 8, 2015.

Bialystok, Ellen, Fergus Craik, and Gigi Luk. 2008. "Cognitive Control and Lexical Access in Younger and Older Bilinguals," *Journal of Experimental Psychology: Learning, Memory, and Cognition* 34: 859–73.

Bialystok, Ellen, Fergus I. M. Craik, Cheryl Grady, Wilkin Chau, Ryouhei Ishii, Atsuko Gunji, and Christol Pantev. 2005. "Effect of Bilingualism on Cognitive Control in the Simon Task: Evidence From MEG," *NeuroImage* 24: 40–49. http://www.elsevier.com/locate/ynimg. Accessed July 29, 2015.

Bialystok, Ellen, Gigi Luk, Kathleen F. Peters, and Sujin Yang. 2010. "Receptive Vocabulary Differences in Monolingual and Bilingual Children," *Bilingualism: Language and Cognition* 13(4): 525–31.

Bialystok, Ellen, and Michelle M. Martin. 2004. "Attention and Inhibition in Bilingual Children: Evidence From the Dimensional Change Card Sort Task," *Developmental Science* 7(3): 325–39.

Blanco, María. 2010. "Before Brown, There Was Mendez: The Lasting Impact of *Mendez V. Westminster.*" Washington, D.C.: Immigration Policy Center, American Immigration Council. http://www.immigrationpolicy.org/sites/default/files/docs/Mendez_v._Westminster _032410.pdf. Accessed June 10, 2015.

Bolton, Herbert Eugene. 1919. *Kino's Historical Memoir of Pimería Alta: 1683–1711*, Volume 1. Cleveland: The Arthur H. Clark Company.

Bonnet, Andreas. 2004. *Chemie im bilingualen Unterricht: Kompetenzerwerb durch Interaktion.* [Chemistry in bilingual education]. Opladen, Germany: Leske + Budrich.

———. 2012. "Towards an Evidence Base for CLIL: How to Integrate Qualitative and Quantitative as well as Process, Product and Participant Perspectives in CLIL Research," *International CLIL Research Journal* 1(4): 65–78. http://www.icrj.eu/14/article7.html. Accessed November 16, 2015.

Boone, Elizabeth Hill. 2010. "Foreword." In *Indigenous Intellectuals: Knowledge, Power, and Colonial Culture in Mexico and the Andes*, edited by Gabriela Ramos and Yarinna Yannakakis, ix–xvii. Durham, NC: Duke University Press.

Bourke, John G. 2010. *On the Border with Crook.* London: Bison Press.

Bredenbröker, W. 2000. *Förderung der fremdsprachlichen Kompetenz durch bilingualen Unterricht* [Promotion of foreign language competence through bilingual education]. Frankfurt: Bern.

Breidbach, Stephan, and Britta Viebrock. 2012. "CLIL in Germany: Results from Recent Research in a Contested Field of Education," *In Focus: International CILIL Research Journal* 1(4): 1–16. Accessed November 12, 2015.

Briggs, Charles L. 1988. *Competence in Performance: The Creativity of Tradition in Mexicano Verbal Art.* Philadelphia: University of Pennsylvania Press.

Brooks, James E. 2003. *Captive Cousins: Slavery, Kinship and Community in the Southwest Borderlands.* Chapel Hill: University of North Carolina Press.

Brown, Tracy L. 2013. *Pueblo Indians and Spanish Colonial Authority in Eighteenth-Century New Mexico.* Tucson: University of Arizona Press.

Brownson, Carelton L., ed. 1999. Xenophon, *Anabasis.* Book I, Sections 2–5. http://www.perseus .tufts.edu/hopper/text?doc=Perseus%3Atext%3A1999.01.0202. Accessed April 21, 2015.

Bryc, Katarzyna, Eric Y. Durand, J. Michael Macpherson, David Reich, and Joanna L. Mountain. 2015. "The Genetic Ancestry of African Americans, Latinos, and European Americans across the United States," *American Journal of Human Genetics* 96(1): 37–53.

Buchweitza, Augusto, and Chantel Prat. 2013. "The Bilingual Brain: Flexibility and Control In The Human Cortex," *Physics of Life Reviews* 10(4): 428–43.

Burciaga, José Antonio. 1992. *Drink Cultura: Chicanismo*. Santa Barbara, CA: Capra Press.

Bureau of the Census. 2011. American Community Survey. https://www.census.gov/prod /2013pubs/acs-22.pdf. Accessed October 6, 2015.

Bureau of the Census, American Fact Finder, Community Facts. 2010. http://factfinder .census.gov/faces/nav/jsf/pages/community_facts.xhtml?src=bkmk#none. Access November 30, 2015.

Caesar, Julius. 1869. *The Works of Julius Caesar, Gallic Wars*, translated by W. A. McDevitte and W. S. Bohn. http://www.sacred-texts.com/cla/jcsr/dbg4.htm. Accessed April 21, 2015.

Calderón, Margarita, and Argelia Carreón. 2000. *A Two-Way Bilingual Program: Promise, Practice, and Precautions*. Report No. 47, 1–57. Center for Research on the Education of Students Placed At Risk (CRESPAR), www.csos.jhu.edu. Accessed August 22, 2015.

California Department of Education. 2015. Facts about English Learners in California— CalEdFacts. http://www.cde.ca.gov/ds/sd/cb/cefelfacts.asp. Accessed July 22, 2015.

Calvo, Alejandra, and Ellen Bialystok. 2014. "Independent Effects of Bilingualism and Socioeconomic Status on Language Ability and Executive Functioning," *Cognition* 130(3): 278–88.

Campbell, Howard, and Josiah McC. Heyman. 2007. "Slantwise: Beyond Domination and Resistance on the Border," *Journal of Contemporary Ethnography* 36(1): 3–30. http:// pdxscholar.library.pdx.edu/cgi/viewcontent.cgi?article=1009&context=rri_facpubs. Accessed July 5, 2015.

Campa, Arthur L. 1997. *Hispanic Culture in the Southwest*. Norman: University of Oklahoma Press.

Canagarajah, Suresh. 1999. *Resisting Linguistic Imperialism in English Teaching*. Oxford: Oxford University Press.

———. 2013. *Translingual Practice*. London: Routledge.

Carter, Thomas P. 1970. *Mexican Americans in Schools: A History of Educational Neglect*. New York: College Entrance Examination Board.

Cassidy, Megan. 2016. "Sheriff Joe Arpaio in Contempt of Federal Court, Judge Rules." *Arizona Republic*, May 16. http://www.azcentral.com/story/news/local/phoenix/2016/05/13 /arpaio-contempt-federal-court-ruling/77833232. Accessed May 25, 2016.

Castle, Stephen, and Aurelien Breeden. 2015. "Britain and France Scramble as Channel Becomes Choke Point in Migration Crisis," *New York Times*, July 29. http://www.nytimes.com /2015/07/30/world/europe/britain-and-france-scramble-as-channel-crossing-attempts-by -migrants-continue.html. Accessed July 30, 2015.

Catálogo de las lenguas indígenas nacionales: Variantes lingüísticas de México (National Catalogue of Indigenous Languages: Linguistic Variation of Mexico). 2008. *Diario Oficial* (Primera Sección) 31. Instituto Nacional De Lenguas Indígenas.

Chávez, Fray Angelico. 1992. *Origins of New Mexico Families: A Genealogy of the Spanish Colonial Period*. Santa Fe: Museum of New Mexico Press.

———. 1995. *The Domínguez Escalante Journal: Their Expedition Through Colorado, Utah, Arizona, and New Mexico in 1776*. Translated by Fray Angelico Chávez and edited by Ted J. Warner. Salt Lake City: Utah University Press.

Chávez, Leo. 2001. *The Latino Threat: Constructing Immigrants, Citizens, and the Nation*. Palo Alto: Stanford University Press.

Clay, M. M. 1993. *An Observation Survey of Early Literacy Achievement*. Portsmouth, NH: Heinemann Education.

Coe, Michael D. 1973. *The Maya Scribe and His World*. New York: The Grolier Club.

Coers, W. C. 1934. "Comparative Achievement of White and Mexican Junior High School Pupils," *Peabody Journal of Education* 12(4): 157–62.

Cole Brousseau, Georgia. 1993. "Bridging Three Centuries: One of the Most Progressive and Advanced Systems in the United States." Tucson: Tucson Unified School District http://tusd1.org/contents/distinfo/history/history9305.asp. Accessed July 18, 2015.

Collier, Virginia P., and Wayne P. Thomas. 2004. "The Astounding Effectiveness of Dual Language Education for All," *NABE Journal of Research and Practice* 2(1): 1–20.

———. 2005. "The Beauty of Dual Language Education," *TABE Journal* 8(1): 1–6.

———. 2010. "Helping Your English Learners in Spite of No Child Left Behind." *Teachers College Record, March 17*.

Collier, Virginia P., Wayne P. Thomas, and J. V. Tinajero. 2006. "From Remediation to Enrichment: Transforming Texas Schools Through Dual Language Education." *TABE Journal* 9(1): 23–34.

Combs, Mary. C. 2014. "Self-Inflicted *Reductio ad Absurdum*: Pedagogies and Policies of the Absurd in the State of Arizona." In *Raza Studies: The Public Option for Educational Revolution*, edited by J. Cammarota and A. Romero, 63–90. Tucson: University of Arizona Press.

Comunidad Pacifica en Resistencia. 2011. "Las dos caras de la migración en Guerrero," *Problematicas*, November 19. http://comunidadpacificaen-resistencia.blogspot.com/2011/08/las-dos-caras-de-la-migracion-en.html. Accessed May 20, 2016.

Cordova, Randy. 2017. "Marriage Is Messy in 'You're Killing Me Susan,'" *Arizona Republic*, March 3.

Cortés Vargas, Daniel, María de Ibarrola, Marco A. Delgado Fuentes, Mery Hamui, Pablo Latapí Sarre, Aldo Muñoz, Carlos Muñoz Izquierdo, Maira Pavón Tadeo, Marisol Silava Laya, and Sylvia Schmelkes. 2008. "La educación indígena en México: Inconsistencias y retos" (3/4), *Observatorio Ciudadano de la Educación*. Universidad Nacional Autónoma de México.

Crawford, James. 2000. "English-Only vs. English-Only: A Tale of Two Initiatives: California and Arizona." http://www.languagepolicy.net/archives/203-227.htm. Accessed September 12, 2015.

———. 2002. Census 2000: A Guide for the Perplexed. http://www.languagepolicy.net /articles/census02.htm. Accessed July 12, 2014.

———. 2006. "Official English Legislation: Bad For Civil Rights, Bad For America's Interests, And Even Bad For English." Testimony before the House Subcommittee on Education Reform, July 26. http://www.elladvocates.org/documents/englishonly/Crawford_Official _English_testimony.pdf and Reprinted in *Advocating for English Learners, Selected Essays*, Toronto: Multilingual Matters LTD. Accessed July 12, 2014.

———. 2008. "Monolingual and Proud of It." Originally published in the *Guardian* (UK). Reprinted in *Advocating for English Learners, Selected Essays*, Toronto: Multilingual Matters, Ltd.

Crystal, David. 1997. *English as a Global Language*. Cambridge: Cambridge University Press.

Cuello, José. 1982. "Beyond the 'Borderlands' is the North of Colonial Mexico: A Latin-Americanist Perspective to the Study of the Mexican North and the United States Southwest." In *Continuity and Change in Latin America*. PCCLAS Proceedings 9:18.

Cummins, Jim. 1998. "Immersion Education for the Millennium: What Have We Learned from 30 Years of Research on Second Language Immersion?" In *Learning Through Two Languages: Research and Practice*, edited by M. R. Childs and R. M. Bostwick, 34–47. Second Katoh Gakuen International Symposium on Immersion and Bilingual Education. Katoh Gakuen, Japan.

Curtis, F.S. 1927. "Spanish Arms and Armor in the Southwest," *New Mexico Historical Review* 2(2): 107–33.

Dana, Richard H. 1984. "Intelligence Testing of American Indian Children: Sidesteps in Quest of Ethical Practice," *White Cloud Journal* 3(3): 35–43.

Davis, Jeffrey, and Samuel Supalla. 1995. "A Sociolinguistic Analysis of Sign Language Use in a Navajo Family." In *Sociolinguistics in Deaf Communities*, edited by Cecil Lucas. Washington, D.C.: Gallaudet University.

Dawson, Alexander S. 2012. "Histories and Memories of the Indian Boarding Schools in Mexico, Canada, and the United States," *Latin American Perspectives* 39(5): 80–99.

de Obregón, Baltasar. 1988. *Historia de los Descubrimientos Antiguos y Modernos de la Nueva España Escrita por el Conquistador en el Año de 1584*. México: Porrua.

de Varennes, Fernand. 2012. "Language, Rights and Opportunities: The Role of Language in the Inclusion and Exclusion of Indigenous Peoples." Submission on the role of languages and culture in the protection and promotion of the rights and identity of Indigenous peoples to the UN Expert Mechanism on the Rights of Indigenous People, February 17. https:// www.academia.edu/2361057/Language_Rights_and_Power_The_Role_of_Language_in _the_Inclusion_and_Exclusion_of_Indigenous_Peoples. Accessed June 12, 2015.

de Velasco Rivero, Pedro J. 1987. *Danzar o Morir: Religión y resistencia al la dominación en la cultura Tarahumara*. 2nd ed. México: Universidad Iberoamericana.

Deacon, Terrence W. 2012. *Incomplete Nature: How Mind Emerged from Matter*. New York: W. W. Norton.

Dejong, David H. 1993. *Promises of the Past: A History of Indian Education in the United States.* Golden, CO: North American Press.

Del Castillo, Adelaida. 2005. "Cultural Citizenship," *New Dictionary of the History of Ideas.* http://www.encyclopedia.com/doc/1G2-3424300116.html. Accessed July 17, 2015.

Delgado-Larocco, E. L. 1998. "Classroom Processes in a Two-Way Immersion Kindergarten Classroom." PhD diss., University of California.

Dell'Amore, Christine. 2014. "Sixty Languages at Risk of Extinction in Mexico—Can They Be Kept Alive?" *National Geographic*, April 12. http://news.nationalgeographic.com/news /2014/04/140410-mexico-languages-speaking-cultures-world-zapotec. Accessed April 22, 2015.

Denetdale, Jennifer. 2007. *The Long Walk: The Forced Navajo Exile.* New York: Chelsea House Publications.

Derrida, Jacques. 1974. *Of Grammatology.* Translated by G.C. Spivak. Baltimore: Johns Hopkins University Press.

Diamond, Jared. 2010. "The Benefits of Multilingualism," *Science*, October 15, 330, 332–33. http://science.sciencemag.org/content/330/6002 Accessed August 11, 2015.

Dickerson, R. F. 1919. "Some Suggestive Problems in the Americanization of Mexicans." *Pedagogical Seminary* 26(3): 288–93.

Di Peso, Charles C. 1974. *Casas Grandes: A Falen Trading Center of the Gran Chichimeca*, Vol. 2, *Medio Period.* Dragoon: The Amerind Foundation.

Dozier, Edward P. 1970. *The Pueblo Indians of North America.* New York: Holt, Rinehart and Winston.

Dutcher Mann, Kristin. 2010. *The Power of Song: Music and Dance in the Mission Communities of Northern New Spain, 1590–1810.* Stanford: Stanford University Press and Berkeley: The Academy of American Franciscan History.

Ebright, Malcolm, and Rick Hendricks. 2006. *The Witches of Abiquiu: The Governor, the Priest, The Genizaro Indians, and the Devil.* Albuquerque: University of New Mexico Press.

Eggan, Fred. 1979. "Pueblos: Introduction." In *Handbook of North American Indians: Southwest*, Vol. 9, edited by Alfonso Oritz, 224–35. William C. Sturtevant, General Editor. Washington, DC: Smithsonian Institution.

Escamilla, Kathy. 1987. "The Relationship of Native Language Reading Achievement and Oral English Proficiency to Future Achievement in Reading English as a Second Language." PhD diss., University of California, Los Angeles.

———. 2013. *Biliteracy from the Start: Literacy Squared in Action.* Philadelphia: Caslon Publishing.

Espinosa, Aurelio M. 1975. "Speech Mixture in New Mexico: The Influence of the English Language on New Mexican Spanish." In *El Lenguaje de los Chicanos: Regional and Social Characteristics Used by Mexican Americans*, edited by E. Hernández Chávez, A. D. Cohen and A. F. Beltramo, 99–114. Arlington: Center for Applied Linguistics.

Fabbro, F. 2001. "The Bilingual Brain: Cerebral Representation of Languages." *Brain and Language* 79(2): 211–22.

Farah Ibáñez, José Luis. Interview. Chair of the Department of Applied Mathematics of the Instituto Tecnologico Autonomo de Mexico in Mexico City, August 18, 2015.

Fedewa, Marilyn H. 2009. *María of Ágreda: Mystical Lady in Blue*. Albuquerque: University of New Mexico Press.

Fehrenbach, T. R. 1974. *Comanches: The Destruction of a People*. New York: Alfred A. Knopf.

Ferguson, Margaret W. 2003. *Dido's Daughters: Literacy, Gender, and Empire in Early Modern England and France*. Chicago: University of Chicago Press.

Fernández-Gilbert, Arturo. 2010. "From Voice to Print: Language and Social Change in New Mexico, 1880–1912." In *Spanish of the U.S. Southwest: A Language in Transition*, edited by S. Rivera-Mills and D. J. Villa, 45–62. Madrid: Iberoamericana.

———. 2012. "The Politics of Spanish and English in Territorial New Mexico." XXIII Congreso del Español en los Estados Unidos, Sacramento, California, March 17.

Flint, Richard. 2009. "Without Them, Nothing Was Possible: The Coronado Expedition's Indian Allies." *New Mexico Historical Review* 84 (1): 65–118.

Flores, Ralph M. 2004. *The Horse in the Kitchen: Stories of a Mexican-American Family*. Albuquerque: University of New Mexico Press.

Flores Cano, Enrique. 2014. *Memoria Mexicana*. México D. F.: Fondo de Cultura Economica.

Folsom, Ralph Brewster. 2014. *The Yaquis and the Empire: Violence Spanish Imperial Power, and Native Resistance in Colonial Mexico*. New Haven, CT: Yale University Press.

Forbes, Jack D. 2010. "Black Pioneers: The Spanish-Speaking Afro-Americans of the Southwest." In *The Afro-Latin@ Reader*, edited by Miriam Jímenez Román and Juan Flores, 27–37. Durham, NC: Duke University Press.

Ford, Richard I. 1983. "Inter-Indian Exchange in the Southwest." In *Handbook of North American Indians: Southwest*, Vol. 10, edited by A. Ortriz, 711–22. W. C. Sturtevant, General Editor. Washington, D.C.: Smithsonian Institution.

Foster, William C. 1995. *Spanish Expeditions into Texas: 1689–1768*. Austin: University of Texas Press.

Foucault, Michel. 1980. *Power/Knowledge: Selected Interviews and Other Writings 1972–1977*. Edited by Colin Gordon. Translated by Colin Gordon, Leo Marshall, John Mepham, and Kztte Soper. New York: Vintage Books.

———. 1982. "The Subject and Power." In *Michel Foucault: Beyond Structuralism and Hermeneutics*, 2nd ed., edited by H. D. Dreyfus and P. Rabinow, 208–26. Chicago: University of Chicago Press.

Fraga, Luis R., John A. García, Rodney E. Hero, Michael Jones-Correa, Valerie Martínez-Ebers, and Gary Segura. *Redefining America: Findings from the 2006 Latino National Survey*, Presentation for the Woodrow Wilson International Center for Scholars, PowerPoint,

December 8, 2006, updated February 2, 2007. http://depts.washington.edu/uwiser/LNS .shtml. Accessed July 27, 2015.

Fraga, Luis R., John A. Garcia, Rodney E. Hero, Michael Jones-Correa, Valerie Martínez-Ebers, and Gary Segura. 2010. *Latino Lives in America: Making it Home*. Philadelphia, PA: Temple University Press.

Fratiglioni, L., S. Paillard-Borg, and B. Winblad. 2004. "An Active and Socially-Integrated Lifestyle in Late Life Might Protect Against Dementia," *Lancet Neurology* 3: 343–53.

Freeman, Yvonne S., and David E. Freeman 1996. *Teaching Reading and Writing in Spanish in the Bilingual Classroom*. Portsmouth, NH: Heinemann.

Frontex. 2014. Risk Analysis 2014. Frontex European Agency for the Management of Operational Cooperation at the External Borders of the Member States of the European Union. Warsaw: Poland. http://frontex.europa.eu/assets/Publications/Risk_Analysis/Annual _Risk_Analysis_2014.pdf. Accessed July 30, 2015.

Gabaldon, Salvador, and Carlos Ovando. 2011. "Restrictive English-Only Policies in a Globalizing World: The Conflictive Case of Arizona Orchestrated by a Conservative Political Agenda." In *In the Shadow of Neoliberalism: Thirty Years of Educational Reform in North America*, edited by Lilian Olmos, Carlos Alberto Torres, and Rich Van Heertum. Potomac: Bentham eBooks.

Galindo, D. Leticia, and Maria Dolores Gonzales. 1999. *Speaking Chicana: Voice, Power, and Identity*. Tucson: University of Arizona Press.

Gallegos, Bernardo P. 1992. *Literacy, Education, and Society in New Mexico, 1693–1821*. Albuquerque: University of New Mexico Press.

García, Eugene E. 2005. *Teaching and Learning in Two Languages: Bilingualism and Schooling in the United States*. New York: Teachers College.

García, Eugene E., Mehmet Dali Öztürk, and J. Luke Wood. 2009. "The Critical Condition Of Latino Education In Arizona." State of Latino Arizona. Tempe: Arizona State University, 41–53.

García, Eugene E., Mehmet Dali Öztürk, and J. Luke Wood. 2012. The Critical Condition of Latino Education in Arizona. PowerPoint presentation, Conference on the Critical Condition of Latino Education in Arizona, March 1. Tempe: Arizona State University.

García, Ofelia, and Li Wei. 2014. *Translanguaging: Language, Bilingualism, and Education*. New York: Palgrave.

García-Vázquez, Enedina, Luis Vásquez, Isable C. López, and Wendy Ward. 2010. "Language Proficiency and Academic Success: Relationships Between Proficiency in Two Languages and Achievement Among Mexican American Students." *Bilingual Research Journal: The Journal of the National Association for Bilingual Education* 21(4): 395–408. Accessed August 14, 2015.

Garduño, Everardo. 2004. *La disputa por la tierra—la disputa por la voz: Historia Oral del movimiento agrario en el valle de Mexicali*. Mexicali: Universidad Autónoma de Baja California.

Garis, Roy L. 1930. "The Mexican Invasion." *Saturday Evening Post*, April 19, 43, 44.

Garretson, O. K. 1928. "A Study of Causes of Retardation in a Small Public School System in Arizona," *Journal of Educational Psychology* 19(1): 31–40.

Garth, Thomas R. 1925. "A Review of Race Psychology." *Psychological Bulletin* 22: 343–64.

———. 1927. "The Intelligence of Mexican Children." *School and Society* 27 (December): 791–94.

———. 1930. "A Review of Race Psychology." *Psychological Bulletin* 27(5): 329–56.

———. 1934. "The Intelligence and Achievement of Mexican Children." *Journal of Abnormal Social Psychology* 29(2): 222–29.

Gayle, Damien. 2012. "Map Reveals the Different Languages Written in Tweets Across the U.S. (. . . and Unsurprisingly Most of Them Use English)," *Daily Mail*. http://www.dailymail .co.uk/sciencetech/article-2222966/Twitter-map-reveals-different-languages-used-Twitter -users-U-S-unsurprisingly-use-English.html. Accessed November 30, 2016.

Gelt, Jessica. 2017. "Bilingual Magic Carpet Ride," *Los Angeles Times*, January 12. https://www .pressreader.com/usa/los-angeles-times/20170113/282626032375705. Accessed January 14, 2017.

Genesee, Fred. 1994. *Integrating Language and Content: Lessons from Immersion. Educational Practice Report 11*. Santa Cruz: National Center for Research on Cultural Diversity and Second Language Learning. http://www.ncbe.gwu.edu/miscpubs/ncrcdsll/epr11.htm36700 50903418793. Accessed July 30, 2015.

Giudicelli, Christope. 2006. "Un Cierre de Fronteras . . . Taxonómico Tepehuanes y Tarahumaras Después de la Guerra de los Tepehuanes, 1616–1631." http://www.unicen.edu.ar /iehs. Accessed April 28, 2015.

Glass, John. 1975. "A Survey of Native Middle American Pictorial Documents," *Handbook of Middle American Indians* 14: 3–80.

Glass, John, in collaboration with Donald Robertson. 1975. "A Census of Native Middle American Pictorial Manuscripts," *Handbook of Middle American Indians* 14: 81–252.

Gómez-Quiñones, Juan. 1973. *Sembradores, Ricardo Flores Magón y el Partido Liberal Mexicano: A Eulogy and Critique*. Los Angeles: Aztlan Publications, Chicano Studies Center, University of California, Los Angeles.

González, Gilbert G. 2013. *Chicano Education in the Era of Segregation*. Houston: University of North Texas Press.

González, Norma. 2000. "The Funds of Knowledge for Teaching Project." Reprint. In *Classics of Practicing Anthropology 1978–1998*, edited by Patrick J. Higgins and J. Anthony Paredes, 247–54. Oklahoma City: Society for Applied Anthropology.

———. 2001. *I Am My Language: Discourses of Women and Children in the Borderlands*. Tucson: University of Arizona Press.

González, Norma, and Cathy Amanti. 1997. "Teaching Anthropological Methods to Teachers: The Transformation of Knowledge," In *The Teaching of Anthropology: Problems, Issues, and*

Decisions, edited by Conrad Kottak, Jane J. White, Richard H. Furlow, and Patricia C. Rice, 353–59. Mountain View, CA: Mayfield Publishing.

González, Norma, Luis C. Moll, and Cathy Amanti, eds. 2005. *Funds of Knowledge: Theorizing Practices in Households, Communities and Classrooms*. Mahwah, NJ: Lawrence Erlbaum Associates.

Gordon, Ian. 2012. *The Immigration Hardliner Family Tree: A Guide to the Funders, Think Tanks, Lawyers, and Politicians Behind Harsh Arizona-Style Legislation*. March/April. http://m.mother jones.com/politics/2012/03/john-tanton-anti-immigration-laws. Accessed August 21, 2015.

Gramsci, Antonio. 1971. *Selections from the Prison Notebooks*. Edited and translated by Quintin Hoare and Geoffrey Nowell Smith. New York: International Publishers.

———. 1973. *Letters from Prison*. Edited and translated by Lynne Lawner. New York: Harper and Row.

Green, C. S., and D. Bavelier. 2003. "Action Video Game Modifies Visual Selective Attention," *Nature* 423: 534–37.

Greenberg, James B. 1990. "Funds of Knowledge: Historical Constitution, Social Distribution, and Transmission." In *Restructuring to Promote Learning in America's Schools: Selected Readings*, Vol. 2, edited by William T. Pink, Donna S. Ogle, and Beau F. Jones, 317–26. Elmhurst, IL: North Central Regional Educational Laboratory.

Greenberg, James B., and Thomas K. Park. 1994. "Editor's Preface," *Political Ecology* 1: 1–12. http://jpe.library.arizona.edu/volume_1/foreword.pdf. Accessed February 3, 2014.

Greene, J. 1998. *A Meta-Analysis of the Effectiveness of Bilingual Education*. Claremont: Tomás Rivera Policy Center. Available: http://uark.edu/ua/der/People/Greene/Meta_Analysis _Bilingual_Education.pdf. Accessed December 2014.

Gutiérrez, Ramón A. 1991. *When Jesus Came, the Corn Mothers Went Away: Marriage, Sexuality, and Power in New Mexico, 1500–1846*. Stanford: Stanford University Press.

Hackett, Charles Wilson. 1942. *Revolt of the Pueblo Indians of New Mexico and Otermins's Reconquest*. Albuquerque: University of New Mexico Press. Vol. 1. Public Domain, Google-digitized. http://www.hathitrust.org/access_use#pd-google. Accessed February 19, 2015.

Hadley, Diana, Thomas H. Naylor, and Mardith K. Schuetz-Miller, eds. 1997. *The Presidio and Militia on the Northern Frontier of New Spain. Volume 2, part 2: The Central Corridor and the Texas Corridor, 1700–1765*. Tucson: University of Arizona Press.

Hämäläinen, Pekka. 2008. *The Comanche Empire*. New Haven, CT: Yale University Press.

Hammond, George Peter, and Agapito Rey. 1953. *Don Juan Oñate: Colonizer of New Mexico, 1595–1628*. Albuquerque: University of New Mexico Press.

Hank López, Enrique. 1967. "Back to Bachimba," *Horizon* 9(1): 81.

Hanson-Smith, Elizabeth. 1997. "Technology in the classroom: practice and promise in the 21st century." TESOL Professional Papers 2, Language Teaching Research, 2(2).

Harrington, J. P. 1920. "Old Indian Geographical Names Around Santa Fe, New Mexico." Bancroft: University of California, Berkeley. Reprinted from the *American Anthropologist*

22(4): 341–59. https://archive.org/stream/oldindiangeograpooharrrich/oldindiangeo grapooharrrich_djvu.txt. Accessed April 25, 2016.

Hart Treviño, Elva. 1999. *Barefoot Heart: Stories of a Migrant Child.* Tempe: Bilingual Press.

Haury, Emil. 1986. "The Greater American Southwest." In *Emil W. Haury's Prehistory of the American Southwest*, edited by J. Jefferson Reid and David E. Doyle, 18–46. Tucson: University of Arizona Press.

Hawley Ellis, Florence. 1979. "Isleta Pueblo," In *Handbook of North American Indians: Southwest*, Vol. 9, edited by Alfonso Ortiz, 438–49. William C. Sturtevant, General Editor. Washington, D.C.: Smithsonian Institution.

Heath, Shirley Brice. 1972. *La Politica del Lenguage en México: De la Colonia a la Nación.* México: Instituto Nacional Indigenista.

Heyman, Josiah, and Amado Alarcón. 2017. "Spanish-English Bilingualism in Uneven and Combined Relations." In *The U.S.-Mexico Transborder Region: Cultural Dynamics and Historical Interactions*, edited by Carlos G. Vélez-Ibáñez and Josiah Heyman, 157–68. Tucson: University of Arizona Press.

Hidalgo, Margarita. 2006. "Language Policy: Past, Present, and Future." In *Mexican Indigenous Languages at the Dawn of the Twenty-First Century*, edited by Margarita Hidalgo, 357–69. Berlin: Druyter.

Hill, Jane H. 1993a. "Hasta La Vista, Baby: Anglo Spanish in the American Southwest," *Critique of Anthropology* 13(2): 145–76.

———. 1993b. "Is It Really 'No Problemo'?" In *SALSA I: Proceedings of the First Annual Symposium about Language and Society-Austin. Texas Linguistic Forum* 33:1–12, edited by Robin Queen and Rusty Barrett.

———. 1995. "Mock Spanish: A Site for the Indexical Reproduction of Racism in American English." Electronic document. University of Chicago Lang-Culture Site. http://www.cs .uchicago.edu/discussions/1-c. Accessed June 20, 2015.

———. 1998. "Language, Race, and White Public Space," *American Anthropologist* 100(3): 680–89.

———. 2001. "Proto-Uto-Aztecan: A Community of Cultivators in Central Mexico?" *American Anthropologist* 103(4): 913–34.

———. 2013. "Race and Language in a Reality-Based World," The 2013 Wells Fargo Distinguished Lecture, School of Transborder Studies, Arizona State University:, April 4.

———. 2015. "Tom Horn is Studying Spanish: Neo-liberal Theories of Language and Culture and the Struggle for Symbolic Resources." In *Visiones de Acá y Allá: Implicaciones de la política antimigrante en las comunidades de origen mexicano en Estados Unidos y México*, edited by Carlos Vélez-Ibáñez, Roberto Sánchez Benítez, and Mariángela Rodríguez Nicholls, 77–102. México: Universidad Nacional Autónoma de México y Universidad Autónoma de Ciudad Juárez.

Hill, Merton E. 1925. *The Development of an Americanization Program*. Ontario, Canada: Board of Trustees of Chaffey Union High School and Chaffey Junior College.

Holtby, David V. 2008. Overview of the Federal Presence in New Mexico 1900–1945. Center for Regional Studies. Albuquerque: University of New Mexico. http://hdl.handle.net/1928 /6711. Accessed July 17, 2015.

Horsman, Reginald. 1981. *Race and Manifest Destiny: The Origins of American Racial Anglo-Saxonism*. Cambridge: Harvard University Press.

Horwitz, Stan. 2011. "Justice Sues Ariz. Sheriff Joe Arpaio, Saying He Violated Hispanics' Rights.," *Washington Post*, May 1.

Hudzia, James J., Duchame S. Albaugh, S. Karama, M, Spottswoodm E. Crehan, A. C. Evans, and K. N. Botteron. 2014. "Cortical Thickness Maturation and Duration of Music Training: Health-Promoting Activities Shape Brain Development," *Journal of the American Academy of Child & Adolescent Psychiatry* 53(11): 1153–1162.e2. http://www.sciencedirect.com /science/article/pii/S0890856714005784. Accessed July 18, 2015.

Hutchins, John M. 2014. *Coronado's Well-Equipped Army: The Spanish Invasion of the American Southwest*. Yardley: Westholme Publishing.

Huysmans, J. 2000. "The European Union and the Securitization of Migration." *Journal of Common Market Studies* 39(5): 751–77.

Instituto Nacional de Lenguas Indígenas (INALI). 2008. *Catálogo de las lenguas indígenas nacionales: Variantes lingüísticas de México con sus autodenominaciones y referencias geo-estadísticas*. January 14. Diario Oficial de la Federación (in Spanish) (México: Imprenta del Gobierno Federal, SEGOB) 652 (9):22–78 (first section), 1–96 (second section), 1–112 (third section). www.inali.gob.mx/pdf/CLIN_completo.pdf. Accessed June 1, 2015.

Jiménez, Luis. 2006. *El Gran Norte de México. Una Frontera Imperial en la Nueva España (1540–1820)*. Madrid: Editorial Tebar.

Jiménez, Tomás R., and Laura López-Sanders 2011. "Unanticipated, Unintended, and Unadvised: The Effects of Public Policy on Unauthorized Immigration." *Pathways* (Winter): 3–7.

Johnson, L. W. 1938. "A Comparison of the Vocabularies of Anglo-American and Spanish High School Pupils," *Journal of Educational Psychology* 29(2): 135–44.

Julyan, Robert. 1996. *The Place Names of New Mexico*. Albuquerque: University of New Mexico Press.

Kanellos, Nicolás. 2000. *A Brief History of Hispanic Periodicals in the United States*. Houston: Arte Público Press. http://docs.newsbank.com/bibs/KanellosNicolas/Hispanic_history.pdf.

Kanellos, Nicolas, and Helvetia Martell. 2000. *Hispanic Periodicals in the United States, Origins to 1960: A Brief History and Comprehensive Bibliography*. Houston: Arte Público Press.

Kelly, Henry W. 1940. "Franciscan Missions of New Mexico 1740–1760," *New Mexico Historical Review* 15(4): 345–68.

Kessell, John L., Rick Hendricks, and Meredith D. Dodge, eds. 1992. *By Force of Arms: The Journals of don Diego de Vargas, New Mexico, 1691–1693*. Albuquerque: University of New Mexico Press.

Klimentidis, Y., C. Miller, and M. D. Shriver. 2009. "Genetic admixture, self-reported ethnicity, self-estimated admixture, and skin pigmentation among Hispanics and Native Americans," *American Journal of Physical Anthropology* 138(4): 375–83.

Knaut, Andrew L. 1997. *The Pueblo Revolt: Conquest and Resistance in Seventeenth-Century New Mexico*. Norman: University of Oklahoma. From "Declaration of Pedro Naranjo of the Queres Nation, San Felipe," December 19, 1681, *Revolt* 2: 246.

Koball, Heather, Randy Capps, Krista Perreira, Andrea Campetella, Sarah Hooker, Juan Manuel Pedroza, William Monson, Sandra Herta. 2015. *Health and Social Service Needs of US-Citizen Children with Detained or Deported Immigrant Parents*. Urban Institute and the Migration Policy Institute. http://www.migrationpolicy.org/research/health-and-social-service-needs-us-citizen-children-detained-or-deported-immigrant-parents. Accessed November 19, 2016.

Kramer, A. F., Louis Bherer, Stanley J. Colcombe, Willie Dong, and William T. Greenough 2004. "Environmental influences on cognitive and brain plasticity during aging," *Journals of Gerontology* 59(9): 940–57.

Krizman, Jennifer, Erika Skoe, Viorica Marian, and Nina Kraus. 2014. "Bilingualism Increases Neural Response Consistency and Attentional Control: Evidence for Sensory and Cognitive Coupling," *Brain & Language* 128(1): 34–40.

Krogstad, Jens Manuel, and Ana González-Barrera. 2015. "A Majority of English-Speaking Hispanics in the U.S. are Bilingual," *Fact Tank: News in the Numbers*. Pew Research Center. March 24. http://www.pewresearch.org/fact-tank/2015/03/24/a-majority-of-english-speaking-hispanics-in-the-u-s-are-bilingual/. Accessed March 27, 2015.

Lamadrid, Enrique. 2008. "Rutas del Corazón: Pilgrimage and Cultural Commerce on the Camino Real de Tierra Adentro," *New Mexico Historical Revie* 83(4): 423–49.

Lamb, E. 1930. "Racial Differences in Bimanual Dexterity of Latin and American Children," *Child Development* 1(3): 204–31.

Lamsfuss-Schenk, Stefanie. 2008. *Fremdverstehen im bilingualen Geschichtsunterricht: Eine Fallstudie*. Frankfurt am Main: Peter Lang.

Leal, Luis 1954. "La Cucaracha," *Revista de la Universidad de México* 5(Enero): 15–17. http://www.revistadelauniversidad.unam.mx/ojs_rum/index.php/rum/article/view/6146/7384. Accessed July 1, 2105.

LeBlanc, Steven A. 2003. "Conflict and Language Dispersal: Issues and a New World Example." In *Examining the Farming/Language Dispersal Hypothesis*, edited by Peter Bellwood and Charles Renfrew, 357–65. Cambridge: McDonald Institute for Archaeological Research.

———. 2008. "The Case for an Early Farmer Migration into the Greater American Southwest." In *Archaeology Without Borders: Contact, Commerce, and Change in the U.S. Southwest and Northwestern Mexico*, edited by Laurie D. Webster, and Maxine E. McBrinn, with Eduardo Gembos Carrera, 107–42. Boulder: University Press of Colorado.

Leonard, Irving A. 1953. *Los Libros del Conquistador*. Ciudad de México: Fondo de Cultural Economica. Translation of *Book of the Brave: Being an Account of Books and of Men in the*

Spanish Conquest and Settlement of the Sixteenth Century World. Cambridge, MA: Harvard University Press.

——. 1992. *Being an Account of Books and of Men in the Spanish Conques and Settlement of the Sixteenth-Century New World*. Berkeley: University of California Press.

Letras Libres. 2014. "Migrantes indígenas, un tema pendiente." *Letras Libres*, September 25. http://www.letraslibres.com/blogs/frontera-adentro/migrantes-indigenas-un-tema -pendiente. Accessed April 22, 2015.

Letter of Coronel Mendoza to Virrey Cruillas in the Summary Description of AZTM, AGN, Vol. 069, ff. 057–069.

Lightfoot, Kent G. 2006. *Indians, Missionaries, and Merchants: The Legacy of Colonial Encounters on the California Frontiers*. Berkeley: University of California Press.

Lindholm-Leary, Kathryn J., and Graciela Borsato. 2002. "Impact of Two-Way Immersion on Students' Attitudes Toward School and College," Center For Applied Linguistics. http:// www.cal.org/twi/pdfs/impact-of-two-way-immersion-on-students-attitudes-toward -school-and-college.pdf. Accessed August 16, 2015.

Lipscomb, Andrew A. 1904. *The Writings of Thomas Jefferson*. Vol. 6. Washington, D.C.: Thomas Jefferson Memorial Association.

Liptak, Adam. 2017. "President's Pardon of Arpaio Follows the Law, Yet Challenges It," *New York Times*, August 27: 1.

Lockridge, Kenneth A. 1974. *Literacy in Colonial New England: An Enquiry into the Social Context of Literacy in the Early Modern West*. New York: W. W. Norton.

Loeb, Catherine. 1980. "La Chicana: A Bibliographic Survey," *Frontiers: A Journal of Women's Studies* 5(2): 59–74.

Lomas, Clara. 2003. "Transborder Discourse: The Articulation of Gender in the Borderlands in the Early Twentieth Century," *Frontiers: A Journal of Women's Studies* 24(2–3): 51–74. http://muse.jhu.edu/journals/fro/summary/v024/24.210mas.html. Accessed July 14, 2015.

Lomelí, Francisco A. 1993. "Contemporary Chicano Literature, 1959–1990." In *Handbook of Hispanic Culture-Literature*, edited by Francisco Lomelí, 86–108. Houston: Arte Público Press.

Long, J. C. 1991. "The Genetic Structure of Admixed Populations," *Genetics* 127: 417–28.

López, Ronald. 1968 "Los Repatriados." Seminar paper, History Department, University of California, Los Angeles.

Lucero, Stanley A. 2009. "Tlaxcalan Indians," *Nuestras Raíces* 21(2): 13–19.

Lumholtz, Carl. 1894. "Tarahumari Dances and Plant-Worship." *Scribner's Magazine* 16(4): 438–56.

Lynch, Sarah N. 2007. "Hispanics Change Face of Mormon Faith," *East Valley Tribune* (AZ). May 30. http://www.rickross.com/reference/mormon/mormon394.html.

Mabry, Jonathan, John P. Carpenter, and Guadalupe Sánchez. 2008. "Archaeological Models of Early Uto-Aztecan Prehistory in the Arizona-Sonora Borderlands." In *Archeology Without Borders: Contact, Commerce, and Change in the U.S. Southwest and Northwestern Mexico*, edited by Laura D. Webster and Maxine E. McBrinn, 155–83. Boulder: University Press of Colorado.

Mabry, Jonathan B., and William E. Doolittle. 2008. "Modeling the Early Agricultural Frontier in the Desert Borderlands." In *Archaeology Without Borders: Contact, Commerce, and Change in the U.S Southwest and Northwestern Mexico,* edited by Laurie Webster and Maxine E. McBrinn, with Eduardo Garriboa Carrera, 55–88. Boulder: University Press of Colorado.

MacDonald, Victoria-María. 2004. *Latino Education in the United States: A Narrated History from 1513–2000.* New York: Palgrave Macmillan.

Macias, Anna. 1980. "Women and the Mexican Revolution, 1910–1920," *Americas* 37(1): 53–82. http://www.jstor.org/stable/981040. Accessed October 7, 2015.

Magallanes Castañeda, Irma Leticia 2001. "Rebeliones de los indios Tarahumaras en Nueva Vizcaya durante el siglo XVII." http://www.chihuahuamexico.com/index.php?option= com_content&task=view&id=1652&Itemid=38. Accessed April 6, 2015.

Makoni, Sinfree, and Alastair Pennyook, eds. 2006. *Disinventing and Reconstituting Languages.* Bristol, U.K.: Multilingual Matters.

Manuel, Herschel T. 1965. *Spanish-Speaking Children of the Southwest, Their Education, and the Public Welfare.* Austin: University of Texas Press.

Martínez, Glenn A. 2006. *Mexican Americans and Language: Del dicho al hecho.* Tucson: University of Arizona Press.

Martínez, R.A. 2010. "Spanglish as Literacy Tool: Toward an Understanding of the Potential Role of Spanish-English Code-Switching in the Development of Academic Literacy," *Research in the Teaching of English* 45(2): 124–49.

Martínez-Cortés, Gabriela, Joel Salazar-Flores, Laura Gabriela Fernández-Rodríguez, Rodrigo Rubi-Castellanos, Carmen Rodríguez-Loya, Jesús Salvador Velarde-Félix, José Franciso Muñoz-Valle, Isela Parra-Rojas, and Héctor Rangel-Villalobos. 2012. "Admixture and Population Structure in Mexican-Mestizos Based on Paternal Lineages," *Journal of Human Genetics* 57(9): 568–74. Epub. Jul 26, 2012.

Massey, Douglas S. 2006. "Mexican Migration Slides." The Distinguished Wells Fargo Lecture. School of Transborder Studies, Arizona State University, April 21.

Maturana, Humberto R., and Francisco J. Varela. 1987. *The Tree of Knowledge: The Biological Roots of Human Understanding.* Boston: New Science Library.

Matus, Max. 2016. Dialogos Desde la Frontera. https://www.youtube.com/watch?v=oW9UY 5CR8nc&list=PL6MJBd6DK54GlWitAkxiISsVL-80ay-1u&index=9Utube. Accessed November 30, 2016.

McCaa, Robert. 2000. "The Peopling of Mexico from Origins to Revolution." In *A Population History of North America,* edited by Michael R. Haines and Richard H. Steckel, 241–304. Cambridge: Cambridge University Press,.

McGrath, G. D., and Willard Abraham. 1960. *Investigation of Mental Retardation and Pseudo Mental Retardation in Relation to Bilingual and Sub-Cultural Factors.* Tempe: Arizona State University, College of Education.

McKenna, Teresa. 1997. *Migrant Song: Politics and Process in Contemporary Chicano Literature.* Austin: University of Texas Press.

McMahon, Sister Thomas Marie C. S. J. 1952. "The Sisters of St. Joseph of Carondelet: Arizona's Pioneer Religious Congregation, 1870–1890." Master's thesis, St. Louis University. http:// parentseyes.arizona.edu/carondelet/mcmahon_chapter5.html. Accessed July 26, 2015.

Mecham, J. Lloyd. 1926. "The Second Spanish Expedition to New Mexico," *New Mexico Historical Review* 1(3): 265–91.

Mechelli, Andrea, et al. 2004. "Neurolinguistics: Structural plasticity in the bilingual brain," *Nature* 432(October): 757. http://faculty.washington.edu/losterho/mechelli_12_vmb.pdf. Accessed September 23, 2015.

Medina Miguel, Ángel 1987. *Doctrina Cristiana Para Instrucción de los Indios: Redactada por Pedro de Córdoba*. Salamanca: Editorial San Esteban.

Meier, Gabriela. 2010. "Two-Way Immersion Education in Germany: Bridging the Linguistic Gap," *International Journal of Bilingual Education and Bilingualism* 13(4): 419–37. Accessed July 30, 2015.

———. 2012. "Recent Findings and Developments in Bilingual Education." Presentation. http://www.mecd.gob.es/reinounido/dms/consejerias-exteriores/reino-unido/formacion -del-profesorado/Seminario-del-espa-ol/Presentation-Meier-Liverpool_3/Presentation %20Meier%20Liverpool_3.pdf. Accessed July 30, 2015.

Menjívar, Cecilia, and Leisy J. Abrego. 2012. "Legal Violence: Immigration Law and the Lives of Central American Immigrants," *American Journal of Sociology* 117(5): 1380–1421. http:// www.jstor.org/stable/10.1086/663575. Accessed July 22, 2015.

Meriam, Junius L. 1933. "An Activity Curriculum in a School of Mexican Children," *Journal of Experimental Education* 1(4): 304–8.

Meyer, Doris. 1996. *Speaking for Themselves: Neomexicano Cultural Identity and the Spanish-Language Press, 1880–1920*. Albuquerque: University of New Mexico Press.

Miller, Edward, and John Hatcher. 2014. *Medieval England: Towns, Commerce and Crafts: 1086–1348*. New York: Routledge Press.

Mingers, John 1991. "The Cognitive Theories of Maturana and Varela," *Systems Practice* 4(4).

Molina, Miguel Angel. 1987. *Doctrina Christiana para Instrucción de los Indios*. 1544 and 1546. Salamanca: Editorial San Esteban.

Moll, Luis C., Cathy Amanti, Denorah Neff, and Norma Gonzáez. 1992. "Funds of Knowledge for Teaching: Using a Qualitative Approach to Connect Homes and Classrooms," *Theory into Practice* 31: 132–41.

Moll, Luis C., and Norma González. 1997. "Teachers as Social Scientists: Learning about Culture from Household Research." In *Race, Ethnicity, and Multiculturalism*, edited by P. M. Hall, 89–114. New York: Garland Press.

Montaño, Mary. 2001. *Tradiciones Nuevomexicanas: Hispano Arts and Culture of New Mexico*. Albuquerque: University of New Mexico Press.

Montejano, David. 1987. *Anglos and Mexicans in the Making of Texas, 1836–1986*. Austin: University of Texas Press.

Moorhead, Max L. 1975. *The Presidio: Bastion of the Spanish Borderlands*. Norman: University of Oklahoma Press.

Moreno, Joseph. 2008. "The Tradition Continues: The Matachines Dance of Bernalillo, New Mexico." http://www.townofbernalillo.org/matachines.htm. Accessed August 15, 2015.

Moses, Michele S. 2000. "Why Bilingual Education Policy Is Needed: A Philosophical Response to the Critics," *Bilingual Research Journal: The Journal of the National Association for Bilingual Education* 24(4): 333–54.

Mumme, Stephen P. 1999–2000. "US-Mexico Borderlands Studies at the Millennium," *IBRU Boundary and Security Bulletin* (Winter): 102–5.

Myers-Scotton, Carol. 1993. *Social Motivations for Code Switching: Evidence from Africa*. Oxford: Oxford University Press.

National Education Association. 1966. *The Invisible Minority: Report of The NEA-Tucson Survey On the Teaching of Spanish to the Spanish-Speaking*, Washington, D.C.: Department of Rural Education, National Education Association.

Native Heritage Project. 2013. Las Castas—Spanish Racial Classifications. Posted June 15. http://nativeheritageproject.com/2013/06/15/las-castas-spanish-racial-classifications/. Accessed April 22, 2015.

Nez, Chester, with Judith Schiess Avila. 2011. *Code Talker*. New York: Berkeley Caliber.

Nicholson, H. B. 2002. "Fray Bernardino de Sahagún: A Spanish Missionary in New Spain, 1529–1590." In *Representing Aztec Ritual: Performance, Text, and Image in the Work of Sahagún*, edited by Eloise Quiñones Keber, 21–39. Boulder: University of Colorado Press.

Nieto-Phillips, John. 2004. *The Language of Blood: The Making of Spanish American Identity in New Mexico: 1880s–1930s*. Albuquerque: University of New Mexico Press.

Office of Immigration Statistics. 2014. *Yearbook of Immigration Statistics*. U.S. Department of Homeland Security. https://www.dhs.gov/yearbook-immigration-statistics. Accessed July 20, 2015.

Officer, James E. 1987. *Hispanic Arizona: 1536–1856*. Tucson: University of Arizona Press.

Olavarría, María Eugenia. 1995. "Creatividad y sincretismo en un ritual yaqui," *Alteridades* 5(9): 71–76.

Olivas, Jose Agaito Olivas. 1858 (Circa). Sabino Olivas Family Papers. New Mexico State Record Center and Archives, Santa Fe, New Mexico.

Ovando, Carlos J. 2014. "The Conflicted Origins and Conflicts of Spanish in the United States." In *The Future of Spanish in the United States: The Language of Hispanic Migrant Communities*, edited by Jose Antonio Alonso, Jorge Durand, and Rodolfo Gutierrez. Madrid: Editorial Ariel.

Page, Helán E., and Brooke Thomas. 1994. "White Public Space and the Construction of White Privilege in U.S. Health Care: Research Concepts and a New Model of Analysis," *Medical Anthropology Quarterly* 8(1): 109–16.

Paredes, Américo. 1958. *With His Pistol in His Hand: A Border Ballad and Its Hero*. Austin: University of Texas Press.

Park, Joseph E. 1961. "The History of Mexican Labor in Arizona during the Territorial Period." Master's thesis, University of Arizona.

Paschal, Franklin C., and Louis R. Sullivan. 1925. "Racial Influences in the Mental and Physical Development of Mexican Children," *Comparative Psychology Monographs* 3(14): 1–76.

Passel, Jeffrey S., and D'Vera Cohn. 2009. *A Portrait of Unauthorized Immigrants in the United States: A Report*. Washington, D.C.: Pew Research Center, Hispanic Trends.

Passel, Jeffrey S., D'Vera Cohn, and Mark Hugo López. 2011. "Census 2010: 50 Million Latinos Hispanics Account for More Than Half of Nation's Growth in Past Decade," Washington, D.C.: Pew Hispanic Research Center.

Pelayo, Cervantes, Icela, Elisabeth Valenzuela, Marilyn Newton-Wright, and Jesús Jurado. 2013. *New Mexico Bilingual Multicultural Education and Title III Programs Technical Assistance Manual SY 2013–2014*. Bilingual Multicultural Education Bureau. http://ped.state.nm .us/ped/BilingualDocs/SY%202013-2014. BMEB Technical Assistance Manual.pdf. New Mexico Public Education Department, Bilingual Multicultural Education Bureau, Title III Programs.

Pellicer, Dora, Bárbara Cifuentes, and Carmen Herrera. 2006. "Legislating Diversity in Twenty-First-Century Mexico." In *Mexican Indigenous Languages at the Dawn of the Twenty-First Century. Contributions to the Sociology of Language*, no. 91, edited by Margarita G. Hidalgo, 127–68. Berlin: Mouton de Gruyter.

Perales, Monica. 2006. "El Paso Laundry Strike." In *Latinas in the United States: A Historical Encyclopedia*, Vol. 2, edited by Vicki L. Ruiz and Virginia Sánchez Korrol, 228–29. Bloomington: Indiana University Press.

Perani, Daniela, Jubin Abitalebi, Eraldo Paulesu, Simona Brambati, Paola Scifo, Stefano F. Cappa, and Ferrui Fazio. 2003. "The role of age of acquisition and language usage in early, high-proficient bilinguals: An fMRI study during verbal fluency," *Human Brain Mapping* 19(3): 170–82.

Pérez, Bertha. 2004. *Becoming Biliterate: A Study of Two-Way Bilingual Immersion Education*. Mahwah, NJ: Lawrence Erlbaum Associates.

Perez de Villagra, Gaspar. 1992. *Historia de la Nueva Mexico, 1610*. Translated by Miguel Encinias 1620. Albuquerque: University of New Mexico Press.

Perry, Susan. 2008. "The Bilingual Brain." *Society for Neuroscience*. September. http://www .brainfacts.org/sensing-thinking-behaving/language/articles/2008/the-bilingual-brain/. Accessed August 8, 2015.

Perttula, Timothy K. 1992. *The Caddo Nation: Archaeological and Ethnohistoric Perspectives*. Austin: University of Texas Press.

Petron, Mary A. 2003. "'I'm Bien Pocha': Transnational Teachers of English in Mexico." PhD diss., University of Texas, Austin.

Pfefferkorn, Ignatz [Ignaz, Ignacio]. 1989. *Sonora: A Description of the Province*. Translated by Theodore E. Treutlein. Tucson: University of Arizona Press. Originally published in 2 vols. 1794–1795.

Planas, Roque. 2012. "Neither Banned or Allowed: Mexican American Studies in Limbo." http://latino.foxnews.com/latino/news/2012/04/19/neither-banned-nor-allowed -mexican-american-studies-in-limbo-in-arizona. Accessed July 26, 2014.

Popenoe Paul, and Roswell Hill Johnson. 1933. *Applied Eugenics*. New York: Macmillan.

Pratt, Mary Louise. 1992. *Imperial Eyes: Travel Writing and Transculturation*. New York: Routledge.

Price, Alkes L., Nick Patterson, Fuli Yu, David R. Cox, Alicja Waliszewska, Gavin J. McDonald, Arti Tandon, et al. 2007. "A Genomewide Admixture Map for Latino Populations," *American Journal of Human Genetics* 80(June): 1024–36.

Programa del Encuentro Binacional de Investigadores. 2014. "Cultura y Comunidad" Museo del Vino, Valle de Guadalupe. Ensenada, Baja California. September 10, 11, 12.

Ramírez, J. David. 2000. "A Research Symposium on High Standards in Reading for Students from Diverse Language Groups: Research, Bilingualism and Literacy: Problem or Opportunity?" *A Synthesis of Reading Research on Bilingual Students: Practice & Policy*, Proceedings, April 19–20. Washington, D.C.: U.S. Department of Education, Office of Bilingual Education and Minority Languages Affairs.

Rangel-Ortiz, Luis Xavier. 2008. "Sociocultural Identity and Self Conceptualizations of Mexican Transnational Entrepreneurs (MTNE) in San Antonio, Texas." PhD diss., University of Texas, San Antonio.

Rausch, Jr., George J. 1962. "The Exile and Death of Victoriano Huerta," *Hispanic American Historical Review* 42(2): 133–51. http://www.jstor.org.ezproxy1.1ib.asu.edu/stable/2510294. Accessed July 1, 2015.

Reff, Daniel T. 1991. *Disease, Depopulation and Culture Change in Northwestern New Spain, 1518–1764*. Salt Lake City: University of Utah Press.

Riley, Carroll L. 1971. "Early Spanish-Indian Communication in The Greater Southwest," *New Mexico Historical Review* 46(4): 285–314.

———. 2005. *Becoming Aztlán: Mesoamerican Influences in the Greater Southwest, AD 1200– 1500*. Salt Lake City: University of Utah Press.

Rivas-Rodríguez, Maggie 2015. *Texas Mexican Americans and Postwar Civil Rights*. Austin: University of Texas Press.

Roberts, Kenneth L. 1928a. "Wet and Other Mexicans," *Saturday Evening Post*. February 4, 10–11.

———. 1928b. "The Docile Mexican," *Saturday Evening Post*, March 10, 39–41.

Rodríguez, Alma Dolores. 2007. "Prospective Bilingual Teachers' Perceptions of the Importance of their Heritage Language," *Heritage Language Journal* 5(1): 172–87.

Rodríguez, Sylvia. 1996. *The Matachines Dance: Ritual Symbolism and Interethnic Relations in the Upper Rio Grande Valley*. Albuquerque: University of New Mexico Press.

———. 2009. *The Matachines Dance: The Ritual of the Indian Pueblos and the Mexicano/Hispano Communities*. Santa Fe: Sunstone Press.

Rodríguez Marín, Francisco. 1883. "La Cucaracha." Cantos Populares Españoles Recogidos, Ordenados e Ilustrados por Francisco Rodríguez Marín. Sevilla: Francisco Álvarez y Ca. https://en.wikipedia.org/wiki/La_Cucaracha#Revolutionary_lyrics. Accessed June 25, 2015.

Rogers, Tim. 2016. "Obama has deported more immigrants than any other president. Noh's running up the score." Fusion. http://fusion.net/story/252637/obama-has-deported-more -immigrants-than-any-other-president-now-hes-running-up-the-score. Accessed November 19, 2016.

Rolstad, Kellie, Jeff MacSwan, and Kate S. Mahoney. 2012. "The Ineffectiveness of English Immersion in Arizona," *International Journal of Language Studies* 6(2): 137–50. http:// www.terpconnect.umd.edu/~rolstad/ijls2012.pdf.

Román, Miriam Jímenez, and Juan Flores, eds. 2010. *The Afro-Latin@ Reader*. Durham, NC: Duke University Press.

Romano-V., Octavio Ignacio. 1969a. "The Historical and Intellectual Presence of Mexican-Americans," *El Grito: A Journal of Contemporary Mexica-American Thought* 2(2): 31–46.

———. 1969b. "Goodbye Revolution—Hello Slum." In *El Espejo—The Mirror: Selected Mexican American Literature*, 76–82. Berkeley: Quinto Sol Publications.

Ronstad, Federico José María. http://en.wikipedia.org/wiki/Federico_Jos%C3%A9_Mar%C3 %ADa_Ronstadt. Accessed April 12, 2015.

Rosaldo, Renato. 1989. *Culture and Truth: The Remaking of Social Analysis*. Boston: Beacon Press.

———. 1994. "Cultural Citizenship and Educational Democracy," *Cultural Anthropology* 9(3): 402–11. http://www.jstor.org/stable/656372. Accessed July 17, 2015.

Roseberry, William. 1994. "Hegemony and the Language of Contention." In *Everyday Forms of State Formation: Revolution and the Negotiation of Rule in Modern Mexico*, edited by Gilbert M. Joseph and Daniel Nugen, 355–66. Durham, NC: Duke University Press.

Rospide, María Margarita. 1995. "La Real Cédula del 10 de mayo de 1770 y La Enseñanza del Castellano: Observaciones sobre su Aplicación en el Territoriao Altoperuano," 1415–1448. Memoria del X Congreso del Instituto Internacional de Historia del Derecho Indiano. Accessed March 5, 2015. http://bibliohistorico.juridicas.unam.mx/libros/2/819 /22.pdf.

Ruhlam, Jana, Leila Gass, and Barry Middleton. 2014. "Contemporary Land-Cover Change from 1973 to 2000 in the Madrean Archipelago Ecoregion." Madrean Archipelago, July 28. Accessed March 21, 2015. http://landcovertrends.usgs.gov/west/eco79Report.html.

Sabes, Jovita. 2010. "Empire, Indians, and the Negotiation for the Status of City in Tlaxcala, 1521–1550." In *Negotiation within Domination: New Spain's Indian Pueblos Confront the Spanish State*, edited by Ethelia Ruiz Medrano and Susan Kellogg, 19–41. Boulder: University of Colorado Press.

Saldívar, Ramón. 2006. *The Borderlands of Culture: Américo Paredes and the Transnational Imaginary*. Durham, NC: Duke University Press.

San Miguel, Jr., Guadalupe. 1987. *"Let All of Them Take Heed": Mexican Americans and the Campaign for Educational Equality in Texas, 1910–1981*. Austin: University of Texas Press.

Sánchez, George I. 1967. *Forgotten People: A Study of New Mexicans*. Albuquerque: Calvin Horn Publisher, Inc.

Sánchez, Rosaura. 1994. *Chicano Discourse*. Houston: Arte Público Press.

Sander, William. 2001. "The Effects of Catholic Schools on Religiosity, Education, and Competition." Occasional Paper No. 32. National Center for the Study of Privatization in Education: 1–38. Teachers College, Columbia University.

Santiestevan, Stina. 1991. "Use of the Spanish Language in the United States: Trends, Challenges, and Opportunities." ERIC ED335176. ERIC Clearinghouse on Rural Education and Small Schools, Charleston.

Scheiner Diane L., John Keilp, Monica Rivera Mindt, Ainsley K. Burke. María A. Oquendo, and J. John Mann. 2014. "Verbal learning deficits in posttraumatic stress disorder and depression," *Journal of Trauma Stress* 27(3): 291–98. Accessed July 18, 2015.

Schmid, Carol L. 2001. *Politics of Language: Conflict, Identity, and Cultural Pluralism in Comparative Perspective*. Oxford: Oxford University Press.

Schneider, Jane, and Rayna Rapp. 1995. *Articulating Hidden Histories: Exploring the Influence of Eric R. Wolf*. Berkeley: University of California Press.

Schwaller, John F., with Helen Nader. 2014. *The First Letter from New Spain: The Lost Petition of Cortés and His Company, June 20, 1519*. Austin: University of Texas Press.

Scott, James C. 1977a. "Protest and Profanation: Agrarian Revolt and the Little Tradition," part 1. *Theory and Society* 4(1): 1–38.

———. 1977b. "Protest and Profanation: Agrarian Revolt and the Little Tradition," part II. *Theory and Society* 4(2): 211–46.

———. 1990. *Domination and the Arts of Resistance: Hidden Transcripts*. New Haven, CT: Yale University Press.

Secretaría de Gobernación. 1940. *Seis Años de Gobierno al Servicio de México, 1934–1940*. México: Nacional Impresora S.A.

Servín, Manuel P. 1978. "The Legal Basis for the Establishment of Spanish Colonial Sovereignty: The Act of Possession," *New Mexico Historical Review* 53(4): 295–303.

Shaul, David Leedom. 2014. *A Prehistory of Western North America: The Impact of Uto-Aztecan Languages*. Albuquerque: University of New Mexico Press.

Sheldon, William H. 1924. "The Intelligence of Mexican Children," *School and Society* 19: 139–42.

Sheridan, Thomas E. 1986. *Los Tucsonenses: The Mexican Community of Tucson, 1854–1941*. Tucson: University of Arizona Press.

Shofield, Robert S. 1968. "The Measurement of Literacy in Pre-Industrial England." In *Literacy in Traditional Societies*, edited by J. Goody, 311–25. Cambridge: Cambridge University Press.

Shohamy, Elana. 2006. *Language Policy: Hidden Agendas and New Approaches*. London: Routledge.

Silva-Zolezzi, Irma, Alfredo Hidalgo-Miranda, Jesús Estrada-Gil, Juan Carlos Fernández-López, Laura Uribe-Figueroa, Alejandra Contreras, Eros Balam-Ortiz, Laura del Bosque-Plata, David Velázquez-Fernández, Cesar Lara, Rodrigo Goya, Enrique Hernández-Lemus, Carlos Davila, Eduardo Barrientos, Santiago March, and Gerardo Jiménez-Sánchez. 2009. "Analysis of Genomic Diversity in Mexican Mestizo Populations to Develop Genomic Medicine in Mexico." *Proceedings of the National Academy of Sciences* 106(21): 8611–16.

Simons, Marc. 1964. "Tlascalans in the Spanish Borderlands," *New Mexico Historical Review*. 39(2): 101–10.

Sisneros, Samuel. n.d. Complete Genizaro Petition by Los Genizaros to populate the old Pueblo of Sandia, 1733, SANM I, Roll 6, Frames 687–96. Transliterated and translated by Samuel Sisneros, Archivist, Zimmerman Library, Albuquerque, NM. November 2014. Unpublished manuscript.

Sisneros, Samuel. Found Archive, Zimmerman Library, without Origination. June 10, 2015, communication. Documents not identified or listed.

Sisneros, Samuel E. Interviews. 2014. October 15 and November 15.

———. 2013. "The Armendárizes: A Transnational Family in New Mexico and Mexico," *New Mexico Historical Review* 88(1): 15–39.

Slavin, Robert E., and Alan Cheung 2005. "A Synthesis of Research on Language of Reading Instruction for English Language Learners," *Review of Educational Research* 75(2): 247–84.

Slavin, Robert E., Nancy Madden, Margarita Calderón, Anne Chamberlain, and Megan Hennessy. 2010. "Reading and Language Outcomes of a Five-Year Randomized Evaluation of Transitional Bilingual Education." http://www.edweek.org/media/bilingual_pdf.pdf. Accessed August 12, 2015.

Snow, C. E., M. S. Burns, and P. Griffin, eds. 1998. *Preventing Reading Difficulties in Young Children*. Washington, D.C.: National Academy Press.

Sosa, Suárez, and Margarita y Cristina Henríquez Bremer 2012. *Instituto Nacional Indigenista: Comisión Nacional para el Desarrollo de los Pueblos Indígenas, 1948–2012*. México: Comisión Nacional para el Desarrollo de los Pueblos Indígenas.

Spell, Lota M. 1927. "Music Teaching in New Mexico in the Seventeenth Century: The Beginnings of Music Education in the United States," *New Mexico Historical Review* 442(1): 27–37.

Spicer, Edward H. 1962. *Cycles of Conquest: The Impact of Spain, Mexico, and the United States on the Indians of the Southwest, 1533–1960*. Tucson: University of Arizona Press.

Staff, Roger T., Alison D. Murray, Ian J. Deary, and Lawrence J. Whalley. 2004. "What Provides Cerebral Reserve?" *Brain* 127(5): 1191–99.

Stanley, Grace C. 1920. "Special Schools for Mexicans," *Survey* 44: 714–15.

Stavans, Ilan. 2003. *Spanglish: The Making of a New American Language*. New York: HarperCollins.

Stavenhagen, Rodolfo. 1990. "Linguistic Minorities and Language Policy in Latin America: The Case of Mexico." In *Linguistic Minorities and Literacy: Language Policy Issues in Developing Countries*, edited by Florian Coulmas, 56–62. Berlin: Mouton Publishers.

Stoddard, Elwynn R. 1975. "The Status of Borderland Studies: Sociology and Anthropology," *Social Sciences Journal* 12(3): 38; January 1976, 13(1): 29–54.

———. 1984. "Functional dimensions of informal border networks," *Border Perspectives* 8. Center for Inter-American and Border Studies. El Paso: University of Texas, El Paso.

———. 1986. "Border studies as an emergent field of scientific inquiry: scholarly contributions of U.S.-Mexico borderlands studies," *Journal of Borderlands Studies* 1(1): 1–33.

———. 1989. "Developmental Stages of U.S.-Mexico Borderlands Studies." In *Borderlands in Africa: A Multidisciplinary and Comparative Focus in Nigeria and West Africa*, edited by A. I. Asiwaju and P. O. Adeniyi, 403–24. Lagos: University of Lagos Press.

———. 1991. "Frontiers, borders and border segmentation: toward a conceptual clarification," *Journal of Borderland Studies* 6(1): 1–22.

———. 2001. *U.S.-Mexico Borderlands Issues: The Bi-National Boundary, Immigration and Economic Policies*. El Paso: Promontory.

———. 2005. *U.S.-Mexico Borderlands as a Multicultural Region*. El Paso: Promontory.

Stoddard, Elwynn R., Richard L. Nostrand, and Jonathan P. West, eds. 1982. *Borderlands Sourcebook: A Guide to the Literature on Northern Mexico and the American Southwest*. Norman: University of Oklahoma Press.

Suárez, Mario. 2004. *Chicano Sketches: Short Stories by Mario Suárez*. Tucson: University of Arizona Press.

Swartz, Marc J. 1966. "Introduction." In *Political Anthropology*, edited by Marc J. Swartz, Victor Turner, and Arthur Tuden, 1–47. Chicago: Aldine Press.

———. 2010. "At Dawn's Edge: Tulum, Santa Rita, and the Floral Symbolism in the International Style of Late Postclassic Mesoamerica." In *Astronomers, Scribes, and Priests Intellectual Interchange between the Northern Maya Lowlands and Highland Mexico in the Late Postclassic Period*, edited by Gabrielle Vail and Christine Hernández, 145–91. Washington, D.C.: Dumbarton Oaks.

Taylor, Paul, Mark Hugo López, Jessica Martínez, and Gabriel Velasco. 2012. "When Labels Don't Fit: Hispanics and Their Views of Identity." Executive Summary, Pew Research Center, Hispanic Trends. http://www.pewhispanic.org/2012/04/04/when-labels-dont-fit-hispanics-and-their-views-of-identity. Accessed July, 22, 2015.

Texas Beyond History. n.d. "Indians, Missionaries, Soldiers, and Settlers: History of the El Paso Valley." http://www.texasbeyondhistory.net/paso/history.html. Accessed July 19, 2015.

Thomas, Wayne, and Virginia P. Collier. 2003a. "Reforming Education Policies for English Learners: Research Evidence from U.S. Schools," *Multilingual Educator* 4(1): 16–19. Covina, CA: California Association for Bilingual Education.

——. 2003b. "The Multiple Benefits of Dual Language," *Educational Leadership* 61(2): 61–64.

Tinker Salas, Miguel. 1992. "Sonora: The Making of a Border Society, 1880–1910," *Journal of the Southwest* 34(4): 429–56.

——. 1997. *The Shadow of the Eagles: Sonora and the Transformation of the Border during the Porfiriato*. Berkeley: University of California Press.

Torres-Guzmán, María E. 2002. "Dual Language Programs: Key Features and Results," *Directions in Language & Education* 14 (Spring): 1–16, Washington, D.C: National Clearinghouse for Bilingual Education.

Torres-Olave, Blanca Minerva. 2012. "Imaginative geographies: identity, difference, and English as the language of instruction in a Mexican university program," *Higher Education: The International Journal of Higher Education Research* 63(3): 317–35.

Treviño, Adrian, and Barbara Gilles. 1994. "A History of the Matachines Dance," *New Mexico Historical Review* 69(2): 105–22. https://ejournals.unm.edu/index.php/nmhr/issue/view /364. Accessed May 5, 2015.

Trujillo, Michael L. 2008. "Remembering and Dismembering in Northern New Mexico." *Aztlán: A Journal of Chicano Studies* 33(2): 91–99. http://www.academia.edu/231413 /OñateSalazar. Accessed April 21, 2015.

Turner, Victor W. 1974. *Dramas, Fields, and Metaphors: Symbolic Action in Human Society*. Ithaca: Cornell University Press.

Two-Way Bilingual Immersion Programs in the U.S. Center for Applied Linguistics, Washington, D.C. http://www.cal.org/twi/directory/. Accessed August 16, 2015.

United States-Mexico Border Health Commission. "Border Region." http://www.borderhealth .org/border_region.php, Accessed July 15, 2015.

Urciuoli, Bonnie. 1996. *Exposing Prejudice: Puerto Rican Experiences of Language, Race, and Class*. Boulder, CO: Westview Press.

U.S. Commission on Civil Rights. 1972. "Language Rights and New Mexico Statehood." In *The Excluded Student: Educational Practices Affecting Mexican Americans in the Southwest*, 78–82. Washington, D.C.: Government Printing Office. http://www.nmhcpl.org/uploads /what_the_N_M_Constitution_says.pdf. Accessed July 17, 2015.

——. 2011. *English Only Policies in the Workplace*. Washington D.C.: Government Printing Office. http://www.usccr.gov/pubs/English_Only_Policies_Report-July2011.pdf. Accessed July 10, 2014.

Valdés, Guadalupe. 1997. "Dual-Language Immersion Programs: A Cautionary Note Concerning the Education of Language-Minority Students," *Harvard Educational Review* 67: 391–429.

———. 2003. *Expanding Definitions of Giftedness: The Case of Young Interpreters from Immigrant Communities*. Mahwah, NJ: Lawrence Erlbaum Associates.

Valencia, Richard R. 2002. *Chicano School Failure and Success: Past, Present, and Future*. New York: Routledge.

Valencia Reyes, Alicia. 2009. *Diagnóstico sobre las necesidades educativas de los estudiantes migrantes Mexicanos-Estadounidenses en retorno al Estado de Morelos*. Cuernavaca: Instituto de la Educación Básica del Estado de Morelos.

Valenzuela, M. J., and P. Sachdev. 2006. "Brain reserve and dementia: A systematic review," *Psychological Medicine* 36(4): 441–54.

van Bers, Bianca M. C. W., Ingmar Visser, Tessa J. P. van Schijndel, Dorothy J. Mandell, and Maartje E. J. Raijmakers. 2011. "The Dynamics of Development on the Dimensional Change Card and Sorting Task," *Developmental Science* 14 (5): 960–71.

van Gennep, Arnold. 1960. *The Rites of Passage*. Translated by M. B. Vizedom and G. L. Caffee. Chicago: University of Chicago Press.

Varela, F. 1979. *Principles of Biological Autonomy*. New York: Elsevier-North Holland.

———. 1980. "Describing the Logic of the Living. The Adequacy and Limitations of the Idea of Autopoiesis." In *Autopoiesis, Dissipative Structures and Spontaneous Social Orders, AAAS Selected Symposium 55*, edited by M. Zeleny, 36–48. Boulder, CO: Westview Press.

———. 1981. "Autonomy and Autopoiesis." In *Self-Organising Systems: An Interdisciplinary Approach*, edited by G. Roth and H. Schwegler. Frankfurt: Campus Verlag.

———. 1984. "Two Principles for Self-Organization." In *Self-Organization and the Management of Social Systems*, edited by H. Ulrich and G. Probst, 25–32. Frankfurt: Springer.

———. 1989. "Reflections on the Circulation of Concepts Between a Biology of Cognition and Systemic Family Therapy," *Family Processes* 28(1): 5–24.

Varela, F., H. Maturana, and R. Uribe. 1974. "Autopoiesis: The Organization of Living Systems, Its Characterization and a Model," *Biosystems* 5(1): 87–196.

Vásquez-Cunningham, Pat. 2011. 318th annual Fiestas de San Lorenzo. Posted on September 10. https://pvcfoto.files.wordpress.com/2011/09/pvc081011d3.jpg. Accessed April 2015.

Velasco Ortiz, Laura. 2014. "Organización y liderazgo de migrantes indígenas en México y Estados Unidos. El caso del FIOB," *Migracion y Desarrollo* 23: 97–125. http://www.scielo.org.mx/scielo.php?script=sci_arttext&pid=S1870-75992014000200004. Accessed April 22, 2016.

Velasco Rivero, Pedro de. 1987. *Danzar O Morir: Religión y Resistencia a la Dominación en la Cultura Tarahumara*. México: Centro de Reflexión Teológica.

Vélez-Ibáñez, Carlos G. 1969. "El Milagro." In *El Espejo-The Mirror: Selected Mexican American Literature*, edited by Octavio Ignacio Romano-V., 124–27. Berkeley: Quinto Sol Publications.

———. 1970. "Que Cres? The Themes and Ramifications of Racism in the Chicano Southwest." San Diego. Unpublished essay.

———. 1983. *Rituals of Marginality: Politics, Process, and Culture Change in Central Urban Mexico: 1969–1974*. Berkeley: University of California Press.

———. 1993. "Ritual Cycles of Exchange: The Process of Cultural Creation and Management in the U.S. Borderlands." In *Celebrations of Identity: Multiple Voices in American Ritual Performance*, edited by Pamela R. Frese, 120–43. Westport: Bergin and Garvey.

———. 1996. *Border Visions: Mexican Cultures of the Southwest United States*. Tucson: University of Arizona Press.

———. 2010. *An Impossible Living in a Transborder World: Culture, Confianza, and Economy of Mexican-Origin Populations*. Tucson: University of Arizona Press.

———. 2011. "Política y Economía Transfronteriza: Migración, Contradicciones y Consecuencias por una Prisma Experiencial y Regiones de Refugio Como Estructuras de Desigualdad." In *Economía, política y cultura transfronteriza: 5 Ensayos*, edited by Roberto Sánchez Benítez, 9–33. Nuevo Leon: Consejo Estatal de Ciencia y Tecnología de Nuevo Leon.

———. 2014a. "Spanish Literacy and Language in the Southwest United States: Hegemonic Language Politics from the Colonial Period to the Present." In *The Future of Spanish in the United States: The Language of Hispanic Migrant Communities*, edited by José Antonio Alonso, Jorge Durand, and Rodolfo Gutiérrez, 45–104. Madrid: Editorial Ariel.

———. 2014b. "Ethnicity Estimate for Carlos Vélez-Ibáñez: DNA Tests for Ethnicity & Genealogical DNA Testing." Ancestry DNA. http://dna.ancestry.com/ethnicity/02E93706 -EC10-45DC-B219-3F32EC738B5F. Accessed August 24, 2014.

———. 2015. "The Genographic Project," *National Geographic*. https://genographic.national geographic.com/results/dashboard. Accessed February 1, 2015.

———. 2017a. "Continuity and Contiguity of the Southwest North American Region: The Dynamics of a Common Political Ecology." In *The U.S.-Mexico Transborder Region: Cultural Dynamics and Historical Interactions*, edited by Carlos G. Vélez-Ibáñez and Josiah Heyman, 11–43. Tucson: University of Arizona Press.

———. 2017b. "The Hegemony of Language and Its Discontents: Spanish Impositions from the Colonial to the Mexican Period." In *The U.S.-Mexico Transborder Region: Cultural Dynamics and Historical Interactions*, edited by Carlos G. Vélez-Ibáñez and Josiah Heyman, 134–56. Tucson: University of Arizona Press.

Vélez-Ibáñez, Carlos G., Paul Espinoza, James García, Marta Sánchez, and Michelle Martínez. 2009. "The Arts." *State of Latino Arizona*, 76–87. Tempe: Arizona Board of Regents.

Vélez-Ibáñez, Carlos G., and James B. Greenberg. 1992. "Formation and Transformation of Funds of Knowledge Among U.S. Mexican Households," *Anthropology and Education Quarterly* 23(4): 313–35.

Vélez-Ibáñez, Carlos G., and Josiah Heyman. 2017. "Introduction." In *The U.S.-Mexico Transborder Region: Cultural Dynamics and Historical Interactions*, edited by Carlos G. Vélez-Ibáñez and Josiah Heyman, 11–43. Tucson: University of Arizona Press.

Vélez-Ibáñez, Carlos G., L. C. Moll, N. González, and C. Amadi. 1992. *Funds of Knowledge for Educational Development: An elaboration of an anthropological and educational collaborative dissemination project*. Report submitted to the W.K. Kellogg Foundation. Tucson: Bureau of Applied Research in Anthropology, University of Arizona.

Vélez-Ibáñez, Carlos G., and Carlos J. Ovando. 2009. Secondary school practice teacher's interviews in the state of Guerrero.

Vélez-Ibáñez, Carlos G., and Elsie Szecsy. 2014. "Politics, Process, Culture and Human Folly: Life among Arizonans and the Reality of a Transborder World," *Journal of Borderlands Studies* 29(4): 404–17.

Veltman, C. 1988. *The Future of the Spanish Language in the United States*. Washington, D.C.: Hispanic Policy Development Project. ERIC Document Reproduction Service No. ED 295 485.

Vianna, Oliveira. 1959. *Raça e assimilaçao*. Río de Janeiro: José Olympia.

Vigil, Diego. 1980. *From Indians to Chicanos: A Sociocultural History*. St Louis: C. V. Mosby Company.

Vygotsky, L. S. 1987. "Thinking and Speech." In *The Collected Works of L. S. Vygotsky, Volume 1: Problems of General Psychology*, edited by R. W. Rieber and A. S. Carton, 39–285. New York: Plenum Press. Original work published 1934.

Warman, Arturo. 1972. *La danza de moros y cristianos*. Mexico: Secretaría de Educación Pública.

Waters Yarsinske, Amy. 2004. *All for One & One for All: A Celebration of 75 Years of the League of United Latin American Citizens (LULAC)*. Virginia Beach: Donning Company Publishers. Accessed November 19, 2016. http://lulac.org/about/history/.

Weber, David J. 1973. *Foreigners in Their Native Land: Historical Roots of the Mexican Americans*. Albuquerque: University of New Mexico Press.

———. 1992. *The Spanish in North America*. New Haven, CT: Yale University Press.

———. 2005. "The Spanish Borderlands, Historiography Redux," *History Teacher* 39(1): 43–56. www.historycooperative.org/jounralsht39.1/weber.html. Accessed July 19, 2015.

Weber, Devra. n.d. "Wobbly Magonistas: Re-Envisioning Internationalist and Transnational Movements through Mexican Lenses." Unpublished manuscript.

Weber, Devra, Roberto Melville, and Juan Vicente Palerm. 2002. *Manuel Gamio: El Migrante Mexicano, La Historia de su Vida: Entrevistas Completas, 1926–1927*. México: Miguel Ángel Porrúa.

Weigand, Phil C. 1997. "La Turquesa," *Arqueologia Mexicana* 5(27): 26–33.

———. 2008. "Turquoise: Formal Economic Interrelationships between Mesoamerica and the Southwest United States." In *Archeology Without Borders*, edited by Laura D. Webster and Maxine E. McBrinn, 343–53. Boulder: University Press of Colorado.

West, Guy A. 1936. "Race Attitudes among Teachers In The Southwest," *Journal of Abnormal and Social Psychology* 31: 331–37.

Wheelwright, Jeff. 2012. *The Wandering Gene and the Indian Princess: Race, Religion, and DNA.* New York: W. W. Norton.

White, Sam 2014. "Cold, Drought, and Disaster: The Little Ice Age and the Spanish Conquest of New Mexico," *New Mexico Historical Review* 89(4): 425–58.

Widmer, Randolph. 1994. "'Review of the Caddo' by Thomas Pertulla," *Ethnohistory* 41: 476–78.

Williams, Raymond. 1977. *Marxism and Literature.* Oxford: Oxford University Press.

Wilson, Christopher E. 2011. Working Together: Economic Ties Between the United States and Mexico. Washington, D.C.: Mexico Institute, Woodrow Wilson International Center for Scholars.

Winn, Conchita Hassell. 2010. "Spanish-Language Newspapers." In *Handbook of Texas Online* (http://www.tshaonline.org/handbook/online/articles/ees18). Texas State Historical Association. Accessed June 18, 2015.

Wolf, Eric R. 1983. "The People Without History." Lecture to the University Faculty Senate 125th Plenary Session, City University of New York, December 13.

———. 2010. *Europe and the People Without History.* Berkeley: University of California Press.

Wood, Peter H. 2010. "The Earliest Africans in North America." In *The Afro-Latin@ Reader,* edited by Miriam Jímenez Román and Juan Flores, 19–26. Durham, NC: Duke University Press.

Wright, Melissa W. 2006. *Disposable Women and Other Myths of Global Capitalism.* New York: Routledge.

Yetman, David, and David Leedom Shaul. 2010. *The Ópatas: In Search of a Sonoran People. Southwest Center Series.* Tucson: University of Arizona Press.

Young, Julia G. 2012. "Cristero Diaspora: Mexican Immigrants, the U.S. Catholic Church, and Mexico's Cristero War, 1926–1929," *Catholic Historical Review* 98(2): 271–300. http://muse .jhu.edu/journals/cat/summary/vo98/98.2.young.html. Accessed July 14, 2015.

———. 2015. *Mexican Exodus: Emigrants, Exiles and Refugees of the Cristero War.* Oxford: Oxford University Press.

Zamora, Emilio. 1980. "Sarah Estela Ramírez: Una Rosa Roja en el Moviemiento." In *Mexican Women in the United States,* edited by Magdalena Mora and Adelaida R. del Castillo, 163–69. Los Angeles: Chicano Studies Research Center, University of California, Los Angeles.

Zamora, Gloria. 2009. *Sweet Nata: Growing Up in Rural New Mexico.* Albuquerque: University of New Mexico Press.

Zentella, Ana Celia. 2003. "'José, Can You See?': Latino Responses to Racist Discourse." In *Bilingual Games: Some Literary Investigations,* edited by Doris Sommer, 51–68. New York: Palgrave.

Zavella, Patricia. 2001. "Silence Begins at Home." In *Telling to Live: Latina Feminist Testimonios,* edited by Latina Feminist Group, 43–54. Durham, NC: Duke University Press.

Zeta Acosta, Oscar. 1973. *The Revolt of the Cockroach People*. San Francisco: Straight Arrow Books.

TITLED WEB PAGES

"Bacadéhuachi." n.d. PueblosAmerica.com. http://en.mexico.pueblosamerica.com/i/bacade huachi. Accessed September 18, 2015.

"Belgium." 2015. *The World Factbook*. https://www.cia.gov/library/publications/the-world -factbook/geos/be.html. Accessed July 30, 2015.

"California Proposition 58, Non-English Languages Allowed in Public Education (2016)." https://ballotpedia.org/California_Proposition_58,_Non-English_Languages_Allowed _in_Public_Education_(2016). Accessed November 19, 2016.

"Chumacero." http://apellidosespanoles.blogspot.com/2013/06/zorrilla-y-chumacero.html. Accessed May 10, 2015.

Diario Official 2014. "Comision Nacional para el Desarrollo de los Pueblos Indigenas." http:// www.cdi.gob.mx/programas/2014/programa-especial-de-los-pueblos-indigenas-2014-2018 .pdf. Accessed July 25, 2015.

"El Corrido Mexicano. Las historias detrás de los corridos en México: La Cucaracha." n.d. http://corridomexicano.com/letras/la-cucaracha.html. Accessed July 1, 2015.

"Estevanico Facts." http://biography.yourdictionary.com/estevanico. Accessed December 22, 2016.

"Geo-Mexico, the Geography and Dynamics of Modern Mexico." May 29, 2014. http://geo -mexico.com. Accessed April 10, 2015.

"Indians, Missionaries, Solderies, and Settlers: History of the El Paso Valley." 2015. http://www .texasbeyondhistory.net/paso/history.html. Accessed March 1, 2015.

"La Cucaracha." https://en.wikiepedia.org/wiki/LaCucaracha#Revolutionary#Lyrics. Accessed May 10, 2015.

"Language Spoken at Home and English-Speaking Ability by State: 2011." American Community Survey. Table 4, U.S. Census Bureau, 2011. https://www.census.gov/prod/2013pubs /acs-22.pdf. Accessed August 20, 2015.

"The Madrean Archipelago" (Sky Island Region). http://madrean.org/region.php. Accessed April 25, 2015.

"Mapping Mediterranean Migration." September 15, 2014. *BBC News*. http://www.bbc.com /news/world-europe-24521614. Accessed July 30, 2015.

McKay, Robert 2010. "Mexican Americans and Repatriation." Texas State Historical Association. https://tshaonline.org/handbook/online/articles/pqmyk. Accessed, June 9, 2015.

"Mexican Group Denounces Rights Violations against Yaqui Tribe Tomas Rojo, spokesman of the Yaqui Tribe, denounces the Independence Aqueduct in front of Mexico's Supreme

Court." 2015. http://www.telesurtv.net/english/news/Mexican-Group-Denounces-Rights
-Violations-against-Yaqui-Tribe-20150211-0033.html. Accessed June 15, 2015.

"Mexican State on Texas Border Mandates All Children Learn English." 2009. *The Guardian*,
February 5. http://www.theguardian.com/world/2009/feb/05/tamaulipas-texas-mexico
-us-border-english. Accessed July 27, 2015.

"Migrantes indígenas, un tema pendiente," *Letras Libres*. 2014. http://www.letraslibres.com
/blogs/frontera-adentro/migrantes-indigenas-un-tema-pendiente. Accessed July 10, 2016.

"Niños saturan escuelas en Sonora por la Ley SB1070." 2010. *El Universal*. Ni%C3%B1°s%20
saturan%20escuelas%20en%20Sonora%20por%20la%20Ley%20SB1070.htm. Accessed
November 19, 2016.

"On Language Ability and Executive Functioning." *Cognition 130*: 278–88. www.elsevier.com
/locate/COGNIT. Accessed August 5, 2015.

Ordinances For the Discovery, the Population and the Pacification of the Indies." *The Laws
of the Indies*. http://codesproject.asu.edu/sites/default/files/THE%20LAWS%20OF%20
THE%20INDIEStranslated.pdf. Accessed July 25, 2016.

Our Lady of Refuge Catholic School. http://www.olorschoolep.org. Accessed July 27, 2015.

"Reggaetón Music," 2016. Don Quijote Language School. http://www.donquijote.org/culture
/puerto-rico/music/reggaeton-music Accessed December 5, 2016.

"Se duplica arresto de rarámuris en EU." *El Universal*. April 17, 2016. http://www.eluniversal
.com.mx/articulo/periodismo-de-investigacion/2016/04/17/se-duplica-arresto-de
-raramuris-en-eu. Accessed April 30, 2016.

"Special Eurobarometer 386." 2012. *Europeans and their Languages*. Brussels: European Commission. http://ec.europa.eu/public_opinion/index_en.htm. Accessed, July 28, 2012.

"Tarahumaras protestan contra Javier Corral en el Senado." 2015. *Monitor Naciona*l (5 de
marzo). http://www.monitornacional.com/tarahumaras-protestan-contra-javier-corral-en
-el-senado. Accessed April 30, 2016.

"Town of Bernalillo." http://www.city-data.com/city/Bernalillo-New-Mexico.html. Accessed
May 5, 2014.

"US Hispanic Population by Origin Sources." U.S. Decennial Census 1970, 1980, 1990, 2000,
2010. https://www.census.gov/population/hispanic/files/hispanic2006/Internet_Hispanic
_in_US_2006.pdf.

UNTITLED WEB PAGES

City-data.com, Bernalillo, NM. n.d.a http://www.city-data.com/city/Bernalillo-New-Mexico
.html. Accessed July 5, 2015.

City-Data.com, Bernalillo, NM. n.d.b. http://www.city-data.com/crime/crime-Bernalillo
-New-Mexico.html. Accessed November 15, 2015.

http://imagine2050.newcomm.org/wp-content/uploads/2010/11/john_tanton. Accessed February 2, 2015.

http://www.international.ucla.edu/languages/heritagelanguages/journal/volume5-1.asp. Accessed July 18, 2015.

http://www.observatorio.org/comunicado2915s/EducDebate15_EducacionIndigena_3.html. Accessed June 13, 2015.

http://www.revistadelauniversidad.unam.mx/ojs_rum/index.php/rum/article/view/6146/7384. Accessed July 1, 2105.

https://theintermediateperiod.wordpress.com/2013/10/29/back-to-bachimba. Accessed June 9, 2015.

http://transborder.bts.gov/programs/international/transborder/TBDR_BC/TBDR_BCQ.html. Accessed December 18, 2014.

http://travel.trade.gov/view/m-2013-I-001/index.html. Accessed November 2014.

http://www.visitmexico.com/en/copper-canyon.

INDEX

ABOUT THE AUTHOR

Carlos G. Vélez-Ibáñez is Regents' Professor of the School of Transborder Studies and School of Human Evolution and Social Change at Arizona State University. His numerous honors include the 2004 Robert B. Textor and Family Prize for Excellence in Anticipatory Anthropology and the 2003 Bronislaw Malinowski Medal. Vélez-Ibáñez was named as corresponding member of the Mexican Academy of Sciences (Miembro Correspondiente de la Academia Mexicana de Ciencias) in 2015, and he is the author of *An Impossible Living in a Transborder World: Culture, Confianza, and Economy of Mexican-Origin Populations*, among numerous other monographs and edited works.